W9-BNP-642

Preface

THE NASSI / LEVY SPANISH TWO YEARS, NEW EDITION is designed to give students a comprehensive review and thorough understanding of the elements of the Spanish language and the highlights of Spanish-American cultures. Abundant and varied exercises help students master each phase of the work.

This NEW EDITION, contains the following features:

1. A proficiency-oriented communicative approach.
2. Grammatical topics are presented in smaller increments and exercises devoted to practice, drill, and mastery of these topics immediately follow the grammatical explanation.
3. The exercises are set in contexts that are both functional and realistic. Many of them are personalized to stimulate student response and internalization of the concepts under study.
4. The exercises are graded from easy to more challenging and provide opportunities for personalized self-expression by the learner.
5. There is an abundance of artwork used to elicit specific grammar topics and vocabulary.
6. Alternative-assessment activities, called **Actividades**, are introduced to enable students to show both their proficiency and creativity, while performing contextually organized tasks in the target language.

ORGANIZATION

For ease of study and reference, the book is divided into six parts. In Parts One through Three, the chapters are organized around related grammatical topics. The three chapters in Part Four are devoted to word building, synonyms and antonyms, and thematic vocabulary. Part Five covers geography, history, literature, art, music, architecture, science, and life-style. Part Six provides material for comprehensive practice and testing of the speaking, listening, reading, and writing skills.

GRAMMAR

Each grammar chapter deals fully with one major topic or several closely related ones. Explanations of structures are brief and clear. All points of grammar are illustrated by many examples, in which the key elements are typographically highlighted.

This second year review of Spanish covers a basic grammar sequence. Care has been taken to avoid the use of overly complex, structural elements. To enable students to concentrate on the structural practice, the vocabulary has been carefully controlled and systematically "recycled" throughout the chapters.

EXERCISES

For maximum efficiency in learning, the exercises directly follow the points of grammar to which they apply. Carefully graded, the exercises proceed from simple assimilation to more challenging manipulation of elements and communication. To provide students with meaningful practice of a grammar topic, the exercises are set in contexts that are functional, realistic, and communicative. Many are also personalized to stimulate student response and internalization of the concepts under study.

While the contents of the exercises afford extensive oral practice, the book's format also encourages reinforcement through written student responses, including English-to-Spanish exercises intended to sharpen composition skills. The grammatical chapters conclude with Mastery Exercises, in which all grammatical aspects in the chapter are again practiced in recombinations of previously covered elements. The communicative situations for each exercise and the directions are given in English.

FLEXIBILITY

The topical organization and the integrated completeness of each chapter permit the teacher to follow any sequence suitable to the objectives of the course and the needs of the students. This flexibility is facilitated by the detailed table of contents at the front of the book and the comprehensive grammatical index at the back. Teachers and students will also find the book useful as a reference source.

CULTURE

The cultural chapters in Part Five are presented in Spanish. Every effort has been made to keep the narratives clear and readable and to provide a wealth of cultural information. Each cultural chapter includes exercises designed to facilitate and check learning.

OTHER FEATURES

In order to help students demonstrate their performance in Spanish, almost all chapters in Parts One to Three contain alternative-assessment activities. Although these activities are grammatically organized, they are open-ended and enable students to demonstrate their proficiency in using the grammatical elements in personalized, contextually organized tasks.

The Appendix features complete model verb tables and the principal parts of common irregular verbs, as well as basic rules of Spanish punctuation, syllabication, and pronunciation. Spanish-English and English-Spanish vocabularies and a comprehensive Index complete the book.

The NASSI / LEVY SPANISH TWO YEARS, NEW EDITION presents a comprehensive coverage of the elements of Spanish, clear and concise explanations, extensive contextualized practice materials, functional vocabulary, interesting cultural narratives in Spanish, and performance-oriented assessment activities, will help students strengthen their skills in the Spanish language. As students pursue proficiency, they will also gain valuable insights into the cultures of the Spanish-speaking world.

THE NASSI · LEVY SPANISH TWO YEARS

WORKBOOK EDITION

New Edition

Stephen L. Levy
Head, Foreign Language Department
Roslyn (New York) Public Schools

Robert J. Nassi
Former Teacher of Spanish
Los Angeles Valley Junior College
Los Angeles, California

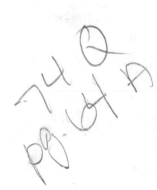

AMSCO SCHOOL PUBLICATIONS, INC.
315 Hudson Street / New York, N.Y. 10013

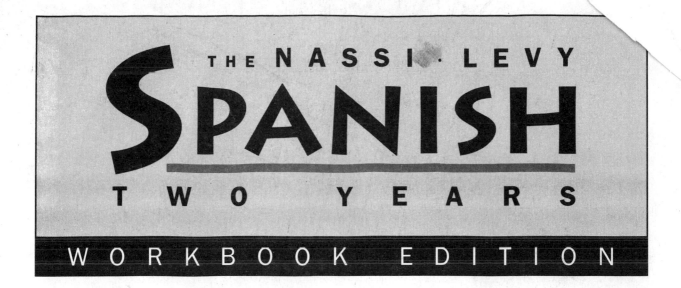

With grateful acknowledgement to coauthor,
Bernard Bernstein

To Sergio,
El alma no tendría un arcoiris si los ojos no tuvieran lágrimas.
Q.E.P.D.

S.L.L.

Text design by A Good Thing
Cover photograph of Ecuador, Quito, Church of San Francisco and Plaza
by Tony Stone Images, Inc.
Illustrations by Felipe Galindo

Please visit our Web site at:
www.amscopub.com

When ordering this book, please specify *either* **R 707 W** *or*
NASSI / LEVY SPANISH TWO YEARS, Workbook Edition

ISBN 1-56765-480-0
NYC Item 56765-480-X

Copyright © 2001 by Amsco School Publications, Inc.

No part of this book may be reproduced in any form
without written permission from the publisher.

Printed in the United States of America

4 5 6 7 8 9 10 07 06 05 04 03 02 01

Contents

Part One
Verbal Structures

Part Two
Nouns, Pronouns, and Prepositions

Part Three
Adjective / Adverb and Related Structures

Part Four
Word Study

Part Five
Spanish and Spanish-American Civilizations

Part one

Verbal Structures

Chapter 1

Present Tense of Regular Verbs

[1] REGULAR VERBS

a. The present tense of regular verbs is formed by dropping the infinitive ending (*-ar, -er, -ir*) and adding the following personal endings:

-o, -as, -a, -amos, -áis, -an for -ar verbs
-o, -es, -e, -emos, -éis, -en for -er verbs
-o, -es, -e, -imos, -ís, -en for -ir verbs

	bailar *to dance*	comer *to eat*	vivir *to live*
yo	bail*o*	com*o*	viv*o*
tú	bail*as*	com*es*	viv*es*
Ud., él, ella	bail*a*	com*e*	viv*e*
nosotros, -as	bail*amos*	com*emos*	viv*imos*
vosotros, -as	bail*áis*	com*éis*	viv*ís*
Uds., ellos, ellas	bail*an*	com*en*	viv*en*

b. The present tense has the following meanings in English.

yo como — *I eat, I'm eating, I do eat*
usted baila — *you dance, you're dancing, you do dance*
ellos viven — *they live, they're living, they do live*

NOTE:

1. In a negative statement, **no** follows the subject and goes immediately before the verb.

   Ellos no comen a las doce. — *They don't eat at twelve o'clock.*

2. In a question, the subject usually follows the verb.

   ¿Comen ellos a las doce? — *Do they eat at twelve o'clock?*
   ¿No comen ellos a las doce? — *Don't they eat at twelve o'clock?*

3. Unless required for clarity or for emphasis, subject pronouns are usually omitted.

   Colecciono discos. — *I collect records.*
   ¿Colecciona Ud. discos también? — *Do you collect records too?*

[2] COMMON *-AR* VERBS

ayudar *to help*
bajar *to go down, descend*
borrar *to erase*
buscar *to look for, seek*
caminar *to walk*
cantar *to sing*
coleccionar *to collect*
comprar *to buy*
contestar *to answer*
cultivar *to cultivate*
dejar *to let, allow, leave*
descansar *to rest*
desear *to want, wish*
enseñar *to teach, show*
entrar *to enter*
escuchar *to listen (to)*
esperar *to wait for, await, hope, expect*
estudiar *to study*

explicar *to explain*
gritar *to shout*
hablar *to speak, talk*
hallar *to find*
invitar *to invite*
llenar *to fill*
llevar *to carry, wear*
mirar *to look (at)*
necesitar *to need*
pagar *to pay (for)*
pasar *to pass, spend (time)*
patinar *to skate*
practicar *to practice*
preguntar *to ask*
preparar *to prepare*
quitar *to take away*
regresar *to return*
sacar *to take out; to take (photo)*
tomar *to take, eat, drink*
trabajar *to work*
usar *to use*
viajar *to travel*
visitar *to visit*

EXERCISE A. Alfredo is describing what happens in his classes at school. Express in complete sentences what he says.

EXAMPLE: yo / prestar atención Yo **presto** atención.

1. la maestra / enseñar la lección La maestra enseña la lección.
2. los alumnos / escuchar a la maestra Los alumnos escuchan a la maestr
3. Javier / contestar las preguntas Javier contesta las preguntas
4. yo / buscar las palabras en el diccionario Yo busco las palabras en el diccionar
5. tú / preguntar muchas cosas Tú preguntas muchas cosas.
6. Gloria / entrar en la clase tarde Gloria entra en la clase tarde.
7. la clase / preparar la tarea La clase prepara la tarea.
8. nosotros / estudiar mucho Nos estudiamos mucho.

EXERCISE B. While talking to your grandmother on the telephone she asks you what everyone in the family is doing at this moment. Tell her.

EXAMPLE: Felipe / mirar la televisión Felipe **mira** la televisión.

1. mi hermana / pasar la aspiradora ____________________
2. mamá / preparar la comida ____________________
3. Luis / trabajar en el jardín ____________________
4. papá / lavar el carro ____________________
5. Rosita y yo / escuchar discos ____________________
6. Adela / tocar el piano ____________________

EXERCISE C. Use the cues provided to write negative sentences.

EXAMPLE: los niños / coleccionar insectos Los niños **no coleccionan** insectos.

1. las niñas / montar en bicicleta ____________________
2. los amigos / caminar en el parque ____________________

3. Pierre y yo / nadar en la piscina ______________________________

4. Kyoko / comprar un suéter ______________________________

5. yo / viajar en autobús ______________________________

EXERCISE D. **Write a list of seven things you and your classmates do not do in school. Use the following suggestions or create your own.**

escuchar discos	preparar la tarea	arreglar el monopatín
visitar otras clases	gritar en la clase	mirar por la ventana
hablar en voz alta	descansar en la clase	

EXAMPLE: Yo no miro por la ventana.

1. ______________________________
2. ______________________________
3. ______________________________
4. ______________________________
5. ______________________________
6. ______________________________
7. ______________________________

EXERCISE E. **Your father is watching his favorite program and isn't paying close attention to what you are telling him. After each statement, he asks a question. Tell what he asks in response to the statements below.**

EXAMPLES: Rogelio gana muchos trofeos.
¿**Gana Rogelio** muchos trofeos?

Yo colecciono insectos.
¿**Coleccionas tú** insectos?

1. Guy y Lázaro toman muchos refrescos. ______________________________
2. Evelyn practica un deporte. ______________________________
3. Gustavo escucha música clásica. ______________________________
4. Yo patino con monopatines. ______________________________
5. Lucy y Sean cantan en el coro. ______________________________
6. Marco descansa en una hamaca. ______________________________
7. Beto y yo sacamos muchas fotos. ______________________________

[3] COMMON *-ER* VERBS

aprender *to learn*	**correr** *to run*	**leer** *to read*
beber *to drink*	**creer** *to believe*	**prometer** *to promise*
comer *to eat*	**deber** *to have to (should, ought); to owe*	**responder** *to answer*
comprender *to understand*	**esconder** *to hide (something)*	**vender** *to sell*

EXERCISE F. **Gladys and a friend describe what different people are doing at the beach. Tell what they say.**

EXAMPLE: un hombre / vender refrescos Un hombre **vende** refrescos.

1. los niños / correr en la playa Los niños corren en la playa.
2. tú / aprender a nadar Tú aprendes a nadar.
3. Sofía / beber mucho jugo Sofía bebe mucho jugo.
4. Rafael y yo / leer una revista Rafael y yo leemos una revista.
5. yo / esconder la pelota Yo escondo la pelota.
6. nosotros / comer en un café Nos comemos en un café.
7. el salvavidas / responder a muchas preguntas el salvavidas responde a muchas pregunt
8. Cristina / prometer correr en una carrera Cristina promete correr en una carrera

EXERCISE G. **After Anabel's friends leave, her younger sister asks her a lot of questions. Answer the sister's questions according to the cues provided.**

EXAMPLE: ¿Quién responde a la carta? (*mamá*) **Mamá responde** a la carta.

1. ¿Quién corre en el parque todos los días? (*Diego*)

2. ¿Quiénes comen muchos dulces? (*tú y yo*)

3. ¿Quién lee las tiras cómicas? (*tú*)

4. ¿Quiénes beben muchos refrescos? (*Gabriela y Carlos*)

5. ¿Quién debe estudiar más? (*yo*)

6. ¿Quién promete estudiar mucho? (*Donald*)

7. ¿Quiénes aprenden a patinar en monopatín? (*Ramona e Isabel*)

EXERCISE H. **Luis and his friend Víctor always disagree with each other. Tell what Luis says and what Víctor responds.**

EXAMPLE: deber comprar una bicicleta nueva (*Samuel*)

LUIS: Samuel debe comprar una bicicleta nueva.
VÍCTOR: Samuel no debe comprar una bicicleta nueva.

1. esconder el dinero / Anita

   LUIS: ______________________________

   VÍCTOR: ______________________________

2. aprender a hablar japonés / Oscar

   LUIS: ______________________________

   VÍCTOR: ______________________________

3. prometer visitar la biblioteca / Esteban y Pablo

   LUIS: ______________________________

   VÍCTOR: ______________________________

4. comer mucha fruta / Adriana

   LUIS: ______________________________

   VÍCTOR: ______________________________

5. leer el periódico todos los días / nosotros

   LUIS: ______________________________

   VÍCTOR: ______________________________

6. correr en un maratón / Silvia y Luz

   LUIS: ______________________________

   VÍCTOR: ______________________________

EXERCISE I. **An exchange student asks you questions about the school and the students. Answ[er] her questions using the cues provided in parentheses.**

EXAMPLES: ¿Dónde comen los estudiantes? (*la cafetería*)
Los estudiantes **comen en** la cafetería.

¿Lees tú muchas revistas? (*no*)
No, **no leo** muchas revistas.

1. ¿Deben Uds. beber refrescos en la clase? (*no*)

   ____

2. ¿Aprenden muchos estudiantes a hablar español? (*sí*)

   ____

3. ¿Dónde corres tú? (*el gimnasio*)

   ____

4. ¿Qué lee el profesor en la clase de inglés? (*los exámenes*)

   ____

5. ¿Quién esconde los libros del profesor? (*Felipe*)

____

6. ¿Quiénes responden a las preguntas del profesor? (*los alumnos*)

____

7. ¿Prometes tú ayudarme en la clase de inglés? (*sí*)

____

[4] COMMON *-IR* VERBS

abrir *to open*
asistir a *to attend*
cubrir *to cover*
decidir *to decide*
describir *to describe*
dividir *to divide*
escribir *to write*
insistir (en) *to insist on*
partir *to leave, depart*
permitir *to permit, allow*
recibir *to receive*
subir *to go up, climb; to raise*
sufrir *to suffer*
vivir *to live*

EXERCISE J. **To celebrate "el cinco de mayo," Tamara decides to have a party at her home. Express what she tells a friend about the party.**

EXAMPLE: yo / abrir los refrescos — Yo **abro** los refrescos.

1. yo / decidir dar una fiesta — Yo decido dar una fiesta.

2. mis padres / permitir la fiesta — Mis padres permite la fiesta.

3. tú y yo / escribir las invitaciones — Tú y yo escribamos las invitaciones.

4. tú / cubrir la mesa con un mantel mexicano — Tú cubres la mesa con un mantel mexicano.

mi mamá / insistir en preparar tacos y enchiladas — Mi mamá insiste en preparar tacos y enchiladas.

6 mis hermanos / decidir no ayudarme — Mis hermanos deciden no ayudarme.

7. odos los amigos / asistir a la fiesta — Todos los amigos asisten a la fiesta.

EXCISE K. **Gregory could not attend the team's first game today. Ramon and Peter tell him about it. Write what they say.**

1. Eluipo / asistir a un partido imrtante ______________________________

2. El enador / dividir el equipo en grupos ______________________________

3. Gon / insistir en ser el jefe ______________________________

4. Juan rique / decidir ser antipát ______________________________

5. El autobús / partir tarde ____________________

6. Nosotros / recibir los uniformes ____________________

7. Yo / subir al autobús tarde ____________________

8. Tú / describir las jugadas ____________________

EXERCISE L. **Imagine you are an exchange student in his/her first day of class. Your classmate David asks you several questions. Answer his questions negatively.**

EXAMPLE: ¿Vives con una familia que habla español? No, **no vivo** con una familia que habla español.

1. ¿Escriben tus padres cartas todos los días? ____________________

2. ¿Asistes tú a muchos conciertos? ____________________

3. ¿Viven Uds. cerca de la escuela? ____________________

4. ¿Insiste la familia en muchas reglas? ____________________

5. ¿Permiten ellos muchas libertades en la casa? ____________________

6. ¿Descubres tú muchas cosas nuevas? ____________________

EXERCISE M. **Lee is an avid joker and always responds to what you say with a question. Write the questions she asks for each statement you make.**

EXAMPLE: Los hermanos Silva viven en Costa Rica. ¿**Viven** los hermanos Silva en Costa Rica?

1. Ellos asisten a un campamento de tenis.

____

2. Yo decido practicar con ellos.

____

3. Ángel escribe muchas tarjetas a sus amigos en Costa Rica.

____

4. Luisa cubre los regalos con un mantel.

____

5. Nosotros siempre dividimos la cuenta.

____

6. El tren para la ciudad parte a las tres y quince.

____

7. Tú insistes en contestar con preguntas.

____

MASTERY EXERCISES

EXERCISE N. **Gabriel is a fast talker and, when he speaks, one statement or question always follows another even if they are not related. Complete his statements / questions with the appropriate form of the verbs given.**

1. (*practicar*) Yo practico el piano cada tarde. ¿Qué practicas tú? Elias practica el fútbol americano.

2. (*vender*) Este señor vende globos. Esos niños venden limonada. Nosotros no vendemos nada.

3. (*sufrir*) El equipo sufre cuando no gana. Mi perro sufre cuando hace calor. ¿ sufren los gatos también?

4. (*prometer*) Yo prometo llegar a tiempo. Andrés promete trabajar mucho. ¿Qué prometes tú?

5. (*viajar*) Tú siempre viajares en autobús. María viajara en taxi. ¿En qué viajamos nosotros?

6. (*dividir*) Nosotros dividimos los gastos. Tú divides el trabajo. El señor Ramos no divide la cuenta.

EXERCISE O. **A young cousin asks you many questions about school. Answer his questions as indicated.**

1. ¿Entras tú a la escuela a tiempo? (*sí*)

____

2. ¿Quiénes saludan a la profesora? (*los alumnos*)

____

3. ¿Quién explica la lección? (*la profesora*)

____

4. ¿Usa la clase mucho tiempo en la biblioteca? (*no*)

____

5. ¿Reponden Uds. en inglés o en español?

____

6. ¿Dóne comes tú? (*la cafetería*)

____

7. ¿DeberUds. trabajar mucho? (*sí*)

____

8. ¿Asisten tú y tus amigos a las mismas clases? (no)

____

9. ¿Lees tú el periódico en la escuela? (a veces)

____

10. ¿Reciben Uds. buenas notas en los exámenes? (*sí*)

____

EXERCISE P. Tell who does the following activities.

yo	correr tres millas cada día
tú	practicar un deporte
mi amigo	leer muchas novelas
mis padres	asistir a una clase de baile
mi hermana y yo	escribir poemas

EXAMPLE: Pedro **ayuda** en casa.

1. ____

2. ____

3. ____

4. ____

5. ____

EXERCISE Q. You are talking about a new friend. Express the following sentences in Spanish.

1. She lives near the school. Ella vive cerca de la escuela.

2. She speaks Spanish and French. Ella habla español y francia.

3. Now she is learning English. Ahora ella aprende ingles.

4. She practices many sports. Ella practica muchos deportes.

5. We attend the same exercise class. Asistimos la misma clase de ejercicio.

6. She runs one mile every day. Ella corre una mile todos las días.

7. She insists on drinking a lot of water. Ella insiste en beber mucho agua.

8. Her parents don't understand English well. Sus padres no comprenden ingles bien.

9. They want to study English. Ellos desean estudiar ingles.

10. They read three newspapers each day. Ellos leen tres periodicos cada día.

11. Her father responds in Spanish but her mother responds in English. Su padre responde en español pero su madre responde en ingles.

12. They take pictures of many things. Sacan fotos de muchas cosas.

13. My friend explains the photos. Mi amigo explica las fotos.

14. We spend a lot of time together. Pasamos mucho tiempo juntos.

15. She promises to help me speak Spanish well. Ella promete ayudarme hablo español bien.

ACTIVIDADES

1. How many things do you do on a given day? Write a paragraph in Spanish in which you describe eight different activities you do on a specific day. Include the people with whom you do some of them and try to use a different verb for each activity.

2. Write a list of the chores you do around the house during the week and on the weekend. List eight chores using a different verb for each one.

3. Summer vacation has just begun. Write a paragraph in Spanish of at least ten sentences in which you describe some of the activities you usually do in the summer, the places you visit and the people with whom you do these things. Use as many different verbs as you can.

Chapter 2
Present Tense of Stem-Changing Verbs

[1] STEM-CHANGING *-AR* AND *-ER* VERBS

a. Many verbs that contain *e* in the stem change the *e* to *ie* in all present tense forms except those for *nosotros* and *vosotros.*

b. Many verbs that contain *o* in the stem change the *o* to *ue* in all present tense forms except those for *nosotros* and *vosotros.*

c. This change occurs in the syllable directly before the verb ending.

d. The verbs *cerrar, defender, contar,* and *volver* have regular endings in the present tense.

	cerrar *to close*	defender *to defend*	contrar *to count*	volver *to return*
yo	c*ie*rro	def*ie*ndo	c*ue*nto	v*ue*lvo
tú	c*ie*rras	def*ie*ndes	c*ue*ntas	v*ue*lves
Ud., él, ella	c*ie*rra	def*ie*nde	c*ue*nta	v*ue*lve
nosotros, -as	cerramos	defendemos	contamos	volvemos
vosotros, -as	cerráis	defendéis	contáis	volvéis
Uds., ellos, ellas	c*ie*rran	def*ie*nden	c*ue*ntan	v*ue*lven

NOTE: All stem-changing verbs that change *e* to *ie* or *o* to *ue* are identified in the end vocabulary by (*ie*) or (*ue*) after the verb.

Common Stem-Changing Verbs

E to *IE*

atravesar *to cross*
calentar *to heat*
cerrar *to close*
comenzar *to begin*
confesar *to confess*
defender *to defend*
despertarse *to wake up*
empezar *to begin*
encender *to light*
entender *to understand*
gobernar *to govern*
nevar *to snow*
pensar *to think; to intend*
perder *to lose*
quebrar *to break*
querer *to want; to wish; to love*
sentarse *to sit down*
temblar *to tremble*

O to *UE*

acordarse (de) *to remember*
acostarse *to go to bed*
almorzar *to (eat) lunch*
contar *to count*
costar *to cost*
devolver *to return, to give back*
encontrar *to find, to meet*
envolver *to wrap up*
jugar (ue) *to play*
llover *to rain*
morder *to bite*
mostrar *to show*
mover *to move*
oler (hue) *to smell*
poder *to be able, can*
probar *to prove, to try, to test*
recordar *to remember*
sonar *to sound*
soñar con *to dream*
volar *to fly*
volver *to return*

EXERCISE A. **Thomas and his friends are talking about the future. Tell what each one intends to do.**

EXAMPLE: Thomas / visitar a España — Thomas **piensa** visitar a España.

1. Elena / estudiar enfermería — ~~Elena~~ Elena piensa estudiar enfermería
2. Ellos / ser jugadores de béisbol — ~~Ellos piensan ser jugadores de béisbol~~
3. yo / escribir una novela — Yo pienso escribir una novela.
4. Kyoto / volver al Japón — ~~Kyoto piensa volver al Japón~~
5. Gabriel y yo / visitar un parque de atracciones — Gabriel y yo pensamos visitar un parque
6. tú / ganar un campeonato — ~~Tú piensas ganar un campeonato~~
7. los hermanos Silva / trabajar con su padre — Los hermanos Silva piensan trabajar con su padre.
8. Ignacio / ser abogado — ~~Ignacio piensa ser abogado.~~

EXERCISE B. **Tell what language each of these people understands.**

EXAMPLE: Vicenzo / italiano — Vicenzo **entiende** italiano.

1. Marcel / francés — Marcel entiende francés.
2. Natasha / ruso — ____________
3. Sofía y Josefina / rumano — Sofía y Josefina entienden rumano.
4. Hans y yo / alemán — ____________
5. Tú / portugués — Tú entiendes portugués.
6. Uds. / chino — ____________
7. Ahmed / árabe — Ahmed entiende árabe
8. el señor Kim / coreano — ____________

EXERCISE C. **Tell where each of these people eats lunch.**

EXAMPLE: Carmen / cafetería de la escuela — Carmen **almuerza en** la cafetería de la escuela.

1. los primos / parque — Los primos almuerzan en el parque
2. Papá / oficina — ____________
3. yo / comedor — Yo almuerzo en el comedor.
4. Sasha y Felipe / restaurante — ____________
5. tú / café de la plaza — Tú almuerzas en el café de la plaza.

6. mis abuelos y yo /al aire libre ______________________
7. el médico / hospital El médico almuerza en el hospital.
8. el salvavidas / la playa ______________________

EXERCISE D. **Tell at what time each person returns home.**

EXAMPLE: Florence / a las ocho Florence **vuelve** a casa a las ocho.

1. yo / a las cuatro Yo vuelvo a ~~las~~ casa a las cuarto.
2. mis padres / a las siete ~~Mis padres vuelven a casa a las siete.~~
3. mi hermano / a la una Mi hermano vuelve a casa a la una.
4. tú / a la medianoche ~~Tú vuelves a casa a la medianoche.~~
5. Richard y Charles / a las once Richard y Charles vuelven a casa a las once.
6. Romi y yo / a las nueve ~~Romi y yo volvemos a casa a las nueve~~

EXERCISE E. **Tell who does or doesn't do each of the following things.**

EXAMPLE: los soldados / defender la patria Los soldados **defienden** la patria.

1. los niños / no atravesar la calle solos Los niños no atraviesan la calle solos.
2. el portero / cerrar las puertas ~~El portero cierra las puertas.~~
3. yo / soñar con unas vacaciones en la playa Yo ~~sueño~~ sueño con unas vacaciones en la playa.
4. el perro / no morder al niño ~~El perro no muerde al niño.~~
5. tú / encender la luz del patio Tú enciendes la luz del patio.
6. Roberto y yo / no pensar jugar al tenis esta tarde ______________________
7. yo / calentar la sopa Yo caliento la sopa.
8. tú / devolver el regalo a la tienda ______________________
9. Uds. / empezar a ahorrar dinero Uds. empiezan a ahorrar dinero
10. nosotros / no probar la comida japonesa ______________________

EXERCISE F. **Answer the questions a Spanish-speaking pen pal asks you about you and your friends. Use the cues provided.**

1. ¿Piensan Uds. asistir a la universidad? (*sí*)

____

2. ¿Te acuestas tarde todos los días? (*no*)

____

3. ¿Juegan Uds. al fútbol cuando llueve? (*no*)

____

4. ¿Piensas tú que el presidente gobierna bien? (*sí*)

____

5. ¿Pierde frecuentemente el equipo de béisbol de tu escuela? (*no*)

____

6. ¿Quieren tú y tus amigos visitar mi país? (*sí*)

____

7. ¿Puedes recordar los cumpleaños de todos tus amigos? (*no*)

____

8. ¿Cuentan tus amigos contigo? (*sí*)

____

e → ie

[2] STEM-CHANGING *-IR* VERBS

a. Some *-ir* verbs that contain an *e* in the stem change the *e* to *ie* or to *i* in all present-tense forms, except those for *nosotros* and *vosotros.*

b. Some *-ir* verbs that contain an *o* in the stem change the *o* to *ue* in all present-tense forms, except those for *nosotros* and *vosotros.*

c. The change occurs in the syllable directly before the verb ending.

d. The verbs *sentir, dormir,* and *pedir* have regular endings in the present tense.

	sentir *to regret*	**dormir** *to sleep*	**pedir** *to ask for*
yo	s*ie*nto	d*ue*rmo	p*i*do
tú	s*ie*ntes	d*ue*rmes	p*i*des
Ud., él, ella	s*ie*nte	d*ue*rme	p*i*de
nosotros, -as	sentimos	dormimos	pedimos
vosotros, -as	sentís	dormís	pedís
Uds., ellos, ellas	s*ie*nten	d*ue*rmen	p*i*den

NOTE: All stem-changing verbs that change *e* to *ie, e* to *i,* or *o* to *ue* are identified in the end vocabulary by (*ie*), (*i*), or (*ue*) after the verb.

Common Stem-Changing Verbs

E to *IE*

preferir *to prefer* **referir** *to tell; to narrate* **sentir** *to regret, be sorry; to feel*

O to *UE*

dormir *to sleep* **morir(se)** *to die*

[handwritten conjugation box: yo duermo, dormimos nosotros (ros); tú duermes; él/ella/Ud. duerme, duermen ellos/ellas/Uds.]

E to I

despedirse (de) *to take leave (of),* *to say goodbye (to)*	**reír(se)** *to laugh*	**sonreír(se)** *to smile*
impedir *to prevent*	**reñir** *to quarrel; to scold*	**vestirse** *to get dressed,* *to dress (oneself)*
medir *to measure*	**repetir** *to repeat*	
pedir *to ask for, request; to order (food)*	**servir** *to serve*	

NOTE: The verbs *reír* and *sonreír* have an accent mark over the *i* in all the present tense forms: *río, ríes, ríe, reímos, reís, ríen.*

EXERCISE G. You and your friends are planning a day's outing but can't decide where to go. Tell what each person prefers.

EXAMPLE: Carina / ir a la piscina Carina prefiere ir a la piscina.

1. Esther / sentarse en un café. *Esther se sienta en un café*

2. Berta y Homero / mirar la televisión *Berta y Homero miran la televisión*

3. Yo / visitar un museo *Visito*

4. Uds. / caminar en el parque *Caminan*

5. Tú / ir al estadio *Vas*

6. Roberto y yo / ver una película *Vemos*

EXERCISE H. Teddy is describing how the members of his family sleep. Tell what he says.

EXAMPLE: mi padre / con la boca abierta Mi padre **duerme** con la boca abierta.

1. yo / con los ojos cerrados *duermo*

2. mi hermano / con un ojo abierto *duerme*

3. mis abuelos / en la silla - chair *duermen*

4. tú / boca abajo *duermes*

5. mi tía Aurora / tranquilamente *duerme*

6. mis hermanos y yo / profundamente *dormimos*

EXERCISE I. You and several friends are in a Spanish restaurant. Tell what each person orders.

EXAMPLE: Alex / arroz con pollo Alex **pide** arroz con pollo.

1. Marisa / paella *pide*

2. Eddie y Verónica / mariscos *piden*

3. yo / una chuleta de cerdo *pido*

4. Larry / cocido *pide*

5. tú / caldo gallego ______________________________

6. nosotros / flan de postre ______________________________

EXERCISE J. Tell when each of these people laughs.

EXAMPLE: Marina / lee las tiras cómicas Marina **ríe cuando** lee las tiras cómicas.

1. tú / escuchas un chiste ______________________________

2. Amelia / tiene miedo ______________________________

3. Arthur y Freda / cometen un error ______________________________

4. mis amigos y yo / vemos algo cómico ______________________________

5. yo / mi hermana canta ______________________________

6. muchas personas / están nerviosas ______________________________

EXERCISE K. Sondra is writing a story about her grandmother. Help her complete it by writing the appropriate form of the verbs indicated in the spaces provided.

Mi abuela siempre ________ (*1.* referir) muchos cuentos de su infancia y de su adolescencia. A veces ella ________ (*2.* repetir) el mismo cuento cinco veces. Ella no nos ________ (*3.* reñir) cuando nosotros se lo ________ (*4.* recordar). Muchas veces ella ________ (*5.* vestirse) en ropa antigua mientras ________ (*6.* referir) el cuento. Ella ________ (*7.* sentarse) en una silla en la sala y mis primos y yo ________ (*8.* sentarse) en el piso frente a su silla. Ella siempre ________ (*9.* comenzar) el cuento con la misma introducción y nosotros ________ (*10.* sonreír). Ninguno de mis primos ________ (*11.* dormirse) durante el cuento. Las tías nos ________ (*12.* servir) leche y galletas y mis primos Héctor y Felipe siempre ________ (*13.* pedir) más. A veces los cuentos son cómicos y Felipe ________ (*14.* reír) muchísimo. Entonces mi abuela le ________ (*15.* reñir) porque él ________ (*16.* impedir) terminar el cuento. Cuando ella termina el cuento, ella ________ (*17.* despedirse) de nosotros con estas palabras: «Yo lo ________ (*18.* sentir) mucho, pero es el fin del cuento.» Me gustan sus cuentos y yo se los ________ (*19.* repetir) a mis amigos. Son cuentos alegres porque nadie ________ (*20.* morir) en ellos.

[3] VERBS ENDING IN *-IAR* AND *-UAR*

a. Some verbs ending in *-iar* and *-uar* have a written accent mark on the *i* (*í*) or the *u* (*ú*) in all present-tense forms, except those for *nosotros* and *vosotros.*

	enviar *to send*	**continuar** *to continue*
yo	**env*ío***	**contin*úo***
tú	**env*ías***	**contin*úas***
Ud., él, ella	**env*ía***	**contin*úa***
nosotros, -as	**enviamos**	**continuamos**
vosotros, -as	**enviáis**	**continuáis**
Uds., ellos, ellas	**env*ían***	**contin*úan***

NOTE:

1. The verbs *anunciar, averiguar, cambiar, copiar, estudiar, iniciar, limpiar, odiar, principiar,* and *pronunciar* are exceptions and have no accents on the *i* or the *u*.
2. All *-iar* and *-uar* verbs that have an accent on the *i* or *u* are identified in the end vocabulary by (*í*) or (*ú*) after the verb.

b. Verbs like *enviar* and *continuar*

confiar (en) *to rely (on), to confide (in)*
guiar *to guide, to drive (a vehicle)*
resfriarse *to catch a cold*
variar *to vary*
actuar *to act*
graduarse *to graduate*
situar *to place, to locate*

EXERCISE L. Lenny's sister is away at school and it's her birthday. Tell what everyone sends to her.

EXAMPLE: su abuela / besos Su abuela **le envía** besos.

1. yo / una tarjeta de cumpleaños ______________________
2. sus padres / dinero ______________________
3. su novio / flores ______________________
4. su hermana / globos ______________________
5. sus amigos / un telegrama ______________________
6. tú / un disco compacto ______________________
7. todo el mundo / felicitaciones ______________________

EXERCISE M. June is a busy month for the Vargas family. Everyone seems to be graduating. Tell where they are graduating from.

EXAMPLE: la hermana mayor / la universidad La hermana mayor **se gradúa de** la universidad.

1. el hermano menor / la primaria ______________________
2. Elena y Rosa / la secundaria ______________________
3. la prima Olivia / el jardín de niños ______________________
4. la tía Raquel / la Facultad de Leyes ______________________

5. tú / la Facultad de Medicina ______________________________

6. los primos Tony y Celso / la escuela vocacional ______________________________

EXERCISE N. Answer the questions a Spanish-speaking exchange student asks you.

1. ¿Guías el automóvil de tu familia?

____

2. ¿Continúas las clases de español este año?

____

3. ¿Envían tus amigos regalos de cumpleaños?

____

4. ¿Guían tus amigos su propio carro?

____

5. ¿Te resfrías fácilmente?

____

6. ¿Varías tu horario a menudo?

____

7. ¿Actúan tus amigos y tú en las obras de teatro de la escuela?

____

8. ¿Te gradúas de la secundaria este año?

____

[4] VERBS ENDING IN *-UIR*

a. Verbs ending in *-uir* (but not *-guir*) insert a *y* in the stem before the present-tense endings.

huir *to flee*			
yo	huyo	nosotros, (-as)	huimos
tú	huyes	vosotros, (-as)	huís
Ud., él ,ella	huye	Uds./ellos/ellas	huyen

Concluimos

NOTE: All verbs ending in *-uir* that add a *y* are identified in the end vocabulary by (*y*) after the infinitive.

b. Common Verbs Ending in *-UIR*

concluir *to conclude*
construir *to construct, to build*
contribuir *to contribute*
destruir *to destroy*
distribuir *to distribute*
influir *to influence*
sustituir *to substitute*

EXERCISE O. **One of the clubs in your school is sponsoring a toy drive for charity. Tell what each person contributes.**

EXAMPLE: Roger / una pelota Roger **contribuye** una pelota.

1. el señor Olmeda / un rompecabezas ______________________
2. Franco / un juguete ______________________
3. Lisa y Janet / dos animales de peluche ______________________
4. yo / un guante de béisbol ______________________
5. tú / una pelota de voleibol ______________________
6. mi hermano y yo / un juego de damas ______________________

EXERCISE P. **The following observations are made at a public town-hall meeting. Complete each one with the appropriate form of the verb in parentheses.**

1. Los políticos (*influir*) ______________ mucho en la vida del pueblo.
2. Los perros (*destruir*) ______________ las plantas y las flores de los parques.
3. Mi vecino (*construir*) ______________ una fuente grande entre las dos casas.
4. Lázaro y yo (*distribuir*) ______________ muchos folletos a favor de la conservación.
5. Muchas veces tú (*sustituir*) ______________ una idea por otra.
6. Los comerciantes (*contribuir*) ______________ mucho dinero a las obras públicas.
7. La reunión (*concluir*) ______________ con muchos aplausos.

MASTERY EXERCISES

EXERCISE Q. **Tell who does the following things.**

preferir ver una telenovela	servir el café	graduarse de la escuela
pensar viajar en el verano	guiar el carro	no resfriarse
acostarse temprano	resolver el problema	actuar en una película
morder un hueso		

1. Mi hermano mayor ______________________.
2. El bebé ______________________.
3. Los matemáticos ______________________.
4. Yo ______________________.
5. La actriz ______________________.

6. El perro ____.

7. Tú ____.

8. Mi mamá ____.

9. El mesero ____.

10. Los médicos ____.

EXERCISE R. **Match the situation in column A with an appropriate reaction in column B. Then, using that reaction, write what these people do.**

EXAMPLE: Papá está muy cansado. dormir la siesta
Papá **duerme** la siesta.

A	B
Yo recuerdo que es el cumpleaños de mi novia.	a. jugar al tenis y al voleibol
Alicia tiene que llegar a la escuela a las 7:30.	b. reír mucho
Mi mamá quiere comprar una alfombra nueva.	c. volver a la tienda
Los niños están muy contentos.	d. enviar una tarjeta
El arquitecto necesita una casa más grande.	e. medir el cuarto
A Susana le gustan los deportes.	f. despertarse temprano
Tú compras dos regalos pero necesitas tres.	g. construir una casa grande

1. ____

2. ____

3. ____

4. ____

5. ____

6. ____

7. ____

EXERCISE S. **Use the cues provided to answer the questions a friend asks you.**

1. ¿Cuántas horas duermes cada noche? (*ocho*)

____

2. ¿Cuándo te acuestas? (*tarde*)

____

3. ¿Cuándo te despiertas? (*temprano*)

____

4. ¿Dónde almuerzan tus amigos y tú? (*la cafetería de la escuela*)

____

5. ¿Cuánto cuesta el almuerzo? (*dos dólares*)

____

6. ¿Cuándo sonríes? (*estoy contento*)

____

7. ¿Qué trabajo tienes los sábados? (*distribuir folletos*)

____

EXERCISE T. Raúl is talking about his father. Express what he says in Spanish.

1. My father constructs houses.

____

2. He meets a lot of people.

____

3. They ask for houses with large rooms.

____

4. He includes several very large rooms in the plans.

____

5. Each room costs about $15,000.

____

6. They begin the construction in the spring.

____

7. They do not work when it snows or rains.

____

8. If the weather is bad they lose a lot of time.

____

9. Sometimes they move very large trees.

____

10. I am able to help him during the vacations.

____

11. They always intend to finish on time.

____

12. My father doesn't sleep very much.

____

13. Sometimes he quarrels with the other workers but they usually laugh a lot.

____

14. He works outdoors but he doesn't catch cold often.

____

15. He relies a lot on the other workers.

____

ACTIVIDADES

You are traveling in Spain with your family. Write a letter in Spanish to a friend at home in which you relate the people you meet on the trip, what you want to do during the trip, how you are managing in a Spanish-speaking country, the foods you are trying, and other interesting details. Try to use as many of the verbs as you can from this chapter.

Chapter 3
Verbs with Spelling Changes in the Present Tense

[1] VERBS ENDING IN *-CER* AND *-CIR*

a. Most verbs whose infinitives end in *-cer* and *-cir* have the ending *-zco* in the first-person singular of the present tense. This pattern occurs only if a vowel precedes the *c* in the infinitive.

	ofrecer *to offer*	**producir** *to produce*
yo	ofre*zco*	produ*zco*
tú	ofreces	produces
Ud., él, ella	ofrece	produces
nosotros, -as	ofrecemos	producimos
vosotros, -as	ofrecéis	producís
Uds., ellos, ellas	ofrecen	producen

b. If a consonant precedes the *c* in the infinitive, the ending *-zo* is used in the first-person singular of the present tense.

vencer *to conquer, defeat*			
yo	venzo	nosotros	vencemos
tú	vences	vosotros	vencéis
Ud., él, ella	vence	Uds., ellos, ellas	vencen

NOTE: Verbs with these spelling changes are identified in the end vocabulary by (*z*) or (*zc*) after the infinitive.

c. Common Verbs with Spelling Changes

1. *-CER* Verbs (like *ofrecer*)

agradecer *to thank (for)*
aparecer *to appear*
conocer *to know (a person)*
desaparecer *to disappear*
merecer *to deserve*
nacer *to be born*
obedecer *to obey*
ofrecer *to offer*
padecer *to suffer*
parecer *to seem*
permanecer *to remain*
pertenecer *to belong*
reconocer *to recognize*

2. *-CER* Verbs (like *vencer*)

convencer *to convince*
ejercer *to exert, to exercise, to practice (a profession)*
vencer *to conquer, to defeat*

3. *-CIR* Verbs

conducir *to lead, to drive*
producir *to produce*
reducir *to reduce*
traducir *to translate*

NOTE: The verbs *hacer* and *decir* are exceptions.

EXERCISE A. **Tell who obeys and who follows rules.**

EXAMPLE: los soldados / el toque de queda Los soldados **obedecen** el toque de queda.

1. el chofer / el semáforo rojo ____________________
2. el perro / a su dueño ____________________
3. los ciudadanos / las leyes ____________________
4. yo / a mis padres ____________________
5. tú / al entrenador del equipo ____________________
6. Sabrina y yo / las reglas del juego ____________________

EXERCISE B. **The president of the freshman class is mentioning the places in the school with which each of them is already familiar.**

EXAMPLE: Humberto / la biblioteca Humberto **ya conoce** la biblioteca.

1. Sarita y Mercedes / el teatro ____________________
2. Felipe / la cafetería ____________________
3. Ralph y yo / el gimnasio ____________________
4. tú / la piscina ____________________
5. yo / los laboratorios ____________________
6. Miguel / la oficina del director ____________________

EXERCISE C. **The Spanish Club is planning for a visit by Spanish-speaking exchange students to their school. Tell what the members volunteer to translate for them.**

EXAMPLE: Ruth / el manual estudiantil Ruth **traduce** el manual estudiantil.

1. yo / el menú de la cafetería

____

2. Larry / los anuncios diarios

____

3. Nilda e Inés / las reglas de seguridad

____

4. Ana y yo / la tarea

____

5. tú / un artículo del periódico estudiantil

____

6. Bárbara / el horario de los partidos de fútbol

____

EXERCISE D. **Using the suggestions, tell the profession each of these people practices.**

SUGGESTIONS: actor, maestro, médico, entrenador personal, pintor, mecánico, mesero

EXAMPLE: Alfredo les enseña a las personas en el gimnasio.
Alfredo ejerce la profesión de **entrenador personal.**

1. Mi hermana le enseña a los alumnos.

____

2. Mi madre cura a los enfermos.

____

3. Mi tío arregla los carros.

____

4. Yo trabajo en un restaurante y les sirvo a los clientes.

____

5. Tú pintas muchos cuadros bonitos.

____

6. Gladys y yo trabajamos en el teatro.

____

EXERCISE E. **Complete with the appropriate form of the verbs indicated the letter that Gabriel wrote to Guy shortly after his arrival in Santander.**

Querido Guy,

Yo ______ (*1.* agradecer) mucho toda tu ayuda antes de la hora del viaje. ______ (*2.* parecer) que yo ______ (*3.* padecer) de la mala costumbre de dejarlo todo para el último momento. Tú ______ (*4.* parecer) mi único buen amigo. Mis otros amigos ______ (*5.* desaparecer) cuando más los necesito. Esta ciudad ______ (*6.* ofrecer) mucho para el turista. Hay museos, teatros, cines, parques, playa y restaurantes buenos. Yo ya ______ (*7.* conocer) los restaurantes baratos y los cafés donde se reúnen los jóvenes. El chofer del autobús en que viajamos ______ (*8.* conducir) muy rápido y ______ (*9.* parecer) que no ______ (*10.* obedecer) las señales de tránsito. El guía ______ (*11.* traducir) todo y ______ (*12.* permanecer) con el grupo todo el día. El ______ (*13.* aparecer) antes del desayuno y no ______ (*14.* desaparecer) hasta después de la cena. Yo ______ (*15.* pertenecer) a un grupo de jóvenes divertidos y nosotros ______ (*16.* reconocer) que tenemos los mismos intereses. Nos levantamos temprano y ______ (*17.* ejercer) en el parque—corremos dos millas cada día. Ellos me ______ (*18.* convencer) a permanecer en España por más tiempo. Es todo por ahora. Hasta pronto, mi buen amigo.

Saludos de,
Gabriel

[2] VERBS ENDING IN *-GER* AND *-GIR*

a. Most verbs whose infinitives end in *-ger* and *-gir* have the ending *-jo* in the first-person singular of the present tense.

b. This pattern occurs to preserve the original sound in accordance with the rules for Spanish pronunciation.

	proteger *to protect*	**dirigir** *to direct*
yo	prote*j*o	diri*j*o
tú	proteges	diriges
Ud., él, ella	protege	dirige
nosotros, -as	protegemos	dirigimos
vosotros, -as	protegéis	dirigís
Uds., ellos, ellas	protegen	dirigen

NOTE: Verbs with these spelling changes are identified in the end vocabulary by (*j*) after the infinitive.

c. Common -*GER* and -*GIR* Verbs

coger *to seize, to catch*
escoger *to choose*
proteger *to protect*
recoger *to pick up, to gather*
corregir (i) *to correct*
dirigir *to direct*
dirigirse *to make one's way toward, to address*
elegir (i) *to elect*

EXERCISE F. **Everyone is helping to pick up after the party. Tell what each person picks up.**

EXAMPLE: Gina / vasos Gina **recoge** los vasos.

1. Anthony / platos sucios ______________________
2. Javier y Joan / discos compactos ______________________
3. yo / decoraciones ______________________
4. Frida y yo / botellas vacías ______________________
5. Tú / papeles ______________________
6. Alice / velas ______________________

EXERCISE G. **At summer camp everyone has to choose a sport. Tell which sport each person chooses.**

SUGGESTIONS: el béisbol, la equitación, el fútbol, el golf, la natación, el voleibol

EXAMPLE: A Carlos le gusta jugar con una o dos personas. Carlos **escoge el tenis.**

1. A mí me gusta ir a la playa cuando hace mucho calor.
   Yo ______________________.
2. A Robert le gusta correr y patear una pelota.
   Robert ______________________.

3. A Manny y a José les gusta caminar mucho y meter una pelota en un hoyo.
Manny y José ____ .

4. A ti te gusta montar a caballo.
Tú ____ .

5. A Pablo y a mí nos gusta batear pelotas.
Pablo y yo ____ .

6. A Daniel le gusta pasar una pelota de un lado de la red a otro.
Daniel ____ .

EXERCISE H. Use the cues provided to tell who directs what activity.

EXAMPLE: el policía / dirigir el tránsito El policía **dirige** el tránsito.

1. Susana / dirigir una orquesta ______________________

2. Enrique /dirigir a los actores ______________________

3. tú / dirigir una banda ______________________

4. yo / dirigir a los mecánicos ______________________

5. mis padres / dirigir a los jardineros ______________________

6. Carol y yo / dirigir al perro ______________________

[*3*] VERBS ENDING IN *-GUIR*

a. Most verbs whose infinitives end in *-guir* have the ending *-go* in the first-person singular of the present tense.

b. This pattern occurs to preserve the original sound in accordance with the rules for Spanish pronunciation.

distinguir *to distinguish*			
yo	**distingo**	**nosotros**	**distinguimos**
tú	**distingues**	**vosotros**	**distinguís**
Ud., él, ella	**distingue**	**Uds., ellos ,ellas**	**distinguen**

NOTE: Verbs with these spelling changes are identified in the end vocabulary by (*g*) after the infinitive

c. Common -*GUIR* Verbs

conseguir (i) *to get, to obtain, to succeed in*
distinguir *to distinguish*
extinguir *to extinguish*
perseguir (i) *to pursue*
seguir (i) *to follow, to continue*

EXERCISE I. **Complete each statement with an appropriate form of *distinguir* to explain each person's doubt.**

1. Los padres de Héctor siempre lo castigan. Héctor no ________________ entre lo bueno y lo malo.
2. ¿Es una corbata verde o azul? Yo no ________________ los colores.
3. El gato duerme todo el día y quiere jugar por la noche. El gato no ________________ entre el día y la noche.
4. ¿Es un mango o una papaya? Nosotros no ________________ los sabores.
5. ¿Es un teatro o una iglesia? Tú no ________________ bien los edificios.
6. ¿Es un diamante o una esmeralda? La señora no ________________ las piedras preciosas.

EXERCISE J. **Combine the words in the two columns to tell who does what (use the verb *seguir*).**

yo	los consejos de los profesores
el atleta	la misma carrera que nuestro padre
la señora	las instrucciones del médico
los enfermos	la misma ruta a la ciudad
tú	una dieta muy estricta
mis hermanos y yo	un régimen de ejercicios
el chofer	la receta

EXAMPLE: Tú / la receta Tú **sigues** la receta.

1. ____
2. ____
3. ____
4. ____
5. ____
6. ____

MASTERY EXERCISES

EXERCISE K. **Beto's little brother always wants to be the center of attention. He contradicts everything he hears. Tell what he says.**

EXAMPLE: El policía persigue al ladrón. ¡No! **Yo** persigo al ladrón.

1. Elena sigue el plano de la ciudad.

____

2. Rogelio y yo cogemos la pelota.

____

3. El profesor corrige la frase.

____

4. Mamá conoce a los nuevos vecinos.

____

5. El niño explorador merece una medalla.

____

6. Geraldo y Larry nunca obedecen las señales de tránsito.

____

7. Tú nunca recoges las hojas en el jardín.

____

8. Los bomberos extinguen el fuego.

____

9. Susan escoge una bicicleta azul.

____

10. Aniluz consigue un boleto para el concierto.

____

11. El perro siempre desaparece cuando hay un problema.

____

12. José convence a sus padres fácilmente.

____

EXERCISE L. **Answer the questions your new friend asks you.**

1. ¿Escoges con cuidado a tus amigos ?

____

2. ¿Les agradeces a tus amigos los favores que ellos te hacen?

____

3. ¿Distingues entre la realidad y el sueño?

____

4. ¿Corriges tus faltas?

____

5. ¿Vences a tus rivales?

____

6. ¿Proteges a tus hermanos?

____

7. ¿Conoces a tus vecinos?

____

8. ¿Ofreces ayuda en casa?

____

9. ¿Desapareces cuando hay algo que hacer?

____

10. ¿Consigues buenas notas en todas las clases?

____

11. ¿Obedeces a tus padres?

____

12. ¿Conduces un automóvil?

____

13. ¿Recoges tus libros antes de salir de casa?

____

14. ¿Sigues las noticias todos los días?

____

15. ¿Padeces de dolor de cabeza?

____

EXERCISE M. **Manuel is running for president of the student government. Help him express what he plans to say at the election assembly.**

1. Today the students elect a president of the student government.

____

2. The new president remains in the office for one year.

____

3. I seize this opportunity to address you.

____

4. The president leads the daily work of the student government.

____

5. It seems like a difficult assignment.

____

6. We choose from three candidates.

____

7. I offer my experience and services.

____

8. I recognize that I have defects but I deserve your support.

____

9. If we work together we produce good results.

____

10. All candidates convince the public.

____

11. I follow the rules.

____

12. The candidate that gets the most votes wins.

____

13. I deserve to win.

____

14. I appreciate your attention.

____

ACTIVIDADES

1. Imagine that you are at a summer camp. Write a letter to a friend in which you describe your experience there. Write at least ten sentences in Spanish, using as many verbs from this chapter as possible.

You may use the following:

Dateline:	**19 de julio de** ______
Salutation:	**Querido(-a)** ____________ :
Closing:	**Tu amigo(-a),**

2. Find ten pictures in a magazine or newspaper that reflect the action of ten of the verbs presented in this chapter. Paste each picture on a sheet of paper and write a sentence below each one to describe it.

Chapter 4

Verbs Irregular in the Present Tense

[1] VERBS WITH IRREGULAR *YO* FORMS

a. In the present tense, the following verbs have irregular *yo* forms:

caber	*to fit*	*quepo,* cabes, cabe, cabemos, cabéis, caben
dar	*to give*	*doy,* das, da, damos, dais, dan
hacer	*to make, to do*	*hago,* haces, hace, hacemos, hacéis, hacen
poner	*to put, to place*	*pongo,* pones, pone, ponemos, ponéis, ponen
saber	*to know*	*sé,* sabes, sabe, sabemos, sabéis, saben
salir	*to go out* (leave)	*salgo,* sales, sale, salimos, salís, salen
valer	*to be worth*	*valgo,* vales, vale, valemos, valéis, valen
ver	*to see, to watch*	*veo,* ves, ve, vemos, veis, ven

b. The *yo* form of *caer* (to fall) and *traer* (to bring) has an *i* between the stem and the first-person singular ending (*-go*). Their other forms are regular.

caer	*to fall*	*caigo,* caes, cae, caemos, caéis, caen
traer	*to bring*	*traigo,* traes, trae, traemos, traéis, traen

EXERCISE A. **Your friend Edgar is telling his parents all the things he can now do after attending camp for the first time. Tell what he says:**

EXAMPLE: hacer la cama Yo **sé** hacer la cama.

1. trabajar en la computadora ______________________
2. patinar en monopatín ______________________
3. montar a caballo ______________________
4. jugar al voleibol ______________________
5. tocar el violín ______________________
6. identificar las estrellas ______________________

EXERCISE B. **A group of young people are telling what they do after school. Express what each one says.**

EXAMPLE: Silvia / hacer la tarea Yo **hago** la tarea.

1. Humberto / hacer ejercicios hago
2. Amelia / ver mi programa favorito veo
3. Peter / salir con mis amigos salgo
4. Virginia / poner las cosas en su lugar pongo
5. Alejandro / dar de comer a los gatos doy

EXERCISE C. **Your sister received the following e-mail message from a friend who lives in Madrid, but the communication wasn't clear. Help her decipher the message by filling in the missing words.**

Querida amiga:

Todos los días yo ______ (*1.* hacer) planes diferentes para pasar las vacaciones de verano. Aquí te ______ (*2.* poner) el plan más reciente. ______ (*3.* salir) de Madrid el 10 de julio en el vuelo 400 de Iberia. Te ______ (*4.* dar) el número de teléfono de mi tía: 892 61 12. Yo te ______ (*5.* ver) pronto. Saludos.

Emilio

EXERCISE D. **Jeremy is trying to decorate and organize his room but things aren't going well for him. Describe what's happening.**

EXAMPLE: el reloj / de la chimenea — El reloj **cae** de la chimenea.

1. la tarea / en la cesta de basura ______
2. los discos / detrás del mueble ______
3. las cortinas / de las ventanas ______
4. el fútbol / debajo de la cama ______
5. los carteles / de la pared ______
6. el refresco / al suelo ______

EXERCISE E. **Guillermo is organizing a party to celebrate the end of the school year. Tell what his friends bring to the party.**

EXAMPLE: Gerardo / los discos — Gerardo **trae** los discos.

1. tú / los refrescos ______
2. Marisol / las palomitas ______
3. Alicia y yo / los sándwiches ______
4. yo / el tocadiscos ______
5. Kenji / los adornos ______
6. Tony y Yolanda / los platos ______

[2] VERBS WITH IRREGULAR PRESENT-TENSE FORMS

The following verbs are irregular in the present tense:

decir	*to say, to tell*	digo, dices, dice, decimos, decís, dicen
estar	*to be*	estoy, estás, está, estamos, estáis, están
ir	*to go*	voy, vas, va, vamos, váis, van

oír	*to hear*	**oigo, oyes, oye, oímos, oís, oyen**
ser	*to be*	**soy, eres, es, somos, sois, son**
tener	*to have*	**tengo, tienes, tiene, tenemos, tenéis, tienen**
venir	*to come*	**vengo, vienes, viene, venimos, venís, vienen**

EXERCISE F. **It's the first day of summer vacation. Tell where the following people go.**

EXAMPLE: Margarita / al centro comercial — Margarita **va** al centro comercial.

1. Luis / a la playa ______________________________

2. mis hermanos / al parque ______________________________

3. Gloria / al cine ______________________________

4. yo / al centro ______________________________

5. Esteban y José / al museo ______________________________

6. Migdalia y yo / al restaurante ______________________________

EXERCISE G. **You are showing a friend some photographs of your trip to Mexico. Tell where each person is in the photos.**

EXAMPLE: Lina y Beatriz están delante de la iglesia.

1. Ernesto y Lorenzo ______________________________
______________________________.

2. Yo ______________________________
______________________________.

3. Mis padres ______________________________
______________________________.

4. Ruthie ______________________________
______________________________.

5. Roberto y yo ______________________________
______________________________.

6. Yo ______________________________
______________________________.

EXERCISE H. Tell when each of the following people comes to school.

EXAMPLE: los profesores / 7:00 Los profesores **vienen** a las siete.

1. yo / 8:15 ______________________________

2. el director / 7:30 ______________________________

3. mis amigos / 8:30 ______________________________

4. tú / 8:00 ______________________________

5. Armando y yo / 7:45 ______________________________

6. Elena / 9:00 ______________________________

EXERCISE I. Tell each person's profession, according to his / her job description.

EXAMPLE: La señora Ramos da clases. La señora Ramos **es maestra.**

1. La señorita Mateo cuida a los enfermos en su consultorio.
La señorita Mateo ______________________________.

2. Pablo vende cosas en un almacén grande.
Pablo ______________________________.

3. Tú apagas incendios.
Tú ______________________________.

4. Felipe y yo asistimos a la universidad.
Felipe y yo ______________________________.

5. Los señores Alba diseñan edificios.
Los señores Alba ______________________________.

6. Yo cuido a los nadadores en la playa en el verano.
Yo ______________________________.

EXERCISE J. You and several friends are hiking in the woods. Tell what each one hears.

EXAMPLE: Gabriel **oye** el canto de los pájaros.

1. Yo ________________ el ruido de un avión supersónico.

2. Ralph y Ted ____________ los pasos de otros excursionistas.

3. Tú ____________ el zumbido de las abejas.

4. Susan ____________ el sonido de un teléfono.

5. Elias y yo ____________ el viento en las hojas.

EXERCISE K. **Use the phrases below to tell what each person says in the following situations.**

Gracias.	Buen provecho.	Adiós.	Buenos días.
Mucho gusto.	Igualmente.	Hola.	Salud.

EXAMPLE: Lola sale de la casa. Lola dice **adiós.**

1. Entras en la casa de un amigo. Su familia cena.
Yo ____________ .

2. Ricardo acaba de conocer a Carlos y a Jaime.
Él ____________ y Carlos y Jaime ____________ .

3. Tú acabas de estornudar.
Tu mamá ____________ .

4. Antonia contesta el teléfono.
Ella ____________ .

5. Tus padres ven a un vecino.
Ellos ____________ .

6. Tú y tu hermano reciben un regalo de sus abuelos.
Ustedes ____________ .

EXERCISE L. **Describe each picture below using an expression with tener.**

EXAMPLE: Ricky **tiene miedo.**

1. Las chicas ____________
____________ .

2. Alberto ____________
____________ .

3. Tú ______________________________________
______________________________________.

5. Yo ______________________________________
______________________________________.

4. Miriam ______________________________________
______________________________________.

6. Celia y yo ______________________________________
______________________________________.

EXERCISE M. Use the cues provided to answer your friend's questions.

1. ¿Adónde vas mañana? (*a la playa*) ______________________________________

2. ¿Sabes nadar bien? (*sí*) ______________________________________

3. ¿A qué hora sales de la casa? (*7:30*) ______________________________________

4. ¿Tienes que viajar en autobús a la playa? (*sí*) ______________________________________

5. ¿Haces ejercicios en la playa? (*sí*) ______________________________________

6. ¿A quiénes ves allí? (*a mis amigos*) ______________________________________

7. ¿Qué oyes en la playa? (*los gritos de los niños*) ______________________________________

8. ¿A qué hora vienes a la casa? (*3:30*) ______________________________________

EXERCISE N. Complete the note that Marta leaves for her mother.

Querida mamá:

______________ (*1.* ser) mediodía. Yo ______________ (*2.* estar) muy contenta porque Arturo ______________ (*3.* venir) a visitarme. El ______________ (*4.* ser) de Costa Rica y ______________ (*5.* ser) simpático. Nosotros ______________ (*6.* ir) a ir al centro. Yo ______________ (7. tener) que comprar un libro para mi clase de inglés. Puesto que la librería ______________ (*8.* estar) cerca del cine, nosotros ______________ (9. ir) a ver una película. Yo ______________ (10. ir) a estar en casa a eso de las cinco y media.

Nos vemos,
Marta

MASTERY EXERCISES

EXERCISE O. Migdalia describes her host family in Venezuela to a friend. What are the appropriate forms of the missing verbs?

Vivo con una familia muy agradable. ______________ (1. ser) la familia Sagunto. Ellos ______________ (2. ser) de la Argentina pero ahora ______________ (3. estar) en Caracas porque el señor Sagunto trabaja en la Embajada Argentina. La señora Sagunto ______________ (4. ser) periodista. El periodismo ______________ (5. ser) una profesión muy interesante y divertida. Los Sagunto ______________ (6. tener) tres hijos: Raúl ______________ (7. tener) dieciséis años y Pilar e Hilda ______________ (8. tener) catorce. Ellas ______________ (9. ser) gemelas. Su casa ______________ (10. estar) en una parte muy pintoresca de la ciudad. Desde la ventana de mi dormitorio yo ______________ (11. ver) la salida del sol cada mañana porque el dormitorio ______________ (12. dar) al este. También ______________ (13. ver) un parque que ______________ (14. tener) muchos árboles. Nosotros ______________ (15. ir) al parque a menudo, y a veces el perro ______________ (16. ir) también. Coquito ______________ (17. ser) un perro cómico y bien educado, pero a veces yo ______________ (18. oír) sus ladridos a las seis de la mañana, cuando el lechero ______________ (19. venir) a la casa. A la familia le gusta pasar mucho tiempo juntos. Ellos ______________ (20. ser) aficionados al camping y los sábados, temprano por la mañana, ellos ______________ (21. poner) todo el equipo de acampar en su camioneta y ______________ (22. salir) para las montañas o un lago. Yo ______________ (23. ir) con ellos. Yo siempre ______________ (24. traer) mi diccionario conmigo: ______________ (25. ser) un amigo fiel y útil. Nosotros apenas ______________ (26. caber) en la camioneta porque nosotros ______________ (27. traer) tantas cosas: el equipo de acampar, el equipo deportivo y la comida. Durante el fin de semana nosotros ______________ (28. hacer) muchas cosas divertidas al aire libre. Ahora yo ______________ (29. hacer) planes de seguir esta rutina cuando yo ______________ (30. estar) en mi propia casa.

EXERCISE P. **What do you do in each of the following situations? Select the appropriate reaction for each one.**

darles un regalo	hacer la cama
salir aprisa de la casa	ir al parque
ir a la fiesta	tener que estudiar
ver el horario de los estrenos	poner la mesa
oír el pronóstico del tiempo	decir buenas noches

1. Hay una fiesta en casa de Elena.
   Yo ______________________________ .
2. Es el aniversario de mis abuelos.
   Yo ______________________________ .
3. Pienso ir a la playa mañana.
   Yo ______________________________ .
4. Yo pienso ir al cine con mis amigos.
   Yo ______________________________ .
5. El autobús escolar pasa en un minuto.
   Yo ______________________________ .
6. Debo arreglar mi cuarto.
   Yo ______________________________ .
7. Ayudo a mi madre con los preparativos de la cena.
   Yo ______________________________ .
8. Quiero jugar al béisbol.
   Yo ______________________________ .
9. Es hora de acostarme.
   Yo ______________________________ .
10. Hay un examen mañana en la clase de historia.
    Yo ______________________________ .

EXERCISE Q. **A friend stops by your house as you are getting ready to leave on a trip. Answer his questions using the cues provided.**

1. ¿Quién es tu compañero de viaje? (*mi primo*)
   ____
2. ¿Adónde van ustedes? (*España*)
   ____
3. ¿Qué clase de vuelo tienen ustedes? (*directo*)
   ____
4. ¿A qué hora salen ustedes de la casa? (*4:00*)
   ____

5. ¿En cuántas maletas cabe la ropa? (*2*)

6. ¿A qué hora llegan ustedes a España? (*no saber*)

7. ¿Qué traes en la maleta de mano? (*el pasaporte y el dinero*)

8. ¿Qué haces durante el vuelo? (*nada*)

9. ¿Cuánto vale todo el viaje? (*$1,500*)

10. ¿Qué ves por la ventanilla del avión? (*las nubes*)

EXERCISE R. You e-mail your Spanish penpal to tell her your plans for next week. Express the following in Spanish.

1. Next week, I am going to the country.

2. My friends say that it is pretty in autumn.

3. I always hear the weather forecast before I go out.

4. I always leave the house early in the morning.

5. I bring a book with me.

6. I wear sneakers because I fall a lot.

7. I see many different birds and I know how to identify them.

8. I put my things in my backpack.

9. Sometimes several friends come with me.

10. When I am in the country I see mountains.

11. It's a worthwhile experience.

12. I like to be outdoors.

Chapter 5
The Imperative

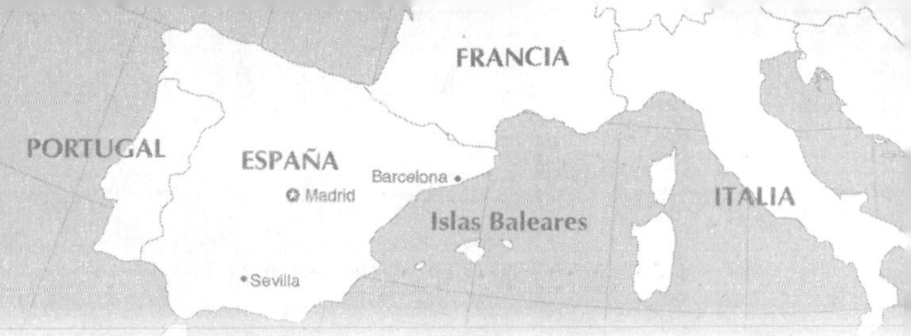

The imperative is the verb form used to give commands.

[*1*] FORMAL COMMANDS

a. Formal commands (*Ud., Uds.*) are used with persons you would normally address with *usted* (strangers, adults).

b. The formal (*Ud.*) command is formed from the *yo* form of the present tense. The final *-o* is changed as follows:

-ar verbs: *-e* for *Ud.* (singular) and *-en* for *Uds.* (plural).

-er verbs:
-ir verbs: } *-a* for *Ud.* (singular) and *-an* for *Uds.* (plural).

INFINITIVE	PRESENT TENSE	COMMAND FORMS		MEANING
	YO FORM	SINGULAR	PLURAL	
caer	**caigo**	**caiga**	**caigan**	*fall*
comer	**como**	**coma**	**coman**	*eat*
decir	**digo**	**diga**	**digan**	*say*
escribir	**escribo**	**escriba**	**escriban**	*write*
hacer	**hago**	**haga**	**hagan**	*do, make*
huir	**huyo**	**huya**	**huyan**	*flee*
oír	**oigo**	**oiga**	**oigan**	*hear*
poner	**pongo**	**ponga**	**pongan**	*put*
salir	**salgo**	**salga**	**salgan**	*leave*
tener	**tengo**	**tenga**	**tengan**	*have*
tomar	**tomo**	**tome**	**tomen**	*take*
traducir	**traduzco**	**traduzca**	**traduzcan**	*translate*
traer	**traigo**	**traiga**	**traigan**	*bring*
venir	**vengo**	**venga**	**vengan**	*come*
ver	**veo**	**vea**	**vean**	*see*

NOTE:

1. The vowel of the endings of the command forms are the opposite of the vowel endings of the *él / ella / Ud.* form of the present tense: *-e* for *-ar* verbs, and *-a* for *-er* and *-ir* verbs.
2. The subject pronoun (*Ud., Uds.*) follows the verb.
3. In Spanish America, *Uds.* can be either formal or informal (familiar).

c. To form the negative command, place no before the verb.

No griten. *Don't shout.*
No salga ahora. *Don't leave now.*

d. Stem-changing Verbs

The formal command (*Ud.)* is formed from the yo form of the present tense. The final *o-* is changed as follows:

-ar verbs: *-e* for *Ud.* (singular) and *-en* for *Uds.* (plural).

-er verbs:
-ir verbs: } *-a* for *Ud.* (singular) and *-an* for *Uds.* (plural).

E TO *IE* VERBS	PRESENT TENSE YO FORM	COMMAND FORMS SINGULAR	COMMAND FORMS PLURAL	MEANING
pensar	**pienso**	**piense**	**piensen**	*think*
defender	**defiendo**	**defienda**	**defiendan**	*defend*
referir	**refiero**	**refiera**	**refieran**	*tell*

E TO *I* VERBS	PRESENT TENSE YO FORM	COMMAND FORMS SINGULAR	COMMAND FORMS PLURAL	MEANING
medir	**mido**	**mida**	**midan**	*measure*
pedir	**pido**	**pida**	**pidan**	*ask (for)*

O TO *UE* VERBS	PRESENT TENSE YO FORM	COMMAND FORMS SINGULAR	COMMAND FORMS PLURAL	MEANING
contar	**cuento**	**cuente**	**cuenten**	*count*
mover	**muevo**	**mueva**	**muevan**	*move*
dormir	**duermo**	**duerma**	**duerman**	*sleep*

e. Verbs with Spelling Changes

Verbs that end in *-zar, -car,* and *-gar, -ger, -gir,* and *-guir* have spelling changes in the command forms. The spelling change in these verbs occurs to keep the original sound in the infinitive form.

zo→ce
co→que
gar→gue
ger→jo

INFINITIVE	PRESENT TENSE YO FORM	COMMAND FORMS SINGULAR	COMMAND FORMS PLURAL	MEANING
comenzar	**comienzo**	**comience**	**comiencen**	*begin*
practicar	**practico**	**practique**	**practiquen**	*practice*
llegar	**llego**	**llegue**	**lleguen**	*arrive*
escoger	**escojo**	**escoja**	**escojan**	*choose*
corregir	**corrijo**	**corrija**	**corrijan**	*correct*
seguir	**sigo**	**siga**	**sigan**	*follow, continue*

EXERCISE A. You are preparing a recipe for a class cookbook. Complete the recipe with the appropriate form of the verbs indicated.

EXAMPLE: sacar los ingredientes necesarios **Saque** los ingredientes necesarios.

1. poner dos tazas de agua en un caldero de tamaño mediano Ponga ______________________

2. hervir el agua ______________________

3. añadir el arroz, una cucharada de aceite de oliva o margarina y las especias añada
4. revolver bien con un tenedor revuelva
5. volver a hervir el arroz por un minuto Vuelva
6. cubrir el caldero bien cubra?
7. reducir el fuego a fuego lento reduzca
8. cocinar por 25 minutos ~~conci~~ cocine
9. apagar el fuego apague
10. servir en seguida con carne o pollo ______

EXERCISE B. **Your teacher is telling the class what they should do in preparation for a major examination. Complete each statement with the appropriate form of the verb indicated.**

EXAMPLE: estudiar la noche anterior **Estudien** la noche anterior.

1. llegar a tiempo ______
2. traer un bolígrafo y un lápiz ______
3. tomar el asiento asignado ______
4. prestar atención al profesor ______
5. no hablar con su vecino ______
6. abrir el examen al recibir la señal ______
7. leer todo con cuidado ______
8. seguir las instrucciones ______
9. trabajar diligente y rápidamente ______
10. contestar todas las preguntas ______
11. repasar su trabajo ______
12. no salir hasta la hora indicada ______

EXERCISE C. **In preparation for your first driving experience, the driver education teacher gives you the following instructions. Give the appropriate form of the verb indicated.**

EXAMPLE: (*entrar*) ______ en el carro con cuidado.
Entre en el carro con cuidado.

1. (*cerrar*) ______ la puerta del carro.
2. (*ajustar*) ______ el asiento y los espejos.

3. (*abrochar*) ____________________ el cinturón de seguridad.

4. (*poner*) ____________________ la llave en el motor.

5. (*arrancar*) ____________________ el motor.

6. (*mirar*) ____________________ los espejos antes de salir del estacionamiento.

7. (*acelerar*) ____________________ poco a poco.

8. (*usar*) ____________________ las señales de tránsito.

9. (*anticipar*) ____________________ cuando tiene que poner los frenos.

10. (*no mirar*) ____________________ al pasajero.

11. (*conducir*) ____________________ con cuidado.

EXERCISE D. **You have been asked to prepare a radio announcement for the "Restaurante La Reja." Base your radio announcement on the information contained in the newspaper ad shown below. Use the following verbs in your announcement: *bailar, celebrar, compartir, disfrutar, escuchar, llamar, pasar, pedir,* and *probar.***

Si quiere comer bien y pasar un rato agradable al mismo tiempo,

el *Restaurante La Reja* le ofrece:

- Comidas típicas
- Especialidades diarias
- Salón para fiestas privadas
- Ambiente íntimo
- Música en vivo
- Pista de baile

Calle Mayor, 10 Reservaciones: 5-80-90-00

EXAMPLE: Llame al 5-80-90-00 para reservar una mesa.

____

____

____

____

____

____

____

____

[2] Formal Commands of Irregular Verbs

a. The following verbs form the formal (polite) command irregularly:

INFINITIVE	PRESENT TENSE **YO** FORM	COMMAND FORMS SINGULAR	PLURAL	MEANING
dar	**doy**	**dé**	**den**	*give*
estar	**estoy**	**esté**	**estén**	*be*
ir	**voy**	**vaya**	**vayan**	*go*
saber	**sé**	**sepa**	**sepan**	*know*
ser	**soy**	**sea**	**sean**	*be*

NOTE:

1. *Dé* has an accent mark to distinguish it from *de* (of).
2. *Esté* and *estén* have accent marks to indicate that the stress falls on the last syllable.

b. To form the negative command, place *no* before the verb.

No sea descortés. *Don't be impolite.*
No vayan allí. *Don't go there.*

EXERCISE E. **Write the instructions your parent gave when you and various friends went to the theater.**

EXAMPLE: comer antes de entrar en el teatro **Coman** antes de entrar en el teatro.

1. saber la dirección del teatro ______________________
2. ir al teatro en tren ______________________
3. no perder los boletos ______________________
4. ser puntuales ______________________
5. estar allí a las siete y media ______________________
6. dar los boletos al acomodador ______________________

EXERCISE F. **You just joined a tour in Lima, Peru. Write the instructions the tour guide gives to you.**

EXAMPLE: no ir solo al museo No **vaya** solo al museo.

1. saber el número del autobús ______________________
2. estar en el autobús a la hora indicada ______________________
3. ir en grupos de cuatro ______________________
4. no ser impaciente ______________________
5. no volver tarde al autobús ______________________
6. dar una propina al guía ______________________

[3] Informal Commands of Regular Verbs

a. Use of informal commands

Informal commands are used with those people you normally address with the *tú* form (friends, classmates, parents, pets).

b. *Tú* commands

The *tú* command is the same as the *él, ella,* and *Ud.* form of the present tense.

c. *Vosotros* commands

The *vosotros* command is formed by changing the final *-r* of the infinitive to *-d.*

INFINITIVE	TÚ COMMAND	VOSOTROS COMMAND	MEANING
abrir	**abre**	**abri*d***	*open*
cerrar	**cierra**	**cerra*d***	*close*
dar	**da**	**da*d***	*give*
hablar	**habla**	**habla*d***	*speak*
leer	**lee**	**lee*d***	*read*
perder	**pierde**	**perde*d***	*lose*
servir	**sirve**	**servi*d***	*serve*
ver	**ve**	**ve*d***	*see*
volver	**vuelve**	**volve*d***	*return*

NOTE:

1. Subject pronouns are usually omitted.
2. The *vosotros* command is rarely used in Spanish America. The *ustedes* (*Uds.*) command is used instead.

   Lee el libro   *Read the book.*

   Lean el libro.   *Read the book.*

d. All negative familiar commands are expressed by the present subjunctive.

INFINITIVE	TÚ		VOSOTROS	
	AFFIRMATIVE	NEGATIVE	AFFIRMATIVE	NEGATIVE
abrir	**abre**	**no abras**	**abrid**	**no abráis**
cerrar	**cierra**	**no cierres**	**cerrad**	**no cerréis**
dar	**da**	**no des**	**dad**	**no deis**
hablar	**habla**	**no hables**	**hablad**	**no habléis**
leer	**lee**	**no leas**	**leed**	**no leáis**
perder	**pierde**	**no pierdas**	**perded**	**no perdáis**
servir	**sirve**	**no sirvas**	**servid**	**no sirváis**
ver	**ve**	**no veas**	**ved**	**no veáis**
volver	**vuelve**	**no vuelvas**	**volved**	**no volváis**

RCISE G. Your friend Nora has decided to follow a rigorous exercise program. Express the advice you give to her.

E: descansar después de hacer ejercicio   **Descansa** después de hacer ejercicio.

ter ser seria ______________________________

2. correr una milla todos los días ____________________
3. tomar mucha agua ____________________
4. dejar de comer dulces ____________________
5. practicar un deporte ____________________
6. no dormir menos de ocho horas cada noche ____________________
7. seguir la misma rutina todos los días ____________________
8. prestar atención al entrenador ____________________
9. no comer en exceso ____________________
10. no perder la esperanza ____________________

EXERCISE H. **You want everyone attending a party at your home to have a good time. You tell them to do the following:**

EXAMPLE: ¡Tomás, (*tomar*) más refresco! ¡Tomás, **toma** más refresco!

1. ¡Juan, (*comer*) ____________________ otro pedazo de pastel!
2. ¡Grace, (*tocar*) ____________________ otra canción en la guitarra!
3. ¡Emilio, (*bailar*) ____________________ con Inés!
4. ¡Estelita, (*participar*) ____________________ en los juegos!
5. ¡Antonio, (*contar*) ____________________ un chiste!
6. ¡Ricky, (*abrir*) ____________________ tu regalo!

EXERCISE I. **Several friends stayed after the party to help Gregorio clean up. Express what Gregorio told each one to do.**

EXAMPLE: Vinny / sacar la basura ¡Vinny, **saca** la basura!

1. Lisa / guardar los discos ____________________
2. Pedro / recoger los vasos ____________________
3. Emilia / pasar la aspiradora ____________________
4. Paco / descolgar los adornos ____________________
5. Sonia / lavar los platos ____________________
6. Jack / ayudar a Paco ____________________

[4] Informal Commands of Irregular Verbs

a. The following verbs have irregular *tú* commands:

INFINITIVE	TÚ COMMAND	VOSOTROS COMMAND	MEANING
decir	***di***	**decid**	*say, tell*
hacer	***haz***	**haced**	*do, make*
ir	***ve***	**id**	*go*
poner	***pon***	**poned**	*put*
salir	***sal***	**salid**	*leave, go out*
ser	***sé***	**sed**	*be*
tener	***ten***	**tened**	*have*
venir	***ven***	**venid**	*come*

NOTE: The *vosotros* form of these verbs is regular.

EXERCISE J. One of your friends is not doing well in school. After class you tell her what she should do to improve.

EXAMPLE: hacer la tarea todos los días ¡**Haz** la tarea todos los días!

1. poner más atención a los estudios ______________________
2. tener paciencia ______________________
3. ser más diligente ______________________
4. ir a la biblioteca con más frecuencia ______________________
5. venir a mi casa para estudiar juntos(-as) ______________________
6. decirles la verdad a tus padres ______________________

b. The negative familiar command of the following verbs is expressed by the present subjunctive.

INFINITIVE	TÚ		VOSOTROS	
	AFFIRMATIVE	NEGATIVE	AFFIRMATIVE	NEGATIVE
decir	**di**	**no digas**	**decid**	**no digáis**
hacer	**haz**	**no hagas**	**haced**	**no hagáis**
ir	**ve**	**no vayas**	**id**	**no vayáis**
poner	**pon**	**no pongas**	**poned**	**no pongáis**
salir	**sal**	**no salgas**	**salid**	**no salgáis**
ser	**sé**	**no seas**	**sed**	**no seáis**
tener	**ten**	**no tengas**	**tened**	**no tengáis**
venir	**ven**	**no vengas**	**venid**	**no vengáis**

EXERCISE K. Jenny is going to visit her penpal Christina in San José, Costa Rica. Express what Jenny's mother tells her not to do.

EXAMPLE: no tener miedo No **tengas** miedo.

1. no estar nerviosa No estas nerviosa.

2. no ponerse de mal humor — No pongas de mal humor
3. no decir cosas absurdas — No digas cosas absurdas.
4. no hacer más trabajo para la mamá de Cristina — No hagas más trabajo para la mamá de Cristina
5. no salir sola por la noche — No salgas sola por la noche.
6. no ir de compras todos los días — No vayas de compras todos los días.
7. no ser descortés — No seas descortés

[5] COMMANDS WITH OBJECT PRONOUNS

a. **Object pronouns (including reflexive pronouns) are attached to the affirmative command. A written accent mark is generally required on the vowel that is stressed.**

Dígale la verdad.	*Tell him the truth.*
Escríbanles pronto.	*Write to them soon.*
Siéntate.	*Sit down.* sentarse
Lávense las manos.	*Wash your hands.* lavarse

b. **In negative commands, the object pronoun precedes the verb.**

No le diga la verdad.	*Don't tell him the truth.*
No les escriban pronto.	*Don't write to them soon.*
No te sientes.	*Don't sit down.*
No se laven las manos.	*Don't wash your hands.*

EXERCISE L. **Ricky has a new puppy and is trying to train him. Use the familiar command of the verbs in parentheses to express the commands Ricky gives the puppy.**

EXAMPLE: (*venir*) ¡ ven aquí! **¡Ven** aquí!

1. (*sentarse*) ¡ [crossed out] ! Siéntate
2. (*darme la pata*) ¡ dámte la pata!
3. (*traerme la pelota*) ¡ traénte la pelota!
4. (*buscar el hueso*) ¡ buscan el hueso!
5. (*quedarse*) ¡ quedanse !
6. (*caminar despacio*) ¡ caminan despacio!
7. (*prestar atención*) ¡ prestan atención!
8. (*mover la cola*) ¡ moven la cola!
9. (*ladrar*) ¡ ladran !
10. (*ponerse de pie*) ¡ ponense de pie!

EXERCISE M. **Ricky's brother likes to hassle Ricky by telling the dog not to do what he is told. Express what he says by making the commands in Exercise L negative.**

EXAMPLE: (*venir*) ¡ ______________ aquí! ¡**No vengas** aquí!

1. ______________________________
2. ______________________________
3. ______________________________
4. ______________________________
5. ______________________________
6. ______________________________
7. ______________________________
8. ______________________________
9. ______________________________
10. ______________________________

EXERCISE N. **Eileen is babysitting her younger brother. Express in Spanish what her mother tells her to do while she babysits.**

EXAMPLE: Si Víctor tiene sed, (*darle jugo*), (*no darle refresco*).
Si Víctor tiene sed, **dale** jugo, **no le des** refresco.

1. Si Víctor tiene sueño, (*acostarlo*) en la cuna, (*no dejarlo*) en el sofá.

____

2. Si él tiene frío, (*ponerle*) un suéter, (*no ponerle*) una chamarra.

____

3. Si él tiene hambre, (*darle*) una galleta, (*no darle*) chocolates.

____

4. Si él empieza a llorar, (*abrazarlo*), (*no gritarle*).

____

5. Si él quiere salir, (*decirle*) que no puede, (*no sacarlo*) a la calle.

____

MASTERY EXERCISES

EXERCISE O. **You are helping your sister prepare for a trip. Use the cues to give her some good suggestions.**

EXAMPLE: no olvidar tu pasaporte ¡No **olvides** tu pasaporte!

1. comprar cheques de viajero ______________________________

2. hacer las maletas con anticipación ______________________

3. lavar la ropa que vas a llevar ______________________

4. no esperar hasta el último momento ______________________

5. terminar tu trabajo ______________________

6. no perder el boleto de avión ______________________

7. decir adiós a tus abuelos ______________________

8. escoger revistas para leer durante el vuelo ______________________

EXERCISE P. **You give advice to your friends. Use the expression in parentheses to tell them what you say.**

EXAMPLE: ALAN: Acabo de recibir mi licencia de conducir.
TÚ: (*no conducir rápidamente*) No conduzcas rápidamente.

1. GISELA: Quiero comprar los aretes que vimos en la joyería.
TÚ: (*decírselo a tus padres y esperar tu cumpleaños*)
____

2. GREG: Saqué una buena nota en el último examen.
TÚ: (*seguir estudiando y hacerlo otra vez en el próximo examen*)
____

3. LISA: Mañana es la carrera y quiero ganar.
TÚ: (*tener confianza y no estar nerviosa*)
____

4. RAÚL: Está lloviendo y no quiero mojarme.
TÚ: (*no salir; quedarse en casa*) ______________________

5. VANESSA: Toda mi familia está enferma.
TÚ: (*no venir a mi casa esta tarde*) ______________________

6. ANTONIO: Elena no puede acompañarme a la fiesta.
TÚ: (*no preocuparse; ir solo*) ______________________

7. MARISSA: Salgo en un viaje mañana por la mañana.
TÚ: (*hacer la maleta ahora*) ______________________

8. ALEX: Jane nos invitó a Tom y a mí a un baile pero tenemos otro compromiso.
TÚ: (*decirle la verdad*) ______________________

EXERCISE Q. **Mrs. Huerta is having guests for dinner. Express in Spanish what she tells her children to do.**

1. Please help me in the kitchen. ______________________

2. Hugo, set the table, please. ______________________

3. Don't put the forks on the right. ______________________

4. Silvia, please wash the vegetables. ______________________

5. Miriam, close the refrigerator door. ______________________

6. Hugo, don't forget the napkins. ______________________

7. Miriam, arrange the flowers and put them on the table. ______________________

8. Silvia and Hugo, don't sit down yet. ______________________

9. Hugo, please go to the store and buy ice cream. ______________________

10. Silvia, take the dish out of the oven. ______________________

11. Be careful, the dish is hot. ______________________

12. Miriam, leave the bread on the table. ______________________

13. Miriam and Silvia, please serve the soup. ______________________

14. Hugo, please remove the dirty dishes from the table. ______________________

15. Take them into the kitchen. ______________________

ACTIVIDADES

1. Using commands, make a list of ten things your classmates should do and should not do to demonstrate school spirit.
2. The Spanish Club is soliciting ads for its magazine. Prepare an ad for two local merchants to be placed in the magazine, e.g., a restaurant, a florist, etc.
3. It's safety month in your school. Prepare a list of what students should do or not do in case of a fire, if they witness an accident, etc.

Chapter 6

Preterit Tense of Regular Verbs

The preterit tense is used to narrate an action or event in the past.

[1] REGULAR -AR VERBS

a. The preterit tense of regular *-ar* verbs is formed by dropping the infinitive ending *-ar* and adding the personal endings *-é, -aste, ó, amos, -asteis,* and *-aron.* The preterit tense has the following meanings in English:

Ud. bailó *you danced, you did dance*

Yo conté *I counted, I did count*

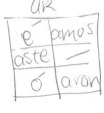

	bailar *to dance*	**contar** *to count*
yo	**bail*é***	**cont*é***
tú	**bail*aste***	**cont*aste***
Ud., él, ella	**bail*ó***	**cont*ó***
nosotros, -as	**bail*amos***	**cont*amos***
vosotros, -as	**bail*asteis***	**cont*asteis***
Uds., ellos, ellas	**bail*aron***	**cont*aron***

b. In the preterit, the nosotros ending (*-amos*) is the same as in the present tense: *regresamos* (we return, we returned).

c. Most verbs that are stem-changing (*o* to *ue; e* to *ie*) do not change the stem in the preterit tense:

(contar) Present: cuento Preterit: conté

d. Verbs that end in *-car, -gar,* and *-zar* have a spelling change in the *yo* form. In *-car* and *-gar* verbs, this change occurs to keep the original sound of the *c* and *g,* respectively. The change occurs in *-zar* verbs because *z* rarely precedes *e* or *i* in Spanish.

tocar yo to*qué*

llegar yo lle*gué*

comenzar yo comen*cé*

[2] FREQUENTLY USED -AR VERBS IN THE PRETERIT

aceptar *to accept*
acompañar *to accompany*
acostarse *to go to bed*
admirar *to admire*
asar *to roast*
cerrar *to close*
cobrar *to collect*
cocinar *to cook*
colgar *to hang*
comprar *to buy*
contar *to count*
conversar *to converse*
copiar *to copy*
cortar *to cut*
desayunarse *to have breakfast*
elevar *to raise, to lift*
encontrar *to find, to meet*
enviar *to send*
espantar *to frighten, to scare*
estudiar *to study*
examinar *to examine*
hablar *to speak*
inflar *to inflate*
jugar *to play (a sport, game)*

lavar *to wash*
llorar *to cry, to weep*
mirar *to look at*
pasar *to pass, to spend time*
pensar *to think, to intend*
planchar *to iron*
preparar *to prepare*
prestar *to lend*
pronunciar *to pronounce*
robar *to rob*
sacar *to take out*
tocar *to play (an instrument)*
trabajar *to work*
visitar *to visit*

EXERCISE A. **Lucy is describing what everyone did in preparation for the party. Use the cues to express what she says.**

EXAMPLE: mi mamá / preparar la comida — Mi mamá **preparó** la comida.

1. Gabriel / comprar los refrescos — Gabriel compró los refrescos.
2. Susie y Glenda / limpiar la sala — Susie y Glenda
3. yo / colgar las decoraciones — Colgué las decoraciones.
4. Richy y yo / inflar los globos — Richy y yo inflamos los globos.
5. tú / lavar los vasos — Tú lavaste los vasos.
6. Miriam y Silvia / enviar las invitaciones — Miriam y Silvia enviaron las invitaciones.

EXERCISE B. **When school resumes in September, some friends are talking about what they and other students did during the summer. Express what they say.**

EXAMPLE: yo / trabajar en la oficina de un abogado — Yo **trabajé** en la oficina de un abogado.

1. Manuel / visitar a sus primos en Venezuela — Manuel visitó a sus primos en Venezuela
2. Blanca y Virginia / tomar cursos en la universidad — Blanca y Virginia tomaron cursos en la universidad
3. tú / viajar con tu familia — Tú viajaste con tu familia.
4. Alex y yo / cantar en un coro — Alex y yo cantamos en un coro.
5. yo / comenzar a estudiar el violín — Comencé a estudiar el violín.
6. Efraín / jugar en un equipo de béisbol — Efraín jugó en un equipo de béisbol.

EXERCISE C. **You and a group of friends are in a restaurant. One of your friends is helping you figure out the check. Answer her questions.**

1. ¿Quién ordenó hamburguesas y papas fritas? (*Milton y Jaime*)
Milton y Jaime ordenaron hamburguesas...
2. ¿Quién tomó dos tés helados? (*Laura*)
Laura tomó dos tés helados.
3. ¿Quién desayunó huevos fritos y tocino? (*tú*)
Tú desayunaste huevos fritos y tocino.

4. ¿Quién probó el plato especial del día? (*Carlos y yo*)
Carlos y yo probamos el plato especial del día.

5. ¿Quién pagó la cuenta? (*yo*)
Pagé la cuenta.

EXERCISE D. **Tell what these people did in each of these circumstances. Use the suggestions provided.**

SUGGESTIONS:

~~estudiar mucho~~	~~cortar las flores~~	~~tocar la trompeta~~
~~lavar el carro~~	pagar la cuenta	llorar mucho
~~tomar un refresco~~		

EXAMPLE: Hay un examen en mi clase de matemáticas.
Estudié mucho.

1. La niña no encontró a su mamá en la tienda.
Ella lloró mucho. .

2. Tenía sed.
Yo tomé un refresco. .

3. El carro de mi papá se llenó de lodo.
Mi papá lavó el carro. .

4. Había muchas flores en el jardín de mi abuela.
Mi abuela cortó las flores. .

5. Compré una raqueta de tenis.
Yo pagué la cuenta. .

6. Había un concierto en mi clase de música.
Yo toqué un concierto en mi clase de música. .

EXERCISE E. **You did not attend the latest family function. Your little sister tells you in her usual non-stop fashion what happened there. Complete her monologue with the appropriate form of the verbs indicated.**

Nosotros llegamos (*1.* llegar) a la fiesta temprano. Yo ayudé (*2.* ayudar) a mi tía a poner la mesa. Cuando mis primos llegaron (*3.* llegar), yo empecé (*4.* empezar) a jugar con ellos pero yo no jugué (*5.* jugar) con ellos por mucho tiempo porque yo acompañé (*6.* acompañar) a mi tío al supermercado. Nosotros viajamos (*7.* viajar) en motocicleta. Nosotros pasamos (*8.* pasar) mucho tiempo allí y mi tío pagó (*9.* pagar) con su tarjeta de crédito. Tío y yo regresamos (*10.* regresar) a la casa en la moto y Felipe sacó (*11.* sacar) una fotografía de nosotros cuando entramos (*12.* entrar) en la casa con las manos llenas de paquetes. Sarita tocó (*13.* tocar) el piano cuando Pablo cantó (*14.* cantar) feliz cumpleaños a Mirta. Nosotros ___admiramos___ (15. admirar) sus regalos pero a ella no le ___gustaron___ (16. gustar) todos. Yo ___jugué___ (17. jugar) con el perro del vecino pero de repente me ___espanté___ (18. espantar). ___Ladré___ (19. ladrar) mucho y yo ~~gritamos~~ ___grité___ (20. gritar).

Toda la familia ___cenó___ (21. cenar) a las cinco porque ___comenzó___ (22. comenzar) a llover. Yo ___regresé___ (23. regresar) a casa en el carro de Pablo. Yo ___pasé___ (24. pasar) un buen rato hoy. Y tú, ¿cómo ___pasaste___ (25. pasar) el día?

[3] Regular *-er* and *-ir* Verbs

a. The preterit tense of regular *-er* and *-ir* verbs is formed by dropping the infinitive ending *-er* or *-ir* and adding the personal; endings *-í, -iste, -ió, -imos, -isteis,* and *-ieron.*

	romper *to break*	**recibir** *to receive*
yo	romp*í*	recib*í*
tú	romp*iste*	recib*iste*
Ud., él, ella	romp*ió*	recib*ió*
nosotros, -as	romp*imos*	recib*imos*
vosotros, -as	romp*isteis*	recib*isteis*
Uds., ellos, ellas	romp*ieron*	recib*ieron*

b. The preterit endings are the same for *-er* and *-ir* verbs.

c. In *-ir* verbs, the first-person plural ending (*-imos*) is the same as in the present tense. In *-er* verbs, however, the endings are different.

d. The accent mark is omitted over the following forms of *ver: vi, vio.*

e. Stem-changing verbs ending in *-er* do not change the stem vowel in the preterit tense. Stem-changing verbs ending in *-ir* have special stem changes in the preterit and are discussed in Chapter 7.

[4] Frequently Used *-er* and *-ir* Verbs in the Preterit

-ER Verbs

aparecer *to appear*
aprender *to learn*
conocer *to know (a person)*
convencer *to convince*
devolver *to return, to give back*
envolver *to wrap*
escoger *to choose*
establecer *to establish*
meter *to put in*
mover *to move*
nacer *to be born*
perder *to lose*
prometer *to promise*
reconocer *to recognize*
romper *to break*
vender *to sell*
ver *to see*
volver *to return*

-IR Verbs

abrir *to open*
aplaudir *to applaud*
asistir *to attend*
decidir *to decide*
interrumpir *to interrupt*
recibir *to receive*
salir *to go out, leave*
sufrir *to suffer*
vivir *to live*

EXERCISE F. Everyone is having a bad day. Tell what happened to each person.

EXAMPLE: el chofer / no ver el otro carro El chofer no **vio** el otro carro.

1. tú / perder las llaves de la casa
Tú perdiste las llaves de la casa.

2. el vendedor / no vender nada
El vendedor no vendó nada.

3. los miembros del grupo / no aprender la canción
Los miembros del grupo no aprendieron la canción.

4. yo / recibir una mala nota en la clase de historia
Recibí una mala nota en la clase de historia.

5. la clase / no reconocer al nuevo maestro de español
La clase no reconozco al nuevo maestro de español.

6. Javier y yo / romper unos platos
Javier y yo rompimos unos platos.

7. una tormenta / interrumpir el concierto al aire libre
una tormenta interrumpo el concierto al aire libre.

EXERCISE G. Tell what you and your family decided to do during the weekend.

EXAMPLE: Alicia y Felicia / nadar / piscina Alicia y Felicia **decidieron** nadar en la piscina.

1. Bobby y yo / bailar — decidimos — Bobby y yo bailamos en la calle.
2. mis padres /ir /cine — mis padres decidieron ir al cine.
3. mi hermano / jugar / voleibol — Mi hermano decidió jugar al voleibol.
4. tú / comprar / suéter — Tú compraste el suéter azul.
5. yo / limpiar / dormitorio — Limpí el dormitorio desorganizado.
6. toda la familia / ir / restaurante — toda la familia decidió ir al restaurante.

EXERCISE H. Complete the note that Raquel sent to a friend after missing a concert. Give the appropriate form of the verbs indicated.

Querida amiga:

Yo prometí (1. prometer) escribirte después de asistir al concierto de nuestro grupo favorito. La verdad es que yo no asistí (2. asistir). Ema y yo compramos (3. comprar) los boletos hace mucho tiempo pero a última hora ella decidió (4. decidir) acompañar a su familia a las montañas y vendió (5. vender) su boleto. Ella se lo vendió (6. vender) a su prima Imelda. Imelda y yo decidimos (7. decidir) ir juntas. Yo salí (8. salir) de la casa con bastante tiempo pero tomé (9. tomar) el autobús equivocado y ___llegé___ (10. llegar) tarde a su casa. Yo ___buscé___ (11. buscar) un taxi pero no ___encontré___ (12. encontrar) ninguno. El padre de Imelda nos ___llevamos___ (13. llevar) al concierto en su carro pero no ___llegé___ (14. llegar) a tiempo. Yo me ___perdí___ (15. perder) todo el concierto e Imelda ___enojaste___ (16. enojarse) conmigo. Nosotras ___volvimos___ (17. volver) a casa muy tristes.

Hasta luego,

Raquel

EXERCISE I. **Answer the questions a reporter from the school newspaper asks you. Use the cues provided.**

1. ¿Cuándo decidiste participar en la excavación arqueológica? (*el año pasado*)

____

2. ¿Cuántas personas asistieron? (*20*)

____

3. ¿Sufriste muchas inconveniencias? (*sí*)

____

4. ¿Cuándo salieron Uds. del país? (*el primero de julio*)

____

5. ¿Dónde viviste durante la excavación? (*tiendas de campo*)

____

6. ¿Encontraron Uds. cosas interesantes? (*sí*)

____

7. ¿Qué hallaste tú? (*una olla*)

____

8. ¿Quién examinó la olla? (*el arqueólogo principal*)

____

9. ¿Cuánto tiempo pasaste allí? (*un mes*)

____

10. ¿Aprendiste mucho? (*sí*)

____

MASTERY EXERCISES

EXERCISE J. **Janet always answers for her sister as well as for herself. Complete the questions and Janet's responses to her mother's questions. Use the verbs indicated.**

EXAMPLE: (*terminar*) ¿Terminaste la tarea?
Sí, yo **terminé** la tarea, pero Gloria no la **terminó**.

1. (*lavar/secar*) ¿ Lavaste tú los platos y los secó Gloria?
   Sí, yo lavé los platos y Gloria los secó.
2. (*practicar*) ¿ Practicaron Uds. el yoga?
   Sí, yo practiqué el yoga, pero Gloria no lo practicó.
3. (*escribir*) ¿ Escribieron Uds. una carta a su tía?
   Sí, yo escribí una carta, pero Gloria no la escribió.
4. (*romper*) ¿ Rompiste tú algo en la cocina?
   No, yo no rompí nada, pero Gloria rompió un vaso.
5. (*devolver*) ¿ devolvieron Uds. los libros a la biblioteca?
   Sí, yo los devolví, pero Gloria no los devolvió.
6. (*convencer*) ¿ convenciste tú a tu padre?
   Sí, nosotras le convencimos.
7. (*asistir*) ¿ Asistieron Uds. a la clase de baile?
   Sí, yo asistí a la clase, pero Gloria no asistió.
8. (*meter*) ¿Quién metió los refrescos en el refrigerador?
   Nosotras metimos los refrescos en el refrigerador.
9. (*jugar*) ¿ Jugaron Uds. al tenis?
   Sí, yo jugué al tenis, pero Gloria jugó al voleibol.
10. (*reconocer*) ¿ Reconociste tú al hijo de mi amiga?
    Sí, yo lo reconocí, pero Gloria no lo reconoció.

EXERCISE K. **Tell who did what activities during the weekend.**

~~mi hermano~~	~~cortar el césped~~
~~mi padre~~	~~lavar el carro~~
~~mi madre~~	~~perder el número de teléfono~~
~~mis padres~~	~~asistir a un concierto~~
~~yo~~	~~ver una película~~
~~tú~~	~~recibir muchos regalos~~
~~mis amigos y yo~~	~~sacar una novela de la biblioteca~~
la Sra. ~~Ortiz~~	~~empezar a trabajar~~
	llegar tarde al teatro
	~~correr en el parque~~

1. Mi hermano cortó el césped en el fin de semana.
2. Tú lavaste el carro en el fin de semana.
3. Yo ví una película en el fin de semana.
4. Mis padres ~~[illegible]~~ corrieron en el parque en el fin de semana.
5. Mi padre asistió a un concierto en el fin de semana.

6. Mi madre perdió el número de teléfono en el fin de semana
7. La Srta. Ortiz llegó tarde el teatro en el fin de semana
8. Mis amigos y yo recibimos muchos regalos, en el fin de semana.
9. yo empeze a trabajar en el fin de semana.
10. Tú sacaste una novela de la biblioteca en el fin de semana.

EXERCISE L. **Ricky describes what happened when he arrived home late from school. Express what he says in Spanish.**

1. When I left school I decided to go to the mall.

2. I tried to call my mother but no one answered the telephone.

3. I met my friend Pedro there.

4. I accompanied him to a videogame store.

5. We looked at many games.

6. I played a new game that I liked a lot.

7. I paid $30 for the game.

8. I walked home because I spent all my money.

9. I arrived home at 8:00 P.M.

10. I put the key into the door but my mother opened the door.

11. She looked at me sternly.

12. She asked: "Where did you spend the afternoon?"

13. I responded: "Pedro and I spent the afternoon at the mall."

14. She punished me.

____

15. The next day I took back the videogame to the store.

____

16. I learned a good lesson.

____

ACTIVIDADES

1. The school newspaper has asked you to do a study of how students spent the summer vacation. Prepare a series of questions in Spanish that you will ask the students about their summer activities.

2. You are doing a social experiment on cause and effect. For each of the statements below, indicate what you think the people did to accomplish the result they achieved.

a. El cuarto de Alicia está limpio y ordenado.
b. Raúl sacó una nota alta en el examen final de química.
c. Ruthie se ve muy bien; no es ni delgada ni gorda, y tiene mucha energía.
d. Jack y Miguel tienen mucho dinero en el banco.
e. Ahora yo uso la computadora para todo.

3. Prepare an entry for your journal in which you describe the activities in which you participated last week. Use as many of the verbs you have learned in the preterit tense as you can.

Chapter 7
Preterit Tense of Stem-Changing and Irregular Verbs

[1] VERBS THAT CHANGE *i* TO *y* IN THE PRETERIT

a. In the preterit, *-er* and *-ir* verbs whose stems end in a vowel change the endings of the third-person singular and plural forms from *-ió* to *-yó* and *-ieron* to *-yeron*, respectively. The *i* has an accent in all the other forms.

	caer *to fall*	creer *to believe*	leer *to read*	oír *to hear*
yo	caí	creí	leí	oí
tú	caíste	creíste	leíste	oíste
Ud., él, ella	ca**yó**	cre**yó**	le**yó**	o**yó**
nosotros, -as	caímos	creímos	leímos	oímos
vosotros, -as	caísteis	creísteis	leísteis	oísteis
Uds, ellos, ellas	ca**yeron**	cre**yeron**	le**yeron**	o**yeron**

b. Other verbs

caer *to fall*	huir *to flee*	oír *to hear*
construir *to construct, to build*	incluir *to include*	poseer *to possess, to own*
creer *to believe*	leer *to read*	
distribuir *to distribute*		

NOTE:

1. Exceptions are *traer, atraer,* and all verbs ending in *-guir.*

2. Verbs that end in *-uir* do not have an accent in the endings *-uiste, -uimos,* and *-uisteis.*

EXERCISE A. Tell from what or whom the following people fled.

EXAMPLE: el ladrón / la policía El ladrón **huyó** de la policía.

1. los ciudadanos / las inundaciones _Los ciudadanos huyeron de las inundaciones_

2. los inmigrantes / la pobreza _huyeron de_

3. yo / la muchedumbre _hui_ _____

4. el chofer / el accidente _huyó_ _____

5. tú / las olas fuertes del mar _huiste_ _____

6. Rebeca y yo / el ruido fuerte del estéreo _huimos_

EXERCISE B. Everyone in school is trying to earn community service credit. Tell what these students did.

EXAMPLE: Otto / el periódico escolar Otto **distribuyó** el periódico escolar.

1. yo / los recados a los profesores

____

2. Emilio / los exámenes en la clase de español

____

3. tú / los libros

____

4. Edgar y José / los premios al terminar el juego

____

5. Gabi / los boletos para la obra de teatro

____

6. Roberta y yo / el jugo a los niños de primer año

____

EXERCISE C. **Some students are telling what they read last night in celebration of the reading month. Tell what each one read based on what you know about them. Use the suggestions below.**

SUGGESTIONS:

la crítica de una película	una revista deportiva
un drama	la sección de anuncios del periódico
un libro de recetas	las tiras cómicas
un guía turístico	

EXAMPLE: Alfredo quiere ser cocinero y dueño de un restaurante.
Alfredo **leyó** un libro de recetas.

1. 'A Gino le gustan los deportes. Practica el fútbol, el tenis y la natación.
Gino ____.

2. Yo pienso visitar a mis primos en Montevideo la semana que viene.
Yo ____.

3. Nicolás quiere ser actor. Siempre va al teatro.
Nicolás ____.

4. Tú no eres seria. No te gustan los libros grandes ni largos.
Tú ____.

5. Patricia y yo vamos al cine con mucha frecuencia.
Nosotros ____.

6. Arnaldo busca un trabajo.
Arnaldo ____.

[2] STEM-CHANGING *-IR* VERBS IN THE PRETERIT

a. Stem-changing verbs ending in -ir change the stem vowel from e to i and o to u in the third-person singular and plural of the preterit.

	pedir *to ask for*	**dormir** *to sleep*
yo	pedí	dormí
tú	pediste	dormiste
Ud., él, ella	pid*ió*	durm*ió*
nosotros, -as	pedimos	dormimos
vosotros, -as	pedisteis	dormisteis
Uds., ellos, ellas	pid*ieron*	durm*ieron*

b. Other verbs that change e to i are:

medir *to measure* — **referir** *to tell* — **sentir** *to feel*
pedir *to ask for* — **reñir** *to argue* — **servir** *to serve*
preferir *to prefer* — **repetir** *to repeat* — **vestir** *to dress*

c. Other verbs that change o to u are:

morir *to die* — **podrir** *to rot*

d. Stem-changing verbs ending in -ar or -er do not change the stress vowel in the preterit tense.

	cerrar *to close*	**mover** *to move*
yo	cerré	moví
tú	cerraste	moviste
Ud., él, ella	cerró	movió
nosotros, -as	cerramos	movimos
vosotros, -as	cerrasteis	movisteis
Uds., ellos, ellas	cerraron	movieron

NOTE: -Ir verbs that have ñ directly before the ending (gruñir, reñir) drop the i of the ending in the third-person singular and plural (riñó, riñeron). The sound of the ending is still regular because of the ñ.

EXERCISE D. **One of your friends doesn't remember what everyone ordered in the restaurant last night. Tell her what each person ordered.**

EXAMPLE: Harry **pidió** una pizza.

1. Annette y Andy pidieron hamburguesas y papas fritas.
2. Yo pedí una ensalada de atún.
3. Pablo pidio un sándwich de jamón y queso.
4. Irma y yo pedimos té helado.

Pedir
pedí pedimos
pediste
pidió pidieron

5. Vicki pidió una ensalada de frutas frescas.

6. Tú pediste un helado de chocolate y fresa.

EXERCISE E. Your mother is telling a friend where all her guests slept when they visited.

EXAMPLE: Beatriz **durmió** en la cama de la abuela.

1. Los hijos de mi hermano durmieron en bolsas de dormir.

2. Mi hermano y su esposa durmieron en el sofá cama.

3. Mi esposo y yo dormimos en nuestra cama.

4. Antonio durmió en un colchón de aire.

5. El bebé durmió en con sus padres.

6. Tú dormiste en tu propia casa.

7. Yo dormí en mi dormitorio.

EXERCISE F. Tell who did these different things. Use the suggestions below.

SUGGESTIONS:

medir el cuarto
pedir más postre
referir cuentos de su juventud
vestir una muñeca
preferir ver la televisión
sentirse mal
repetir la misma frase muchas veces
dormir una siesta
servir la cena
reñir al perro

1. Mi papá ______________________________.

2. La abuela ______________________________.

3. El carpintero ______________________________.

4. Los niños ______________________________.

5. Yo ______________________________.

6. Mi tía ______________________________.

7. Tú y yo ______________________________.

8. Los vecinos ______________________________.

9. Mi mamá ______________________________.

10. Mis hermanos ______________________________.

HW

[3] VERBS IRREGULAR IN THE PRETERIT

a. *I*-stem Verbs in the Preterit

The following verbs have irregular stems and endings:

	hacer *to do, to make* **hic-**	**querer** *to want, to love* **quis-**	**venir** *to come* **vin-**
yo	hice	quise	vine
tú	hiciste	quisiste	viniste
Ud., él, ella	hizo	quiso	vino
nosotros, -as	hicimos	quisimos	vinimos
vosotros, -as	hicisteis	quisisteis	vinisteis
Uds., ellos, ellas	hicieron	quisieron	vinieron

NOTE:

1. The preterit endings of -*i*-stem verbs do not have accent marks.
2. In the third-person singular of *hacer*, the *c* changes to *z* to preserve the original sound.

EXERCISE G. Everyone in the family is very disappointed because their weekend plans didn't work out. Tell what each person wanted to do.

EXAMPLE: Gregorio **quiso** ver el partido de fútbol.

1. Papá ___quiso___ ir a pescar.
2. Mis hermanos ___quisieron___ nadar en la piscina.
3. Mamá ___quiso___ ir de compras.
4. Yo ___quise___ ver una película.
5. Tú ___quisiste___ ir a un restaurante japonés.
6. Mis primos y yo ___quisimos___ jugar al tenis.

EXERCISE H. It's your mother's birthday and everyone in your family wants to surprise her. Complete the statements with the appropriate form of *hacer*, as she tries to learn who did what.

EXAMPLE: Pepe, ¿hiciste el desayuno? No, yo no **hice** el desayuno. Gloria lo hizo.

1. Gloria, ¿ ___hiciste___ tú la limpieza de la casa?
   No, yo no ___hice___ la limpieza; Pepe y Adela la ___hicieron___.
2. Adela, ¡qué bonito pastel ___hiciste___ tú!
   Yo no ___hice___ el pastel; mi abuela lo ___hizo___.
3. ¿Quién ___hizo___ el arreglo de flores?
   Gloria y yo ___hicimos___ el arreglo.

4. Daniel, ¿ hiciste tú el paquete de mi regalo?
No, yo no hice el paquete. El dependiente de la tienda lo hizo .

5. ¿Quién hizo la reservación en el restaurante?
Mi papá hizo la reservación.

EXERCISE I. **You and a friend are talking about Gregory, who broke his leg while skiing. Tell when each person came to see Gregory.**

EXAMPLE: Gregorio **vino** del hospital a las ocho y media de la mañana.

1. Yo vine antes de ir a la escuela.
2. El médico vino por la mañana.
3. Tú viniste al mediodía.
4. Edgar y Mauricio vinieron después de las clases.
5. Raúl y yo vinimos antes de cenar.
6. La maestra de español vino a las siete de la noche.

EXERCISE J. **Use the cues to answer the questions your grandmother asks you about a party that was held in your house.**

1. ¿Cuándo hiciste la fiesta? (*el sábado pasado*)
Hice la fiesta el sábado pasado.
2. ¿Cuántos amigos vinieron a la fiesta? (*10*)
Diez amigos vinieron a la fiesta.
3. ¿Quisiste invitar a más amigos? (*no*)
No, no quise invitar a más amigos.
4. ¿Cómo vinieron a la casa? (*en autobús*)
____
5. ¿Qué hizo tu mamá para la fiesta? (*sándwiches*)
____
6. ¿Hicieron Uds. adornos? (*sí*)
____
7. ¿Cuál de tus amigos no quiso asistir? (*Pablo y Renée*)
Pablo y Renée no quisieron asistir.
8. ¿Quién no quiso bailar? (*Elena*)
Elena no quiso bailar.

b. ***U*-stem Verbs in the Preterit**

The following verbs have irregular stems and endings:

INFINITIVE	STEM	PRETERIT FORMS
andar	**anduv**	**anduve, anduviste, anduvo, anduvimos, anduvisteis, anduvieron**
estar	**estuv**	**estuve, estuviste, estuvo, estuvimos, estuvisteis, estuvieron**
poder	**pud**	**pude, pudiste, pudo, pudimos, pudisteis, pudieron**
poner	**pus**	**puse, pusiste, puso, pusimos, pusisteis, pusieron**
saber	**sup**	**supe, supiste, supo, supimos, supisteis, supieron**
tener	**tuv**	**tuve, tuviste, tuvo, tuvimos, tuvisteis, tuvieron**
traer	**traj**	**traje, trajiste, trajo, trajimos, trajisteis, trajeron**
decir	**dij**	**dije, dijiste, dijo, dijimos, dijisteis, dijeron**
traducir	**traduj**	**traduje, tradujiste, tradujo, tradujimos, tradujisteis, tradujeron**

NOTE:

1. The preterit endings of *u*-stem verbs do not have accent marks.
2. All verbs ending in *-ducir* are conjugated like *traducir.*

	conducir *to drive, to lead*	**producir** *to produce*
yo	**cond*uje***	**prod*uje***
tú	**cond*ujiste***	**prod*ujiste***
Ud., él, ella	**cond*ujo***	**prod*ujo***
nosotros, -as	**cond*ujimos***	**prod*ujimos***
vosotros, -as	**cond*ujisteis***	**prod*ujisteis***
Uds., ellos, ellas	**cond*ujeron***	**prod*ujeron***

EXERCISE K. **Albert is writing a paragraph about something he and a friend did when they were in Madrid. Complete his paragraph with the needed verb forms.**

Cuando Héctor y yo ____________ (*1.* estar) en Madrid visitamos el Museo del Prado. Nosotros ____________ (*2.* andar) por todos los salones del museo. Héctor ____________ (*3.* saber) mucho de la pintura española, pero yo ____________ (*4.* tener) que comprar un libro en la tienda del museo. Yo no ____________ (*5.* poder) llevar mi cámara conmigo por el museo; por eso la ____________ (*6.* poner) en mi mochila en el guardarropa del museo. Héctor visitó el museo el mes pasado y él ____________ (7. poder) visitar un salón especial. Este día el salón ____________ (*8.* estar) cerrado al público. Héctor y yo ____________ (*9.* poder) regresar al museo dos veces, pero yo nunca ____________ (*10.* poder) ver el salón especial.

Poder — to be able to

EXERCISE L. Jack and some friends spent a day at a new amusement park. Use the following phrases to tell what each person was able to do there.

montar a caballo jugar muchos juegos
subir en los aparatos ganar muchos premios
comer palomitas conducir un carro eléctrico
nadar en una piscina grandísima *drive*
 manejar.

EXAMPLE: Manny **pudo** montar a caballo.

1. Jack _____ pudo conducir un carro eléctrico _____.

2. Raquel y Leslie _____ pudieron montar a cabal _____.

3. Yo _____ pude comer palomitas _____.

4. Alex _____ pudo _____.

5. Tú _____ pudiste _____.

6. Jack y yo _____ pudimos _____.

EXERCISE M. Tell why you and none of your friends went to the football game on Saturday.

EXAMPLE: Elvira **tuvo** que ir de compras. *had to*

1. Gabriela y María _____ tuvieron que _____ visitar a sus abuelos.

2. Yo _____ tuve que _____ trabajar.

3. Tú _____ tuviste que _____ estudiar para un examen.

4. Ricky y Eddy _____ tuvieron que _____ ayudar en casa.

5. Maddy y yo _____ tuvimos que _____ ir al centro.

6. Javier _____ tuvo que _____ llevar el perro al veterinario.

EXERCISE N. Danny is telling his parents where his friends hid an object during a game they played. Tell where each person put the object. Use the suggestions.

en la cocina en la cama del perro dentro de un cajón
debajo del sofá detrás de un libro

EXAMPLE: Emilio lo **puso** en el patio de la casa.

1. Yo _____.

2. Rogelio _____.

3. Carmen y yo _____.

4. Tú _____.

5. Andrés y Pilar _____.

6. Víctor _____.

EXERCISE O. **In preparation for a student trip to Mexico, a group is practicing some polite expressions in Spanish. Use the following phrases to express what each person said in various situations.**

SUGGESTIONS:			
	buenos días	con permiso	gracias
	buenas tardes	salud	por favor
	buenas noches	buen provecho	hasta luego

EXAMPLE: Cuando Hugo entró en la casa por la tarde, él dijo «buenas tardes».

1. Cuando Esteban estornudó, todo el mundo ______________________.
2. Cuando Adela y Luz pasaron entre dos personas, ellas ______________________.
3. Cuando yo saludé a la familia por la mañana, yo ______________________.
4. Cuando pediste un refresco en el café, tú ______________________.
5. Cuando el mesero nos sirvió la cena a Beto y a mí, nosotros ______________________.
6. Cuando Gerardo salió de la casa, él ______________________.
7. Al servir la comida la señora ______________________.

c. The Verbs *dar, ir,* and *ser* in the Preterit

***Dar, ir,* and *ser* are also irregular. *Dar* takes the endings of regular *-er* and *-ir* verbs, but without a written accent in the first- and third-person singular forms. *Ir* and *ser* have the same forms.**

	dar *to give*	**ir** *to go* **ser** *to be*
yo	di	fui
tú	diste	fuiste
Ud., él, ella	dio	fue
nosotros, -as	dimos	fuimos
vosotros, -as	disteis	fuisteis
Uds., ellos, ellas	dieron	fueron

[4] USES OF THE PRETERIT TENSE

a. The preterit tense is used to narrate an action or event that occurred in the past. It may indicate the beginning or end of the action, or the completed action or event begun and finished in the past.

(1) Beginning or End of an Action

Empezamos a bailar.	*We began to dance.*
Cerraron la puerta.	*They closed the door.*

(2) Completed Action

Fui al cine anoche.	*I went to the movies last night.*

b. Some expressions often used with the preterit are:

anoche *last night*	**el año pasado** *last year*
ayer *yesterday*	**el mes pasado** *last month*
anteayer *the day before yesterday*	**la semana pasada** *last week*

EXERCISE P. **Before shutting off the computer for the night, you look at your calendar to check that you did everything in your list of things to do. Tell what you did today.**

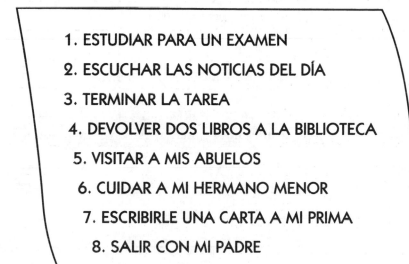

1. ESTUDIAR PARA UN EXAMEN
2. ESCUCHAR LAS NOTICIAS DEL DÍA
3. TERMINAR LA TAREA
4. DEVOLVER DOS LIBROS A LA BIBLIOTECA
5. VISITAR A MIS ABUELOS
6. CUIDAR A MI HERMANO MENOR
7. ESCRIBIRLE UNA CARTA A MI PRIMA
8. SALIR CON MI PADRE
9. LEER UN ARTÍCULO

1. ______________________________

2. ______________________________

3. ______________________________

4. ______________________________

5. ______________________________

6. ______________________________

7. ______________________________

8. ______________________________

9. ______________________________

10. ______________________________

EXERCISE Q. **Upon returning to school in September, various students are discussing the summer vacation. Tell where each student went.**

EXAMPLE: Virginia **fue a** España.

1. Pedro fue a Puerto Rico.
2. Yo fui a la granja de mis abuelos.
3. Donald fue a Canadá.
4. Los hermanos fueron a un campamento de tenis.
5. Tú fuiste a acampar en las montañas.
6. Anita y yo fuimos a un congreso sobre el medio ambiente.

EXERCISE R. **A friend was absent from school yesterday. Answer the questions she asks you.**

1. ¿Estuvo ausente otro alumno?

   ____

2. ¿Fue la clase de historia a escuchar el debate?

   ____

3. ¿Viniste a tiempo a la escuela?

   ____

4. ¿Trajiste muchos libros a la escuela hoy?

   ____

5. ¿Hiciste el trabajo para hoy?

   ____

6. ¿Pusiste todos los nombres en el trabajo?

   ____

7. ¿Leyeron Uds. muchos artículos del periódico?

   ____

8. ¿Anduviste por la calle Moya después de las clases?

   ____

9. ¿Diste el trabajo al maestro?

   ____

10. ¿Tradujeron Uds. los anuncios al español?

   ____

EXERCISE S. **A friend is trying to help you remember when you did different things. Using the information provided, tell what he asks and give your response.**

EXAMPLE: conducir el carro / anoche / el domingo pasado
¿**Condujiste** el carro anoche?
No, **conduje** el carro el domingo pasado.

1. ir al cine / la semana pasada / anteayer

¿ ____ ?

____

2. dar un paseo por el parque / el mes pasado / ayer

¿ ____ ?

____

3. jugar al tenis / esta mañana / el mes pasado

¿ ____ ?

____

4. pescar en el lago / el domingo pasado / el verano pasado

¿ ____ ?

____

5. estar en el centro / anteayer / anoche

¿ ____ ?

____

MASTERY EXERCISES

EXERCISE T. **You just realized that you misplaced your wallet. Write a series of ten sentences in Spanish in which you retrace your activities during the day to help you locate the wallet.**

EXAMPLE: Almorcé en un café y pagué la cuenta. Luego fui a la biblioteca y pasé dos horas allí. Conduje el carro de mi mamá. . .

____

____

____

____

____

____

EXERCISE U. You and your friend Gladys go to a school dance. Gladys isn't very happy. Read the description of the dance and then rewrite it, changing the verbs to the preterit.

Mi amiga Gladys y yo vamos a un baile de la escuela. El baile tiene lugar en el gimnasio del colegio. Ella quiere ir al baile pero Shawn no la invita. En el baile, Gladys ve a Shawn y quiere bailar con él, pero Shawn prefiere bailar con otras chicas. Hay un concurso de baile y Gladys no puede participar en él. Busca una pareja pero no tiene suerte. Durante un intermedio ve a Shawn. Él va hacia ella. Se pone muy contenta. Cree que Shawn toma otra decisión. Shawn anda rápidamente y nos pasa sin mirarnos. Va al bar y pide un refresco. Gladys se da cuenta de esto y huye del gimnasio. Yo la sigo y tomamos un taxi de regreso a casa.

____

____

____

____

____

____

EXERCISE V. Lee describes something that happened last night. Help him express it in Spanish.

1. Last night I couldn't write a news story. ______________________
2. I began to work at 8:00 but I stopped working at 8:10. ______________________
3. There was a thunderstorm. ______________________
4. When I heard the thunder I shut off the computer. ______________________
5. A bolt of lightning fell near the house. ______________________
6. We lost electricity. ______________________
7. My younger sister began to scream. ______________________
8. I looked for her in the darkness. ______________________
9. We went to the basement. ______________________
10. My parents came too. ______________________
11. My father brought a flashlight and some candles. ______________________
12. We had to leave the basement immediately. ______________________
13. My mother couldn't prepare dinner. ______________________
14. We put a candle on a table and played several games. ______________________

15. The dog heard a noise and she began to bark. ____________________________________

16. My father climbed the stairs. ____________________________________

17. Someone suddenly knocked on the door. ____________________________________

18. It was a policeman. ____________________________________

19. He gave my father another flashlight and more candles. ____________________________________

20. When the rain stopped we went outside. ____________________________________

21. I never finished the news story but I described what happened last night. ____________________________________

ACTIVIDADES

1. Prepare an entry for your journal, in which you describe what you did yesterday. Divide your entry into what you did in the morning, the afternoon, and last night. Provide at least four different activities for each time period.

2. A famous alumnus is coming to your school to talk to the student body. You are going to interview him for the school newspaper. Prepare ten questions you will ask him. Use the suggestions provided.

EXAMPLE: ¿Quiénes influyeron su interés por la música?

SUGGESTIONS:					
	cuándo	qué	(a) quién(es)	dónde	adónde
	por qué	cuánto(s)	andar	conocer	empezar
	estar	hacer	influir	ir	poder
	poner	querer	saber	tener	venir

3. Role-play the interview with a classmate. Take notes on his answers and then write the article for the Spanish section of the school newspaper.

Chapter 8

Imperfect Tense

[1] The Imperfect Tense of Regular Verbs

a. The imperfect tense of regular verbs is formed by dropping the ending (*-ar, -er, -ir*), and adding the following endings:

	pensar *to think*	**volver** *to return*	**sufrir** *to suffer*
yo	**pens*aba***	**volv*ía***	**sufr*ía***
tú	**pens*abas***	**volv*ías***	**sufr*ías***
Ud., el, ella	**pens*aba***	**volv*ía***	**sufr*ía***
nosotros, -as	**pens*ábamos***	**volv*íamos***	**sufr*íamos***
vosotros, -as	**pens*abais***	**volv*íais***	**sufr*íais***
Ud., ellos, ellas	**pens*aban***	**volv*ían***	**sufr*ían***

b. Verbs that are stem changing in the present tense do not change the stem vowel in the imperfect.

c. In the imperfect, *yo, Ud., él* and *ella* have the same form. Subject pronouns are used if necessary to clarify the meaning of the verb.

EXERCISE A. **Tell where each person used to walk to.**

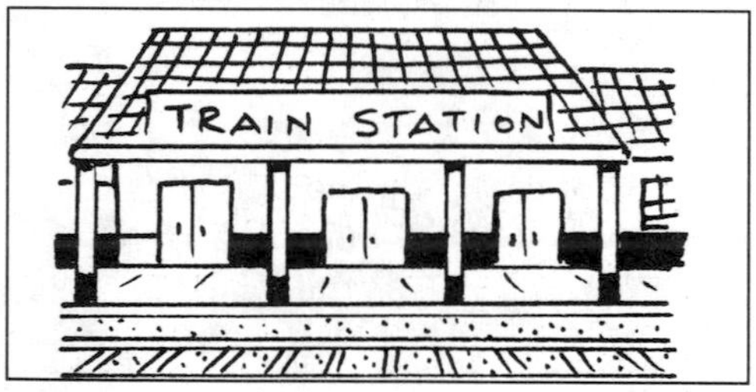

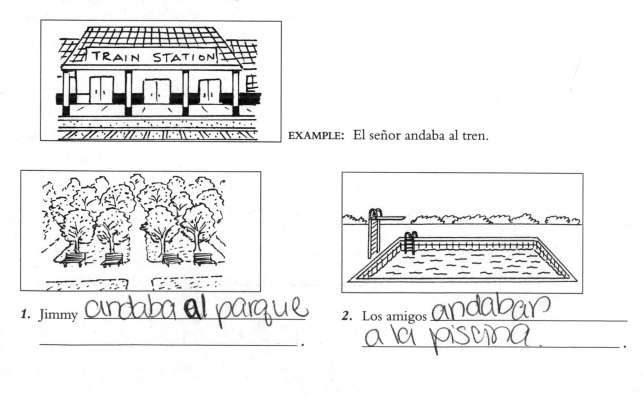

EXAMPLE: El señor andaba al tren.

1. Jimmy andaba al parque
________________________.

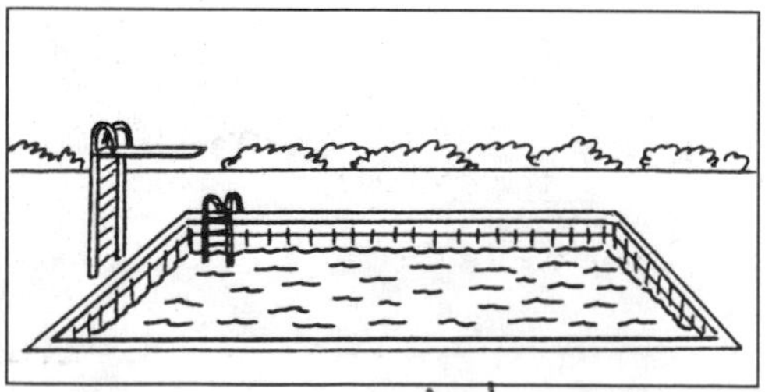

2. Los amigos andaban
a la piscina.

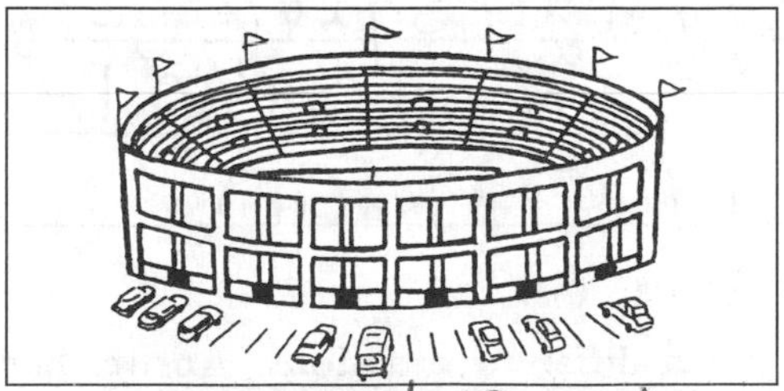

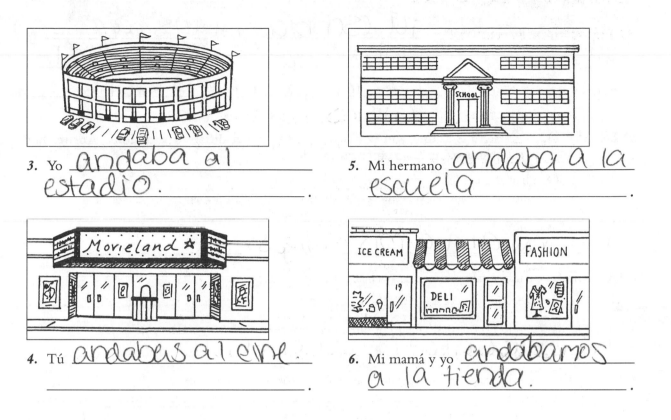

3. Yo *andaba al estadio.*

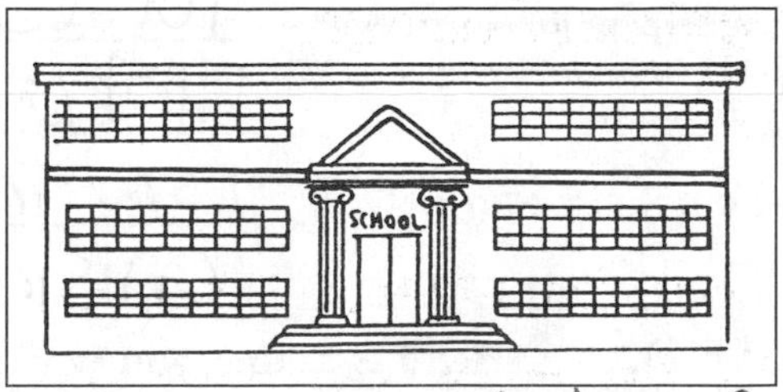

5. Mi hermano *andaba a la escuela* .

4. Tú *andabas al cine* .

6. Mi mamá y yo *andábamos a la tienda.*

EXERCISE B. Tell who used to drink these beverages.

EXAMPLE:　Dora / agua　　　Dora **bebía** agua.

1. el bebé / leche
2. las señoras / té helado
3. tú / té caliente con limón
4. Andy y yo / chocolate
5. yo / batidos de frutas
6. Irma e Hilda / refrescos dietéticos

El bebé bebía leche.
Las señoras bebían té helado.
Tú bebías té caliente con limón.
Andy y yo bebíamos chocolate
Yo bebía batidos de frutas
Irma e Hilda bebían refrescos dietéticos

EXERCISE C. A group of friends are talking about things they used to write. Tell what they wrote.

EXAMPLE:　Genaro / canciones　　　Genaro **escribía** canciones.

1. yo / versos
2. Elena y su hermana / cuentos infantiles
3. Richie / cartas a su amigo

Yo escribía versos.
Elena y su hermana escribían cuentos infantiles
Richie escribía cartas a su amigo

4. tú / reglas para juegos nuevos Tú escribías reglas para juego

5. Yoko y yo / refranes Yoko y yo escribíamos refranes

6. Marta y Rosa / chistes Marta y Rosa escribían chistes

EXERCISE D. **A friend is asking you what you used to do in different situations. Answer her questions using the responses provided.**

EXAMPLE: ¿Qué hacías cuando no tenías tarea? (*ver la televisión*)
Cuando no tenía tarea yo **veía** la televisión.

odd

1. ¿Qué hacías cuando tus padres salían? (*invitar a mis amigos*)
cuando mis padres salían, yo invitaba a mis amigos.

2. ¿Qué hacías cuando estabas enfermo? (*guardar cama*)

3. ¿Qué hacías cuando no querías hablar con un amigo por teléfono? (*no contestar el teléfono*)
No contestaba el teléfono.

4. ¿Qué hacías cuando tus padres te preguntaban adónde ibas? (*decir la verdad*)

5. ¿Qué hacías cuando perdías un partido? (*felicitar al ganador*)
cuando perdía un partido yo felicitaba al ganador.

6. ¿Qué hacías cuando no hacía buen tiempo? (*no salir de la casa*)

EXERCISE E. **Some people are talented and did two things simultaneously. Tell what the following people were doing at the same time.**

EXAMPLE: escuchar la radio / estudiar
Felipe **escuchaba** la radio mientras **estudiaba.**

1. silbar / trabajar
El señor Perón silbaba mientras trabajaba.

2. hablar por teléfono / cocinar
Mi mamá hablaba por teléfono mientras cocinaba.

3. cantar / bañarse
Yo cantaba mientras me bañaba.

4. reír / pelear
Los niños reían mientras peleaban.

5. dormir / estar en la clase de historia
Tú dormías mientras estabas en la clase de español.

6. hablar / comer
Romi y yo ____.

EXERCISE F. **You and some friends are remembering the part-time jobs you all had while going to school. Tell who did what.**

Gary	distribuir folletos
Felipe y Juan	cortar el césped
Alicia	cuidar a los niños del vecino
yo	entregar pizza a domicilio
Mirta y yo	contestar el teléfono en una oficina
tú	lavar carros

EXAMPLE: Pedro **lavaba** platos todos los sábados.

1. ____

2. ____

3. ____

4. ____

5. ____

6. ____

EXERCISE G. **Tell how frequently these people did these activities.**

EXAMPLE: Esteban / mirar la televisión / todos los días
Esteban **miraba** la televisión todos los días.

1. Miriam / enviar tarjetas a sus amigos / siempre

____

2. José y Clemente / jugar al fútbol / todos los sábados

____

3. yo / telefonear a mi mejor amiga / cada noche

____

4. Estela y yo / visitar las tiendas / de vez en cuando

____

5. Mi familia / comer en un restaurante / con frecuencia

____

6. tú / escribir poemas / a veces

____

[2] Verbs Irregular in the Imperfect Tense

There are three irregular verbs in the imperfect tense: *ir, ser,* and *ver.*

	ir *to go*	**ser** *to be*	**ver** *to see*
yo	**iba**	**era**	**veía**
tú	**ibas**	**eras**	**veías**
Ud., el, ella	**iba**	**era**	**veía**
nosotros, -as	**íbamos**	**éramos**	**veíamos**
vosotros, -as	**ibais**	**erais**	**veíais**
Uds., ellos, ellas	**iban**	**eran**	**veían**

EXERCISE H. **Tell where these people used to go. Include an expression to indicate with what frequency they did this.**

EXAMPLE: Eduardo / la piscina Eduardo **iba** a la piscina **cada tarde.**

1. Martina / el centro comercial Martina iba al centro comercial con frecuencia.
2. yo / el gimnasio Yo iba al gimnasio mucho
3. Hugo y Vicente / el salón de videojuegos Hugo y Vicente iban al salón de videojuegos cada semana.
4. tú / el parque de diversiones Tú ibas al parque... mucha
5. Joan y Joyce / el café Joan y Joyce iban al café cada mañana
6. Víctor y yo / el club de golf Víctor y yo nunca íbamos al club de golf.

EXERCISE I. **Jacqueline and a friend are looking at a class photograph from elementary school. Tell what they say about different people they recognize in the photo.**

EXAMPLE: Clara / cómico Clara **era** cómica.

1. Roberto / guapo Roberto era guapo.
2. Jeff y Ed / divertido Jeff y Ed eran divertidos
3. tú / muy serio Tú eras muy serio.
4. Lance / alto y fuerte Lance era alto y fuerte.
5. yo / tímido Yo era tímida.
6. Ginny y yo / buenos amigos Ginny y yo eran buenos amigos

EXERCISE J. **Tell what type of movies these people used to see.**

EXAMPLE: Miguel / películas policíacas Miguel **veía** películas policíacas.

1. mi mamá y mi tía / películas románticas

Mi mamá y mi tía veían películas románticas.

2. Rigoberto y yo / películas de ciencia-ficción

Rigoberto y yo veíamos películas de ciencia ficción.

3. tú / películas de historia

Tú veías películas de historia.

4. Angel / películas cómicas

Angel veía películas cómicas.

5. yo / películas dramáticas

Yo veía películas dramáticas.

6. mi papá / películas antiguas

Mi papá veía películas antiguas.

EXERCISE K. **Answer the questions a friend asks you about how you used to celebrate your birthday when you were younger.**

1. ¿Tenías una fiesta para celebrar tu cumpleaños?

____

2. ¿Invitaba tu mamá a muchos niños a la fiesta?

____

3. ¿Recibías muchos regalos?

____

4. ¿Apagabas las velas del pastel fácilmente o necesitabas ayuda?

____

5. ¿Jugaban Uds. muchos juegos?

____

6. ¿Ibas al cine a veces?

____

7. ¿Escogías tus propios regalos?

____

8. ¿Te daban tus papás todo lo que pedías?

____

9. ¿Rompían Uds. una piñata en la fiesta?

____

10. ¿Eras feliz?

____

[3] Uses of the Imperfect Tense

The imperfect tense is used:

a. to express what used to happen.

Ellas visitaban a los abuelos todos los domingos.	*They used to visit the grandparents every Sunday.*
Yo jugaba al tenis.	*I played (used to play) tennis.*

b. to express what happened repeatedly in the past.

Yo iba al centro comercial después de las clases.	*I used to go (would go) to the mall after school.*
Raúl y yo hablábamos a diario.	*Raúl and I used to speak (would speak) daily.*

c. to describe what was going on at a particular time.

Yo leía el periódico durante el desayuno.	*I was reading the newspaper during breakfast.*

d. to describe simultaneous actions in the past. *Mientras* is usually used to connect the two actions.

Comía una manzana mientras hacía la tarea.	*I was eating an apple while I did the assignment.*

e. to describe what was going on in the past (imperfect) when something else began or ended (preterit). *Cuando* usually links the two actions.

Yo hablaba por teléfono cuando Ana tocó a la puerta.	*I was speaking on the telephone when Ana knocked on the door.*

f. to describe persons or things in the past.

Felipe era alto y fuerte.	*Philip was tall and strong.*
Los trenes eran modernos.	*The trains were modern.*

g. to express the time of day (the hour) in the past.

Eran las tres.	*It was three o'clock.*

EXERCISE L. **Pilar asked her grandmother to send her a letter describing what life was like when she was young and lived in a small town. The letter didn't arrive in very good shape. Help Pilar complete it by giving the imperfect tense of the verbs that are missing.**

Cuando yo ___era___ (*1.* ser) pequeña, mi familia y yo ___vivíamos___ (*2.* vivir) en un pueblo pequeño. Todas las tiendas ___estaban___ (*3.* estar) en una calle que ___daban___ (*4.* dar) a la plaza principal. Los viernes ___habían___ (*5.* haber) un mercado al aire libre porque muchos campesinos ___venían___ (*6.* venir) al pueblo para vender sus productos. Yo siempre ___acompañaba___ (*7.* acompañar) a mi mamá cuando ella ___iba___ (*8.* ir) de compras. Ella ___llevaba___ (*9.* llevar) una canasta y los vendedores

SER
ESTAR

W
Emotions
I
R
D
O

ponían (*10.* poner) las frutas y las legumbres que nosotros comprabamos (*11.* comprar) en ella. Me gustaba (*12.* gustar) mucho acompañarla. Cerca de la escuela había (*13.* haber) un parque donde los niños ________ (*14.* jugar). El parque tenía (*15.* tener) un subibaja y columpios. Mis hermanos y yo íbamos (*16.* ir) allí todos los domingos. Como todavía no existía (*17.* existir) la televisión, mis hermanos y yo escuchábamos (*18.* escuchar) la radio o leíamos (*19.* leer) libros que pedíamos (*20.* pedir) prestados de la biblioteca. Una vez al mes yo iba (*21.* ir) al cine con mi hermana mayor. Nos fascinábamos (*22.* fascinar) las películas norteamericanas. Cada dos semanas toda la familia ________ (*23.* reunirse) en la casa de mis abuelos. Mi abuela siempre preparaban (*24.* preparar) los platos favoritos de todos los nietos. Todo el mundo tenía (*25.* tener) que ayudar a mis abuelos. En cada reunión, mis primos y yo pasábamos (*26.* pasar) mucho tiempo juntos. Nosotros inventábamos (*27.* inventar) juegos divertidos. La vida de mi pueblo no era (*28.* ser) aburrida.

EXERCISE M. **A lot of activities were going on at the same time at the Hidalgo family reunion. Tell what was happening.**

EXAMPLE: los hombres / jugar al voleibol / las mujeres / charlar
Mientras los hombres **jugaban** al voleibol, las mujeres **charlaban.**

1. Pedro y yo / pescar / Mauricio / nadar en el lago
pedro y yo pescábamos, mauricio nadaba en el lago.

2. Cristina / practicar el baile / los niños / subir a los columpios
Cristina practicaba el baile, los niños subíamos a los columpios.

3. Tim y Greg / practicar la lucha libre / todo el mundo / mirarlos
Tim y Greg practicaban la lucha libre, todo el mundo mirabanlos.

4. mi tío / cocinar / mis tías / poner la mesa
mi tío cocinaba, mis tías ponían la mesa.

5. mi abuelo / dormir la siesta / mi abuela y yo / andar por el parque
mi abuelo dormía la siesta, mi abuela y yo andabamos por el parque.

EXERCISE N. **Something interrupted what these people were doing. Relate each pair of events in a complete sentence.**

EXAMPLE: Ana / preparar la tarea / el teléfono / sonar
Ana **preparaba** la tarea cuando el teléfono **sonó.**

1. tú / regar el césped / los vecinos / llegar
Tú regabas el césped cuando los vecinos llegaron.

2. yo / trabajar en la computadora / la luz/ apagarse

Yo trabajaba en la computadora cuando la luz le apage.

3. la familia / comer en el bosque / un oso / aparecer

La familia comía en el bosque cuando un oso aparece.

4. el equipo / jugar al béisbol / una tormenta / caer

El equipo jugaba al béisbol cuando una tormenta caió.

5. mi padre / dormir la siesta / alguien / tocar a la puerta

Mi padre dormía la siesta cuando alguien toque a la puerta.

6. Elena y yo / nadar en la piscina / nosotros / ver un relámpago

Elena y yo nadábamos en la pisena cuando nosotros vimos un relámpago.

7. Javier / escuchar la radio / un locutor / interrumpir la emisión

Javier escuchaba la radio cuando un locutor interrumpió la emisión

8. el chofer / conducir el taxi / el motor / dejar de funcionar

El chofer conducía el taxi cuando el motor dejó de funcionar.

MASTERY EXERCISES

EXERCISE O. **Rewrite this entry from Eugenio's diary in the imperfect tense.**

Estoy en Venezuela y asisto a un programa especial de verano. Vivo con una familia venezolana. Tienen tres hijos. Dos de ellos son simpáticos y divertidos, pero el menor es muy travieso y a menudo, antipático. Le gusta salirse con la suya y no hay día en que no hace ninguna travesura. Siempre hay muchos gritos en la casa porque el hermano menor molesta mucho a sus hermanos mayores. No hace nada en la casa y sus padres lo consienten mucho. Cuando los amigos de sus hermanos vienen a la casa, él siempre quiere hacer lo que ellos hacen. Los sigue por todas partes. Muchas veces yo voy a su cuarto para hablar con él, pero él siempre cierra la puerta en mi cara. Es divertido ver que esta familia se parece mucho a la mía.

EXERCISE P. **Gladys is describing someone from her childhood. Help her express the following in Spanish.**

1. When I was a little girl, I lived in a big house.
2. There was a small house next to our house.
3. A woman lived alone in the house. Her name was Carmen Alegre.
4. She was old but she said that she was twenty-five years old.
5. She used to spend a lot of time outside.
6. I used to see her almost every day.
7. She knew everyone that lived on the street.
8. Every morning she swept the street.
9. She used to water her garden every day after dinner.
10. She liked flowers very much.
11. Each spring she planted many flowers in her garden.
12. Some mischievous boys used to try to cut the flowers in her garden.
13. She used to come out of the house and ran after them carrying a broom.
14. When it was very hot, she used to sit on her porch.

15. She greeted everyone that passed by her house.

____

16. Sometimes she offered them iced tea or lemonade.

____

17. Many children were afraid of her.

____

18. She really was a kind and pleasant woman.

____

19. I often went to the store for her.

____

20. I liked to talk to her because she told interesting stories.

____

ACTIVIDADES

1. Describe yourself when you were ten years old. Mention your physical and personality characteristics, the activities you enjoyed, and why you enjoyed them. Describe also your friends, your favorite possession, and your favorite pastime(s).

2. Who were your favorite teachers when you were in elementary school? Describe them, tell three things about them, and why you liked them.

Chapter 9
Preterit and Imperfect Tenses Compared

1. The preterit is used to indicate the beginning or the end of an action or event occurring in the past. It may also indicate the complete event (both beginning and end).

Empezó a trabajar.	*He began to work.*
Cesó de llover.	*It stopped raining.*
Visité a María ayer.	*I visited Mary yesterday.*

2. The imperfect is used to indicate the continuance of a situation or event in the past. Neither the beginning nor the end is indicated. Thus, it is used:

a. To express what was happening, used to happen, or happened repeatedly in the past.

¿Qué hacían ellos mientras el niño dormía?	*What were they doing while the child slept (was sleeping)?*
Vivíamos en Madrid.	*We used to live in Madrid.* *We were living in Madrid.*
Yo lo veía a menudo.	*I used to see him often.*

b. To describe persons, things, or situations in the past.

María tenía los ojos azules.	*Mary had blue eyes.*
La imprenta era una máquina útil.	*The press was a useful machine.*

c. To express the time of day in the past.

Eran las ocho.	*It was eight o'clock.*

d. In the construction *hacía + time expression + que + imperfect,* to describe an action or event that began in the past and continued in the past. In questions, how long? is expressed by *¿cuánto tiempo hacía que . . .? + imperfect.*

Hacía una hora que estudiaban.	*They had been studying for an hour.*
¿Cuánto tiempo hacía que Ud. trabajaba?	*How long had you been working?*

e. With the preterit, to describe what was going on in the past (imperfect) when another action or event occurred, that is, began or ended (preterit).

Yo leía cuando mi hermano entró.	*I was reading when my brother entered.*

EXERCISE A. **In each selection the choice of the preterit or imperfect form of the verb is offered. Select the appropriate one.**

1. Cuando Emilio (*llegó, llegaba*) al aeropuerto, se (*dio, daba*) cuenta de que no (*tuvo, tenía*) su boleto. —«¿Dónde lo (*dejé, dejaba*)?»—, (*pensó, pensaba*) Emilio, mientras la agente de la aerolínea (*trató, trataba*) de ayudarlo. Sólo (*hubo, había*) una manera de resolver su problema. (*Tuvo, Tenía*) que comprar otro boleto. (*Buscó, Buscaba*) la cartera en el bolsillo pero no lo (*encontró, encontraba*). (*Fueron, Eran*) ya las dos y cuarto y el avión (*salió, salía*) a las dos y media.

2. (*Fue, Era*) una noche cálida de agosto. (*Fueron, Eran*) las diez de la noche y todavía (*hubo, había*) muchas personas en la playa. Estela (*estuvo, estaba*) en el balcón y desde allí (*pudo, podía*) ver que (*ardieron, ardían*) varias fogatas en la playa. La luz de las llamas de las fogatas (*iluminó, iluminaba*) la escena de la playa. Pero por la oscuridad de la noche no (*se distinguió, se distinguía*) dónde (*comenzó, comenzaba*) el mar y dónde (*terminó, terminaba*) la playa. Estela (*oyó, oía*) claramente las voces de las personas en la playa y el ruido de las olas que (*se rompieron, se rompían*) al tocar la orilla.

3. Lucy siempre (*pasó, pasaba*) muchas horas leyendo revistas de músicos contemporáneos. En una ocasión (*leyó, leía*) la historia de uno de sus cantantes favoritos. El artículo (*dijo, decía*) que el cantante nunca (*demostró, demostraba*) ningún interés discernible hacia la música. El (*asistió, asistía*) a la universidad y (*decidió, decidía*) estudiar leyes. Le (*gustaron, gustaban*) los deportes, especialmente el fútbol. (*Jugó, Jugaba*) con frecuencia y (*fue, era*) muy buen futbolista. Un día, mientras (*condujo, conducía*) su carro, (*tuvo, tenía*) un accidente automovilístico. (*Pasó, Pasaba*) dos meses en el hospital. Al volver a casa, (*comenzó, comenzaba*) a estudiar la guitarra y (*compuso, componía*) varias canciones. Cuando (*pudo, podía*) volver a la universidad, (*terminó, terminaba*) sus estudios y (*llegó, llegaba*) a ser abogado. (*Abandonó, Abandonaba*) la idea de ser abogado y (*grabó, grababa*) un disco de sus canciones. Y así (*se hizo, se hacía*) famoso este cantante.

EXERCISE B. **Raúl never straightened up his room. His mother took a photograph of his room to show him what he wasn't doing. Then Raúl showed her a photo he took of the room. Using the first photo, tell what Raúl wasn't doing. Then, using the second photo, tell what he did. Use the suggestions below.**

EXAMPLE: Raúl no arreglaba su cuarto. Raúl **arregló** su cuarto.

SUGGESTIONS: (no) colgar la ropa en el armario	(no) apagar el estéreo
(no) poner los libros en el librero	(no) guardar los zapatos en el armario
(no) hacer la cama	(no) arreglar su cuarto
(no) sacar la basura	

____

____

____

____

____

____

EXERCISE C. **Complete the passage below with the appropriate form of the verbs indicated in the preterit or imperfect tenses.**

Él ________ (*1.* conocer) a Mariana una sola vez, pero su imagen ________ (*2.* quedar) profundamente grabada en su memoria. Ella ________ (*3.* ser) alta, esbelta y joven. ________ (*4.* tener) los ojos claros y una sonrisa simpática. Ella y sus amigas ________ (*5.* pasar) una semana en un hotel cerca de donde él ________ (*6.* alquilar) un cuarto mientras ________ (7. asistir) a la universidad. Sus pasos ________ (*8.* cruzarse) casi todos los días a la hora de la comida. El ________ (*9.* soler) comer en un restaurante pequeño cerca de la pensión y las jóvenes ________ (*10.* desayunar) allí cada día. ¡Qué bonito ________ (*11.* ser) poder desayunar a la hora en que todo el mundo ________ (*12.* almorzar)! ________ (*13.* pensar). ________ (*14.* querer) saber cómo ella ________ (*15.* llamarse), pero no ________ (*16.* atreverse) a acercarse a su mesa para presentarse. Un día le ________ (*17.* llegar) el momento propicio. El ________ (*18.* ir) a la caja para pagar la cuenta y cuando ella ________ (*19.* levantarse) y ________ (*20.* acercarse) a la caja en el mismo momento. Por un instante ________ (*21.* quedarse) inmóvil y ________ (*22.* sentir) que su boca ________ (*23.* ponerse) muy seca. Ella le ________ (*24.* sonreír) y él ________ (*25.* decidir) aprovecharse de la oportunidad. Le ________ (*26.* hacer) una señal de pasar primero a la caja y ella le ________ (*27.* dar) las gracias. Entonces, el joven ________ (*28.* tratar) de decirle algo pero las palabras no ________ (*29.* salir) de su boca. Ella ________ (*30.* hacer) un comentario sobre el tiempo, pero él sólo ________ (*31.* poder) contestarle con un movimiento de la cabeza. Ella ________ (*32.* fijarse) en los libros que él ________ (*33.* traer) y le ________ (*34.* preguntar) si ________ (*35.* ser) estudiante. Ahora ________ (*36.* saber) que si no le ________ (*37.* responder), la oportunidad sería perdida para siempre.

EXERCISE D. **Antonio is interested in knowing how long his friends had been doing different activities. Prepare the questions he asks.**

EXAMPLE: Jaime / ser miembro del equipo de fútbol
¿Cuánto tiempo hacía que Jaime era miembro del equipo de fútbol?

1. Renaldo / actuar en los dramas de la escuela

____

2. tus abuelos / pasar el invierno en la Florida

____

3. tú / competir en los concursos

____

4. Angela y Gerardo / ser novios

____

5. June y yo / jugar al boliche todos los viernes por la noche

____

6. Uds. / asistir a los conciertos

____

7. Vicente / montar a caballo

____

EXERCISE E. **Answer the questions in Exercise D using the information provided.**

EXAMPLE: (*dos años*) Hacía dos años que Jaime era miembro del equipo de fútbol.

1. (*un año*) ______________________________
2. (*cinco años*) ______________________________
3. (*seis meses*) ______________________________
4. (*dos semanas*) ______________________________
5. (*cinco semanas*) ______________________________
6. (*tres meses*) ______________________________
7. (*diez años*) ______________________________

EXERCISE F. **Your father wants to know why you didn't answer the telephone when he called. Answer the questions he asks.**

1. ¿Dónde estabas cuando sonó el teléfono?

____

2. ¿Qué hacías?

____

3. ¿Quiénes estaban contigo?

____

4. ¿Tenían Uds. el estéreo puesto?

____

5. ¿Oíste cuando el vecino llamó a la puerta?

____

6. ¿Por qué no contestaste el teléfono cuando yo llamé?

____

MASTERY EXERCISES

EXERCISE G. **You are helping your younger brother write a report on a hero for his Spanish class. Complete his report by providing the appropriate form of the verb given in the preterit or imperfect tense.**

El padre Miguel Hidalgo ______________ (*1.* ser) un gran patriota mexicano. ______________ (*2.* ser) el primer jefe de la lucha por la independencia. México ______________ (*3.* ser) entonces una colonia española. Los mexicanos no ______________ (*4.* poder) tomar parte en el gobierno. Los gobernadores ______________ (*5.* ser) todos españoles, nombrados por el rey de España. Muchos ______________ (*6.* aceptar) puestos solamente para hacerse ricos, a costa de los mexicanos. El deseo de liberar a su patria ______________ (*7.* inflamar) el corazón de Hidalgo, que entonces ______________ (*8.* ser) sacerdote de la pequeña aldea de Dolores. En 1810 ______________ (*9.* organizar) un partido patriótico cuyo objeto ______________ (*10.* ser) trabajar y luchar por la independencia. Ellos ______________ (*11.* formar) un ejército y ______________ (*12.* avanzar) sobre Guanajuato, una ciudad grande y rica, fortificada y defendida por los españoles. Por el heroísmo de Hidalgo, los revolucionarios ______________ (*13.* poder) vencer a los españoles. Hidalgo ______________ (*14.* fortificar) la ciudad y la ______________ (*15.* hacer) centro de la revolución. En seguida ______________ (*16.* empezar) a llegar miles de mexicanos, que ______________ (*17.* querer) juntarse a las fuerzas patrióticas. Con la ayuda de éstos, Hidalgo ______________ (*18.* poder) continuar la lucha.

EXERCISE H. **Mrs. Duarte asks her son Joey many questions when he returns from school. Answer the questions she asks him.**

1. ¿Diste la tarea a tu maestra?

____

2. ¿Encontraste a muchos amigos esta mañana mientras ibas a la escuela?

____

3. ¿A qué hora llegaste a la escuela?

____

4. ¿Atravesaste muchas calles hoy para llegar a la escuela?

____

5. ¿Cuando entraste en la casa ahora, colgaste tu abrigo en el armario?

____

EXERCISE I. **Answer the questions a new friend asks you about what you were like when you were younger.**

1. ¿Cuando eras niño(-a), soñabas con viajar?

____

2. ¿Siempre obedecías a tu mamá?

____

3. ¿Poseías una bicicleta?

____

4. ¿Les tiraban piedras tú y tus amigos a los otros niños?

____

5. ¿Interrumpías a tus padres cuando ellos hablaban?

____

EXERCISE J. **A new student in your class has been asked to write a description of his first day in your school. Express what he said in Spanish.**

1. I had been waiting on the corner for the bus for fifteen minutes.

____

2. The bus finally arrived.

____

3. There were so many students on the bus that I could not sit down.

____

4. One student offered to share his seat with me.

____

5. We began to speak.

____

6. He told me that he had just come to the school also.

____

7. He was from El Salvador.

____

8. When I arrived at school, I went to the office.

____

9. A very nice lady gave me my schedule.

____

10. A student accompanied me to my first class.

____

11. When I entered the room, the class was watching a movie.

____

12. The teacher and I went into the hall, and she welcomed me.

____

13. We returned to the classroom and she intoduced me to the other students.

____

14. They were polite and friendly.

____

15. I sat down and listened while the class discussed the movie.

____

Chapter 10
The Future Tense

[1] THE FUTURE TENSE OF REGULAR VERBS

The future tense is formed by adding to the infinitive the following endings:

	ayudar *to help*	**aprender** *to learn*	**abrir** *to open*
	I shall (will) help, you will help, etc.	*I shall (will) learn, you will learn, etc.*	*I shall (will) open, you will open, etc.*
yo	**ayudar*é***	**aprender*é***	**abrir*é***
tú	**ayudar*ás***	**aprender*ás***	**abrir*ás***
él, ella, Ud.	**ayudar*á***	**aprender*á***	**abrir*á***
nosotros, -as	**ayudar*emos***	**aprender*emos***	**abrir*emos***
vosotros, -as	**ayudar*éis***	**aprender*éis***	**abrir*éis***
Uds. ellos, ellas	**ayudar*án***	**aprender*án***	**abrir*án***

NOTE:

1. In English, the future tense is expressed by means of the helping verb *will* or *shall*.

   Estaré en la escuela mañana. — *I shall be in school tomorrow.*
   ¿Cenarás conmigo esta noche? — *Will you have dinner with me tonight?*

2. All the endings have an accent mark, except *-emos*.

EXERCISE A. **Everyone is making plans for the following day. Tell what each person will do.**

EXAMPLE: Marta / visitar a una amiga — Marta **visitará** a una amiga.

1. yo / jugar al voleibol ______________________

2. Felipe y Martín / remar en el lago ______________________

3. mis padres / comer en un restaurante ______________________

4. tú / ir de compras ______________________

5. Uds. / ver una película ______________________

6. Jimmy y yo / asistir a un concierto ______________________

EXERCISE B. **As one year ends and a new one is about to begin, several friends discuss their plans for the new year. Tell what each one will do.**

EXAMPLE: Andrés / buscar un trabajo — Andrés **buscará** un trabajo.

1. Vicki / terminar sus estudios ______________________

2. Esteban y yo / viajar a México ______________________

3. tú / aprender a conducir ______________________

4. yo / leer «El Quijote» __________

5. Ofelia y Arturo / correr en un maratón __________

6. Gisela / tocar en una orquesta __________

EXERCISE C. **Your father follows the same routine every day. Tell what he will do tomorrow.**

EXAMPLE: apagar el reloj despertador — Mi papá **apagará** el reloj despertador.

1. levantarse de la cama en seguida __________

2. bañarse y luego vestirse __________

3. comer el desayuno con mi mamá __________

4. ir al trabajo __________

5. conducir el carro __________

6. asistir a una reunión en su oficina __________

7. llamar a mi mamá a mediodía __________

8. volver a casa a las seis __________

9. cenar con toda la familia __________

10. sentarse en la sala __________

11. leer el periódico __________

12. oír las noticias __________

13. dormirse en el sillón __________

[2] The Future Tense of Irregular Verbs

Some verbs form the future tense by adding the future personal endings (*-é, -ás, -á, -emos, -éis, -án*) to an irregular stem.

a. **The following verbs drop the *e* of the infinitive ending before adding the endings of the future:**

caber *to fit*	**cabré, cabrás, cabrá, cabremos, cabréis, cabrán**
haber *to have (also an auxiliary verb)*	**habré, habrás, habrá, habremos, habréis, habrán**
poder *to be able*	**podré, podrás, podrá, podremos, podréis, podrán**
querer *to want, wish*	**querré, querrás, querrá, querremos, querréis, querrán**
saber *to know*	**sabré, sabrás, sabrá, sabremos, sabréis, sabrán**

EXERCISE D. **You and some friends are going on a school trip to Spain. Tell what each person will be able to do there. Use the verb *poder* in each sentence.**

EXAMPLE: Ema / hablar español todo el día — Ema **podrá** hablar español todo el día.

1. Michael / ir a una corrida de toros ______
2. Celia y Laura / visitar el museo del Prado ______
3. Verónica y yo / comprar muchos recuerdos ______
4. yo / comer paella ______
5. tú / ver programas de televisión en español ______
6. Uds. / conocer a muchos jóvenes españoles ______

EXERCISE E. **You are organizing a school dance. Answer the questions some classmates ask you about it.**

1. ¿Cabrán todos los estudiantes en el gimnasio?

______

2. ¿Habrá mucha comida y bebidas?

______

3. ¿Cuándo sabrás cuántas personas asistirán al baile?

______

4. ¿Querrás nuestra ayuda la noche del baile?

______

5. ¿Podrán los músicos tocar nuestras canciones favoritas?

______

b. **The following verbs replace the *e* or *i* of the infinitive ending with a *d* before adding the endings of the future:**

poner *to put*	**pondré, pondrás, pondrá, pondremos, pondréis, pondrán**
salir *to leave, go out*	**saldré, saldrás, saldrá, saldremos, saldréis, saldrán**
tener *to have*	**tendré, tendrás, tendrá, tendremos, tendréis, tendrán**
valer *to be worth*	**valdré, valdrás, valdrá, valdremos, valdréis, valdrán**
venir *to come*	**vendré, vendrás, vendrá, vendremos, vendréis, vendrán**

c. **The following verbs drop the *e* and *c* of the infinitive before adding the endings of the future:**

decir *to say, tell*	**diré, dirás, dirá, diremos, diréis, dirán**
hacer *to do, make*	**haré, harás, hará, haremos, haréis, harán**

[3] USES OF THE FUTURE TENSE

The future tense is used:

a. To express future time.

¿A qué hora llegará el tren? — *At what time will the train arrive?*

b. To express wonderment or probability in the present time.

¿Qué hora será? — *I wonder what time it is.*

Será la una. — *It is probably one o'clock.*

EXERCISE F. Before leaving for Costa Rica, you receive an e-mail message from a friend who was an exchange student in your school. Complete his message with the future tense of the verbs indicated.

¡Por fin Uds. ______ (1. venir) a San José! Nosotros ______ (2. salir) juntos durante los días que Uds. ______ (3. estar) aquí. Yo ______ (4. tener) mucho gusto en mostrarles mi ciudad a Uds. ______ (5. querer) regresar a San José durante las próximas vacaciones. Mi papá ______ (6. poner) un carro a sus órdenes. Nosotros ______ (7. poder) hablar de las semanas que pasé en su escuela y también ______ (8. hacer) un viaje a la playa. Ya ______ (9. decir) Uds. qué bonito es mi país. Es un viaje largo pero ______ (10. valer) la pena. Hasta pronto.

EXERCISE G. Tell what these people will do when something happens to change their plans.

EXAMPLE: Tú y un amigo piensan ir al cine, pero él está enfermo. (*ir solo al cine*)
Yo **iré** solo al cine.

1. Manuel quiere correr en el parque, pero hace mucho calor. (*nadar en la piscina*)
   Él ______.
2. Sara piensa ir de compras con una amiga, pero ella dice que no tiene dinero. (*prestarle dinero*)
   Su amiga ______.
3. Dos amigos van al cine para ver una película y cambiaron la película. (*ver la otra película*)
   Ellos ______.
4. Vas a salir con tus amigos, pero tus padres no te prestan el carro. (*no salir*)
   Yo ______.
5. Tu hermana se durmió mientras preparaba un pastel. El pastel se quemó. (*hacer otro pastel*)
   Ella ______.
6. Inés iba a trabajar durante el verano, pero salió mal en una clase. (*tener que tomar la clase durante el verano*)
   Ella ______.

MASTERY EXERCISES

EXERCISE H. **Sam invited a group of friends to his house. His younger brother is very inquisitive and asks questions about everything Sam says. Write the questions his brother probably asks.**

EXAMPLE: Unos amigos vienen a la casa esta noche. (*¿quiénes?*)
¿Quiénes **vendrán**?

1. Van a llegar a las ocho. (*llegar a tiempo*)
____

2. Voy a poner algunos discos compactos en el estéreo. (*¿qué?*)
____

3. Debo hacer algo de comer para ellos. (*¿qué?*)
____

4. Quiero atenderlos bien. (*¿por qué?*)
____

5. Puedo poner algunos adornos. (*¿dónde?*)
____

6. Alex viene con Diana. (*¿con quién?*)
____

EXERCISE I. **You and several friends are talking about the future. Answer their questions.**

1. ¿Dónde vivirás en el futuro? ______________________________
2. ¿Qué clase de trabajo tendrás? ______________________________
3. ¿Ganarás mucho dinero? ______________________________
4. ¿Vendrás a ver a tus amigos a menudo? ______________________________
5. ¿Harás muchos viajes al extranjero? ______________________________
6. ¿Podrás ahorrar mucho dinero? ______________________________
7. ¿Pondrás el dinero en la Bolsa? ______________________________
8. ¿Sabrás hacer buenas inversiones con tu dinero? ______________________________

EXERCISE J. **Your mother is planning a large holiday celebration. Using the verbs indicated, tell what each family member will do to help.**

1. Yo le ______________ qué hacer a cada persona. (*decir*)

2. Todo el mundo _________________ que arreglar su cuarto. (*tener*)

3. Alicia _________________ la mesa. (*poner*)

4. El abuelo _________________ ayudar con la limpieza. (*querer*)

5. Tú _________________ los adornos. (*hacer*)

6. Víctor y su papá _________________ al supermercado. (*salir*)

7. Los invitados _________________ a las cuatro. (*venir*)

8. La abuela y yo _________________ a qué hora poner todo en el horno. (*saber*)

9. Yo _________________ descansar antes de la llegada de los invitados. (*poder*)

EXERCISE K. **Answer the questions a friend asks you on the school bus in the morning.**

1. ¿A qué hora saldrás de la escuela hoy?

____

2. ¿A qué hora estarás en casa esta tarde?

____

3. ¿Podrás ir al cine esta noche?

____

4. ¿Tendrás que estudiar para un examen mañana?

____

5. ¿Qué harás mañana después de las clases?

____

6. ¿Podrás ir al centro conmigo?

____

7. ¿Sabrás si Gus podrá ir al centro también?

____

8. ¿Dónde pasarás el fin de semana?

____

9. ¿En qué fecha vendrán tus primos a verte?

____

10. ¿Te gustará tomar un refresco conmigo en el café?

____

EXERCISE L. **You are on a city tour and there is a Spanish-speaking family. The tour guide doesn't speak Spanish. Help her express the following in Spanish.**

1. The bus will leave at one o'clock.

____

2. I will explain everything.

____

3. We will visit many interesting places.

____

4. You will be able to go into the museum.

____

5. You will have to buy tickets to enter the museum.

____

6. The tickets probably cost three dollars per person.

____

7. You will not be able to take photos in the museum.

____

8. You will have to leave your cameras on the bus.

____

9. I will be on the bus.

____

10. The children will not be able to visit the museum alone.

____

11. You will have forty-five minutes to visit the museum.

____

12. There will be a guide in the museum that speaks Spanish.

____

13. We will also pass many interesting buildings.

____

14. You will know the names of the buildings because I will say them in Spanish.

____

15. The tour will end at six o'clock.

____

16. We will return to the hotel.

____

17. There will be no time to shop.

____

18. There will be another tour tomorrow.

____

19. I will sell tickets for the other tour.

____

20. We will be very happy to see you again tomorrow.

____

ACTIVIDADES

1. What will the world be like in twenty-five years? How old will you be? What will you be doing? Will the same problems still exist? Peace throughout the world? The environment? New inventions? Space? New problems? Write a paragraph in Spanish in which you tell what you think the world will be like in twenty-five years. Address as many of the topics listed above. Be sure to use the future tense of as many regular and irregular verbs as you can.

2. Your parents have promised you a trip to any place in the world as a graduation gift. However, they want to know why you selected that destination. Write a letter to them in which you tell them your desired destination, why you want to go there, what you will see, learn, and be able to do there, how long you will need to spend there, etc. You may wish to consult the Internet for information about your chosen destination that you can include in the letter. Use the future tense as often as you can in the letter.

Chapter 11
The Conditional Tense

[1] REGULAR VERBS

a. The conditional tense is formed by adding to the infinitive the following endings:

	viajar *to travel*	**comer** *to eat*	**permitir** *to permit*
yo	viajar*ía*	comer*ía*	permitir*ía*
tú	viajar*ías*	comer*ías*	permitir*ías*
Ud., él, ella,	viajar*ía*	comer*ía*	permitir*ía*
nosotros, -as	viajar*íamos*	comer*íamos*	permitir*íamos*
vosotros, -as	viajar*íais*	comer*íais*	permitir*íais*
Uds., ellos, ellas	viajar*ían*	comer*ían*	permitir*ían*

b. In English, the conditional tense is expressed by means of the helping verb *would.*

¿Adónde viajarías? — *Where would you travel to?*
Viajaría a la América del Sur. — *I would travel to South America.*

c. All the endings have an accent mark on the *i* of the ending.

EXERCISE A. Several friends are speculating about what they would do if they had unlimited funds. Tell what each one would do.

EXAMPLE: Pablo / comprar un carro de modelo deportivo
Pablo **compraría** un carro de modelo deportivo.

1. Virginia / dar dinero a los pobres ______________________
2. Eddie y Roger / vivir en una isla tropical ______________________
3. Dennis y yo / ayudar a nuestras familias ______________________
4. tú / ir de compras todos los días ______________________
5. yo / ser dueño de una compañía grande ______________________
6. Franco / no trabajar ______________________

EXERCISE B. You are a member of an ecology club in your school. Tell what everyone would do to protect the environment.

EXAMPLE: todo el mundo / reciclar la basura — Todo el mundo **reciclaría** la basura.

1. Jenny / conservar el agua

____

2. yo / proteger las flores y las plantas del parque

____

3. Enrique y yo / usar el transporte público

____

4. tú / no tirar papeles en el piso

____

5. Selene y Rocío / montar en bicicleta

____

6. la comunidad / organizar un programa de reciclaje

____

EXERCISE C. Tell what these people would do in this situations.

EXAMPLE: Mi amiga no me llama. (*llamarla*) Yo la **llamaría.**

1. El abuelo de Carlos está en el hospital. (*ir a visitarlo*)
   Carlos iría a visitarlo.

2. Es el cumpleaños de mi hermano. (*comprarle un regalo*)
   Yo le compraría un regalo.

   lose expensive
3. Mi tía perdió un anillo muy caro. (*ofrecer una recompensa*)
   Ella ofrecería una recompensa.

4. El cajero les dio demasiado cambio a Vinny y a Tony. (*devolver el dinero*)
   Ellos ____.

5. Nosotros tenemos boletos para un concierto pero no podemos asistir. (*dar los boletos a unos amigos*)
   Nosotros ____.

6. Tu padre no puede pintar la casa solo. (*ayudarle a pintar la casa*)
   Tú ____.

[2] VERBS IRREGULAR IN THE CONDITIONAL TENSE

Some verbs form the conditional tense by adding the conditional personal endings to an irregular stem.

a. The following verbs drop the *e* of the infinitive ending before adding the endings of the conditional:

caber	*to fit*	**cabría, cabrías, cabría, cabríamos, cabríais, cabrían**
haber	*to have (auxiliary verb)*	**habría, habrías, habría, habríamos, habríais, habrían**
poder	*to be able*	**podría, podrías, podría, podríamos, podríais, podrían**
querer	*to want, wish*	**querría, querrías, querría, querríamos, querríais, querrían**
saber	*to know*	**sabría, sabrías, sabría, sabríamos, sabríais, sabrían**

b. The following verbs replace the *e* (or *i*) of the infinitive ending with a *d* before adding the endings of the conditional:

poner *to put*	pondría, pondrías, pondría, pondríamos, pondríais, pondrían
salir *to leave, go out*	saldría, saldrías, saldría, saldríamos, saldríais, saldrían
tener *to have*	tendría, tendrías, tendría, tendríamos, tendríais, tendrían
valer *to be worth*	valdría, valdrías, valdría, valdríamos, valdríais, valdrían
venir *to come*	vendría, vendrías, vendría, vendríamos, vendríais, vendrían

c. The following verbs drop the *e* and *c* of the infinitive before adding the endings of the conditional:

decir *to say, tell*	diría, dirías, diría, diríamos, diríais, dirían
hacer *to do, make*	haría, harías, haría, haríamos, haríais, harían

NOTE: When *would* is used in the sense of *used to,* it is expressed by the imperfect tense, not the conditional.

Siempre nos ayudaba. *He always would (used to) help us.*

EXERCISE D. Janice and her friends have had a very busy school year. Express what they would know how to do if they had had more time. Use the verb saber in your answers.

EXAMPLE: Janice / patinar en hielo — Janice **sabría** patinar en hielo.

1. Ralph y Perry / esquiar ______________________
2. yo / conducir ______________________
3. Ellas / patinar en monopatín ______________________
4. Felice y yo / jugar al tenis ______________________
5. tú / navegar ______________________
6. Mitch / montar a caballo ______________________

EXERCISE E. You and your younger brother are waiting in the crowded dentist's office. To help distract him while you wait, you give him two lists. One contains the members of your family; the other contains activities they would prefer. Tell who would prefer what.

Papá	ir a la playa o a las montañas
Mamá	hacer un castillo en la arena o nadar en el mar
Sally	jugar al golf o al tenis
Richie	dar o recibir regalos
Tío Juan	pasar las vacaciones con la familia o con tus amigos
yo	comer en una cafetería o un restaurante elegante
tú y yo	poner el dinero en el banco o gastarlo visitar al dentista o ir a la heladería

EXAMPLE: Yo iría a la heladería.

1. ______________________________
2. ______________________________

3. ______________________________

4. ______________________________

5. ______________________________

6. ______________________________

7. ______________________________

8. ______________________________

EXERCISE F. **You have been out of the country for over a month and haven't seen a local newspaper in all that time. Tell what you would know or do if you had a local newspaper. Use the suggestions.**

SUGGESTIONS:
saber cuándo comienzan las baratas en las tiendas
poder seguir las tiras cómicas
hacer el crucigrama
leer las últimas noticias
hacer comentario sobre un suceso local
ver los anuncios de las tiendas
enterarse de las noticias locales
saber los tantos de los equipos de béisbol

EXAMPLE: Yo podría seguir las tiras cómicas.

1. ______________________________

2. ______________________________

3. ______________________________

4. ______________________________

5. ______________________________

6. ______________________________

7. ______________________________

EXERCISE G. **You and your sister listened to a message your father left on the answering machine but neither of you understood it. Tell what you thought he said.**

EXAMPLE: él / llegar a casa en dos horas El **llegaría** a casa en dos horas.

1. nosotros / deber esperarlo para cenar

____

2. no haber trenes hasta la mañana debido a un accidente

____

3. él / alquilar un carro

____

4. tu mamá / poder buscarlo en la estación

____

5. tú / no saber nada por dos horas

____

6. él / tener que pasar la noche en un hotel

____

7. él y un vecino / venir en autobús

____

8. todo el mundo / no caber en el primer tren de la mañana

____

9. los pasajeros / no salir del tren

____

10. él / volver a llamar más tarde

____

[3] USES OF THE CONDITIONAL TENSE

The conditional is used:

a. To express what would or could happen in the future or to make a polite request.

Pagaría mucho por las joyas.	*I would pay a lot for the jewelry.*
Me gustaría ver una corbata de seda.	*I would like to see a silk tie.*

b. To express wonderment or probability in the past.

¿Qué hora sería?	*I wonder what time it was.*
Sería la una.	*It was probably one o'clock.*

NOTE: **The future tense is commonly used in combination with the present or future tense; the conditional, with a past tense.**

Dice que irá.	*He says he will go.*
Dijo que iría.	*He said he would go.*

EXERCISE H. **You are planning a trip with the travel agent. Answer her questions.**

1. ¿Adónde iría Ud.? ______________________________

2. ¿Cuántas personas harían el viaje? ______________________________

3. ¿Cuándo podrían Uds. salir? ______________________________

4. ¿En qué fecha querrían regresar? ______________________________

5. ¿Harían excursiones allí? ______________________________

6. ¿Cuántas excursiones harían Uds.? ______________________________

7. ¿Cuánto dinero querría Ud. gastar en el viaje? ______________________________

8. ¿Tendría Ud. que alquilar un carro? ______________________________

9. ¿Quién podría llevarlos al aeropuerto? ______________________________

10. ¿Pagaría Ud. con un cheque personal o con una tarjeta de crédito? ______________________________

EXERCISE I. **You are reading an ad for a health club. Tell five things you would do if you were a member.**

EXAMPLE: Yo usaría las máquinas de entrenamiento.

1. ______________________________

2. ______________________________

3. ______________________________

4. ______________________________

5. ______________________________

MASTERY EXERCISES

EXERCISE J. **You and a friend are going to Costa Rica to visit your friend's family. You send her this e-mail message. Complete the message with the appropriate form of the verbs indicated in the conditional.**

El agente de viajes me dijo que el avión ______________ (1. salir) a las siete de la noche. Nosotros ______________ (2. tener) que estar en el aeropuerto dos horas antes y me ______________ (3. gustar) estar allí a la hora indicada. Así nosotras ________ (4. escoger) los asientos con calma. También yo ________ (5. querer) comprar algo para tu familia en la tienda Libre de Aduanas. Entendí que tus padres te ________ (6. llevar) al aeropuerto. ¿Qué ________ (7. decir) ellos si yo les ________ (8. pedir) un favor muy grande? ¿ ________ (9. poder) Uds. pasar por mí camino al aeropuerto? Así yo no ________ (10. tener) que buscar un taxi y nosotras ________ (11. llegar) juntas al aeropuerto. Contéstame.

EXERCISE K. A friend calls you after school. Answer the questions.

1. ¿Qué hora sería cuando te acostaste anoche?

   ____

2. ¿Cómo sabrías que el maestro estaría ausente?

   ____

3. ¿Sabías a qué universidad asistiría Pedro?

   ____

4. ¿Les aseguró el maestro que no recibirían un examen?

   ____

5. ¿Les prometiste a tus padres que estudiarías más?

   ____

6. ¿Les dijiste a tus amigos cuándo caería tu cumpleaños?

   ____

7. ¿Adónde querrías ir para celebrar tu cumpleaños?

   ____

8. ¿Escogiste los regalos que te gustaría recibir?

   ____

9. ¿Cuánto valdría un reloj como el que tenía Kyoko?

   ____

10. ¿Dónde pondrías un reloj tan caro cuando jugabas al tenis?

    ____

EXERCISE L. Your summer vacation is over and it feels as if it passed very quickly. Tell five things you would do differently next vacation.

EXAMPLE: No me acostaría tan tarde cada noche.

1. ____

2. ____

3. ____

4. ____

5. ____

EXERCISE M. **A Spanish-speaking friend of your father is coming to your house for dinner. He owns a company and you would like to work there during the summer vacation. You are planning what you will say to him. Express the following in Spanish.**

1. I promised my father that I would earn money during the summer.

2. My teacher told me that if I could speak Spanish during the summer it would help me.

3. I would like to have a job in your office. I would work hard.

4. I would prefer to work from Monday to Friday.

5. I would arrive at 8:00 A.M. and I would leave at 5:00 P.M.

6. I would need one hour for lunch.

7. I would open the mail and answer the telephone.

8. What other tasks would I have?

9. How much would you pay me?

10. Could you recommend another office?

ACTIVIDADES

1. You are planning to study in a Spanish-speaking country during the summer. Write a letter to the director of a special program for foreigners in which you request information concerning the program. In your letter, provide information concerning your plans and goals. Also, obtain information concerning the program (duration, requirements, cost, etc.), living accommodations, travel options, etc. Write at least ten sentences in Spanish, using the conditional.

For your convenience, use the following:

Dateline: **2 de junio de ______**
Salutation: **Estimado(-a) ____________ :**
Closing: **Atentamente,**

2. Tell what you would do in the situations shown in the pictures below.
For each situation write at least three sentences in Spanish using the conditional.

1. ______________________________

____

____

2. ______________________________

____

____

3. ______________________________

____

____

4. ______________________________

____

____

5. ______________________________

____

____

Chapter 12
The Gerund and the Progressive Tenses

In Spanish, the gerund (*el gerundio*) is generally equivalent to the English present participle, or *-ing* verb form.

[1] The Gerund of Regular Verbs

Regular verbs form the gerund by dropping the infinitive endings and adding *-ando* (*-ar* verbs) and *-iendo* (*-er* and *-ir* verbs).

trabajar:	trabajando	*working*	vivir:	viviendo	*living*
aprender:	aprendiendo	*learning*			

[2] Gerunds Ending in *-yendo*

Irregular *-er* and *-ir* verbs with stems ending in a vowel form their gerunds by adding *-yendo.*

caer:	cayendo	*falling*	ir:	yendo	*going*
construir:	construyendo	*constructing*	leer:	leyendo	*reading*
creer:	creyendo	*believing*	oír:	oyendo	*hearing*
destruir:	destruyendo	*destroying*	traer:	trayendo	*bringing*
huir:	huyendo	*fleeing*			

[3] Irregular Gerunds

a. In the gerund, stem-changing *-ir* verbs change their stem vowel from *e* to *i* and from *o* to *u*.

decir:	diciendo	*saying, telling*	pedir:	pidiendo	*asking for*
dormir:	durmiendo	*sleeping*	sentir:	sintiendo	*feeling, regretting*
morir:	muriendo	*dying*	venir:	viniendo	*coming*

b. Other verbs of this type are:

conseguir:	consiguiendo	*obtaining*	repetir:	repitiendo	*repeating*
corregir:	corrigiendo	*correcting*	servir:	sirviendo	*serving*
mentir:	mintiendo	*lying*	vestir:	vistiendo	*dressing*

c. The gerund of the verb *poder* is *pudiendo.*

[4] Uses of the Gerund

The gerund is often the equivalent of *by* + *present participle.*

Trabajando, se gana dinero.	*By working, one earns money.*
Estudiando, aprendes mucho.	*By studying, you learn a lot.*

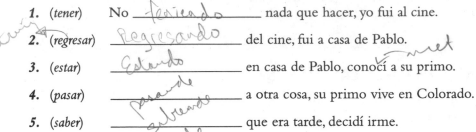

EXERCISE A. **Beto is describing what he did last night. Complete each statement with the gerund of the verb indicated.**

EXAMPLE: (*mirar*) ____________________ la televisión, me dormí.
Mirando la televisión, me dormí.

1. (*tener*) No ____________________ nada que hacer, yo fui al cine.
2. (*regresar*) ____________________ del cine, fui a casa de Pablo.
3. (*estar*) ____________________ en casa de Pablo, conocí a su primo.
4. (*pasar*) ____________________ a otra cosa, su primo vive en Colorado.
5. (*saber*) ____________________ que era tarde, decidí irme.
6. (*dar*) ____________________ las gracias, pedí permiso y salí.

EXERCISE B. **Complete each statement with the gerund of the verb indicated.**

1. (*construir*) ____________________ casas, el señor Paván se hizo rico.
2. (*leer*) ____________________ libros, Elsa conoció otras culturas.
3. (*oír*) ____________________ la noticia, le llamé a mi tío.
4. (*creer*) ____________________ el chisme, Alicia lo contó a sus amigas.
5. (*decir*) ____________________ eso, se acabó la entrevista.
6. (*dormir*) ____________________ por ocho horas, Alex se sintió mejor.
7. (*repetir*) ____________________ el poema varias veces, la niña lo aprendió de memoria.
8. (*pedir*) ____________________ ayuda, yo aprendí a usar la computadora.
9. (*huir*) ____________________ del perro, el cartero se cayó.
10. (*traer*) ____________________ su traje de baño, Gregorio pudo nadar en la piscina.

[5] PROGRESSIVE TENSES

The progressive tenses are used to talk about an action that is (was or will be) in progress or is continuing at the moment indicated. The gerund is used with forms of the verbs *estar, seguir,* and *continuar,* and with verbs of motion.

Los niños **están llorando.**	*The children are crying.*
Él **estaba leyendo.**	*He was reading.*
Siguen escribiendo.	*They continue writing.*
Continuaban hablando.	*They continued speaking.*
Entró gritando.	*He entered shouting.*

NOTE: **The present participles of *estar, ir,* and *venir* are not usually used to form the progressive tenses. Instead, the simple tenses are used.**

Ella **viene** aquí.	*She is coming here.*
Rosa **iba** al parque.	*Rosa was going to the park.*

EXERCISE C. **Your school is celebrating a physical fitness day. Tell what each person is doing.**

EXAMPLE: Enrique / levantar pesas — Enrique **está levantando** pesas.

1. Carmen / montar en bicicleta — Carmen está montando en
2. Felipe y Rosa / correr en la pista — están corriendo
3. yo / hacer ejercicios — estoy haciendo
4. Imelda y yo / nadar en la piscina — estámos nadando
5. Ruth / practicar yoga — está practicando
6. todos los muchachos / jugar al voleibol — están jugando

EXERCISE D. **It's seven o'clock in the evening. Tell which member of your family is doing these activities.**

EXAMPLE: lavar los platos — Mi hermano **está lavando** los platos.

1. sacar al perro ______
2. leer el periódico ______
3. mirar la televisión ______
4. jugar a las damas ______
5. hacer la tarea ______
6. oír la radio ______
7. tocar el piano ______
8. escribir cheques ______

EXERCISE E. **The Spanish club in your school is having a dinner to celebrate *"El Día de la Raza."* Tell what everyone is busy doing.**

EXAMPLE: colgar los adornos / Ricky y Guillermo
Ricky y Guillermo **están colgando** los adornos.

1. poner las mesas / John y Lucy ______
2. calentar el arroz con pollo / Sofía ______
3. enfriar los refrescos / Lázaro ______
4. arreglar las flores / yo ______
5. escoger la música / tú ______
6. traer más sillas / Mirta y yo ______

EXERCISE F. **You are working in a day care center. Tell what everyone is doing.**

EXAMPLE: Arturito / decir su primera palabra
Arturito **está diciendo** su primera palabra.

1. el bebé / dormir la siesta ______________________________
2. Sarita / vestir una muñeca ______________________________
3. tres niños / repetir el alfabeto ______________________________
4. yo / pedir ayuda ______________________________
5. Frances y yo / servir jugo a los niños ______________________________
6. los padres / venir por sus hijos ______________________________

EXERCISE G. **You want to know what different people were doing at nine o'clock last night. Answer the questions using the cues in parentheses.**

EXAMPLE: ¿Qué estaba haciendo Nelson? (*leer una novela*)
Nelson **estaba leyendo** una novela.

1. ¿Qué estaba haciendo Andrés? (*mirar la television*)
____
2. ¿Qué estaban haciendo Joan y Joyce? (*dormir*)
____
3. ¿Qué estaba haciendo su mamá? (*despedirse de los invitados*)
____
4. ¿Qué estabas haciendo? (*trabajar en la cafetería*)
____
5. ¿Qué estaba haciendo tía Pilar? (*vestir al bebé*)
____

EXERCISE H. **You are telling your mother about your visit to the circus with some friends. Tell how each one left the circus.**

EXAMPLE: tú / reír Tú saliste **riendo.**

1. Ana / llorar ______________________________
2. Tomás y Pedro / gritar ______________________________
3. yo / temblar ______________________________
4. Irma y yo / correr ______________________________
5. tú / decir chistes ______________________________
6. Michelle y Ema / brincar ______________________________

EXERCISE I. **You are going to a camp reunion. Prepare the questions you will ask your friends about themselves and other campers who are not present.**

EXAMPLE: correr en el maratón / tú ¿Sigues **corriendo** en el maratón?

1. coleccionar insectos / Gustavo ______________________________
2. tomar clases de baile / tú y tu hermana ______________________________
3. construir aviones en miniatura / Perry ______________________________
4. aprender a hablar español / tú ______________________________
5. ser buenos amigos / Ralph y Vicente ______________________________
6. pedir más comida / tú ______________________________
7. oír ruidos / la señorita Tess ______________________________

MASTERY EXERCISES

EXERCISE J. **A friend sent you an e-mail message in which she describes her visit to her grandparents' home. Complete her message with the appropriate form of the verbs provided.**

Cuando llegué a casa de mis abuelos, todo el mundo estaba ______________ (1. hacer) algo. Mi abuelo estaba ______________ (2. cortar) el césped y continuó ______________ (3. trabajar) en el jardín hasta la hora de la comida. Mi abuela estaba ______________ (4. cocinar) y siguió ______________ (5. preparar) muchos platillos para la comida. Tía Isabel estaba ______________ (6. cortar) flores en el jardín y pasó una hora y media ______________ (7. poner) las flores por toda la casa. Mis primos estaban ______________ (8. jugar) en el patio y nosotros seguimos ______________ (9. pasar) un buen rato allí hasta la llegada de Marcela. Ella es mi prima, pero le gusta molestar a los primos mayores mientras ellos tratan de divertirse. Mi primo José estaba ______________ (10. revisar) el carro de mi abuelo y pasó media hora ______________ (11. reparar) el limpiaparabrisas. Cuando llegué, el perro estaba ______________ (12. dormir) debajo de una mesa pero pasó toda la tarde ______________ (13. ladrar) y ______________ (14. pedir) comida a todo el mundo. Todavía me duele la cabeza.

EXERCISE K. **You arrive late to a party at one of your friend's home. Tell what you saw when you arrived. Write at least five sentences.**

EXAMPLE: Antonio **estaba tocando** la guitarra. Fred **estaba bailando** con Irma.
El perro **estaba durmiendo** en un rincón de la sala.

____

____

____

____

____

EXERCISE L. **Complete the letter that James wrote to a friend shortly after moving into the college dormitory. Write the gerund of the verb that is needed to complete each statement.**

caer	dormir	leer	poner
cambiar	escribir	llover	terminar
construir	hacer	mentir	trabajar
decir	hacer	oír	vivir

Querido Rafael:

Estoy ______________ esta carta en vez de estar ______________ las mil cosas que debo estar ______________. Cuando llegué aquí ayer estaba ______________. Pasé la tarde ______________ un estante para mis libros. Mientras estaba ______________ yo estaba ______________ la radio. El locutor estaba ______________ que las estaciones están ______________ porque las hojas ya están ______________ de los árboles. No estoy ______________ cuando te digo que ______________ solo no es fácil. Cada día continuaré ______________ más cosas en su lugar. Pasaré esta tarde ______________ y ______________. ¿Qué estás ______________ en este momento?

EXERCISE M. **You are going to describe a hotel training program in which you are enrolled to a group of Spanish-speaking students. Express the following in Spanish.**

1. Many people are already working in the hotel at 6:30 A.M.

____

2. The telephone operators are answering the telephones.

____

3. The chefs are preparing breakfast.

____

4. The waiters are serving breakfast in the restaurant.

5. Other waiters are bringing breakfast to a guest's room.

6. The doorman is obtaining taxis for some guests.

7. Several guests are asking for information about the city.

8. The tour buses are waiting at the door.

9. The tour guides are telling the tourists the itinerary for the day.

10. The chambermaids are knocking on the doors and cleaning the unoccupied rooms.

11. Many guests are leaving.

12. New guests will be arriving soon.

13. Other guests are still sleeping in their rooms.

14. Bellboys are bringing the guests' luggage to the lobby.

15. Other guests are paying the bill.

16. They are building one hundred new rooms.

ACTIVIDADES

1. Using a picture from a magazine that contains several people doing different things, make a list of what each person in the picture is doing at that moment. Use the present progressive.
2. Write a letter to a friend in which you describe what you will be doing during the forthcoming summer. Use the present progressive and the verbs *continuar* and *seguir* in the letter.

Chapter 13
The Past Participle; Compound Tenses

[1] The Past Participle

a. Past Participles of Regular Verbs

The past participle of regular verbs is formed by dropping the infinitive ending and adding *-ado* or *-ido:*

INFINITIVE	PAST PARTICIPLE	MEANING
visitar	**visit*ado***	*visited*
aprender	**aprend*ido***	*learned*
vivir	**viv*ido***	*lived*

b. Past Participles Ending in *-ído*

The past participles of *-er* and *-ir* verbs with stems ending in a vowel have an accent mark.

INFINITIVE	PAST PARTICIPLE	MEANING
caer	**ca*ído***	*fallen*
creer	**cre*ído***	*believed*
leer	**le*ído***	*read*
oír	**o*ído***	*heard*
reír	**re*ído***	*laughed*
traer	**tra*ído***	*brought*

c. Irregular Past Participles Ending in *-to*

The following verbs have irregular past participles ending in *-to.*

INFINITIVE	PAST PARTICIPLE	MEANING
abrir	**abier*to***	*opened*
cubrir	**cubier*to***	*covered*
descubrir	**descubier*to***	*discovered*
escribir	**escri*to***	*written*
morir	**muer*to***	*died*
poner	**pues*to***	*put*
romper	**ro*to***	*broken*
ver	**vis*to***	*seen*
volver	**vuel*to***	*returned*

The following verbs have irregular past participles ending in *-cho.*

INFINITIVE	PAST PARTICIPLE	MEANING
decir	**di*cho***	*said*
hacer	**he*cho***	*done, made*

EXERCISE A. **Gladys leaves a note for her parents. Complete the note with the appropriate past participles of the verbs indicated.**

Ricky yo yo hemos ___salido___ . Hemos ___decidido___ ver una película y nos
 1. (salir) *2.* (decidir)

hemos ___ido___ al cine. He ___dado___ de comer al gato y ya lo ha
 3. (ir) *4.* (dar) *already*

___comido___ todo. Hemos ___seguido___ todas sus instrucciones: hemos ___sacado___
 5. (comer) *6.* (seguir) *7.* (sacar)

la basura, hemos _____ todas las luces, hemos _____ las ventanas.
 8. (apagar) *9.* (cerrar)

He _____ la carne del congelador y la he _____ en la mesa de la cocina.
 10. (sacar) *11.* (dejar)

También he _____ el piso. Y no hemos _____ nada. ¡Hemos
 12. (barrer) *13.* (romper)

_____ muy buenos!
 14. (ser)

EXERCISE B. **You are planning to call the Spanish-speaking exchange student who is ill at home. Complete the questions you will ask with the past participle of the verbs indicated.**

1. ¿Has ___tomado___ la medicina? (*tomar*)

2. ¿Has ___bebido___ mucho jugo de naranja? (*beber*)

3. ¿Has ___comido___ sopa de pollo? (*comer*)

4. ¿Has _____ en cama todo el día? (*permanecer*)

5. ¿Has _____ la siesta? (*dormir*)

6. ¿Has _____ con otros amigos? (*hablar*)

7. ¿Has _____ la tarea de matemáticas? (*recibir*)

8. ¿Ya has _____ la tarea? (*hacer*)

9. ¿Has _____ el periódico de hoy? (*leer*)

10. ¿Has _____ a ver al médico? (*volver*)

11. ¿Qué ha _____ el médico? (*decir*)

12. ¿Qué restricciones te ha _____ el médico? (*poner*)

[2] THE PRESENT PERFECT TENSE

a. The present perfect tense is formed by the present tense of the verb *haber* (to have) and a past participle.

yo	he
tú	has
él, ella, Ud.	ha
nosotros, -as	hemos
vosotros, -as	habéis
ellos, ellas, Uds.	han

visitado/aprendido/vivido

b. **To make a verb in the perfect tenses negative, place *no* before the verb *haber.* To make a verb interrogative, place the subject after the past participle.**

No han vivido allí.	*They haven't lived there.*
¿Ha visto Ud. la película?	*Have you seen the film?*
Yo **no** me he bañado todavía.	*I haven't bathed myself yet.*

NOTE: **Nothing comes between the verb *haber* and the past participle. Pronouns (reflexive and object) come before the verb *haber.***

c. **The present perfect tense is used to describe an action that began in the past and continues up to the present or an action that took place in the past but is connected with the present.**

EXERCISE C. Tell who has done the following things.

EXAMPLE: Mario / viajar a Italia muchas veces — Mario **ha viajado** a Italia muchas veces.

1. Pierre / visitar a París ______________________
2. Yo / ir al circo cada año ______________________
3. Raúl y Gregorio / nadar en el mar Caribe ______________________
4. Mi familia y yo / salir en un crucero ______________________
5. Tú / volar en un avión supersónico ______________________
6. Amir / ver las pirámides de Egipto ______________________

EXERCISE D. You and your family are going to a family wedding. Your mother wants to know how close to being ready everyone is. Tell who has or has not done the following preparations.

Use *ya* or *todavía no* in your statements.

mi papá	afeitarse
mi mamá	bañarse
mi hermana mayor	peinarse
mi hermano	ponerse el maquillaje
mi abuela	ponerse la corbata
yo	vestirse

1. ______________________
2. ______________________
3. ______________________
4. ______________________
5. ______________________
6. ______________________

EXERCISE E. **You are looking at a family album with a cousin. Tell what has happened to the people in the photographs.**

EXAMPLE: ¡Cuánto (Cómo) ha crecido Jerry!

1. ____.

2. ____.

3. ____.

4. ____.

EXERCISE F. **A friend is showing you some photos from her trip to Mexico. You know someone who has been there or done the things in the photos. Tell who has done these things or has been to these places.**

1. Ronnie / subir a la pirámide ______________________________

2. mis padres / visitar el castillo de Chapultepec ______________________________

3. Celia y yo / comprar muchas cosas ______________________________

4. yo / nadar en las playas de Acapulco ______________________________

5. yo / volver a ese restaurante muchas veces ______________________________

EXERCISE G. **Answer the questions a classmate asks you. Use the cues provided.**

1. ¿Has llegado temprano a la escuela? (*sí*)

____

2. ¿Has estudiado para el examen de biología? (*todavía no*)

____

3. ¿Has visto al maestro de español hoy? (*ya*)

____

4. ¿Has hecho el experimento correctamente? (*sí*)

____

5. ¿Han preparado Uds. la tarea para la clase de historia? (*no*)

____

6. ¿Has leído los capítulos asignados? (*ya*)

____

[3] THE PLUPERFECT TENSE

a. The pluperfect tense is formed by the imperfect tense of the verb *haber* (to have) and a past participle.

yo	había	visitado/aprendido/vivido
tú	habías	
él, ella, Ud.	había	
nosotros, -as	habíamos	
vosotros, -as	habíais	
ellos, ellas, Uds.	habían	

b. The pluperfect tense is used to describe an action that was completed in the past before another action took place. I have visited

Yo los había visitado antes. *I had visited them before.*

Nunca le habían escrito. *They had never written to her.*

EXERCISE H. **Tell what the Valera children had done before their parents returned from vacation.**

EXAMPLE: Alicia / lavar la ropa Alicia **había lavado** la ropa.

1. Guillermo / cortar el césped ____________________
2. Alicia y Guillermo / arreglar la casa ____________________
3. tú / pasar la aspiradora ____________________
4. Inés y yo / hacer un pastel ____________________
5. yo / poner flores en la sala ____________________
6. todos los hijos / ir al supermercado ____________________

EXERCISE I. **You are attending a local civic ceremony in which several community members are being honored. Tell what each one had done to merit the award.**

EXAMPLE: el alcalde / bajar los impuestos El alcalde **había bajado** los impuestos.

1. Juan Gálvez / organizar un programa de reciclaje

____

2. un bombero / salvar a una familia en un incendio

____

3. la señora Bustelo / abrir un centro para ancianos

____

4. el director de la escuela / poner un semáforo en la esquina de la escuela

____

5. el jefe de la policía / disminuir el número de crímenes

____

EXERCISE J. **Nothing ever seems to go right for Silvia. Tell what already happened in each of these situations that relate to her nephew's birthday party.**

EXAMPLE: Ella llegó a la estación del metro a las ocho y cuarto.
el tren / salir a las ocho y doce
El tren **ya había salido** a las ocho y doce.

1. Silvia llegó tarde a la fiesta de cumpleaños de su sobrino.
los invitados / cantar «Feliz cumpleaños»
____

2. No pudo entrar en la juguetería.
los empleados / cerrar la tienda
____

3. Sacó el pastel del horno.
el pastel / quemarse
____

4. Iba a colgar una piñata.
los niños / romper otra piñata
____

5. Le dio un regalo a su sobrino.
el sobrino / abrir todos los regalos
____

6. Quería leerle un cuento a su sobrino.
el sobrino / leer ese cuento
____

MASTERY EXERCISES

EXERCISE K. **Tell what you and a friend have done before going on a camping trip. Use the suggestions or be original.**

SUGGESTIONS:

doblar la tienda
sacar la brújula
empacar la mochila
ir de compras
hacer una reservación en el campamento
confirmar la reservación
poner pilas nuevas en la linterna
conseguir un mapa
pedir permiso a los padres
volver a empacar el equipo varias veces
buscar la mejor ruta
leer el pronóstico de tiempo en el periódico

1. ______________________________

2. ______________________________

3. ______

4. ______

5. ______

6. ______

7. ______

8. ______

9. ______

10. ______

EXERCISE L. **You were left to babysit your mischievous younger brother and sister while your parents went to the movies. Your parents are furious with you because of how they found the house when they returned. Tell what you had done before you fell asleep.**

1. darles de comer a los hermanos ______
2. poner los platos en el lavaplatos ______
3. sacar la basura ______
4. apagar las luces y el televisor ______
5. acostar a los hermanos ______
6. hacer la tarea ______
7. cerrar la puerta ______

EXERCISE M. **You are writing a letter to a friend in which you describe a visit you made to your old neighborhood. Express the following in Spanish.**

1. Finally, I have returned to my old neighborhood.

   ______

2. I hadn't been there in a long time.

   ______

3. They have made many changes.

   ______

4. They have closed the elementary school that I had attended for six years.

   ______

5. They have built a very large and modern elementary school.

   ______

6. They have also planted many trees and plants in the park where I had played with my friends.

____

7. Shortly before I moved, they had closed the factory.

____

8. My friends and I had broken many windows in the factory.

____

9. The factory had contaminated the air.

____

10. In its place they have opened a large shopping mall.

____

11. I hadn't thought about my days in the elementary school for a long time.

____

ACTIVIDADES

1. You are applying to an exchange program in Costa Rica and have to describe the things you have done in school in addition to your studies. Write a paragraph in Spanish in which you describe the extra-curricular activities, community service, and/or sports activities in which you have participated.

2. For each of the newspaper article headlines below, tell what the people involved had done to deserve a spot in the news.

a. Camacho ofrece concierto de violín en el Teatro de Bellas Artes.
b. Joven devuelve dinero encontrado en el parque.
c. Joven de 16 años gana el maratón de San Pedro.
d. El presidente y 3.000 jóvenes se reúnen hoy en la capital.
e. Escasez de aceite y azúcar en los supermercados.
f. Harán simposio referido a temas de derecho de familia.
g. Se inauguran 5 nuevas escuelas primarias.
h. ¡Adictas al ejercicio!
i. Peligro: vida sedentaria.
j. Habrá acuerdo con camioneros.

Chapter 14
Ser and *Estar*

Spanish has two different verbs, *ser* and *estar,* that both correspond to the English verb "to be." The use of each one depends on the context.

[*1*] Uses of *Ser*

Ser is used:

a. to express a characteristic, a description, or an identification.

El pastel **es bueno.**	*The cake is good.*
La maestra **es estricta.**	*The teacher is strict.*
El alumno **es inteligente.**	*The student is intelligent.*
La señora Romero **es rica.**	*Mrs. Romero is rich.*
¿Quién es? Es Pablo.	*Who is it? It's Pablo.*

b. to express occupation or nationality.

Elvira **es abogada.**	*Elvira is a lawyer.*
Mis hermanos **son vendedores.**	*My brothers are salesmen.*
Julio **es español.**	*Julio is Spanish.*
Melinda **es argentina.**	*Melinda is Argentine.*

c. to express time and dates.

Son las ocho.	*It is eight o'clock.*	**Es el veinte de octubre.**	*It's October 20.*
Es mediodía.	*It's noon.*	**Es el primero de enero.**	*It's January 1.*

d. with *de,* to express origin, possession, or material.

Sus padres **son de Venezuela.**	*His parents are from Venezuela.*
El aceite de oliva **es de España.**	*The olive oil is from Spain.*
Es el reloj **de Lucy.**	*It's Lucy's watch.*
Ese carro **es de mi abuelo.**	*That car is my grandfather's.*
La camisa **es de algodón.**	*The shirt is made of cotton.*
La pulsera **es de plata.**	*The bracelet is made of silver.*

NOTE:

1. **Adjectives used with *ser* must agree with the subject in number and gender.**

Las naranjas **son sabrosas.**	*The oranges are flavorful.*
El edificio **es muy alto.**	*The building is very tall.*

2. **In questions, adjectives usually follow the verb.**

¿Son nuevos los zapatos?	*Are the shoes new?*

3. The adjective *feliz* is generally used with *ser.*

   El bebé es feliz. *The baby is happy.*

4. The forms of *ser* are summarized in the section on irregular verbs in the Appendix, page 449.

EXERCISE A. **You are the president of the Spanish club in your school. After the first meeting, you and a friend are talking about the new members. Tell what you say about them using the correct form of *ser* and the suggested adjectives below.**

SUGGESTIONS:

aburrido	celoso	guapo	responsable
antipático	divertido	independiente	simpático
bonito	gracioso	inteligente	tímido

EXAMPLE: Felipe **es** guapo y responsable.

1. Gladys ______________________________

2. Ramón y Tom ______________________________

3. Milton y Celia ______________________________

4. Donald ______________________________

5. Dennis y Raquel ______________________________

6. Rita ______________________________

7. Andrea y Elena ______________________________

8. Joseph ______________________________

EXERCISE B. **Jeff is attending a youth conference. After introducing himself and telling his nationality, he presents the other people in the group. Use the cues to tell what Jeff says.**

EXAMPLE: yo / el Canadá   Yo **soy del** Canadá. **Soy** canadiense.

1. Migdalia / Puerto Rico ______________________________

2. Ricardo y Jaime / Colombia ______________________________

3. Sarita / España ______________________________

4. Claire y Marc / Francia ______________________________

5. Elena y María / la Argentina ______________________________

6. Tú (Roberto) / Guatemala ______________________________

EXERCISE C. **George is going to a formal family function and has laid out the clothing he will wear. Tell what each article of clothing is made of.**

EXAMPLE: pañuelo / seda   El pañuelo **es de** seda.

1. traje / lana ______________________________

2. camisa / algodón ______________________

3. corbata / seda ______________________

4. zapatos, cinturón / cuero ______________________

5. reloj / oro ______________________

6. anillo / plata ______________________

EXERCISE D. **You are cleaning up after a party in your house and find some things that your friends left behind. Tell to whom each of the things belong.**

EXAMPLE: el disco compacto / Álvaro El disco compacto **es de** Álvaro.

1. las llaves / Graciela ______________________

2. la mochila / Hugo ______________________

3. las fotos / Isabel ______________________

4. el estéreo / los hermanos Ramos ______________________

5. la chaqueta / Esteban ______________________

6. la bolsa / Virginia ______________________

EXERCISE E. **While the Garza family was away on vacation all of the clocks in their house stopped at different times. Tell what time it is on each clock.**

EXAMPLE: Son las seis y media.

1. ______________________

3. ______________________

2. ______________________

4. ______________________

5. ______

6. ______

EXERCISE F. **You have just met someone on line in the post office. Answer the questions you are asked.**

1. ¿Cuál es su nombre? ______
2. ¿De dónde es usted? ______
3. ¿Cuál es su nacionalidad? ______
4. ¿Cómo es usted? ______
5. ¿Cuál es su color favorito? ______
6. ¿De qué es la gorra que usa Ud.? ______
7. ¿Es Ud. aficionado(-a) a un equipo o un grupo musical? ______
8. ¿Quién es su actor/actriz favorito(-a)? ______
9. ¿Cómo es su escuela? ______
10. ¿Cómo son sus amigos? ______
11. ¿Cuáles son sus pasatiempos favoritos? ______
12. ¿Qué día es hoy? ______
13. ¿Cuál es la fecha de hoy? ______
14. ¿Qué hora es? ______
15. ¿Cuál es la marca de la computadora que usa Ud.? ______

[2] USES OF *ESTAR*

***Estar* is used:**

a. **to express location or position.**

Buenos Aires **está en la Argentina.**	*Buenos Aires is in Argentina.*
Mi padre **está en la oficina.**	*My father is in the office.*
Los platos **están en la mesa.**	*The dishes are on the table.*
¿Dónde **está la farmacia?**	*Where is the drugstore?*

b. to express a condition or state.

El horno **está** muy caliente.	*The oven is very hot.*
Los hombres **están** sentados.	*The men are seated.*
Gladys **está** triste.	*Gladys is sad.*
¿Cómo **estás**? **Estoy** bien.	*How are you? I'm fine.*
Las ventanas **están** cerradas.	*The windows are closed.*

c. to form the progressive tenses with the present participle.

Los niños **están** jugando al tenis.	*The children are playing tennis.*
Estaba trabajando.	*He was working.*

NOTE:

1. Adjectives used with *estar* agree with the subject in number and gender.

La madre está preocupad**a**.	*The mother is worried.*
Los padres están preocupad**os**.	*The parents are worried.*

2. In questions, the adjective usually follows the verb.

¿Está preocupada la madre?	*Is the mother worried?*
¿Están preocupados los padres?	*Are the parents worried?*

3. Some adjectives may be used with either *ser* or *estar,* but differ in meaning.

Alberto es bueno (malo).	*Albert is good (bad).*	Alberto es listo.	*Albert is clever.*
Alberto está bueno (malo).	*Albert is well (ill).*	Alberto está listo.	*Albert is ready.*

4. The forms of *estar* are summarized in the section on irregular verbs in the Appendix, page 446.

EXERCISE G. **Your younger brother wants to know where these people are. Write the questions he asks and your responses.**

EXAMPLE: el actor / el teatro
¿Dónde **está** el actor? El actor **está** en el teatro.

1. los payasos / el circo

____

2. el médico / el hospital

____

3. los estudiantes / el colegio

____

4. el cocinero / la cocina

____

5. el astronauta / el espacio

____

6. los policías / la calle

____

7. los pilotos / los aviones

____

EXERCISE H. The tournament results are in. Tell how the players feel.

EXAMPLE: Víctor / contento — Víctor **está** contento.

1. Felipe y José / preocupado ______________________
2. Antonio / desilusionado ______________________
3. Linda y Elena / nervioso ______________________
4. Ingrid / sorprendido ______________________
5. Doris y Ema / triste ______________________
6. el entrenador / orgulloso ______________________

EXERCISE I. You received this flyer while attending a world youth conference in Buenos Aires. Answer the questions that a hotel guest asks you about the conference.

Bienvenidos al

XX^mo Congreso Mundial de Jóvenes

Tema:	La juventud moderna	
Lugar:	el Gran Hotel, Buenos Aires	
Fecha:	del 2 al 5 de julio	
Reuniones:	Cada día a las 10, 12, 4 y 6	
Salones:	Primavera, Verano, Otoño, Invierno	
Comidas:	Desayuno:	8:00-10:00 -Salón Amanecer
	Comida:	2:00-4:00 -Salón Principal
	Cena:	8:00-10:00 -Salón Medianoche
Enfermería:	Segundo piso del hotel	

1. ¿Cuándo es el congreso? ______________________
2. ¿En qué hotel está el congreso? ______________________
3. ¿A qué hora es la primera reunión del día? ______________________
4. ¿A qué hora es la última reunión cada día? ______________________
4. ¿En qué salones estarán los congresistas? ______________________

6. ¿A qué hora es el desayuno? ______________________________

7. ¿A qué hora es la comida? ______________________________

8. ¿A qué hora es la cena? ______________________________

9. ¿Dónde está la enfermería? ______________________________

10. ¿Cuál es el tema del congreso? ______________________________

EXERCISE J. **Julio is telling a friend what the members of his family were doing when his father returned home.**

EXAMPLE: Mi mamá estaba cocinando.

1. Elena ______________________________
______________________________.

2. Alex y Enrique ______________________________
______________________________.

3. Mi abuela ______________________________
______________________________.

4. Mi abuelo ______________________________
______________________________.

5. Yo ______________________________
______________________________.

MASTERY EXERCISES

EXERCISE K. **You received a letter from a friend who is spending a year studying in Argentina. Complete it with the appropriate forms of *ser* or *estar.***

Querida amiga:

No puedo creer que yo ______ (1.) en la Argentina. Hay quince jóvenes en el grupo y nosotros ______ (2.) estudiando en un colegio muy bueno. ______ (3.) una escuela antigua y la arquitectura de la escuela ______ (4.) de estilo clásico. Vivo con una familia muy simpática. Los miembros de la familia ______ (5.) los señores Rivas y sus tres hijos. Los nombres de los hijos ______ (6.) Rafael, Hilda y Verónica. Rafael ______ (7.) el mayor. El señor Rivas ______ (8.) arquitecto y la señora ______ (9.) doctora. Su casa ______ (10.) amplia y ______ (11.) situada en las afueras de Buenos Aires.

Tampoco puedo creer que ______ (12.) el 10 de enero y hace calor. Ya sabes que la Argentina ______ (13.) en el hemisferio sur y cuando ______ (14.) invierno en los Estados Unidos ______ (15.) verano en el hemisferio sur. ______ (16.) un clima ideal porque no hace muchísimo calor.

Los jóvenes del grupo ______ (17.) muy agradables y divertidos. Cada uno ______ (18.) viviendo en casa de una familia porteña (así se llaman las personas que viven en Buenos Aires). Solamente hay un joven que ______ (19.) desilusionado en el grupo. ______ (20.) un joven bastante aplicado pero ______ (21.) un poco frustrado porque no habla bien el español. Las familias ______ (22.) muy atentas y cariñosas pero hacen muchas preguntas.

Ya ______ (23.) las siete de la noche y debo despedirme de ti. Yo ______ (24.) muy ocupada todos los días porque la vida de un estudiante aquí ______ (25.) muy exigente. Escríbeme pronto.

Tu amiga,

Lucinda

EXERCISE L. **You overhear the following statements in the school cafeteria. Complete them with the appropriate form of *ser* or *estar.***

1. Susana no __________ en la escuela hoy porque __________ enferma.
2. La señora Galván __________ rica porque su joyería __________ de oro.
3. Mi clase de fisica __________ a las diez y cuarto. ¿Qué hora __________ ?
4. El helado de fresa __________ más sabroso que el helado de chocolate.
5. Mi mamá no tiene tiempo para descansar. Siempre __________ muy ocupada.
6. Hoy __________ el tres de julio. Mañana __________ día de fiesta.
7. El maestro de matemáticas va a devolver los exámenes. Todos los alumnos __________ preocupados.
8. La familia de Amir __________ turca, pero ninguno de sus parientes __________ actualmente en Turquía.
9. Esta blusa no __________ mía, __________ de mi hermana mayor.
10. ¿Cuál __________ la fecha de tu cumpleaños? La mía __________ el 20 de marzo.
11. Mis abuelos __________ jubilados. Nunca __________ en casa.
12. El libro que tú __________ leyendo es fabuloso y el fin __________ algo que nunca esperabas.
13. Mi hermano __________ en la universidad también pero no __________ un estudiante diligente.
14. Hace frío aquí porque las puertas __________ abiertas.
15. En esta cafetería la comida que debe __________ caliente siempre __________ fría.

EXERCISE M. **Express in Spanish Joan's description of a day at school.**

1. Today is Wednesday. It is December the first.

 ____

2. It is 11:30 A.M.

 ____

3. It is a beautiful day and I am seated in my history class.

 ____

4. It is a difficult class and the teacher is very demanding.

 ____

5. My friends are also in this class.

 ____

6. I am bored today.

 ____

7. The teacher is reviewing the homework assignment.

___

8. Gladys is reading aloud from the book.

___

9. Kurt is absent today. He isn't well.

___

10. The book that is on my desk is not my book.

___

11. It belongs to Vicky.

___

12. My book is at my aunt's house.

___

13. It is almost noon and I want to be in the cafeteria.

___

14. The food in the cafeteria is not good.

___

me

15. I'm worried because the teacher is looking at me.

Estoy preocupado porque el m. me estar mirando.

estar + ando / iendo

ACTIVIDADES

1. Select an interesting object or person and write a description of it that will enable the reader to guess what or who it is. Use *ser* and *estar* as often as possible in your description.

2. *a.* You are interviewing a new exchange student in school. Prepare ten questions you will ask him/her to find out as much as you can about him/her. Use *ser* and/or *estar* in your questions.

b. Answer these questions as if you were the exchange student.

Chapter 15
Reflexive Verbs

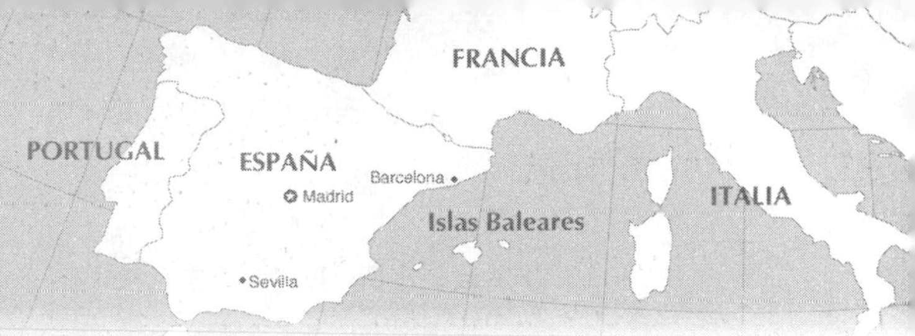

[1] Reflexive Verbs in Simple Tenses

a. A reflexive verb requires a reflexive pronoun (*me, te, se, nos, os, se*) that refers the action of the verb back to the subject.

Yo me baño. *I bathe (myself).*

Ellos se lavan. *They wash (themselves).*

b. Reflexive pronouns generally precede the verb in the simple tenses.

PRESENT TENSE	
yo me baño	**nosotros, -as nos bañamos**
tú te bañas	**vosotros, -as os bañáis**
Ud., él, ella se baña	**Uds., ellos, ellas se bañan**

PRETERIT TENSE	
yo me bañé	**nosotros, -as nos bañamos**
tú te bañaste	**vosotros, -as os bañasteis**
Ud., él, ella se bañó	**Uds., ellos, ellas se bañaron**

IMPERFECT TENSE	
yo me bañaba	**nosotros, -as nos bañábamos**
tú te bañabas	**vosotros, -as os bañabais**
Ud., él, ella se bañaba	**Uds., ellos, ellas se bañaban**

FUTURE TENSE	
yo me bañaré	**nosotros, -as nos bañaremos**
tú te bañarás	**vosotros, -as os bañaréis**
Ud., él, ella se bañará	**Uds., ellos, ellas se bañarán**

CONDITIONAL TENSE	
yo me bañaría	**nosotros, -as nos bañaríamos**
tú te bañarías	**vosotros, -as os bañaríais**
Ud., él, ella se bañaría	**Ud., ellos, ellas se bañarían**

NOTE: When the statement is negative, *no* comes before the reflexive pronoun.

Yo no me bañé. *I didn't bathe.*

c. When a reflexive verb is used as an infinitive, the reflexive pronoun is attached to the end of the infinitive or placed before the conjugated verb. Both forms are accepted.

Voy a lavar**me**.
Me voy a lavar. } *I'm going to wash (myself).*

Queremos acostar**nos** ahora.
Nos queremos acostar ahora. } *We want to go to bed*

d. **When a reflexive verb is used in a progressive tense, the reflexive pronoun is attached to the end of the present participle (gerund) or placed before the conjugated verb. When it is attached to the gerund, an accent mark is required. Both forms are accepted.**

Estoy lavándo**me** la cara.
Me estoy lavando la cara.
} *I am washing my face*

e. **Common reflexive verbs:**

acostarse (ue) *to go to bed*
afeitarse *to shave*
asustarse *to be frightened*
bañarse *to take a bath, bathe*
callarse *to be silent, keep still*
cepillarse *to brush (one's teeth, hair, clothes)*
desayunarse *to have breakfast*
despedirse *to say goodbye, take leave of*
despertarse (ie) *to wake up*
divertirse (ie) *to enjoy oneself, have a good time*
dormirse (ue) *to fall asleep*
ducharse *to take a shower*
enfadarse *to get angry*
enojarse *to get angry*
equivocarse *to be mistaken*
irse *to leave, go away*
marcharse *to leave, go away*
lavarse *to wash oneself*
levantarse *to get up*
llamarse *to be named, be called*
maquillarse *to put on makeup*
pasearse *to take a walk*
peinarse *to comb one's hair*
ponerse *to put on (clothing), become*
quedarse *to stay, remain*
quejarse *to complain*
quitarse *to take off (clothing)*
secarse *to dry oneself*
sentarse (ie) *to sit down*
vestirse (i) *to get dressed*

EXERCISE A. Use the cues to tell what each person is doing.

EXAMPLE: Pedro / peinarse   Pedro **se** peina.

1. Papá / afeitarse ______________________________
2. Arturo e Inés / desayunarse ______________________________
3. tú / vestirse ______________________________
4. yo / cepillarse los dientes ______________________________
5. Renee y yo / maquillarse ______________________________
6. mis abuelos / pasearse en el parque ______________________________

EXERCISE B. Use the cues provided to tell what different people did in different situations.

EXAMPLE: Gloria tuvo hambre a las 8:30 de la mañana. (*desayunarse*)   Gloria **se desayunó.**

1. Miguel tuvo frío en el patio de la escuela. (*ponerse un suéter*)

____

2. Después Miguel tuvo calor. (*quitarse el suéter*)

____

3. Yo escondí la mochila de Sally. (*enojarse*)

4. No me gustó la comida que sirvieron. (*quejarse a la mesera*)

5. Jerry y yo tiramos pintura en la mesa. (*lavarse las manos*)

6. La maestra vio un ratoncito en el piso. (*asustarse*)

7. Tú supiste que nuestro pez se había muerto. (*ponerse triste*)

EXERCISE C. **You have just returned from camp and your grandmother is asking you about it. Answer her questions using the cues provided.**

EXAMPLE: ¿Te despertabas fácilmente todos los días? (*sí*)
Sí, **me despertaba** fácilmente todos los días.

1. ¿Te levantabas de la cama en seguida? (*sí*)

2. ¿Cuántas veces al día te cepillabas los dientes? (*3*)

3. ¿Te peinabas todos los días? (*sí*)

4. ¿Te dormías después de la comida? (*no*)

5. ¿Te paseabas con tus amigos? (*sí*)

6. ¿Cómo se llamaba el consejero de tu grupo? (*Pedro*)

7. ¿Te quejabas a menudo? (*no*)

8. ¿Qué te ponías cuando hacía frío? (*un suéter*)

9. ¿Se sentaban Uds. alrededor de una fogata y cantaban canciones? (*sí*)

10. ¿Te enojabas con tus amigos? (*no*)

EXERCISE D. **You and your family are preparing to go to a family reunion. Tell who wants to do or is going to do the activities listed below. Use the appropriate form of *querer* or *ir a* in your responses.**

mi hermana	vestirse en cinco minutos
yo	afeitarse ahora
papá	secarse el pelo rápidamente
mamá	quedarse en casa
tú	enfadarse
tú y yo	ducharse primero
mis hermanos	maquillarse antes de vestirse
	desayunarse mientras vestirse

EXAMPLE: Mamá **va a** ducharse primero.

1. ______________________________
2. ______________________________
3. ______________________________
4. ______________________________
5. ______________________________
6. ______________________________
7. ______________________________

EXERCISE E. **Describe what each person is doing using the present progressive tense.**

EXAMPLE: Ruth / lavarse el pelo — Ruth **se está lavando** el pelo.
OR Ruth **está lavándose** el pelo.

1. Ernesto / ducharse [handwritten: - take a shower] [handwritten: Ernesto se está duchando]
2. la señora Barca / maquillarse [handwritten: Se está maquillando]
3. Kim y yo / pasearse [handwritten: to put on makeup - passing through] [handwritten: nos estamos pasea]
4. Papá / afeitarse [handwritten: Se está afeitando]
5. Gloria / quedarse en la cama ______________
6. tú / vestirse ______________
7. los niños / divertirse ______________

...IVE VERBS IN COMPOUND TENSES

...tenses like the present perfect and pluperfect, for example, the reflexive ...es before the conjugated form of the helping (auxiliary) verb *haber.*

PRESENT PERFECT	
...bañado	nosotros, -as nos hemos bañado
...bañado	vosotros, -as os habéis bañado
...ella se ha bañado	Uds., ellos, ellas se han bañado

PLUPERFECT	
yo me había bañado	**nosotros, -as nos habíamos bañado**
tú te habías bañado	**vosotros, -as os habéis bañado**
Ud., él, ella se había bañado	**Uds., ellos, ellas se habían bañado**

b. **If the statement is negative, *no* is placed before the reflexive pronoun.**

El **no** se ha lavado. *He hasn't washed himself.*

EXERCISE F. **Imelda is working in a day care center during the summer. She tells the person in charge what she and the children have already done or still haven't done. Tell what she says.**

EXAMPLE: Daniel / despertarse / no levantarse
Daniel ya **se ha despertado** pero todavía no **se ha levantado.**

1. Gladys / bañarse / no secarse

____

2. Hugo y Felipe / vestirse / no ponerse los zapatos

____

3. yo / desayunarse / no sentarse por un minuto

____

4. los niños / lavarse las manos / no peinarse

____

5. el bebé / asustarse / no callarse

____

EXERCISE G. **Tell what the following people had done before they received a telephone call cancelling the party.**

EXAMPLE: Rogelio / afeitarse Rogelio ya **se había afeitado.**

1. los niños / ponerse los disfraces ______________________________
2. Miriam / maquillarse ______________________________
3. yo / enfadarse ______________________________
4. tú / lavarse el pelo ______________________________
5. mi hermana y yo / despedirse de nuestros padres ______________________________

[3] COMMANDS WITH REFLEXIVE VERBS

In affirmative commands, reflexive pronouns follow the verb and are attached to it. In negative commands, reflexive pronouns precede the verb. Affirmative commands with more than two syllables have a written accent over the stressed vowel.

	AFFIRMATIVE COMMANDS	NEGATIVE COMMANDS
tú	**¡Báñate!**	**¡No te bañes!**
Ud.	**¡Báñese!**	**¡No se bañe!**
Uds.	**¡Báñense!**	**¡No se bañen!**

EXERCISE H. You are going to spend the weekend at a friend's house. Tell what your mother tells you to do there.

EXAMPLE: despertarse temprano ¡**Despiértate** temprano!

1. levantarse en seguida ______
2. ducharse rápidamente ______
3. vestirse bien ______
4. desayunarse con la familia ______
5. lavarse las manos antes de comer ______
6. cepillarse los dientes después de comer ______
7. peinarse ______
8. callarse cuando otra persona hable ______
9. despedirse de la familia ______
10. divertirse mucho ______

EXERCISE I. Your mother also tells you what you should not do.

EXAMPLE: quejarse **¡No te quejes!**

1. acostarse tarde ______
2. levantarse a comer durante la noche ______
3. dormirse en el sofá o una silla ______
4. quitarse los zapatos en la sala ______
5. quedarse en la cama después de despertarse ______
6. peinarse en la mesa ______
7. enojarse con tu amigo ______
8. ponerse la gorra en la casa ______
9. irse sin dar las gracias ______

EXERCISE J. **Janet is babysitting her cousins. Use the cues provided to express what she tells them to do.**

EXAMPLE: sentarse en el piso ¡**Siéntense** en el piso!

1. despedirse de sus padres ______________________

2. quedarse en la sala ______________________

3. callarse mientras miran la televisión ______________________

4. ponerse la pijama ______________________

5. cepillarse el pelo antes de acostarse ______________________

6. lavarse la cara y las manos ______________________

7. secarse bien las manos ______________________

8. acostarse a la hora indicada ______________________

EXERCISE K. **Tell what the coach tells his team members they should not do before a big game.**

EXAMPLE: desayunarse mucho ¡**No se desayunen** mucho!

1. acostarse tarde ______________________

2. enojarse si cometen un error ______________________

3. despertarse tarde ______________________

4. ducharse con agua muy caliente ______________________

5. ponerse nerviosos ______________________

6. dormirse delante de la televisión ______________________

7. irse de la cancha sin pedir permiso ______________________

8. callarse cuando el equipo haga un gol ______________________

MASTERY EXERCISES

EXERCISE L. **Complete this dialogue with the appropriate forms of the verbs indicated.**

ALICIA: ______________ (*1.* despertarse), Emma. Tengo miedo. Cuando yo ______________ (*2.* despertarse) hace cinco minutos, yo oí un ruido extraño y yo ______________ (*3.* asustarse) mucho.

EMMA: ______________ (*4.* acostarse) y ______________ (*5.* dormirse), ¿sabes qué hora es?

ALICIA: ________________ , por favor. Yo no puedo ________________ .
6. (levantarse) 7. (dormirse)

EMMA: Ay, yo no quiero ________________ ahora. Nosotros ________________ muy tarde y tengo mucho sueño. ¿Por qué ________________ la bata?
8. (levantarse) 9. (acostarse) 10. (ponerse)

ALICIA: Yo ________________ la bata por dos razones: primero, tengo frío y segundo, podemos bajar a la cocina a ________________ .
11. ponerse 12. (desayunarse)

EMMA: Yo no ________________ ni ________________ a esta hora. Tú siempre ________________ de algo.
13. (vestirse) 14. (desayunarse) 15. (quejarse)

ALICIA: Yo no ________________ de nada. Yo ________________ cuando oí un ruido. Ahora yo ________________ , ________________ el pelo, ________________ , ________________ y ________________ de ti.
16. (quejarse) 17. (espantarse) 18. (bañarse) 19. (lavarse) 20. (peinarse) 21. (vestirse) 22. (despedirse)

EMMA: ¿Adónde vas a esta hora?

ALICIA: Yo ________________ . Regreso a mi propio dormitorio.
23. (irse)

EXERCISE M. **Express in Spanish what Joe says about his friend.**

1. My friend's name is Henry.

____

2. When he comes to my house he doesn't take off his coat.

____

3. I get angry because he is never mistaken.

____

4. He gets up at six o'clock every day.

____

5. He showers and gets dressed in five minutes.

____

6. He never combs his hair.

____

7. I need half an hour to bathe and get dressed.

____

8. He likes to sit in the garden.

____

9. He often falls asleep there.

____

10. I think he goes to bed very late.

____

11. We always have a good time together.

____

12. He is never silent.

____

13. When he leaves, he always says goodbye to my parents.

____

14. We take walks in the park.

____

15. He becomes happy when he sees a dog.

____

ACTIVIDADES

1. Write an entry in your journal in which you describe the activities you do everyday. Use as many reflexive verbs as you can.

2. *a.* Your parent has been hassling you about your daily routine—from the time you wake up in the morning until you go to bed at night. You believe that all people your age act the same way. Prepare a list of 10 questions in Spanish that you will ask several friends to learn if their daily routine is similar to yours.

b. Using the questions you prepared above, interview several friends and ask them the questions. Take notes of their responses. Then, write a note to your parent in which you describe what several of your friends do.

Chapter 16

The Passive Voice

Spanish, like English, has an active and a passive voice. In the active voice, the subject generally performs some action. In the passive voice, the subject is acted upon.

ACTIVE:	La madre **preparó** la comida.	*The mother prepared the meal.*
PASSIVE:	La comida **fue preparada** por la madre.	*The meal was prepared by the mother.*

[1] The Passive Voice in Simple Sentences

If the agent or doer of the action is mentioned or implied, the passive voice is formed by the subject + form of *ser* + past participle + *por* + agent or doer.

Este castillo **fue construido por** el rey.	*This castle was built by the king.*
Muchos árboles **fueron destruidos por** la tormenta.	*Many trees were destroyed by the storm.*
Jorge se encargó de las invitaciones; éstas **fueron mandadas** al día siguiente.	*George took charge of the the invitations; these were (doer, Jorge, implied) sent on the following day.*

NOTE:

1. **In the passive, the past participle is used like an adjective and agrees with the subject in gender and number.**

2. **The agent is usually preceded by *por*. If the past participle expresses feeling or emotion, rather than action, *por* may be replaced by *de*.**

   Es respetado (estimado, amado) **de** todos. *He is respected (esteemed, loved) by all.*

EXERCISE A. The Spanish Club is publishing a yearbook. Tell what each person's role is, was, or will be.

EXAMPLE: Los estudiantes crearon un anuario.
El anuario **fue creado por los estudiantes.**

1. Cindy saca las fotografías. ______________________________
2. Elvira y Jennifer escribirán los poemas. ______________________________
3. Gerardo venderá los anuncios. ______________________________
4. El profesor escribió el prólogo. ______________________________
5. Jack y Silvia hacen los dibujos. ______________________________
6. Gabriela y yo redactamos el anuario. ______________________________
7. Dawn diseñó el volumen. ______________________________
8. Mariluz coordinará la producción del anuario. ______________________________

9. Todos los alumnos contribuirán una selección original. ________________

10. El director de la escuela felicita a todos los alumnos. ________________

EXERCISE B. Tell who did each of the following:

EXAMPLE: el restaurante / cerrar / el Departamento de Salubridad
El restaurante **fue cerrado** por el Departamento de Salubridad.

1. las ventanas / abrir / el portero ________________

2. los adornos / colgar / varios jóvenes ________________

3. la nueva compañía / fundar / unos empleados ________________

4. las calles / cerrar / la policía ________________

5. el presidente / admirar / todos los ciudadanos ________________

6. la música / oír / el público ________________

7. los mayores / respetar / los menores ________________

8. la carta / firmar / el alcalde ________________

9. el cuadro / pintar / un gran artista ________________

10. los árboles / plantar / un grupo de niños ________________

[2] The Passive Voice in Compound Tenses

The passive voice in compound tenses is formed in the same way that it is formed in simple tenses: if the agent or doer of the action is mentioned or implied, the passive voice is formed by the subject + form of *ser* + past participle + *por* + agent or doer. However, the verb *ser* is used in its compound tenses (*ha sido, había sido, habrá sido,* etc.).

Las tiendas han sido abiertas por los dueños los domingos	*The stores have been opened by the owners on Sundays.*
La mesa había sido puesta por el mesero.	*The table had been set by the waiter.*
Los gastos habrán sido pagados por la compañía.	*The expenses will have been paid by the company.*

NOTE:

1. **In the passive, the past participle of the action verb is used like an adjective and agrees with the subject in gender and number.**

2. **The agent is usually preceded by *por.* If the past participle expresses feeling or emotion, rather than action, *por* may be replaced by *de.***

-ar	
é	amos
aste	asteis
ó	aron

-er, -ir	
í	imos
iste	isteis
ió	ieron

EXERCISE C. **Complete this article that will appear in the local newspaper with the appropriate form of the verbs indicated. Use the present perfect, pluperfect or conditional perfect.**

Como resultado de la tormenta, muchos daños descubren (*1.* descubrir) por los ingenieros municipales. Un aviso da (*2.* dar) por el alcalde veinticuatro horas antes de la llegada de la tormenta. En el aviso los lugares que estaban en el ojo de la tormenta identificé (*3.* identificar) por los ingenieros y los científicos. Indicaron que si la información tomé (*4.* tomar) en serio por los habitantes, mucha propiedad no destruió (*5.* destruir) la tormenta. El alcalde alaba (*6.* alabar) de los ingenieros por su acción de avisar a la población y prevenir mucho daño en el pueblo.

EXERCISE D. **You are preparing headlines for several newspaper articles. Using the information provided, write a headline for each one.**

EXAMPLE: la huelga de camioneros / resolver / el presidente

La huelga de camioneros **ha sido resuelta** por el presidente.

1. la fecha del maratón / posponer / las autoridades
La fecha del maratón sido pospone por las autoridades.
2. las clases universitarias / suspender / el decano
Las clases universitarias han sido suspenden por el decano.
3. el precio de la leche / aumentar / los lecheros
El precio de la leche ha sido aumenta por los lechoros.
4. el horario de charlas y debates / anunciar/ un grupo cívico
El horario de charlas y debates ha sido anuncia por un grupo cívico.
5. los candidatos / nombrar / los partidos políticos
Los candidatos habrán sido nombran por los partidos políticos.

[3] THE PASSIVE VOICE WITH *SE*

If the agent or doer is not mentioned or implied and the subject is a thing, the reflexive construction (*se* + verb form for *Ud./él/ella* or *Uds./ellos/ellas*) is used in Spanish to express the passive voice. In such constructions, the subject usually follows the verb.

Aquí **se habla** español.	*Spanish is spoken here.*
Aquí **se hablan** español y alemán.	*Spanish and German are spoken here.*
¿A qué hora **se abren** las tiendas?	*At what time do the stores open?*
De hoy en adelante, **se ofrece** un descuento.	*From today on a discount is offered.*

EXERCISE E. **Tell what happens in these stores.**

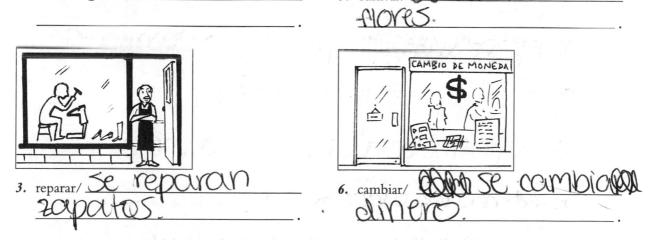

EXAMPLE: hacer/ Se hacen llaves.

1. hacer/ Se hacen los pasteles. ______.

4. preparar/ Se preparan tacos.

2. vender/ Se venden ______.

5. cultivar/ Se cultivan flores.

3. reparar/ Se reparan zapatos.

6. cambiar/ se cambia dinero.

EXERCISE F. **Using the verbs indicated, complete this recipe.**

1. (*necesitar*) Se necesitan 2 pechugas de pollo deshuesadas, 3 cucharadas de aceite, 1/4 taza de salsa soya, 1/2 taza de caldo de pollo, 3 tazas de verduras picadas (zanahoria, habichuelas, coliflor, brócoli) y 1/2 libra de pasta corta.

2. *(cortar)* Se cortan las pechugas en tiras delegadas.

3. *(sofreír)* se sofreín las tiras de pechuga en el aceite.

4. *(sacar)* se sacan las tiras doraditas de pechuga aparte.

5. *(sofreír)* se sofreín las verduras por 2 minutos en el aceite restante.

6. *(revolver)* Se revolven las verduras constantemente.

7. *(agregar)* se agrega el pollo, la salsa soya y el caldo de pollo.

8. *(dejar)* Se deja cocinar 5 minutos.

9. *(cocinar)* Se cocina la pasta al dente.

10. *(escurrir)* Se escurre la pasta.

11. *(mezclar)* se mezcla la pasta con la salsa.

12. *(servir)* Se ~~serve~~ sirve caliente.

EXERCISE G. Answer the questions that friend who is new to your city asks you. Use the cues provided.

1. ¿Dónde se nada aquí? *(la piscina del Club Deportivo)*
   Se nada a la piscina del Club Deportivo.

2. ¿Cuándo se estrenará una nueva película en el cine? *(el jueves próximo)*
   Se estrenara ~~en~~ el jueves proximo.

3. ¿Cuánto se cobra para ver una película? *(7 dólares)*
   Se cobran 7 dólares.

4. ¿Dónde se reparan bicicletas? *(la gasolinera)*
   Se ~~[illegible]~~ reparan a la gasolinera.

5. ¿Hasta qué hora se sirve la comida en el restaurante de la esquina? *(10:00)*
   Se sirve la comida a las diez.

6. ¿Dónde se podrá conseguir un monopatín? *(la tienda de deportes)*
   Se ~~lo~~ podrá a la tienda de deportes.

7. ¿Con qué frecuencia se recoge la basura? *(cada 2 días)*
   Se ~~(la)~~ recoge cada 2 días.

8. ¿A qué hora se cierran las tiendas del centro? *(8:00)*
   Se cierran las tiendas... a las ocho.

9. ¿Dónde se puede correr temprano por la mañana? *(el parque)*
   Se puede (correr...) al parque.

10. ¿Qué fiestas se celebran aquí? *(patrióticas y religiosas)*
    Se celebran patrióticas y religiosas.

MASTERY EXERCISES

EXERCISE H. **Víctor likes to repeat what he hears but he changes the way it was originally said. Tell what he repeats.**

EXAMPLE: Los hombres pintan las casas. Las casas **son pintadas** por los hombres.

1. Su hermano cerró la puerta. ______________________________
2. Virginia no invitó a Gabriel. ______________________________
3. Los niños respetan a sus profesores. ______________________________
4. Pedro pagará la cuenta. ______________________________
5. Mi amigo ayudará a mis hermanas. ______________________________
6. Los padres aman a sus hijos. ______________________________
7. Los profesores estiman a esos alumnos. ______________________________
8. El portero abrirá las puertas de las tiendas a las diez. ______________________________
9. El equipo ganó el trofeo. ______________________________
10. Yo prepararé la comida. ______________________________

EXERCISE I. **Answer the questions a friend asks you as you roam through a new part of town. Use the cues provided.**

1. ¿Qué se fabrica en esa fábrica? (*juguetes*)

   ____

2. ¿Qué se exhibe en el museo hoy? (*obras de Goya*)

   ____

3. ¿Qué se cultiva en ese jardín? (*maíz*)

   ____

4. ¿Qué se anuncia en aquel letrero? (*un baile*)

   ____

5. ¿Qué se sirve en este café? (*pasteles franceses*)

   ____

6. ¿Cuándo se abrirá la nueva estación del metro? (*abril*)

   ____

7. ¿A qué hora se cierran las tiendas aquí? (*9:00*)

   ____

8. ¿Qué idioma se habla en la farmacia? (*español e inglés*)

____

9. ¿Qué se cose allí? (*una bandera*)

____

10. ¿Qué se vende en ese quiosco? (*refrescos*)

____

EXERCISE J. **You are working in a real estate agency during the summer. Express in Spanish the information that the agent gives to prospective buyers.**

1. This town was developed by a man who loved nature. _______________
2. He was respected by the inhabitants. _______________
3. He was also praised by the mayor. _______________
4. The houses were bought by nice people. _______________
5. The houses will be painted by professional painters in the spring. _______________
6. The streets are cleaned every day. _______________
7. Garbage is collected every other day. _______________
8. Mail is delivered in the morning. _______________
9. The grass is cut by the gardener. _______________
10. No loud noises are heard by the homeowners. _______________

ACTIVIDADES

1. You are on the planning committee for homecoming in your school. Prepare a list that will serve as a directory and program for the day's events. For example:

   Se dará un concierto en el auditorio a las cuatro.

   List at least eight activities.

2. Your family received a letter that was mailed five years ago. The envelope of the letter contains postmarks and notes describing the curious journey of the letter. Write a paragraph in Spanish that describes this journey. You may wish to begin with:

   Se echó la carta al buzón en . . . **Fue mandado a Barcelona por el correo.** **Luego. . . .**

   Be sure to use the passive voice in your paragraph.

Chapter 17
The Subjunctive Mood

Chapters 1 through 16 deal with verb tenses in the indicative mood. *Mood* describes the form of the verb that shows the subject's attitude. In this and the next chapter, you will see how the subjunctive mood enables speakers of Spanish to express a variety of attitudes and feelings through the use of different verb forms and constructions.

The indicative mood states facts and expresses certainty or reality. It is based upon knowledge or certainty and is used in main or leading clauses. The subjunctive mood, on the other hand, expresses uncertainty, doubt, wishes, desires, fears, conjecture, supposition, and conditions that are unreal or contrary to fact. It is also in secondary or dependent clauses. Its use is governed by the verb in the main clause or an uncertainty that is implied in some other way. The subjunctive occurs much more frequently in Spanish than in English.

Wish/Desire → Espero que... Quiero que...
Emotion → me gusta que
Impersonal Expressions → Es importante que... Es obvio que...
Recommendations
Doubt
Ojala / OR other expressions

[1] THE PRESENT TENSE SUBJUNCTIVE

a. Regular Verbs

Most verbs form the present tense subjunctive by dropping the ending of the *yo* form of the present indicative (-*o*) and adding the corresponding endings.

	bailar (bail*o*)	vender (vend*o*)	recibir (recib*o*)
yo	bail*e*	vend*a*	recib*a*
tú	bail*es*	vend*as*	recib*as*
Ud., él, ella	bail*e*	vend*a*	recib*a*
nosotros, -as	bail*emos*	vend*amos*	recib*amos*
vosotros, -as	bail*éis*	vend*áis*	recib*áis*
Uds., ellos, ellas	bail*en*	vend*an*	recib*an*

b. Verbs with Irregular *yo* Forms

– swap the e → a

Verbs with irregular *yo* forms in the present tense indicative use the same irregular stem to form the present tense subjunctive.

caber: *quepo,* quepa, quepas, quepa, quepamos, quepáis, quepan
coger: *cojo,* coja, cojas, coja, cojamos, cojáis, cojan
conocer: *conozco,* conozca, conozcas, conozca, conozcamos, conozcáis, conozcan
destruir: *destruyo,* destruya, destruyas, destruya, destruyamos, destruyáis, destruyan
distinguir: *distingo,* distinga, distingas, distinga, distingamos, distingáis, distingan
salir: *salgo,* salga, salgas, salga, salgamos, salgáis, salgan
venir: *vengo,* venga, vengas, venga, vengamos, vengáis, vengan

c. Stem-Changing Verbs

(1) Stem-changing -*ar* and -*er* verbs have the same stem changes in the present tense subjunctive as in the present tense indicative (*e* to *ie, o* to *ue*).

cerrar: c*ie*rre, c*ie*rres, c*ie*rre, cerremos, cerréis, c*ie*rren
volver: v*ue*lva, v*ue*lvas, v*ue*lva, volvamos, volváis, v*ue*lvan

(2) Stem-changing *-ir* verbs have the same stem changes in the present tense subjunctive as in the present tense indicative (*e* to *ie, o* to *ue, e* to *i*). In the *nosotros* and *vosotros* forms, the stem vowel *e* changes to *i* and the stem vowel *o* changes to *u*.

sentir:	s*ie*nta, s*ie*ntas, s*ie*nta, s*i*ntamos, s*i*ntáis, s*ie*ntan
dormir:	d*ue*rma, d*ue*rmas, d*ue*rma, d*u*rmamos, d*u*rmáis, d*ue*rman
repetir:	rep*i*ta, rep*i*tas, rep*i*ta, rep*i*tamos, rep*i*táis, rep*i*tan

(3) Some verbs ending in *-iar* or *-uar* have an accent mark on the *i* or *u* (*í, ú*) in all forms except those for *nosotros* and *vosotros.*

enviar:	env*í*e, env*í*es, env*í*e, enviemos, enviéis, env*í*en
continuar:	contin*ú*e, contin*ú*es, contin*ú*e, continuemos, continuéis, contin*ú*en

d. Verbs with Spelling Changes

In the present subjunctive of verbs ending in *-car, -gar,* and *-zar, c* changes to *qu, g* to *gu,* and *z* to *c*. These spelling changes are the same as those that occur in the *yo* form of the preterit. (See page 55.)

	buscar (bus*qué*)	pagar (pa*gué*)	alzar (al*cé*)
yo	bus*que*	pa*gue*	al*ce*
tú	bus*ques*	pa*gues*	al*ces*
él / ella / Ud.	bus*que*	pa*gue*	al*ce*
nosotros	bus*quemos*	pa*guemos*	al*cemos*
vosotros	bus*quéis*	pa*guéis*	al*céis*
ellos / ellas / Uds.	bus*quen*	pa*guen*	al*cen*

NOTE: To keep its original sound, the *u* in *averiguar* changes to *ü* before *e.* Otherwise, the *u* would be silent, as in *guerra.*

Preterit Tense Indicative:	averigüé
Present Tense Subjunctive:	averigüe

EXERCISE A. **At an orientation for freshmen, the counselor tells them what is important that they do. Express what she says, using the impersonal expression *"Es importante que"* in each statement.**

EXAMPLE: los estudiantes / entrar a tiempo a la escuela
Es importante que los estudiantes **entren** a tiempo a la escuela .

1. cada alumno / preparar la tarea cada día
____

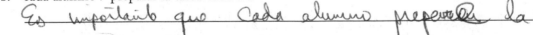

2. Uds. / estudiar para los exámenes
____

3. los alumnos / traer los libros a la clase
____

4. los alumnos y los profesores / comunicarse
____

5. el alumno / no salir de la clase sin permiso
____

6. Uds. y yo / hablar a menudo

____

7. Uds. / aprovecharse de las facilidades de la escuela

____

8. cada uno de Uds. / trabajar al máximo

____

EXERCISE B. **You are babysitting for the first time. Before leaving, the children's mother gives you specific instructions. Express what she tells you, using *Quiero que . . .***

EXAMPLE: Sally / terminar la tarea Quiero que Sally **termine** la tarea.

1. los niños / acostarse a las nueve ______________________

2. nadie / ver la televisión después de las ocho ______________________

3. Enrique y Andy / no pelear ______________________

4. todos / tomar un vaso de leche ______________________

5. Andy / cepillarse los dientes ______________________

6. ellos / obedecerte ______________________

7. tú / contestar el teléfono ______________________

EXERCISE C. **The meteorologist's predictions are rarely accurate. Tell what is projected for the next five days, using *"es probable que . . ."***

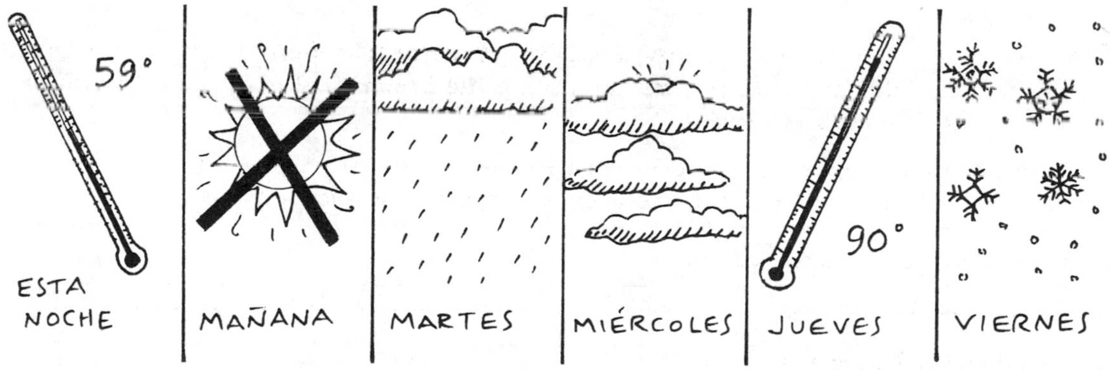

EXAMPLE: Es probable que **haga** fresco esta noche.

1. mañana ______________________

2. martes ______________________

3. miércoles ______________________

4. jueves ______________________

5. viernes ______________________

EXERCISE D. **This is Freddy's first year away at school. He calls home and tells his mother that many students in his dorm have the flu. Tell what his mother advises him, using *"espero que . . ."***

EXAMPLE: comer bien Espero que tú **comas** bien.

1. acostarse temprano ______________________
2. dormir ocho horas ______________________
3. no visitar a los enfermos ______________________
4. tomar las vitaminas ______________________
5. consultar a un buen médico ______________________
6. tomar mucho jugo de naranja ______________________
7. descansar después de las clases ______________________
8. volver a llamarme mañana ______________________

EXERCISE E. **You have a busy day ahead of you. Tell what you have to do, introducing each statement with *"es necesario que . . ."***

estudiar para un examen
escuchar las noticias del día
terminar la tarea
devolver dos libros a la biblioteca
visitar a mis abuelos
cuidar a mi hermano menor
escribirle una carta a mi prima
salir con mis padres
leer un artículo

EXAMPLE: Es necesario que yo **estudie** para un examen.

1. ______________________
2. ______________________
3. ______________________
4. ______________________
5. ______________________
6. ______________________
7. ______________________
8. ______________________

e. Present Tense Subjunctive of Irregular Verbs

The following verbs have irregular forms in the present subjunctive:

dar: **dé, des, dé, demos, deis, den**

estar: **esté, estés, esté, estemos, estéis, estén**

Espero que vayas...

haber:	**haya, hayas, haya, hayamos, hayáis, hayan**
ir:	**vaya, vayas, vaya, vayamos, vayáis, vayan**
saber:	**sepa, sepas, sepa, sepamos, sepáis, sepan**
ser:	**sea, seas, sea, seamos, seáis, sean**

EXERCISE F. **Mrs. Salas is taking her twin sons to a play date. Tell what she tells them before they leave the house. Introduce each statement with *"Quiero que . . ."* or *"Espero que . . ."***

EXAMPLE: no gritar — Quiero (Espero) que Uds. **no griten.**

1. no pelear ____________________
2. compartir los juguetes con los otros niños ____________________
3. ser corteses ____________________
4. no dejar los juguetes en el piso ____________________
5. jugar bien con los otros niños ____________________
6. no ir a decir groserías ____________________
7. decir gracias cuando les ofrecen algo ____________________
8. estar tranquilos ____________________
9. saber portarse bien ____________________
10. no coger los juguetes de los otros niños ____________________

EXERCISE G. **Javier intends to ask Lucy to marry him. Complete the letter he writes to a friend, in which he expresses his feelings.**

Querido Paco:

Yo quiero que Lucy ___se case___ (1. casarse) conmigo. Espero que ella me ___diga___ (2. decir) que sí porque le voy a hacer la pregunta esta noche. Yo no quiero que la boda ___sea___ (3. ser) grande, pero dudo que Lucy ___este___ (4. estar) de acuerdo conmigo. Según ella, cuando dos personas se casan, es importante que todos los parientes y amigos ___asistan___ (5. asistir) a la boda y que ___hayan___ (6. haber) flores, comida, música y baile también. Ella quiere que todo el mundo ____________ (7. divertirse) y que ____________ (8. compartir) ese momento. Es una lástima que nosotros no ____________ (9. poder) escaparnos. Yo dudo que Lucy y yo ____________ (10. comprar) una casa en seguida.

Será necesario que nosotros ______ (11. seguir) trabajando y que ______ (12. empezar) a ahorrar mucho dinero. Es importante que nosotros ______ (13. tener) bastante dinero para comprar lo necesario para amueblar un apartamento. Dudo que ella ______ (14. querer) vivir en la ciudad porque su mamá va a exigir que nosotros ______ (15. vivir) cerca de ella. No me importa porque amo muchísimo a Lucy y sólo espero que nosotros ______ (16. estar) contentos.

Saludos,

Javier

[2] The Present Perfect Subjunctive

a. The present perfect subjunctive is formed by the present subjunctive of *haber* + the past participle of the verb in the dependent clause.

Esperamos que todo **haya salido** bien. *We hope that everything has gone (went) well.*

b. The present perfect subjunctive is used if the verb in the main clause is in the present tense and the dependent verbs refers to an event that has taken place.

Dudo que ellos **hayan escrito** la carta. *I doubt that they have written (wrote) the letter*

EXERCISE H. Inclement weather has affected flight arrivals and departures at the airport. Express what Mr. Neblina says to other passengers.

EXAMPLE: dudo / ningún avión / salir a tiempo hoy
Dudo que ningún avión **haya salido** a tiempo hoy.

1. es probable / muchos vuelos / ser cancelados durante el día

______

2. no me sorprende / los pronosticadores del tiempo / equivocarse otra vez

______

3. me asombra / las colas para los teléfonos / no disminuirse

______

4. temo / las tripulaciones / no poder llegar al aeropuerto

______

5. espero / los técnicos / revisar bien los aviones

______

6. el agente / lamenta / nosotros /no recibir más información sobre los vuelos

______

MASTERY EXERCISES

EXERCISE I. **Tell what a traveler should do before embarking on a trip.**

EXAMPLE: hacer un itinerario **Es preciso** que el viajero **haga** un itinerario.

1. comprar el boleto de avión ______
2. hacer reservación en un hotel ______
3. tener su pasaporte al día ______
4. ir al banco y sacar dinero ______
5. hacer la maleta ______
6. leer libros sobre los lugares que piensa visitar ______
7. despedirse de la familia ______
8. salir temprano de la casa ______
9. estar en el aeropuerto dos horas antes del vuelo ______
10. poner un rollo nuevo en la cámara ______

EXERCISE J. **Tell what these people should do to enjoy good health.**

EXAMPLE: Ernesto / comer bien **Es importante** que Ernesto **coma** bien.

1. Andrea / hacer ejercicio todos los días ______
2. Larry y Tomás / beber mucha agua ______
3. tú / dormir bien ______
4. yo / hacer todo en moderación ______
5. Julie / no fumar ______
6. Victoria / saber descansar ______
7. Joaquín / no estar nervioso ______

EXERCISE K. **You are at a meeting of the school's literary club. Complete the questions and answers with the appropriate form of the present subjunctive.**

1. tener

   ¿Es importante que un autor ______ mucha imaginación?

   Sí, es muy importante que todos los autores ______ mucha imaginación.

2. ser

¿Es preciso que el cuento ______________ verdadero?

No, no es preciso que los cuentos ______________ verdaderos.

3. conocer

¿Es probable que el autor ______________ bien al protagonista del cuento?

Es muy importante que los autores ______________ bien a todos los personajes.

4. saber

¿Es necesario que el autor ______________ desarrollar a los personajes?

Sí, es necesario que los autores ______________ desarrollar a los personajes.

5. haber

¿Es probable que ______________ relación entre la acción del cuento y la vida del autor?

Sí, es probable que ______________ relación entre la acción del cuento y la vida del autor.

EXERCISE L. Joey isn't selling many tickets to a fund-raising event his team is planning. Using the expressions indicated, give the reasons people aren't buying tickets.

1. Es posible que yo ______________
2. Es probable que mi familia ______________
3. Es dudoso que mis amigos ______________
4. Es importante que mi hermano y yo ______________
5. Es una lástima que mi novio ______________
6. Es necesario que nosotros ______________

EXERCISE M. A friend is telling you about one of the school teams. Express what he says in Spanish.

1. It's important that the team wins.

____

2. It's necessary that the players play well.

____

3. It's important that they not commit errors during the game.

____

4. It's important that they practice a lot.

____

5. It's important that the fans attend the games.

____

6. It's important that every student support the team.

____

7. It's necessary that the players arrive on time to the game.

____

8. It's possible that another team has better players.

____

9. It's important that the umpire be fair.

____

10. It's a pity that I'm not a member of the team.

____

ACTIVIDADES

1. Conserving the environment is an important goal in today's society. Using the expressions *"es necesario que…,"* and *"es importante que…,"* prepare a list of eight things you feel people can do to accomplish this goal.
2. Indicate eight things that you feel that people should do as good citizens. Use the expressions *"es necesario que…,"* and *"es importante que…"* to introduce each one.

Chapter 18
Uses of the Subjunctive Mood Tenses

[1] DEPENDENT CLAUSES

The subjunctive in dependent clauses is introduced by the conjunction *que.*

a. The subjunctive tenses are used in a dependent clause when the verb in the main clause expresses advice, command, demand, desire, hope, permission, preference, prohibition, request, suggestion. Here are some common verbs that require the subjunctive.

aconsejar *to advise*
decir *to tell (someone to do something)*
desear *to wish*
esperar *to hope*
exigir *to demand*
mandar *to order*
ordenar *to order*
pedir *to ask, to request*
permitir *to permit, to allow*
preferir *to prefer*
prohibir *to forbid*
querer *to want*
rogar *to request, to beg*
sugerir *to suggest*
suplicar *to implore, to beg*

El profesor **aconseja que** los alumnos **estudien.**	*The teacher advises the students to study (that the students study).*
Juan **quiere que** yo lo **llame** mañana.	*Juan wants me to call him tomorrow (that I call him tomorrow).*
La mamá **desea que** los niños se **acuesten** temprano.	*The mother wants the children to go to bed early (that the children go to bed early).*
Espero que compren la casa.	*I hope that they buy the house.*
Ella **ordena que hagan** la tarea.	*She orders them to do the assignment.*
Él me **pide que** le **pague.**	*He asks me to pay him.*
Mi padre **prohibe que** yo **vea** esa película.	*My father prohibits that I see that film.*
Quiero que Ud. **trabaje** mañana.	*I want you to work tomorrow.*
Ruego que tú me **prestes** atención.	*I beg you to pay attention to me (that you pay attention to me).*
Sugieren que vayamos en taxi.	*They suggest that we go by cab.*

NOTE: **In each of the above sentences, the subject of the main verb is different from the subject of the dependent verb. If the subjects are the same, *que* is omitted and the infinitive form of the dependent verb is used.**

Quiero trabajar mañana. — *I want to work tomorrow.*
Ella espera comprar la casa. — *She hopes to buy the house.*

EXERCISE A. Express what parents ask of their children.

EXAMPLE: los padres / exigir / los hijos / recibir buenas notas
Los padres **exigen** que los hijos **reciben** buenas notas.

1. mi mamá / querer / mis hermanos y yo / ayudar en casa

____

2. mi papá / prohibir / yo / mirar muchos programas de televisión

____

3. los padres / esperar / los hijos / tener éxito en la vida

____

4. mis padres / preferir / yo / trabajar en el verano

____

5. mamá / permitir / tú / comer dulces

____

6. papá / rogar / mi hermana / volver a casa temprano

____

7. los padres / sugerir / Eduardo y Felipe / buscar trabajo

____

8. mis padres / aconsejar / mi hermana / no salir por la noche

____

EXERCISE B. **Use the suggestions provided to express these people's ideas.**

asistir a una buena universidad	preparar la tarea a diario
tener su propio carro	quedarse en casa esta noche
no decir groserías	salir con los amigos
entrar en la sala	ser amable
ganar el campeonato	visitar con más frecuencia

EXAMPLE: Mi mamá prohibe que el perro **entre en la sala.**

1. Felipe quiere que su equipo favorito _______________.
2. Mi abuela desea que mi hermano y yo _______________.
3. Los padres de Sergio prohiben que él _______________.
4. La consejera de Vicki espera que ella _______________.
5. Los padres exigen que sus hijos _______________.
6. Los profesores sugieren que los alumnos _______________.
7. Yo ruego que mi hermana _______________.
8. Los señores dicen que los invitados _______________.
9. Los días escolares mis padres prohiben que yo _______________.
10. El pronosticador del tiempo aconseja que todo el mundo _______________.

b. **The subjunctive is used after verbs of feeling or emotion, such as fear, joy, sorrow, regret, surprise. Such verbs include:**

alegrarse (de) *to be glad*	**sorprenderse (de)** *to be surprised*
lamentar *to be sorry about, to regret*	**temer** *to fear*
sentir *to be sorry, to regret*	**tener miedo (de)** *to fear, to be afraid*

Temen que el gato **se caiga** del árbol.	*They fear that the cat will fall out of the tree.*
Nos alegramos de que tú **vengas.**	*We are happy that you are coming.*
Siento que ella **no esté** aquí.	*I regret that she isn't here.*
Los alumnos **se sorprenden de que no haya** clases hoy.	*The students are surprised that there are no classes today.*

EXERCISE C. **Norma is on a cruise for the first time. Using the verb in parentheses, express her reactions to various things.**

EXAMPLE: Los miembros de la tripulación hablan muchos idiomas. (*sorprenderse*)
Norma **se sorprende de que** los miembros de la tripulación **hablen** muchos idiomas.

1. Los viajeros se visten con mucha elegancia. (*sorprenderse*)

____

2. La comida es muy buena. (*alegrarse*)

____

3. Hay una gran variedad de actividades todos los días. (*sorprenderse*)

____

4. El mar está muy tranquilo. (*alegrarse*)

____

5. Su hermana no la acompaña. (*lamentar*)

____

6. El crucero dura solamente cinco días. (*sentir*)

____

EXERCISE D. **Using one of the following verbs, express what the people feel upon hearing various news items.**

alegrarse	temer	tener miedo de
sorprenderse	sentir	lamentar

EXAMPLE: El presidente visitará muchos países.
Todo el mundo **se alegra de que** el presidente **visite** muchos países.

1. La temporada de tormentas acabará mañana.
Los comerciantes ______________________________ .

2. El premio gordo de la lotería paga diez millones de dólares.
Mi padre ______________________________ .

3. Destruyen muchos edificios antiguos de la ciudad.

Los ciudadanos ____.

4. El equipo favorito no jugará ningún partido en su propio estadio.

Mis amigos ____.

5. Los alumnos no tendrán vacaciones de verano.

Yo ____.

6. No se abren las playas por causa de la contaminación.

Mis amigos y yo ____.

7. El dólar pierde su valor en el mercado mundial.

Los banqueros ____.

8. Hay muchos avances en la investigación de las enfermedades.

Todo el mundo ____.

9. El número de accidentes automovilísticos disminuye con gran velocidad.

La policía ____.

10. El uso de la computadora es uno de los pasatiempos más populares.

Yo ____.

c. The subjunctive is used after verbs expressing doubt, disbelief, and denial, such as:

dudar	*to doubt*	**negar**	*to deny*
no creer	*not to believe*	**pensar**	*to think*

Dudo que vengan temprano.	*I doubt that they will come early.*
Ella **niega que sea** la verdad.	*She denies that it is the truth.*
¿Piensa Ud. **que** él **sea** sincero?	*Do you think he is sincere?*
¿Crees que él **tenga** el dinero?	*Do you believe he has the money?*
No creo que él **tenga** el dinero.	*I don't believe he has the money.*

BUT

Creo que él **tiene** el dinero.	*I believe that he has the money.*

NOTE:

1. **The verbs *creer* and *pensar,* when used interrogatively and negatively, indicate uncertainty and are usually followed by the subjunctive.**

2. ***Creer, pensar, no dudar,* and *no negar* indicate belief or certainty and are usually followed by the indicative.**

Creo (Pienso, No dudo, No niego) que Julia **sabe** la respuesta.	*I believe (I think, I don't doubt, I don't deny) that Julia knows the answer.*

EXERCISE E. **Some friends accompany you on a shopping trip for a wristwatch. Use *dudar, no creer,* or *no pensar* to express their reaction to each wristwatch you look at.**

EXAMPLE: Este reloj cuesta mucho. Rafael **no cree** que este reloj **cueste** mucho.

1. Este reloj vale mucho. Gabi ______________________.
2. Este reloj dura mucho tiempo. Elena y Nora ______________________.
3. Este reloj adelanta mucho. Sam ______________________.
4. Este reloj es de última moda. Tú ______________________.
5. Los números se distinguen fácilmente. Mirta y yo ______________________.

EXERCISE F. **Tell who denies the following statements.**

EXAMPLE: La corte es injusta. (*el juez*) El juez **niega que** la corte **sea** injusta.

1. Los precios aumentan otra vez. (*los comerciantes*)

   ____

2. La princesa se casa con el chofer. (*el rey*)

   ____

3. Los personajes de la novela son verdaderos. (*el autor*)

   ____

4. La huelga es justificada. (*los trabajadores*)

   ____

5. Los pronosticadores del tiempo saben pronosticar el tiempo. (*el público*)

   ____

6. Yo no tengo la culpa. (*el criminal*)

   ____

[2] IMPERSONAL CONSTRUCTIONS

a. **The subjunctive is used after certain impersonal expressions if the dependent verb has an expressed subject.**

es dudoso *it is doubtful*
es importante *it is important*
es imposible *it is impossible*
es una lástima *it is a pity*

es mejor, **más vale**, **es menester** } *it is better*
es necesario, **es preciso** } *it is necessary*

es posible *it is possible*
es probable *it is probable*

Es dudoso que él lo **compre**.	*It is doubtful that he will buy it.*
Es importante que lo **hagamos**.	*It is important for us to do it (that we do it).*

Es necesario que Ud. **coma.** — *It is necessary for you to eat (that you eat).*

BUT

Es necesario comer. — *It is necessary to eat.*

b. **The subjunctive is not used after impersonal expressions that express certainty.**

es cierto *it is certain* **es evidente** *it is evident*
es claro *it is clear* **es verdad** *it is true*

Es verdad que mañana **es** su cumpleaños. — *It is true that tomorrow is her birthday.*
Es cierto que yo **estudio** mucho. — *It is true that I study a lot.*

BUT

No es cierto que yo **estudie** mucho. — *It is not true that I study a lot.*

EXERCISE G. **In your social studies class you have been compiling a list of what candidates for public office should do. Express your reaction to this using the expression indicated.**

EXAMPLE: conocer a todos los electores (*imposible*)
Es imposible que los candidatos **conozcan** a todos los electores.

1. no hacer promesas inalcanzables (*importante*)
Es importante que los candidatos no hagan - - -

2. ser honrados (*necesario*)
Es necesario que sean honrados

3. comprender bien los problemas (*dudoso*)
Es dudoso que - - - comprendan - - -

4. escuchar las quejas de los electores (*preciso*)
____

5. obedecer las leyes (*importante*)
____

6. representar los deseos de los electores (*menester*)
____

7. no ofender a ningún grupo de electores (*imposible*)
____

8. responder a sus apoyadores (*probable*)
____

9. cumplir con su palabra (*dudoso*)
____

10. no meterse en temas ajenos (*mejor*)
____

EXERCISE H. **You are working at the airport and have to prepare a message to passengers who have been delayed due to mechanical problems with the aircraft. Complete the message with the appropriate form of the verbs indicated.**

Es evidente que nosotros ________ (*1.* tener) un problema grande. Es cierto que ________ (*2.* haber) una demora de los aviones porque es importante que los mecánicos ________ (*3.* tener) tiempo suficiente para revisar bien los aviones. Es probable que la demora ________ (*4.* durar) varias horas, pero más vale estar seguros de que todo ________ (*5.* estar) en orden antes de despegar. Es menester que Uds. ________ (*6.* cooperar) con nosotros. Es dudoso que nosotros ________ (*7.* poder) atender las necesidades individuales de cada pasajero, pero más vale ________ (*8.* tratar) de ayudar a unos que a nadie. Es una lástima que muchos de Uds. no ________ (*9.* llegar) a sus destinos a la hora indicada en el horario. Es evidente que muchos de Uds. ________ (*10.* tener) mucha prisa por llegar, pero es imposible ________ (*11.* cambiar) las cosas. Es claro que nosotros ________ (*12.* ir) a hacer todo lo posible para ayudarlos. Si Uds. se alejan de la puerta de salida, es preciso que Uds. ________ (*13.* fijarse) en los anuncios que se darán por altavoz. Es dudoso que el avión ________ (*14.* salir) antes de las nueve de la noche. Es probable que yo ________ (*15.* hacer) otro anuncio dentro de treinta minutos. Muchas gracias por su atención y cooperación.

EXERCISE I. **Imagine that you are a freshman advisor. Tell a group of students about school life and what they should do to succeed.**

EXAMPLE: es probable / Uds. / estar preocupados
Es probable que Uds. **estén** preocupados.

1. es dudoso / Uds. / poder participar en todas las actividades de la escuela

____

2. es necesario / cada estudiante / seguir las reglas de la escuela

____

3. es importante / los alumnos / no llegar tarde a las clases

____

4. es preciso / Uds. / estar bien preparados todos los días

____

5. es mejor / los alumnos / hablar con los profesores

____

6. es importante / nosotros / respetar los derechos de todos los alumnos

____

7. es menester / los profesores / exigir mucho a los estudiantes

____

[3] SEQUENCE OF TENSES

a. **The present tense of the subjunctive mood is generally used if the verb in the main clause is in the present indicative, the future, present perfect, or the imperative (command form).**

Ella **ordena que** ellos **estudien** más.	*She orders them to study more (that they study more).*
Ella **ordenará que** ellos **estudien** más.	*She will order them to study more.*
Ella **ha ordenado que** ellos **estudien** más.	*She has ordered them to study more.*
Ordene Ud. **que** ellos **estudien** más.	*Order them to study more.*

b. **The present perfect subjunctive (*haya hablado* has spoken) is formed by the present subjunctive of *haber* and the past participle of the verb in the dependent clause. The perfect subjunctive is used if the verb in the main clause is in the present tense and the dependent verb represents an event that has taken place.**

No creo que ellos **hayan** salido.	*I do not believe that they have left.*
Niego que ellos **me hayan visto.**	*I deny that they have seen me.*

EXERCISE J. **Mrs. Vega is very nervous about leaving her children with a babysitter. Express what she says to her husband.**

EXAMPLE: no creo / los niños / cenar bien **No creo que** los niños **hayan cenado** bien.

1. espero / los niños / bañarse

Espero que los niños se bañen

2. espero / ellos / no ver ese programa de televisión

Espero que ellos no vayan

3. es importante / Jorge / prestar mucha atención

____

4. dudo / Elvira / preparar la tarea aún

____

5. es probable / Jorge y Víctor / seguir peleando

____

6. ruego / no haber ninguna emergencia

____

7. es evidente / Rosalinda / ser muy responsable

____

8. lamento / nosotros / volver a dejar a los niños en casa

____

9. es dudoso / tú / ayudarme

____

10. es posible / Rosalinda / llamar por teléfono otra vez

____

EXERCISE K. **You and a friend have been communicating over the Internet but you have reached a level of frustration. Complete this message that you send to your friend with the appropriate form of the verbs indicated.**

Querida Marta:

Yo temo que la tecnología moderna ______________ (*1.* poder) terminar con nuestra amistad. En mi mensaje anterior escribí: «Te suplico que ______________ (*2.* comunicarse) conmigo en seguida.» Dudo que tú ______________ (*3.* recibir) ese mensaje, ya que no me contestaste. Es importante que tú y yo ______________ (*4.* hablar) pronto. Prefiero que tú me ______________ (*5.* llamar) por teléfono. Es evidente que nosotros no ______________ (*6.* poder) seguir comunicándonos por el Internet. Espero que te ______________ (7. llegar) esta comunicación. Si me llamas por teléfono, no habrá duda de que la ______________ (*8.* recibir). Si no me llamas pronto, yo trataré de llamarte.

Hasta luego.

MASTERY EXERCISES

EXERCISE L. **Complete the following sentences with your opinions.**

1. Yo prefiero que mis padres ______________.

2. Es necesario que mis hermanos y yo ______________.

3. Tengo miedo de que los profesores ______________.

4. Suplico que mis amigos ______________.

5. No creo que ellos ______________.

6. Es una lástima que mi mejor amigo(a) ______________.

7. Es probable que yo ______________.

8. Espero que toda mi familia ______________.

9. Me alegro de que mi padre ______________________________.

10. Mis padres sugieren que yo ______________________________.

EXERCISE M. Complete this story with the appropriate form of the verbs indicated.

Mañana Pedro va a presentarse a un trabajo por primera vez. Es necesario que él ______________ (*1.* despertarse) temprano el primer día. Él quiere ______________ (*2.* dar) una buena impresión. Su mamá teme que su hijo no ______________ (*3.* oír) el reloj despertador. Ella le ruega a Pedro que ______________ (*4.* acostarse) temprano porque es importante que él ______________ (*5.* estar) alerto en la oficina. Por eso ella prohibe que Pedro ______________ (*6.* salir) con sus amigos por la noche. No permite que él ______________ (*7.* mirar) la televisión hasta muy tarde. Ella quiere que su hijo ______________ (*8.* tener) éxito en el trabajo y que ______________ (*9.* ser) más responsable.

Cuando Pedro asiste a la escuela es necesario que su mamá ______________ (*10.* entrar) en su cuarto para despertarlo. Antes de acostarse ella le dice a Pedro que ______________ (*11.* poner) el reloj despertador para las seis y media de la mañana. Ella le sugiere que ______________ (*12.* usar) dos relojes para despertarse. Ella cree que ______________ (*13.* ser) preciso que Pedro ______________ (*14.* tener) bastante tiempo para desayunar también. Pero a la mañana siguiente, Pedro se despierta tarde. Su mamá teme que Pedro ______________ (*15.* poner) mal el reloj despertador. Es evidente que Pedro no ______________ (*16.* saber) distinguir entre «AM» y «PM» en el reloj.

EXERCISE N. Several friends are planning a ski trip. Express in Spanish what they say.

1. I doubt that it will snow tomorrow.

____

2. I hope that they don't cancel the trip.

____

3. It's neccesary that we pack tonight.

____

4. It's important that we leave early.

____

5. I don't think there will be a lot of traffic.

---

6. They suggest that we take several books with us.

---

7. Tell him to bring his guitar.

---

8. It's doubtful there will be time for that.

---

9. I don't want us to become bored.

---

10. Richie regrets he is not going on the trip.

---

11. I'm surprised that he hasn't changed his mind.

---

12. I hope that we have a good time.

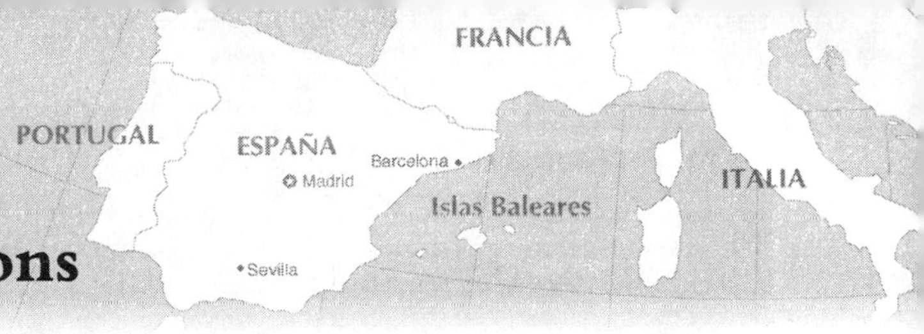

Chapter 19
Common Verbal Expressions

Many Spanish verbs are used in idiomatic expressions. A list of common expressions follows

[1] EXPRESSIONS WITH *HACER*

¿Qué tiempo hace? *How's the weather?*
¿Qué tiempo hace en primavera? — *How's the weather in spring?*

hacer buen/mal tiempo *to be good/bad weather*
Hace buen (mal) tiempo hoy. — *Today the weather is good (bad).*

hacer (mucho) calor/fresco/frío *to be (very) warm/cool/cold (weather)*
Hizo mucho fresco anoche. — *It was very cool last night.*

hacer (mucho) sol *to be (very) sunny*
Hace mucho sol a mediodía. — *It is very sunny at noon.*

hacer (mucho) viento *to be (very) windy*
Hizo viento por la mañana. — *It was windy in the morning.*

hacer el favor de + infinitive *please. . .*
Haga Ud. el favor de pasar la sal. — *Please pass the salt.*

hacer de + occupation *to act as*
Miguel hace de presidente. — *Michael acts as president.*

hacer la maleta (el baúl) *to pack one's suitcase (trunk)*
Hizo la maleta en seguida. — *He packed his suitcase at once.*

hace + time expression + preterit *. . . ago*
Le hablé hace una semana. — *I spoke to her a week ago.*

hacer una pregunta *to ask a question*
El alumno le hizo una pregunta al profesor. — *The student asked the teacher a question.*

hacer un viaje *to take a trip*
Hacen un viaje a México. — *They take a trip to Mexico.*

hacer una visita *to pay a visit*
Le hice una visita a mi tío. — *I paid a visit to my uncle.*

hacerse *to become (through one's own efforts)*
El autor se hizo famoso. — *The author became famous.*

hacerse tarde *to be getting late*
Se hace tarde. — *It's getting late.*

EXERCISE A. **Complete each of the following statements with an expression with *hacer*.**

EXAMPLE: Yo no pude responder cuando el profesor ________________ .
Yo no pude responder cuando el profesor **hizo la pregunta.**

1. Es un buen día para ir a la playa porque hace buen tiempo hoy
2. En la primavera mis abuelos hacen un viaje a Francia.

3. ¿Juan? No sé. ______________________ que no lo veo.

4. ¿ ______________________ ? ¿Necesitaré usar guantes?

5. Cuando Elvira era pequeña, ella siempre ______________________ médica en las obras de la escuela.

6. ______________________ decirme dónde hay un teléfono público.

7. Regresamos a casa en seguida porque ______________________ .

8. Cada domingo, Felipe ______________________ a sus abuelos.

9. Vicki ______________________ porque va a pasar una semana en las montañas.

10. ______________________ y todas las hojas se cayeron de los árboles.

EXERCISE B. **Tell what you like to do in different weather conditions. Use the suggestions provided.**

EXAMPLE: Cuando hace mal tiempo, me gusta leer una novela.

SUGGESTIONS:

quedarme en casa	jugar al tenis
leer una novela	visitar a un amigo
caminar por el parque	esquiar
ir a la playa	ir al cine

1. Cuando ______________________
______________________ .

2. Cuando ______________________
______________________ .

3. Cuando ______________________
______________________ .

4. Cuando ______________________
______________________ .

5. Cuando ______________________________

______________________________.

7. Cuando ______________________________

______________________________.

6. Cuando ______________________________

______________________________.

EXERCISE C. **Neil just returned from a sightseeing trip with his grandparents. Use an expression with *hacer* to tell what he says about the trip.**

______________ (1.) una semana, mis abuelos y yo ______________ (2.) al pueblo donde nació mi abuelo. Pasamos tres días allí. Cada mañana, antes de vestirse, mi abuela ______________ (3.): «¿ ______________ (4.) hoy?» Nos tocó un clima muy variado. Un día ______________ (5.) y la temperatura subió a los noventa grados. Otro día, especialmente por la noche, ______________ (6.) cuando la temperatura bajó a los treinta grados. Pero por lo general, durante el día ______________ (7.) porque ______________ (8.) y también ______________ (9.). Cuando mis abuelos ______________ (10.) para el viaje, metieron ropa ligera y gruesa pero yo no tenía ropa para el frío. Cada día seguimos la misma rutina: nos despertamos temprano y al salir del hotel mi abuelo ______________ (11.) guía. Conocimos la escuela a la cual asistió, el parque donde pasaba su tiempo libre, y los lugares donde se reunía con sus amigos. Me divertí pero le dije: «Abuelito, la próxima vez que yo ______________ (12.) con ustedes, ______________ (13.) comenzar la excursión a mediodía. Me gusta dormir por la mañana.»

[2] EXPRESSIONS WITH *TENER*

tener . . . años *to be . . . years old*
Ella tiene veinte años. — *She is twenty years old.*
¿Cuántos años tiene Ud.? / ¿Qué edad tiene Ud.? — *How old are you?*

tener (mucho) calor *to be (very) warm*
Él tiene (mucho) calor. — *He is (very) warm.*

tener (mucho) frío *to be (very) cold*
Nosotros tenemos (mucho) frío. — *We are (very) cold.*

NOTE: **"To be warm" and "to be cold" translate as *hacer calor* and *hacer frío,* respectively, when referring to the weather, and as *estar caliente* and *estar frío, -a,* respectively, when referring to things.**

tener (mucha) hambre *to be (very) hungry*
¿Tiene Ud. (mucha) hambre? — *Are you (very) hungry?*

tener (mucha) sed *to be (very) thirsty*
Tengo (mucha) sed. — *I am (very) thirsty.*

tener éxito *to be successful*
Ud. siempre tiene éxito. — *You are always successful.*

tener ganas de *to feel like*
Nosotros no tenemos ganas de comer. — *We don't feel like eating.*

tener razón *to be right;* **no tener razón** *to be wrong*
Alfredo tiene razón. — *Alfred is right.*
Pablo no tiene razón. — *Paul is wrong.*

tener sueño *to be sleepy*
¿Tiene Ud. sueño? — *Are you sleepy?*

tener cuidado *to be careful*
Tenga cuidado con el experimento. — *Be careful with the experiment.*

tener prisa *to be in a hurry*
El hombre tiene prisa. — *The man is in a hurry.*

tener (mucho) gusto en *to be (very) glad to*
Tengo (mucho) gusto en conocerle. — *I am (very) glad to know you.*

tener miedo de + infinitive *to be afraid to*
Ella tiene miedo de tocarlo. — *She is afraid to touch it.*
Ella le tiene miedo al perro. — *She is afraid of the dog.*

tener dolor de cabeza (estómago, muelas) *to have a headache (stomachache, toothache)*
Tengo dolor de cabeza. — *I have a headache.*

tener que + infinitive *to have to, must*
Tengo que estudiar. — *I have to (must) study.*

tener mucho (poco, algo) que hacer *to have much (little, something) to do*
Tengo mucho que hacer — *I have much to do.*

tener la bondad de + infinitive *please*
Tenga Ud. la bondad de esperar un momento. — *Please wait a minute.*

tener las manos frías (los ojos cansados) *to have cold hands (tired eyes)*
Él tiene las manos frías (calientes). *His hands are cold (warm).*
Tengo los ojos cansados. *My eyes are tired.*
¿Qué tiene Ud.? *What is the matter with you?*

tener que ver con *to have to do with*
Esto no tiene nada que ver con aquello. *This has nothing to do with that.*

EXERCISE D. Every evening Julia speaks to her best friend on the telephone and gives her the latest gossip about their friends. Express what she says using an expression with *tener*.

1. Luis ____________ ir al cine porque quería ver la película que acaba de estrenar.
2. Sarita no comió nada en la cafetería de la escuela porque ella ____________ .
3. Víctor y Hugo no me vieron cuando corrían por la calle. Ellos ____________ .
4. John ____________ . Bebió más de un litro de agua en diez minutos.
5. Había un perro en la calle y una señora atravesó la calle porque ella le ____________ al perro.
6. Ali se acostó temprano anoche porque ____________ .
7. Grace llamó al dentista anoche porque ella ____________ .
8. Tus primos gemelos, Gustavo y Gloria, celebraron su cumpleaños el domingo. ¿ ____________ ?
9. Le presté un suéter a Raquel porque ella ____________ .
10. Había mucho hielo en la calle. Cuando mi abuelo salió de la casa yo le dije: « ____________ , abuelo».
11. Hoy Jim estaba muy preocupado pero no me contestó cuando le pregunté: «¿ ____________ , Jim?»
12. Vi en el canal del tiempo que la temperatura en San Antonio pasó los cien grados. Los habitantes de San Antonio ____________ , ¿no crees?
13. Cuando mi hermana me pide ayuda, nunca me dice: « ____________ ayudarme».
14. Otra vez no hablo con mi hermano porque él siempre cree que él ____________ .
15. Debemos terminar de hablar porque yo ____________ estudiar para un examen.

EXERCISE E. Gladys is helping her younger brother study for a test. Express what he says in each situation, using an expression with *tener*.

EXAMPLE: Ya han terminado las vacaciones y los jóvenes **tienen que volver a** la escuela.

1. Es medianoche y Felipe no se acuesta aunque él ____________ .
2. Hace mucho calor y Paco está haciendo mucho ejercicio. Él debe ____________ .
3. Los señores andaban lentamente porque no ____________ .
4. Camarero, ____________ de darme una servilleta.

5. Al conocer al padre de su amigo, Jorge le dijo: ____________ en conocerle, señor.

6. Los alumnos estudian mucho porque ellos no ____________ salir mal en el examen.

7. Mirta se desayuna muy temprano, a las seis de la mañana. Ahora es la una de la tarde. Ella debe ____________ .

8. El autobús escolar llega a las siete y diez. Ya son las siete y ocho y Lourdes ____________ porque no quiere perderlo.

9. Al ver el ratoncito, las personas ____________ .

10. La temperatura bajó y los exploradores encendieron un fuego porque ellos ____________ .

EXERCISE F. **Answer the questions that a new neighbor asks you.**

1. ¿Cuántos años tienes? ________________________________

2. ¿Tomas aspirinas cuando tienes dolor de cabeza? ________________________________

3. ¿Tienes frío hoy? ________________________________

4. ¿Tienes que estudiar esta noche para un examen? ________________________________

5. ¿Tienen tus padres razón siempre? ________________________________

6. ¿Tienes hambre por la tarde? ________________________________

7. ¿Qué haces cuando tienes sed? ________________________________

8. ¿Qué haces cuando tienes sueño? ________________________________

9. ¿Tienes cuidado cuando andas en bicicleta en la calle? ________________________________

10. ¿Tienes algo que hacer esta tarde? ________________________________

[3] Expressions with *Dar*

dar a *to face*
Mi ventana da a la avenida. *My window faces the avenue.*

dar con alguien (algo) *to meet, to come upon, to find someone (something)*
Yo di con mi amigo en la calle. *I met my friend on the street.*

dar de comer a *to feed*
Ellos dan de comer a los caballos. *They feed the horses.*

dar la hora (las siete) *to strike the hour (seven)*
El reloj dio las siete. *The clock struck seven.*

dar la mano a alguien *to shake hands with someone*
Carlos le dio la mano. *Charles shook hands with him.*

darse la mano *to shake hands (with each other)*
Los amigos se dan la mano. *The friends shake hands.*

dar las gracias a *to thank*
Ella le dio las gracias al hombre por su bondad. *She thanked the man for his kindness.*

dar los buenos días (las buenas noches) a alguien *to say good morning (good night) to someone*
Yo le doy los buenos días a mi amigo. *I say good morning to my friend.*

dar un paseo *to take a walk or a ride*
Ellos dan un paseo por el parque. *They take a walk (a ride) through the park.*

dar un paseo en automóvil (a caballo) *to take an automobile ride (to go horseback riding)*
Yo doy un paseo en automóvil. *I take an automobile ride.*

EXERCISE G. Vicky is studying in Salamanca, Spain and sends you this postcard. Complete her message with an expression with *dar*.

Querida amiga:

Vivo con una familia simpática. Mi cuarto ________ (1.) un patio grande. Hay un reloj grande en la plaza mayor y el reloj ________ (2.) cada hora. Aquí en España, los amigos ________ (3.) al saludarse. Me gusta ________ (4.) por el centro de la ciudad porque es una ciudad muy antigua y bonita. Ayer yo ________ (5.) un chico que era mi compañero de asiento en el avión. Me invitó a ________ (6.) con él mañana después de las clases. Vamos a ir al parque. Hay muchos pájaros en el parque y muchas personas les ________ (7.). También quiero ________ (8.) por el regalo de viaje que me diste. Es muy bonito y útil. Ya es tarde y voy a acostarme. Voy a ________ (9.).

Saludos,

Vicky

EXERCISE H. Answer the questions a new friend asks you about your customs.

1. ¿Qué hora da el reloj cuando te despiertas todos los días?

____

2. ¿Das un paseo por la mañana?

____

3. ¿Prefieres dar un paseo en carro o a caballo?

____

4. Si das con su amigo(-a) en la calle, ¿se dan Uds. la mano?

____

5. Al despedirse de un amigo, ¿le das la mano?

____

6. ¿Diste con el compañero de clase que buscabas?

____

7. ¿Quién le da de comer a tu perro?

____

8. ¿Les das las gracias a las personas que te ayudan?

____

9. ¿Le das las buenas noches a tu familia antes de acostarte?

____

10. ¿Tu cuarto da a la calle?

____

[4] EXPRESSIONS WITH *HABER*

hay (había, hubo, habrá, habría, ha habido) *there is, there are (there was, there were, there will be, there would be, there has (have) been)*
Había muchos clientes en la tienda. *There were many customers in the store.*

haber lodo (luna, sol, neblina, polvo) *to be muddy (moonlight, sunny, foggy, dusty)*
Hay (mucho) lodo hoy. *It is (very) muddy today.*
Había neblina anoche. *It was foggy last night.*

haber de + infinitive *to be to, to be supposed to*
Han de venir mañana. *They are to come tomorrow.*

hay que + infinitive *one must*
Hay que tener paciencia. *One must have patience.*

hay + noun + **que** + infinitive *there is (there are) + noun + verb*
Hay trabajo que hacer. *There is work to do.*
No hay de qué. *Don't mention it. (You're welcome).*

EXERCISE I. **You are helping a friend study for a test. Complete each statement with one of the following expressions.**

había	han de	hay lodo	hay neblina	hay que
ha de	no hay de qué	hay luna	había polvo	hay . . . que

1. Jaime ____________ venir al anochecer.
2. Cuando alguien me dice «muchas gracias», yo siempre contesto « ____________ ».
3. ____________ callarse para oír.
4. No me gusta dar un paseo después de la lluvia, cuando ____________ en las calles.
5. ____________ una caja de dulces en la mesa.
6. En una noche clara ____________ .

7. ______________ en el aire ayer.

8. Hoy ______________ ; no se ve el sol.

9. En el campo ______________ muchas cosas interesantes ______________ ver.

10. Ellos ______________ estar allí a las once.

[5] Other Verbal Expressions

acabar de **to have just**
Él acaba (acababa) de entrar. — *He has just (had just) entered.*

aprovecharse de *to take advantage of (an opportunity)*
Él se aprovecha de cada oportunidad. — *He takes advantage of each opportunity.*

asistir a *to attend*
Asistimos a la escuela. — *We attend school.*

bajar de *to get off (the train, bus, etc.)*
El pasajero baja del tren. — *The passenger gets off the train.*

burlarse de *to make fun of*
Tú te burlas de la muchacha. — *You make fun of the girl.*

cambiar de *to change (seat, train, mind)*
Él cambia de asiento con su amigo. — *He changes seats with his friend.*
Ella cambió de opinión. — *She changed her mind.*

casarse con *to marry*
Juan se casó con Isabel. — *Juan married Isabel.*

contar con *to rely on, to count on*
Yo cuento con mis amigos. — *I rely on my friends.*

creer que sí (no) *to think so (not)*
Creo que sí. — *I think so.*

cumplir . . . años *to be . . . years old*
Hoy ella cumple quince años. — *Today she is fifteen years old.*

cumplir con (su promesa, su palabra) *to fulfill, to keep (one's promise, one's word)*
Jane siempre cumple con su palabra. — *Jane always keeps her word.*

dedicarse a *to devote oneself to*
Tomás se dedica al trabajo. — *Tomás devotes himself to the work.*

dejar caer *to drop*
Ella dejó caer los platos. — *She dropped the plates.*

dejar de + infinitive *to stop, to fail to*
Él dejó de comer. — *He stopped eating.*
No deje Ud. de hacerlo. — *Don't fail to do it.*

despedirse de *to take leave of, to say goodbye to*
En la estación me despedí de mis amigos. — *In the station I said goodbye to my friends.*

echarse a + infinitive *to begin, to start to*
El niño se echa a llorar. — *The boy begins to cry.*

echar de menos *to miss*
Yo echo de menos a mis amigos. *I miss my friends.*

echar una carta al correo *to mail a letter*
Yo eché la carta al correo ayer. *I mailed the letter yesterday.*

enamorarse de *to fall in love with*
David se enamoró de Dolores. *David fell in love with Dolores.*

entrar en *to enter*
Yo entré en el cuarto. *I entered the room.*

estar a punto de *to be about to* } *to be about to*
estar para
Ellos estaban a punto de salir. *They were about to leave.*

estar de pie *to be standing*
Todos estaban de pie. *All were standing.*

estar por *to be in favor of*
Yo estoy por ir al cine. *I am in favor of going to the movies.*

gozar de *to enjoy*
Él goza de buena salud. *He enjoys good health.*

jugar a *to play (a game)*
Nosotros jugamos al tenis. *We play tennis.*

llegar a ser + noun *to become*
Llegó a ser presidente. *He became president.*

llevar a cabo *to carry out*
La secretaria llevó a cabo las órdenes de su jefe. *The secretary carried out the orders of her boss.*

negarse a + infinitive *to refuse to*
Ella se niega a firmar el cheque. *She refuses to sign the check.*

ocuparse de *to busy oneself with, to be concerned with, to attend to*
La secretaria se ocupa del correo. *The secretary attends to the mail.*

pensar de *to think of (have an opinion about)*
¿Qué piensas de mi nueva bicicleta? *What do you think of my new bicycle?*

pensar en *to think of, to think about (direct one's thoughts to)*
Juan nunca piensa en sus amigos. *John never thinks about his friends.*

poner la mesa *to set the table.*
María pone la mesa. *Mary sets the table.*

ponerse + article of clothing *to put on*
Yo me pongo el abrigo. *I put on my coat.*

ponerse + adjective *to become (involuntarily)*
Ella se puso pálida. *She became pale.*

ponerse a + infinitive *to begin to*
Los niños se pusieron a correr. *The children began to run.*

ponerse el sol *to set (referring to the sun)*
¿A qué hora se pone el sol? *At what time does the sun set?*

ponerse en camino (en marcha) *to start out, to set out*
Ellos se pusieron en camino (en marcha) tarde. *They started out late.*

prestar atención *to pay attention*
Tomás no presta atención en la clase. — *Thomas doesn't pay attention in class.*

querer a *to love (someone)*
Yo quiero a mis padres. — *I love my parents.*

querer decir *to mean*
¿Qué quiere Ud. decir? — *What do you mean?*

quitarse + article of clothing *to take off*
El señor se quita el sombrero. — *The man takes off his hat.*

reírse de *to laugh at*
Ella se ríe del muchacho. — *She laughs at the boy.*

salir bien (mal) *to come out well (poorly), to pass (fail)*
Salí bien en el examen. — *I passed the examination.*

salir *to rise (referring to the sun)*
El sol sale en el este. — *The sun rises in the east.*

salir de *to leave, to go out of*
Salgo de la escuela a las tres. — *I leave school at three o'clock.*

servirse de *to use, to make use of*
Él se sirve de la madera para hacer una mesa. — *He uses the wood to make a table.*

soñar con *to dream of*
Yo sueño con las vacaciones. — *I dream of the vacation.*

subir a *to get on (the train, bus, etc.)*
Yo subo al autobús. — *I get on the bus.*

subir (bajar) la escalera *to go upstairs (downstairs)*
Ella sube la escalera. — *She goes upstairs.*
Ella baja la escalera. — *She goes downstairs.*

tardar en + infinitive *to delay in*
El tren tardó en llegar. — *The train delayed in arriving.*

tratar de + infinitive *to try to*
Yo trato de estudiar. — *I try to study.*

volver a + infinitive *to* + *verb* + *again*
Ella vuelve a cantar. — *She sings again.*

EXERCISE J. **Several friends are discussing different topics. Complete what they say with the appropriate form of the following verbal expressions.**

soñar con	volver a	tardar en	salir mal
negarse a	enamorarse de	pensar de	querer decir
estar para	estar de pie	ponerse	prestar atención
llegar a ser	estar por	reírse de	

1. Freddy ______________ rojo cuando Gloria le besó.

2. Mi padre ______________ prestarme dinero.

3. Yo ______________ porque no hay asientos.

4. Enrique ___________ ganar la carrera.

5. Los videos ___________ llegar a las tiendas. Todavía no las tienen.

6. El hermano de Felipe ___________ mi hermana. Van a casarse.

7. ¿Qué ___________ (Uds.) la película que vimos anoche?

8. Cuando el chico se cayó, nosotros empezamos a ___________ él.

9. Víctor no comprende nada. Siempre me pregunta: «¿Qué ___________ eso?»

10. Elena está muy contenta porque decidió que quiere ___________ enfermera.

11. ¿Quiénes ___________ ir a ver el partido de fútbol mañana?

12. Felipe ___________ llamarme anoche pero yo no estaba en casa.

13. Joey siempre se pierde cuando conduce el carro porque él no ___________ a las instrucciones que le dan.

14. Miguel no puede salir por quince días porque él ___________ en los exámenes.

15. Yo ___________ salir de la casa cuando sonó el teléfono.

EXERCISE K. **Ricky's younger brother likes to ask him a lot of questions. Answer his questions.**

1. ¿Qué quiere decir «amistad»?

____

2. Para llegar al quinto piso, ¿hay que subir o bajar la escalera?

____

3. ¿A qué hora salió el sol ayer?

____

4. ¿Tratas de cocinar algunas veces?

____

5. ¿Te quitas el abrigo al entrar en la casa o al salir de la casa?

____

6. ¿De qué te sirves tú para cortar la carne?

____

7. ¿Quieres a nuestros parientes?

____

8. ¿En dónde entras tú para ver un objeto de arte?

____

9. ¿Te pones enfermo cuando comes frutas verdes?

____

10. ¿Te ocupas tú de los problemas de tus amigos?

____

11. ¿Qué piensas tú de tus maestros?

____

12. ¿Llevas a cabo los quehaceres que te da papá?

____

13. ¿Echas de menos a tus compañeros de clase durante el verano?

____

14. ¿Cumples siempre con tu palabra?

____

15. ¿Echas una carta al correo antes o después de escribirla?

____

MASTERY EXERCISES

EXERCISE L. **Vicente and Elena went shopping together. Complete his description of their shopping trip with an appropriate verbal expression.**

_______________ (*1.* There were) muchas personas cuando Elena y yo _______________ (*2.* to enter) la tienda. Yo _______________ (*3.* to be supposed to) comprar un tocacintas para mi hermano. El domingo él _______________ (*4.* to be) quince años y yo quería _______________ (*5.* to keep my promise) de comprarle un regalo bonito. Nosotros _______________ (*6.* to go downstairs) al sótano, donde venden los aparatos electrónicos. Cuando vi los precios de los tocacintas yo _______________ (*7.* to change one's mind). Elena y yo _______________ (*8.* to begin) buscar otro regalo pero nosotros no _______________ (*9.* to find) nada porque todo estaba carísimo. Yo _______________ (*10.* to love) mucho a mi hermano pero yo no _______________ (*11.* to intend) gastar todo mi dinero en un regalo para él. Yo _______________ (*12.* to think about again) qué le gustaría a él. Mientras tanto, yo _______________ (*13.* to realize) que Elena _______________ (*14.* to become) contenta. Elena decidió _______________ (*15.* to take advantage of) estar en la tienda para buscar algo para sí misma. Ella revisó el directorio de la tienda y _______________ (*16.* to go upstairs) al segundo piso, donde _______________ (*17.* there was) ropa para mujeres. Ella y yo _______________ (*18.* to agree) de reunirnos en media hora. Yo _______________ (*19.* to be about to) _______________ (*20.* to leave) ese departmento cuando vi algo que yo ______ (21. to have to) comprar para mí mismo. Era una videocasetera que estaba en barata. Yo siempre ______ (22. to feel like) tener mi propia videocasetera en mi cuarto. Yo cogí una de las videocaseteras y por fin yo ______ (23. to come upon) un dependiente. Yo le dije que yo ______ (4. to be in a hurry) pero él me dijo que ______ (25. one must) ______ (26. to be patient) porque en ese momento todos los dependientes estaban ocupados. Yo le ______ (27. to thank) por su ayuda y pagué la cuenta en la caja. A mi hermano le compré un video. Dejaré que lo vea en mi cuarto, en la nueva videocasetera. Eso es un buen regalo, ¿verdad?

EXERCISE M. Wong is trying to encourage a friend to go to a special exhibit at the museum. Express in Spanish what he says.

1. It is sunny today but it is cool.

______

2. There will be many people at the museum.

______

3. They have just opened a new exhibit.

______

4. You have to take off your backpack in the museum.

______

5. At the museum there are many things to see.

______

6. We can start out at noon.

______

7. One must attend the exhibit in order to appreciate it.

______

8. There have been many changes.

______

9. There are people who make fun of the pictures they don't understand.

______

10. Don't tell me what your sister thought of the new exhibit.

______

11. I saw the artist's first exhibit ten years ago.

______

12. After many years, the artist became famous.

______

13. People say that I act like the artist's agent.

____

14. It's important to pay attention to the guide.

____

15. We can take a walk after attending the exhibit.

____

16. If we are tired, we can get into a taxi.

____

17. I always keep my word.

____

18. I dream about working in a museum.

____

19. Don't change your mind again!

____

20. I know that you will enjoy the experience.

____

Chapter 20
Negation

[1] NEGATIVES

a. ***No*** **is the most common negative. It always precedes the conjugated verb.**

Ella **no** mira la televisión.	*She doesn't watch television.*
¿**No** leíste esta novela?	*Didn't you read this novel?*

b. Other negatives are:

nada *nothing, (not) anything*	**nunca** *never, (not) ever*
nadie *no one, nobody, (not) anyone*	**jamás** *never, not ... ever, ever*
ni . . . ni *neither . . . nor; not . . . either . . . or . . .*	**tampoco** *neither, not either*
ninguno, -a *no, none, (not) any*	

c. In Spanish double negatives are acceptable and occur frequently. If one of the negatives is ***no*****, it precedes the verb. If** ***no*** **is omitted, the other negative must precede the verb.**

No oigo **nada**.	*I don't hear anything.*	Ella **no** canta **nunca**.	*She never sings.*
Nada oigo.		Ella **nunca** canta.	

d. ***Nadie*** **can be used as the subject or the object of the verb. When** ***nadie*** **is the object of the verb, it is preceded by the preposition** ***a.***

Nadie habla.	*No one speaks.*
No habla **nadie.**	

BUT

No llamo a **nadie.**	*I don't call anyone (anybody).*
A **nadie** llamo.	*I call no one (nobody).*

e. ***Ninguno*** **drops the final** ***-o*** **and takes a written accent mark over the** ***u*** **if it comes immediately before a masculine singular noun. If a preposition comes between** ***ninguno*** **and the noun, the full form is used.**

Ningún equipo ganó.	*No team won.*
Ninguno de los equipos ganó.	*None of the teams won.*
Ninguna persona es perfecta.	*No person is perfect.*

f. ***Jamás*** **in an affirmative question means** ***ever.***

¿Has estado **jamás** en El Paso?	*Have you ever been in El Paso?*

g. Negatives are used after such expressions as ***más que*** **(more than),** ***mejor que*** **(better than),** ***peor que*** **(worse than), and** ***sin*** **(without), to express an affirmative idea.**

más que nunca *more than ever*	**sin decir nada** *without saying anything*
mejor que nadie *better than anyone*	

ODD

EXERCISE A. **You and a friend just returned from an unsuccessful shopping trip and your mother wants to know about it. Answer her questions.**

EXAMPLE: ¿Compraste el regalo para tu hermano? **No, no compré** el regalo para mi hermano.

1. ¿Encontraste los guantes negros? Sí, encontré los guantes negros.
2. ¿Buscaste el suéter para tu abuela? ______
3. ¿Llevaste el cinturón para devolverlo? No, no llevé el cinturón para devolverlo
4. ¿Había muchas personas en las tiendas? ______
5. ¿Compraste videojuegos? No, no compré videojuegos.
6. ¿Comieron Uds. en el centro? ______
7. ¿Gastaste mucho dinero? Sí, gasté mucho dinero.

EXERCISE B. **You are not in the best mood and your sister persists in asking you questions. Answer her questions.**

EXAMPLE: ¿Qué tienes? **No** tengo **nada.**

1. ¿Qué dejaste en el carro? Yo dejé nada.
2. ¿Qué perdiste en la calle? ______
3. ¿Qué comieron tú y Alfonso? Comimos nada.
4. ¿Qué buscas ahora? ______
5. ¿Qué sacaste de mi cuarto? No sacé nada.

EXERCISE C. **Jack is telling his brother the things he and his friends have never done. Tell what he says.**

EXAMPLE: volar en avión (*Jamie*) **Jamie nunca (jamás) ha volado** en avión.

1. montar a caballo (*Susana y Valerie*) Susana y Valerie nunca montaron a caballo.
2. ir a un partido de fútbol (*Gregory*) ______
3. conducir un carro (*yo*) Yo nunca conducí un carro.
4. esquiar en las montañas (*Harry y yo*) ______
5. remar en un lago (*David y Larry*) David y Larry nunca remaron en un lago.
6. correr en un maratón (*tú*) ______

EXERCISE D. **The substitute teacher is describing what happened in one of her classes today. Tell what she says.**

EXAMPLE: tener el libro **Nadie** tuvo el libro.

1. hacer la tarea ______________________________
2. contestar las preguntas ______________________________
3. estar listo para el examen ______________________________
4. saber la materia ______________________________
5. compartir las respuestas correctas ______________________________
6. querer trabajar ______________________________

EXERCISE E. **Mariluz is not paying attention in class. Give her responses to the teacher's questions.**

EXAMPLE: ¿A quién le hablas? **No** le hablo a **nadie.**

1. ¿A quién ayudas? ______________________________
2. ¿A quién saludas? ______________________________
3. ¿A quién le silbas? ______________________________
4. ¿A quién le contestas? ______________________________
5. ¿A quién miras? ______________________________
6. ¿A quién le cuchicheas? ______________________________

EXERCISE F. **It's the beginning of the school year and your mother wants to know what school supplies you have. Answer her questions.**

EXAMPLE: ¿Qué útiles tienes? **No** tengo **ningunos** útiles.

1. bolígrafo ______________________________
2. regla ______________________________
3. compás ______________________________
4. cuadernos ______________________________
5. marcadores ______________________________
6. calculadora ______________________________
7. carpetas ______________________________

-ar

aba	ábamos
abas	abais
aba	aban

EXERCISE G. Gigi is telling her mother what her friends do not do.

EXAMPLE: pasar la aspiradora / lavar los platos / Celia
Celia **no pasa** la aspiradora **ni lava** los platos.

1. sacar al perro / dar de comer al perro / Carmen

____

2. hacer la cama / arreglar su cuarto / Felipe y Rogelio

____

3. preparar la comida / ir de compras / Kim

____

4. secar los platos / planchar la ropa / Miriam y Victoria

____

5. poner la mesa / quitar la mesa / Eugenia

____

EXERCISE H. Sheila is telling Marcos the things she doesn't do or doesn't like to do. Marcos doesn't do these things either. Express what Marcos responds.

EXAMPLE: SHEILA: Yo no sé conducir un carro.
MARCOS: Yo **no** sé conducir tampoco.

1. SHEILA: Yo no monto a caballo.
MARCOS: ______________________________

2. SHEILA: No me gusta visitar los museos.
MARCOS: ______________________________

3. SHEILA: Nunca veo las películas de ciencia-ficción.
MARCOS: ______________________________

4. SHEILA: Yo no juego a muchos deportes.
MARCOS: ______________________________

5. SHEILA: No me gustan las fiestas formales.
MARCOS: ______________________________

EXERCISE I. Janice describes what happened when she accompanied her father downtown. Complete her description with the appropriate negative expressions.

Hoy ____no____ (1.) pude hacer lo que quería porque tuve que acompañar a mi papá a su oficina. La oficina ____no____ (2.) está lejos de la casa, está en el centro. ____Nadie____ (3.) había ido al centro porque era domingo. ____NO____ (4.) vimos ____nadie____ (5.) en el centro:

ninguna (6.) tienda estaba abierta, no había ningunos (7.) trabajadores en el edificio, nadie (8.) se paseaba en las calles del centro. Mi papá no (9.) tenía la llave del edificio y tocó a la puerta. Nadie (10.) contestó. Tampoco (11.) el guardia del edificio apareció. Nosotros no (12.) pasamos mucho tiempo allí. Mi papá buscó un teléfono pero ningún (13.) teléfono de la calle funcionó. Yo tenía mucha sed pero no (14.) pudimos comprar ningún (15.) refresco. ni (16.) los cafés ni (17.) los restaurantes estaban abiertos. Decidimos volver a casa. no (18.) tardamos en llegar porque no (19.) había ningún (20.) tráfico en la carretera. Cuando llegamos a casa, mi papá recibió un recado de un compañero de trabajo. Él había ido a la oficina pero no (21.) pudo entrar tampoco (22.).

[2] Negative Expressions

Some useful negative expressions are:

Ni yo tampoco. *Me neither.*

Ya no vive aquí. *He / She / You (sing. formal) no longer lives here.*

No me cobró más que un dólar. *He / She / You charged me only a dollar.*

de ninguna manera / **de ningún modo**	*by no means*	**ni siquiera**	*not even*
		Creo que no.	*I don't think so.*
No lo creo.	*I don't believe it.*	**¡No me digas!**	*Don't tell me! (You don't say!)*
De nada.	*You're welcome.*	**No me gusta nada.**	*I don't like it at all.*
No es así.	*It is not so.*	**No puede ser.**	*It can't be.*
No es para tanto.	*It's not such a big deal.*	**No puedo más.**	*I can't take it anymore.*
No hay más remedio.	*It can't be helped.*	**¿No te parece?**	*Don't you think so?*
		¿Por qué no?	*Why not?*
No importa.	*It doesn't matter.*		

EXERCISE J. **Use the following expressions to tell how you would respond to the various statements.**

No puede ser.	No hay más remedio.	De ningún modo.
De nada.	Ni yo tampoco.	No puedo más.
No me importa.	No me cobró más que un dólar.	¡No me digas!
No me gusta nada.		ya no

EXAMPLE: ¿Vive la familia Leal en esta casa?
La familia Leal **ya no** vive aquí.

1. Muchas gracias por el regalo.

____

2. Ya llevamos tres horas estudiando para el examen.

____

3. Mañana es el partido y el pronóstico dice lluvia.

____

4. ¿Qué te parece mi corbata nueva?

____

5. Tú vas a acompañarme al centro, ¿verdad?

____

6. ¿Sabías que el hermano de Javier salió con Mirta?

____

7. Yo no quiero ir al concierto el sábado.

____

8. Pagué seis dólares por la pelota.

____

9. Estoy sentado en tu asiento.

____

10. ¡Mira el reloj! ¡Ya son las siete!

____

EXERCISE K. **Alison left the following message on her friend's answering machine. Complete it using the expressions provided below.**

por qué no	ni siquiera	no lo creo
no es para tanto	ni tú tampoco	no te parece
de ninguna manera	no importa	

_______________ (1.) pero anoche me llamó Luis por teléfono. _______________ (2.) nos habíamos saludado cuando me invitó a salir con él. _______________ (3.) pero siempre he dicho que _______________ (4.) saldría con él. Tú siempre has dicho que _______________ (5.) saldrías con él. _______________ (6.) pero le dije que sí iría al baile con él. ¿ _______________ (7.)? Hice bien. ¿ _______________ (8.)? ¡Llámame!

MASTERY EXERCISES

EXERCISE L. **Answer the questions an exchange student asks you. Respond negatively to each question, using an appropriate negative expression.**

1. ¿Cuándo estuviste en España? ______________________
2. ¿Aprendes el latín o el francés? ______________________
3. ¿Qué hacen tú y tus amigos hoy? ______________________
4. ¿Has viajado jamás a Costa Rica? ______________________
5. ¿Vas al museo o a la biblioteca? ______________________
6. ¿Tiene tu amigo algunos libros interesantes? ______________________
7. ¿Qué tienes en la mano? ______________________
8. ¿Cuándo van tus amigos a Sudamérica? ¿Vas tú también? ______________________
9. ¿Tienes algún problema? ______________________
10. ¿A quién visitaste ayer? ______________________

EXERCISE M. **You are talking to a friend on the telephone. Your younger brother comments on everything you say making it negative. Tell what he says.**

EXAMPLE: Yo tengo muchos amigos. Él **no** tiene **ningunos** amigos.

1. Mis amigos vienen a mi casa o yo voy a su casa. ______________________
2. Alguien me invitó a una fiesta. ______________________
3. Yo siempre trabajo. ______________________
4. Yo me atrevo a hacer todo. ______________________
5. Yo tengo un monopatín nuevo. ______________________
6. Yo veo a mis amigos todos los días. ______________________
7. Juana y su prima lo saben. ______________________
8. Yo le expliqué todo. ______________________
9. Yo voy al concierto también. ______________________
10. Sí, todos han vuelto. ______________________

EXERCISE N. **Express in Spanish Hector's comments about a concert he attended last night.**

1. No one heard the concert last night.

____

2. The attendance was worse than ever.

3. They didn't announce the concert anywhere.

4. I couldn't believe it either.

5. Someone said that the group played better than ever.

6. Have you ever attended a concert?

7. This group never plays more than ten songs.

8. No one applauded after the first song.

9. Me neither.

10. None of my friends like to go to concerts.

11. The critics didn't say anything about the concert.

12. By no means will the group give another concert here.

13. It can't be helped.

14. It doesn't matter to me.

15. I don't have any of their records.

ACTIVIDADES

1. You are helping the team coach prepare the players for a special game. Make a list of 10 activities the players should not do before the game. Use as many of the negative words and expressions you have learned as you can.
2. Imagine that you just returned from a weekend camp reunion and that you did not enjoy it at all. Write an entry in your journal in which you describe the disappointing time you had. Use as many of the negative words and expressions you have learned as you can.

Part two

Nouns, Pronouns, and Prepositions

Chapter 21
Nouns and Articles

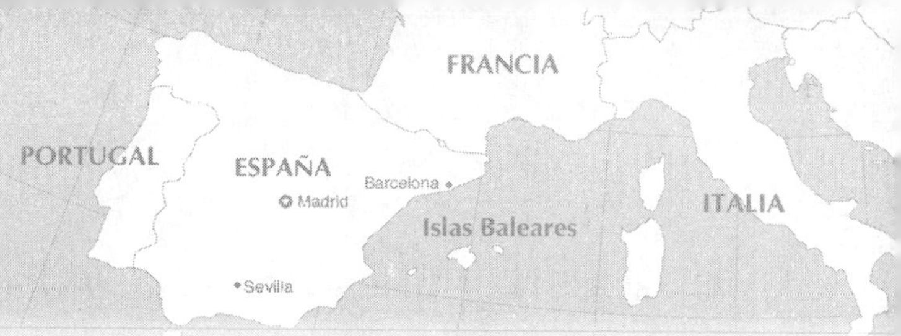

[1] NOUNS

a. Gender of Nouns

1. Most nouns in Spanish are either masculine or feminine. Nouns ending in *-o* and nouns referring to male beings are generally masculine. Nouns ending in *-a, -d, -ión* or *-z* and nouns referring to female beings are generally feminine.

MASCULINE		FEMININE			
libro	*book*	pluma	*pen*	verdad	*truth*
muchacho	*boy*	muchacha	*girl*	nación	*nation*
padre	*father*	madre	*mother*	voz	*voice*

2. Some nouns are either masculine or feminine.

estudiante	*student*
adolescente	*adolescent*

3. Some nouns are gender ambiguous.

mar	*sea*	dote	*dowry; natural gift, talent*
azúcar	*sugar*		

NOTE: Notice the following exceptions.

Feminine nouns ending in *-o*		Masculine nouns ending in *-a*			
mano	*hand*	tranvía	*streetcar*	problema	*problem*
radio	*radio*	clima	*climate*	programa	*programa*
		drama	*drama*	mapa	*map*
		idioma	*language*	poeta	*poet*

4. The gender of nouns ending in a consonant must be learned individually.

MASCULINE		FEMININE	
lápiz	*pencil*	flor	*flower*
papel	*paper*	sal	*salt*

NOTE:

1. The articles used before masculine singular nouns are *el* (the) and *un* (a, an). The articles used before feminine singular nouns are *la* (the) and *una* (a, an).

MASCULINE		FEMININE	
el hombre	*the man*	la mujer	*the woman*
un cuaderno	*a notebook*	una mesa	*a table*

2. The article is generally repeated before each noun in a series.

Necesito un lápiz y una pluma.	*I need a pencil and a pen.*
Compro el suéter y la camisa.	*I buy the sweater and the shirt.*

EXERCISE A. **You are visiting a toy store with a young child. Tell the things that you see there.**

EXAMPLE: la lancha

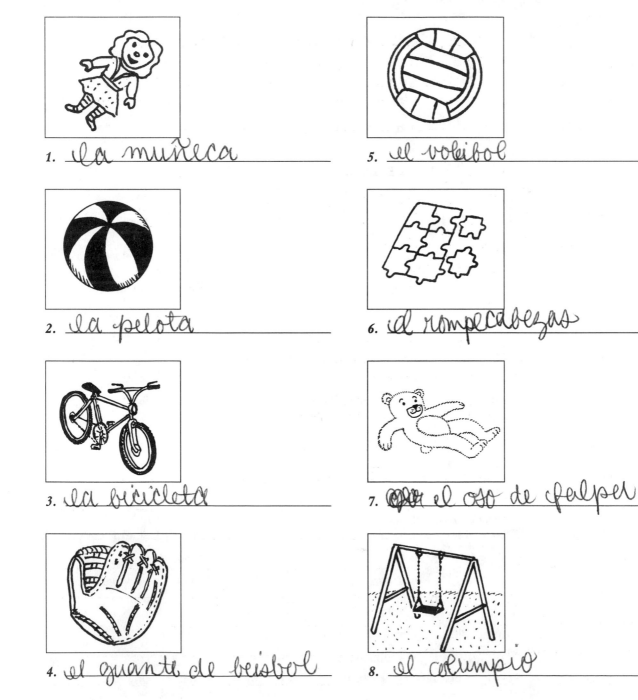

1. la muñeca

2. la pelota

3. la bicicleta

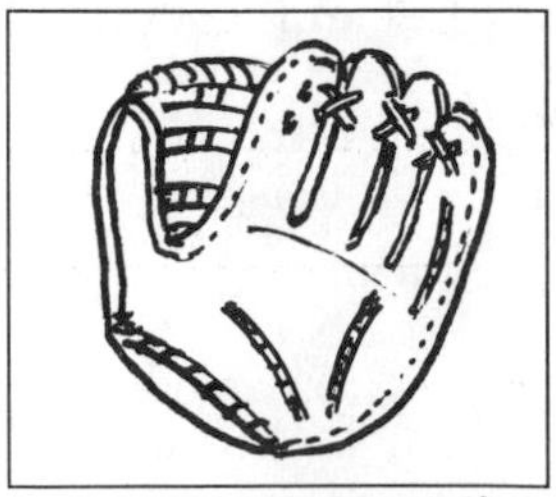

4. el guante de beisbol

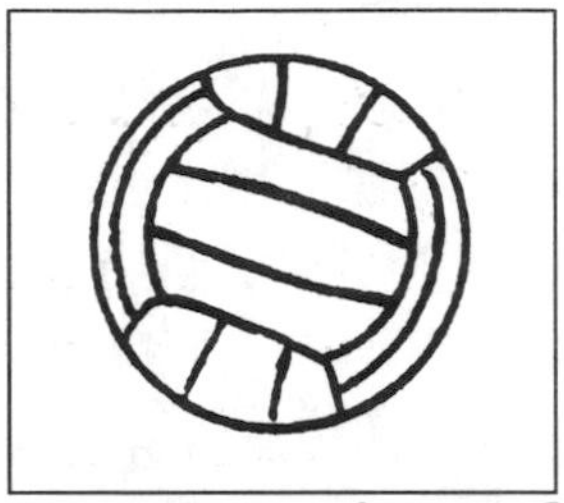

5. el voleibol

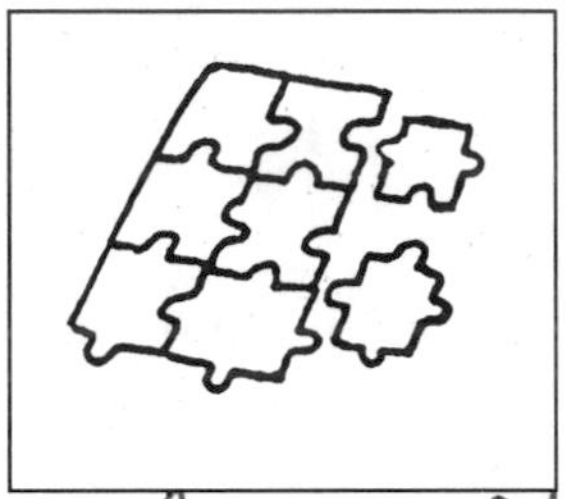

6. el rompecabezas

7. el oso de felpa

8. el columpio

9. el monopatín

10. el anuncio

EXERCISE B. **Tell what each person saw when they first entered a hotel lobby.**

EXAMPLE: Gloria / sofá elegante — Gloria **vio un** sofá elegante.

1. Arturo / restaurante francés — Arturo vio un restaurante francés
2. Esteban y Miriam / lámpara grande — Esteban y Miriam vio una lámpara grande
3. yo / ascensor abierto — Yo vio un ascensor abierto.
4. Lola / espejo antiguo — Lola vio un espejo antiguo.
5. Víctor / pintura moderna — Víctor vio una pintura moderna.
6. Sofía y Linda / alfombra persa — Sofía y Linda vio una alfombra persa.
7. Greg / lista de excursiones — Greg vio una lista de excursiones.
8. Nadia / retrato del dueño — Nadia vio un retrato de dueño.

EXERCISE C. **You are preparing for a vocabulary quiz. Read the definitions and give the appropriate word, and article.**

EXAMPLES: sesenta minutos — **una hora**
el hombre que repara zapatos — **el zapatero**

1. doce meses — un ~~el~~ año
2. un lugar como Cleveland o Dallas — Miami (una ciudad)
3. el hombre que escribe novelas — el autor
4. la parte temprana del día — ~~el noche~~ la mañana
5. el español, el árabe o el japonés — ~~[illegible]~~ las naciones
6. España, Colombia o los Estados Unidos — los idiomas (switch)
7. un instrumento que da la hora — el reloj
8. el lugar donde curan a los enfermos — el hospital
9. la persona que da clases — el/la profesor/a

10. la persona que toma clases — el/la estudiante

11. lo que se usa para escribir y no se borra — la pluma

12. el instrumento para medir — una regla

13. el libro que explica las palabras — el diccionario

14. la máquina que resuelve problemas complicados — una calculatora

15. la lista de las clases de una persona — el programa

16. el vehículo que se usa para viajar rápidamente — el tranvía

17. el lugar donde llegan los trenes — el estación

18. lo que se necesita para ver bien de noche — la linterna

19. lo que las personas usan para ver mejor — los lentes

20. la parte del cuerpo que sirve para escribir — la mano / una

b. Plural of Nouns

1. **Nouns ending in a vowel form the plural by adding *-s*.**

libro	libros	hombre	hombres
tarjeta	tarjetas	clase	clases

2. **Nouns ending in a consonant form the plural by adding *-es*.**

profesor	profesores
flor	flores

3. **Nouns ending in *-z* change *z* to *c* before adding *-es*.**

lápiz	lápices
vez	veces

4. **Nouns ending in *-n* or *-s* add *-es* and an accent mark is added or dropped to keep the original stress.**

joven	j*ó*ven*es*	francés	france*ses*
examen	ex*á*men*es*	nación	nacion*es*

NOTE:

1. ***Países*** **requires the accent mark to preserve the original stress of *país.***
2. **The plural of *plan, planes,* requires no accent mark.**

5. **Nouns ending in *-s* where the final syllable is unstressed remain the same in the plural.**

paraguas	*umbrella*	**paraguas**	*umbrellas*

BUT

mes	*month*	**meses**	*months*

6. The masculine plural form of these nouns may refer to both the male and female members of a group.

los padres	*the fathers, the father and mother, the parents*
los hijos	*the sons, the son and daughter, the children*
los niños	*the little boys, the little boy and girl, the children*
los reyes	*the kings, the king and queen, the rulers*
los señores Luna	*the Luna brothers (for example), Mr. and Mrs. Luna*

EXERCISE D. **Kristy is telling her friends at school about what happened to her during the weekend. Complete what she says with the plural form of the nouns indicated.**

El viernes por la noche unos __amigos__ (*1.* amigo) y yo fuimos a cenar a un restaurante de __mariscos__ (*2.* marisco). Aunque es un restaurante muy grande y hay dos __comedores__ (*3.* comedor) amplios, había muchas __persenas__ (*4.* persona) allí y tuvimos que esperar más de cuarenta __minutos__ (*5.* minuto) para sentarnos a la mesa. Los __meseros__ (*6.* mesero) estaban muy ocupados y por fin nos dieron un menú. Tuvimos que pedir tres __menús__ (*7.* menú) más. Preparan unos __platos__ (*8.* plato) deliciosos con muchas __variedades__ (*9.* variedad) de pescado. Yo pedí un coctel de __camarónes__ (*10.* camarón) para comenzar. Pedimos dos __ensaladas__ (*11.* ensalada), que compartimos entre los cuatro. Como plato principal yo pedí __mejillones__ (*12.* mejillón) en salsa picante. Pedimos tres __postres__ (*13.* postre) y los compartimos también. Tuvimos que pedir la cuenta dos __vezes__ (*14.* vez) porque el mesero estaba muy ocupado.

El resto de la noche no me sentí bien. Me desperté a eso de las tres, sudando y con mucho dolor de estómago. Me temblaban las __manos__ (*15.* mano) y tenía __manchas__ (*16.* mancha) en todo el cuerpo. Desperté a mis __padres__ (*17.* padre) y ellos decidieron llevarme a la sala de __emergencias__ (*18.* emergencia) del hospital. Allí dos __doctores__ (*19.* doctor) me atendieron. Ellos me hicieron muchas __preguntas__ (*20.* pregunta) sobre mis __actividades__ (*21.* actividad) recientes. Querían saber qué __cosas__ (*22.* cosa) había comido y bebido, si tomo __medicamentos__ (*23.* medicamento) y si tengo __alergias__ (*24.* alergia). Después de los __examenes__ (*25.* examen) médicos, me dieron dos __inyecciónes__ (*26.* inyección) y me recetaron unas __píldoras__ (*27.* píldora). Volvimos a casa y me acosté otra vez. Dormí profundamente por ocho __horas__ (*28.* hora) y me desperté perfectamente y con muchas __ganas__ (*29.* gana) de comer.

c. Nouns Describing Materials or Contents

Nouns describing the materials or ingredients of which something is made are preceded by *de.*

un anillo de oro	*a gold ring (a ring of gold)*
una corbata de seda	*a silk tie (a tie of silk)*
un pastel de manzana	*an apple pie (a pie of apple)*
un sándwich de pollo	*a chicken sandwich (a sandwich of chicken)*

EXERCISE E. **Janice and Ralph are going to a formal party. Describe what each wears using the suggestions provided.**

SUGGESTIONS:

un vestido de seda	zapatos de piel
un traje de lana	una corbata de seda
una camisa de algodón	un reloj de oro
un saco de terciopelo	un anillo de plata
un cinturón de piel	

1. Janice lleva ____
____.

2. Ralph lleva ____
____.

EXERCISE F. **You are planning a dinner party and find the following ingredients in the refrigerator. Plan the menu using these ingredients.**

cebollas	pepinos	manzanas
tomates	papas	camarones
carne de res	naranjas	aguacate
lechuga		

UN COCTEL ______________________

UNA SOPA ______________________

UN GUISADO ______________________

UNA ENSALADA ______________________

UN PASTEL ______________________

[2] ARTICLES

a. Definite Articles

There are four definite articles in Spanish that correspond to English *the.*

	SINGULAR	PLURAL
MASCULINE	**el**	**los**
FEMININE	**la**	**las**

Articles agree in number and gender with the nouns they modify.

MASCULINE		FEMININE	
el muchacho	*the boy*	**la** muchacha	*the girl*
los muchachos	*the boys*	**las** muchachas	*the girls*
un muchacho	*a boy*	**una** muchacha	*a girl*
unos muchachos	*some boys*	**unas** muchachas	*some girls*

NOTE:

1. Feminine nouns that begin with the stressed sound of *a* (or ha) take the articles *el* and *un* in the singular. In the plural, the articles are *las* and *unas.*

el agua	*the water*	**las** aguas	*the waters*
un agua	*one water*	**unas** aguas	*some waters*
el ala	*the wing*	**las** alas	*the wings*
un ala	*a wing*	**unas** alas	*some wings*
el hacha	*the ax*	**las** hachas	*the axes*
un hacha	*one ax*	**unas** hachas	*some axes*

BUT

la amistad *friendship*
la alumna *the (female) student* } (Initial *a* is not stressed.)

2. The masculine article *el* contracts with the prepositions *de* and *a,* as follows:

a + el = **al**
de + el = **del**

Va **al** cine.	*He goes to the movies.*
Habla **del** niño.	*He speaks of the child.*

BUT

Va **a la** playa.	*He goes to the beach.*
Habla **de los** niños.	*He speaks of the children.*

3. The neuter article *lo,* used with adjectives, does not vary in form.

lo bueno y **lo** malo — *the good and the bad (that which is good and that which is bad)*

b. Indefinite Articles

There are four indefinite articles in Spanish that correspond to English *a (an), some, several,* and *a few.*

	SINGULAR	PLURAL
MASCULINE	**un**	**unos**
FEMININE	**una**	**unas**

un primo	*a cousin*	**unos** primos	*some cousins*
una camisa	*a shirt*	**unas** camisas	*a few shirts*

EXERCISE G. As you accompany a Spanish-speaking student around your school, he identifies what he sees. Express what he says.

EXAMPLE: gimnasio: **un** gimnasio

1. aula de clase ____________________
2. laboratorios ____________________
3. auditorio ____________________
4. carteles ____________________
5. biblioteca ____________________
6. cafetería ____________________
7. salones de arte ____________________
8. oficinas ____________________
9. computadoras ____________________
10. ascensor ____________________

EXERCISE H. Felipe decided to empty his bookbag. Tell what he took out of it and left on the table.

1. ____
2. ____

3. ______________________________

4. ______________________________

5. ______________________________

6. ______________________________

7. ______________________________

8. ______________________________

9. ______________________________

10. ______________________________

c. Uses of the Articles

The definite article is used:

1. **before the names of languages and other subjects of study, unless the subjects of study follow *hablar, en,* or *de.***

El japonés es una lengua.	*Japanese is a language.*
Estudio el español.	*I study Spanish.*
La fisica es dificil.	*Physics is difficult.*

BUT

El habla español.	*He speaks Spanish.*
Escriben en francés.	*They write in French.*
Mi libro de historia está en casa.	*My history book is at home.*

2. **before titles (except when speaking directly to a person).**

El señor Pardo es alto.	*Mr. Pardo is tall.*
La doctora Pérez está aquí.	*Dr. Pérez is here.*

BUT

Buenas tardes, señor Pardo.	*Good afternoon, Mr. Pardo.*

3. **before the following geographic names.**

la América Central *Central America*	**el Canadá** *Canada*
la América del Norte *North America*	**los Estados Unidos** *the United States*
la América del Sur *South America*	**el Perú** *Peru*
la Argentina *Argentina*	**el Japón** *Japan*
la Florida *Florida*	**la China** *China*

BUT

Alemania *Germany*	**Inglaterra** *England*
España *Spain*	**Italia** *Italy*
Europa *Europe*	**México** *Mexico*
Francia *France*	**Rusia** *Russia*

NOTE: **Current usage tends to omit the definite article before the names of countries.**

Vivo en Estados Unidos. *I live in the United States.*

4. before the days of the week, to express the English word on.

No voy a la escuela los domingos.	*I don't go to school on Sundays.*

5. before the words *escuela, clase,* and *iglesia* when they follow a preposition.

Voy a la escuela.	*I'm going to school.*
Están en la iglesia.	*They are in church.*

6. before parts of the body and articles of clothing.

Se lava las manos.	*She washes her hands.*
Se pone la blusa.	*She puts on her blouse.*

7. before the names of seasons.

Hace calor en el verano.	*It's hot in summer.*

8. before nouns in a general or abstract sense.

Los libros son útiles.	*Books are useful.*
La altura me espanta.	*Height frightens me.*

9. before nouns of weight or measure.

Cuesta diez centavos la libra.	*It costs ten cents a pound.*

10. before certain time expressions and when expressing the time of day.

el mes próximo *next month*

la semana pasada *last week*

Es la una.	*It's one o'clock.*
Te llamaré a las cinco y media	*I'll call you at five thirty.*

11. The indefinite article is used to express the English word *a (an)*.

Tengo un hermano.	*I have a brother.*

12. The indefinite article is omitted before a noun expressing nationality, profession, or occupation when it follows the verb *ser.*

Tomás es alemán.	*Tomás is German.*
Ese hombre es panadero.	*That man is a baker.*
Ella va a ser médico.	*She's going to be a doctor.*

BUT

If the noun is modified, the indefinite article is used.

Deseo ser un ingeniero bueno.	*I want to be a good engineer.*

EXERCISE I. Explain each of the following.

EXAMPLE: chino / lengua El chino **es una** lengua.

1. flan / postre ____________________

2. leche / bebida ____________________

3. química / ciencia ____________________

4. Florida / estado ______

5. América del Sur / continente ______

6. Canadá / nación ______

7. primavera / estación ______

8. melocotón / fruta ______

9. miércoles / día ______

10. consomé / sopa ______

11. maíz / legumbre ______

12. voleibol / deporte ______

EXERCISE J. **Jane is studying new vocabulary words. Express the Spanish word for the following items.**

EXAMPLE: Es un carro.

1. ______

3. ______

2. ______

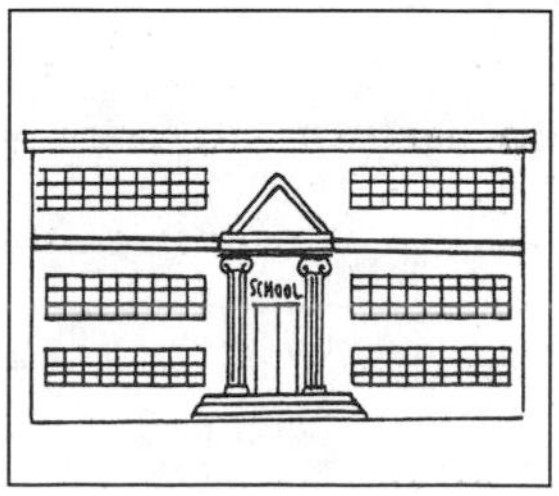

4. ______

5. ______________________

6. ______________________

7. ______________________

8. ______________________

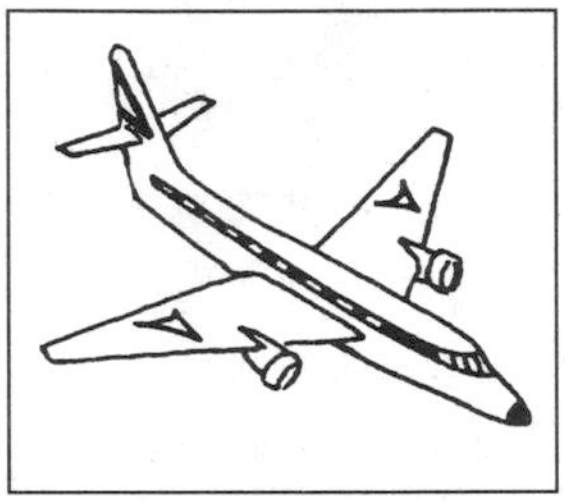

9. ______________________

10. ______________________

EXERCISE K. **Answer the questions a friend asks.**

1. ¿Cuándo celebras tu cumpleaños? ______________________
2. ¿Qué estación prefieres? ______________________
3. ¿Qué deporte te gusta más? ______________________
4. ¿Qué lengua hablan tú y tu familia en casa? ______________________
5. ¿Cuál es tu clase más difícil? ______________________
6. ¿Quién enseña esa clase? ______________________
7. ¿Qué haces los sábados por la tarde? ______________________
8. ¿Qué hora es? ______________________
9. ¿Qué hace tu padre? ______________________
10. ¿Qué países de la América del Sur piensas visitar? ______________________

d. Omission of the Articles

1. **The definite article is omitted:**

   a. before a noun in apposition.

Lima, capital del Perú, es una ciudad interesante.	*Lima, the capital of Peru, is an interesting city.*

   b. with names of rulers.

Carlos Quinto fue un rey español.	*Charles the Fifth was a Spanish king.*

2. **The indefinite article is omitted:**

   a. before an unmodified noun expressing nationality, religion, rank, or occupation following the verb *ser.*

Soy norteamericano.	*I am an American.*
¿Es Ud. protestante?	*Are you a Protestant?*
Carolina es princesa.	*Carolina is a princess.*
Reymundo es dentista.	*Reymundo is a dentist.*
BUT	
Es un abogado famoso.	*He is a famous lawyer.*

   b. with the following words:

cien:	cien dólares *a hundred dollars*
cierto/a:	cierta persona *a certain person*
mil:	mil habitantes *a thousand inhabitants*
otro/a:	otro alumno *another student*
qué:	¡Qué lástima! *What a pity!*
tal:	tal hijo *such a son*

EXERCISE L. Tell how each of these people earns a living.

EXAMPLE: Victoria Alba es **actriz.**

1. Luis Posada es ______________________________
______________________________.

2. La señora Chávez es ______________________________
______________________________.

3. El señor Laredo es ______________________ ______________________.

5. El señor Ferrer es ______________________ ______________________.

4. Virginia Ramos es ______________________ ______________________.

6. Gloria Goya es ______________________ ______________________.

EXERCISE M. Selma visited her father's office and took several messages while she waited for him. Complete the messages she took.

EXAMPLE: Miriam / secretaria / Sra. Vela / llamó
Miriam, secretaria **de la** Sra. Vela, llamó.

1. Vicente Gala / hijo / Sr. Arturo Gala / cambió su cita

____

2. Sr. Pidal / representante / compañía de telecomunicaciones / llamará más tarde.

____

3. Sra. Solana / directora / agencia federal / llamó dos veces

____

4. Ángel López / dueño / periódico «La Palabra» / llegará a las cuatro

____

5. Laura Sotomayor / ayudante / Alicia Baez / dejó otro número de teléfono

____

EXERCISE N. Using the cues provided, answer the questions the registrar asks you as you register for a summer program in Salamanca, Spain.

1. ¿Cuál es su nacionalidad? (*norteamericano*)

____

2. ¿Cuál es su profesión? (*estudiante*)

____

3. ¿Qué clase de estudiante es Ud.? (*diligente*)

____

4. ¿Qué piensa Ud. ser? (*programador de computadoras*)

____

5. ¿En qué hotel se queda Ud.? (*Carlos I*)

____

6. ¿Por qué escogió Ud. ese hotel? (*limpio y céntrico*)

____

7. ¿Cuánto pagó Ud. por el programa de estudios? (*$1.000*)

____

MASTERY EXERCISES

EXERCISE O. **Your Spanish teacher has asked the students to complete the biographical statement he wants to use with his classes next year. Complete his statement with the appropriate articles, if needed.**

Yo soy ______ (1.) señor Valencia. Mi padre es de ______ (2.) Puerto Rico y mi madre es de ______ (3.) Canadá pero yo nací en ______ (4.) Estados Unidos. Asistí a ______ (5.) Universidad de Maryland, donde estudié ______ (6.) lenguas extranjeras: ______ (7.) español y ______ (8.) portugués. Soy bilingüe porque desde chico hablo ______ (9.) inglés y ______ (10.) español. Mis intereses principales son ______ (11.) deportes y ______ (12.) viajar. Soy ______ (13.) buen jugador de ______ (14.) tenis y me gusta ______ (15.) fútbol también. He visitado muchos países extranjeros. De chico pasaba las vacaciones de ______ (16.) invierno en ______ (17.) Puerto Rico y ______ (18.) veranos en ______ (19.) Canadá. También he viajado a ______ (20.) España y a ______ (21.) América del Sur. Visité ______ (22.) Colombia, ______ (23.) Venezuela, ______ (24.) Argentina, ______ (25.) Perú y ______ (26.) Ecuador. Soy ______ (27.) profesor de idiomas extranjeros y creo ser ______ (28.) profesor interesante y divertido. Yo comencé mi carrera de ______ (29.) profesor en ______ (30.) colegio privado, ______ (31.) Colegio Felipe ______ (32.) Segundo. Tengo ______ (33.) sola meta para mis alumnos: poder comunicar en ______________ (34.) otra lengua. Si trabajamos juntos, Uds. podrán lograrla.

EXERCISE P. Cristina is writing to a new E-mail buddy. Express the following in Spanish.

1. I am Peruvian but I wasn't born in Peru. ______________
2. I was born in the United States. ______________
3. My older brother was born in Argentina. ______________
4. I attend high school. ______________
5. I work hard to be a good student. ______________
6. My favorite subjects are English, art, and social studies. ______________
7. I want to be a lawyer. ______________
8. I am a member of the school's debate team. ______________
9. I want to specialize in international law. ______________
10. I want to be a famous lawyer. ______________
11. Last year I participated in a debate competition. ______________
12. I won first place. ______________
13. The prize was $1,000. ______________
14. Ms. Martínez, the team's coach, was very happy and proud. ______________
15. I'll send you another message soon. ______________

ACTIVIDADES

1. Make a list of the school supplies you will need for the new school year. Explain why you will need each item.
2. You are going off to college and are planning what you need for your room in the dormitory. Make a list of the items you will need to furnish your dorm room and explain why each item is necessary.
3. A friend is planning to visit you soon. Write your friend a letter in which you describe the places you can visit together and give a reason for each one.

Chapter 22
Pronouns

[1] SUBJECT PRONOUNS

SINGULAR	PLURAL
yo ***I***	**nosotros, -as** ***we***
tú ***you*** **(familiar)**	**vosotros, -as** ***you*** **(familiar)**
usted (Ud.) ***you***	**ustedes (Uds.)** ***you***
él ***he***	**ellos** ***they*** **(masculine)**
ella ***she***	**ellas** ***they*** **(feminine)**

In Spanish subject pronouns are not used as often as in English. Since the verb ending indicates the subject, subject pronouns are used in Spanish for clarity, emphasis, and politeness.

Ella canta mientras **él** toca el piano.	*She sings while he plays the piano.*
Juan, **yo** debo tomar la decisión.	*Juan, I should make the decision.*
Pase y tome asiento, por favor.	*Please come in and have a seat.*

NOTE:

1. **Even though subject pronouns are usually omitted,** ***usted*** **(*Ud.*), and** ***ustedes*** **(*Uds.*) are often used for politeness.**
2. **The** ***vosotros*** **(familiar plural) form is used in Spain but rarely in Spanish America, where the** ***ustedes*** **form is preferred.**
3. **The English pronoun** ***it*** **is not expressed as a subject in Spanish.**

¿Dónde está? Está allí.	*Where is it? It's over there.*
¿Qué es? Es un disco.	*What is it? It's a record.*

EXERCISE A. Sarita wants to know the sports and games your friends practice. Use the correct subject pronouns in your responses.

EXAMPLE: Lucinda / baloncesto **Ella** practica el baloncesto.

1. Alicia y tú / boliche ______________________
2. Enrique / béisbol ______________________
3. Mirela / tenis ______________________
4. Alberto y Rafael / fútbol americano ______________________
5. tú / ajedrez ______________________
6. Estela y Alba / natación ______________________
7. Gianni / fútbol ______________________
8. Verónica / juego de damas ______________________

EXERCISE B. **A friend at school is asking you about the weekend. Answer his questions using the correct subject pronoun and the cues provided.**

1. ¿Fuiste al cine este fin de semana? (*sí*)

____

2. ¿Fueron Carlos y Eddy también? (*sí*))

____

3. ¿Vieron Uds. una película romántica? (*sí*)

____

4. ¿Prepararon tú y Jaime el proyecto para la clase de historia? (*sí*)

____

5. ¿Saliste tú con tu familia el domingo por la tarde? (*sí*)

____

6. ¿A qué hora regresaron Uds. a casa? (*8:00*)

____

7. ¿Qué vas a hacer el fin de semana que viene? (*trabajar*)

____

8. ¿Cómo son tus compañeros de trabajo? (*simpáticos*)

____

9. ¿Podemos tú y yo salir después del trabajo el sábado? (*sí*)

____

10. ¿Puede ir Silvia también? (*sí*)

____

[2] PREPOSITIONAL PRONOUNS

Prepositions are words that define a relationship to a person, place, or thing.

Common Prepositions

a *to, at*	**entre** *between, among*
cerca de *near*	**hacia** *toward*
con *with*	**para** *for*
contra *against*	**por** *for*
de *of, from*	**sin** *without*
en *in, on*	**sobre** *on top of, over*

When a personal pronoun follows a preposition, it takes the following forms:

SINGULAR	PLURAL
mí *me*	nosotros, -as *us*
ti *you* (familiar)	vosotros, -as *you* (familiar)
usted (Ud.) *you*	ustedes (Uds.) *you*
él *him, it*	ellos *them* (masculine)
ella *her, it*	ellas *them* (feminine)

a. Prepositional pronouns are used as the objects of a preposition, and always follow the preposition.

No es para Uds.; es para nosotros. *It's not for you; it's for us.*

b. The pronouns *mí* and *ti* combine with the preposition *con* as follows:

conmigo *with me* contigo *with you*

NOTE:

1. The forms of the prepositional pronouns are the same as those of the subject pronouns, except for *mí* and *ti.*
2. The forms *conmigo* and *contigo* do not change in gender and number.
3. The familiar plural form *vosotros, -as* is used in Spain but rarely in Spanish America, where the form *ustedes* (*Uds.*) is preferred.

EXERCISE C. **Everyone forgets things sometimes. Tell what these people forgot, using the correct prepositional pronoun.**

EXAMPLE: Mi papá puso las llaves en la mesa del comedor y luego salió de la casa sin **ellas.**

1. Mi mamá me dio dinero para las compras pero yo salí de la casa sin ________ .
2. El niño no pudo encontrar su osito de peluche pero se durmió sin ________ .
3. Mirta dejó la raqueta de tenis en el carro y fue a la cancha de tenis sin ________ .
4. El profesor no metió los exámenes en su mochila y llegó a la clase sin ________ .
5. Yo dejé los anteojos en casa y tuve que ver la película sin ________ .
6. Ayer por la mañana yo perdí el autobús escolar y el autobús escolar salió sin ________ .
7. Claudio no esperó a sus amigos en el estadio y entró en ________ sin ________ .
8. Bob y yo siempre llegamos tarde. Por eso Ken entró en el restaurante sin ________ .

EXERCISE D. **Answer the questions a friend asks you. Use a prepositional pronoun in your responses.**

EXAMPLE: ¿Saliste con Mirta? (*sí*) Sí, yo salí con **ella.**

1. ¿Vas a la fiesta en casa de Lisa y Mirta? (*sí*) ______________________

2. ¿Va Gladys con Frank? (*sí*) ______________________

3. ¿Viven Lisa y Mirta cerca de tu abuela? (*no*) ______________________

4. ¿Puedes ir a la fiesta sin tu hermano? (*no*) ______________________

5. ¿Compraste un regalo para Mirta? (*sí*) ______________________

6. ¿Tomas un taxi conmigo? (*sí*) ______________________

7. ¿Dividimos la cuota entre tú y yo? (*sí*) ______________________

8. ¿Va tu papá por ti por la noche? (*sí*) ______________________

9. ¿Puedo regresar con Uds.? (*sí*) ______________________

10. ¿Todavía piensas en Tommy? (*no*) ______________________

[3] DIRECT OBJECT PRONOUNS

a. **Direct objects tell who or what received the action of the verb and answer the questions whom? or what? Direct object pronouns replace direct objects and agree with them in gender and number.**

SINGULAR	PLURAL
me ***me***	**nos** ***us***
te ***you***	**os** ***you*** **(familiar)**
lo ***him, you*** **(m. formal)** ***it*** **(m.)**	**los** ***them, you*** **(masculine)**
la ***her, you*** **(f. formal);** ***it*** **(f.)**	**las** ***them, you*** **(f.)**

NOTE:

1. ***Le*** **is sometimes used instead of lo.**

2. **The plural form of both** ***le*** **and** ***lo*** **is** ***los.***

b. **The direct object pronoun is usually placed directly before the verb.**

¿Quién lee el libro?	*Who reads the book?*
El alumno **lo** lee.	*The student reads it.*
¿Compró Lola las manzanas?	*Did Lola buy the apples?*
Lola no **las** compró.	*Lola didn't buy them.*

c. **The direct object pronoun precedes the main verb or is attached to an infinitive.**

Vas a escribir una carta.	*You are going to write a letter.*

La vas a escribir.
Vas a escribir**la**. } *You are going to write it.*

Ellos no **te** quieren ver.
Ellos no quieren ver**te**. } *They don't want to see you.*

d. **Direct object pronouns follow the affirmative command, but they come immediately before the verb in the negative command.**

Cómpre**lo**.	*Buy it.*
BUT	
No **lo** compre.	*Don't buy it.*

NOTE: **When the direct object pronoun follows the affirmative command, an accent mark is normally required on the stressed vowel of the verb to keep the original stress. If the affirmative command has only one syllable (*ten*), no accent mark is required (*tenlo*).**

EXERCISE E. **You are trying out for a school team and went for a full physical examination. Answer the questions that a friend asks about the physical. Use direct object pronouns in your responses.**

EXAMPLE: ¿Quién sacó la sangre? (*la enfermera*) La enfermera **la** sacó.

1. ¿Quién hizo la cita? (*mi mamá*) ______________________
2. ¿Quién revisó tu vista? (*el médico*) ______________________
3. ¿Quién dio el examen físico? (*el médico*)
4. ¿Quién sacó las radiografías? (*un técnico*) ______________________
5. ¿Quién llenó el formulario para la escuela? (*una secretaria*) ______________________
6. ¿Quién firmó el formulario? (*el médico*) ______________________
7. ¿Quién escribió la receta para tus anteojos? (*el médico*) ______________________

EXERCISE F. **Before you leave for school, your mother asks you a series of questions. Express her questions and your responses.**

EXAMPLE: apagar el radio

MAMÁ: **¿Lo apagaste?**

TÚ: **Sí, lo apagué.** *OR* **No, no lo apagué.**

1. guardar la ropa sucia

MAMÁ: ______________________

TÚ: ______________________

2. hacer la cama

MAMÁ: ______________________________

TÚ: ______________________________

3. cerrar las ventanas

MAMÁ: ______________________________

TÚ: ______________________________

4. escuchar el pronóstico del tiempo

MAMÁ: ______________________________

TÚ: ______________________________

5. llevar un suéter

MAMÁ: ______________________________

TÚ: ______________________________

6. tomar el desayuno

MAMÁ: ______________________________

TÚ: ______________________________

7. tener todos los libros

MAMÁ: ______________________________

TÚ: ______________________________

EXERCISE G. **You are helping a friend plan a surprise party for her sister. She wants to know what you are going to do.**

EXAMPLE: colgar los adornos (*sí, no*)
¿Vas a colgarlos? (*¿Los vas a colgar?*)
Sí, **voy a colgarlos.** (*Sí, los voy a colgar.*)

OR No, **no voy a colgarlos.** (*No, no los voy a colgar.*)

1. comprar los refrescos (*sí*)

ELLA: ______________________________

TÚ: ______________________________

2. poner la mesa (*no*)

ELLA: ______________________________

TÚ: ______________________________

3. escribir las invitaciones (*sí*)

ELLA: ______________________________

TÚ: ______________________________

4. escoger los discos compactos (*sí*)

ELLA: ______________________________

TÚ: ______________________________

5. invitar a los padres (*no*)

   ELLA: ____________________

   TÚ: ____________________

6. preparar un pastel (*no*)

   ELLA: ____________________

   TÚ: ____________________

EXERCISE H. Your Spanish teacher is telling the class what to do before the first examination. Express what she says.

EXAMPLE: estudiar las lecciones **Estúdienlas.**

1. no dejar los libros en la escuela

2. aprender el vocabulario de memoria

3. traer una pluma

4. practicar los diálogos con un compañero

5. buscar las palabras desconocidas en un diccionario

6. revisar el examen bien

7. no hacer muchas preguntas durante el examen

EXERCISE I. Answer the questions that a friend asks you. Use a direct object pronoun in your responses.

EXAMPLE: ¿Mandas muchas tarjetas?
Sí, **las** mando.
OR No, no **las** mando.

1. ¿Escuchas a tus profesores?
2. ¿Ayudas a tu hermana menor?
3. ¿Compras muchas revistas de deportes?
4. ¿Bebes muchos refrescos?
5. ¿Lees el periódico todos los días?

6. ¿Invitas a tus amigos a ir al cine contigo? ______________________________

7. ¿Quieres buscar nuevos pasatiempos? ______________________________

8. ¿Visitas a tus abuelos con frecuencia? ______________________________

9. ¿Juegas al tenis? ______________________________

10. ¿Piensas vender tu bicicleta? ______________________________

[4] INDIRECT OBJECT PRONOUNS

a. Indirect objects tell to whom or for whom the action of the verb is performed and answer the question to whom? Indirect object pronouns replace indirect objects and agree with them in gender and number.

SINGULAR	PLURAL
me ***to me***	**nos** ***to us***
te ***to you*** **((familiar)**	**os** ***to you*** **((familiar)**
le ***to you*** **(formal),** ***to him, to her***	**les** ***to you*** **((formal),** ***to them*** **(m. & f.)**

NOTE:

1. The forms *le* and *les* are used as both masculine and feminine indirect object pronouns.

2. If the meaning is not clear or if we wish to add emphasis, a phrase with *a* + prepositional pronoun may be used in addition to the indirect object pronouns.

   (Clarity) Yo les escribo a ellas. *I write to them.*

   (Emphasis) A mí me encanta bailar. *I love to dance.*

   Sentences with both indirect object and indirect object pronouns are very common in Spanish.

3. The forms *me, te, nos,* and *os* are also used for direct object pronouns and for reflexive pronouns.

4. The indirect object pronoun may be identified in English by the preposition *to + a person.* The *to* may be expressed or implied.

   Les lee el cuento. *She reads the story to them. (She reads them the story.)*

b. The indirect object pronoun is usually placed before the verb.

Yo te doy el regalo. *I give the gift to you.*

Él me manda un paquete. *He sends a package to me. (He sends me a package.)*

c. When a verb is followed by an infinitive, indirect object pronouns precede the verb or are attached to the infinitive.

¿Me quieres decir algo importante?
¿Quieres decirme algo importante? } *Do you want to tell me something important?*

d. **The indirect object pronoun is attached to the end of an affirmative command, but it is placed before a negative command.**

Dígame la verdad.	*Tell the truth to me. (Tell me the truth.)*
BUT	
No me diga la verdad.	*Don't tell the truth to me. (Don't tell me the truth.)*

NOTE: **When the indirect object pronoun follows and is attached to the affirmative command, an accent mark is normally required on the stressed vowel of the verb in order to keep the original stress.**

EXERCISE J. **You and your brother are talking about the dinner you had with your family in a restaurant last night. The waiter confused everyone's order. Using the cue in parentheses, tell what each person was served.**

EXAMPLE: Mi papá pidió pescado. (*pavo*) El camarero **le** sirvió pavo.

1. Yo pedí papas fritas. (*arroz*) ________________
2. Elvira pidió una hamburguesa. (*ensalada*) ________________
3. Mi abuelo pidió te caliente. (*refresco*) ________________
4. Mi mamá y yo pedimos flan. (*pastel*) ________________
5. Jennifer y Pablo pidieron pollo. (*carne asada*) ________________
6. Tú pediste un coctel de camarones. (*ceviche*) ________________
7. Jamie pidió sopa de verduras. (*consomé*) ________________

EXERCISE K. **John is very upset because although he is always very caring and generous when his friends celebrate their birthdays, they do not reciprocate. Express what he says.**

EXAMPLE: a Verónica / mandar una tarjeta Yo **le** mandé una tarjeta.

1. a Beto / dar un disco compacto

____

2. a Rosa y a Phyllis / llevar flores

____

3. a Lorenzo / comprar boletos para un concierto

____

4. a ti / regalar un monopatín

____

5. a mis primos / mandar una suscripción de revista

____

6. a mí / nadie / dar nada

____

EXERCISE L. **Mandy is not talking to her friends and Janine is trying to "patch things up" between them. Express the suggestions Janine makes and Mandy's responses.**

EXAMPLE: pedir una disculpa a Sara y a Amy
JANINE: Tú puedes **pedirles** una disculpa.
MANDY: Yo no **les voy a pedir** una disculpa.

1. escribir una carta a Valerie
JANINE: ______
MANDY: ______

2. ofrecer una explicación a Janice y a Emma
JANINE: ______
MANDY: ______

3. hablar por teléfono a Gary
JANINE: ______
MANDY: ______

4. dar un regalito a Bárbara y a Alicia
JANINE: ______
MANDY: ______

5. mandar una tarjeta a Héctor
JANINE: ______
MANDY: ______

6. explicar por qué estás enojada conmigo
JANINE: ______
MANDY: ______

EXERCISE M. **Robert found a trunk in the attic of his house. As he goes through its contents with his mother, she tells him what to do with them. Express what his mother says.**

EXAMPLE: dar las fotos / a tu abuela **Dale** las fotos.

1. regalar estas pulseras / a tus tías ______
2. mostrar este anillo / al joyero ______
3. mandar este disco / a tu tío ______
4. ofrecer esta ropa / a una caridad ______
5. dar esta cadena / a mí ______
6. regalar estos libros / a tus amigos ______

EXERCISE N. **Mrs. Núñez is telling her children how to behave at a family reunion. Express what she says.**

EXAMPLE: a tus primos / dar la mano / no gritar **Denles** la mano; no les griten.

1. a su tío / cantar «Las mañanitas» / no cantar otra canción

____

2. a sus primos / contar un chiste / no hacer una broma

____

3. a su tía / ayudar / no dar más trabajo

____

4. a su tío / dar el regalo / no esconder el regalo

____

5. a sus tíos / hablar con cortesía / no contestar groseramente

____

[5] DOUBLE OBJECT PRONOUNS

a. When a verb has two object pronouns, the indirect object pronoun (usually referring to a person) precedes the direct object pronoun (usually a thing).

Pedro me lo da.	*Peter gives it to me.*
Pedro te la da.	*Peter gives it to you.* (fam.)
Pedro se los da.	*Peter gives them to you (him, her, them).*
Pedro nos las da.	*Peter gives them to us.*

NOTE:

1. ***Le* and *les* change to *se* before *lo, la, los, las.***

Pedro le da el libro.	*Peter gives the book to you (him, her).*
Pedro **se lo** da.	*Peter gives it to you (him, her).*

2. **The various meanings of *se* may be clarified by adding *a Ud.* (*Uds.*), *a él* (*ella*), *a ellos* (*ellas*).**

Su padre se lo da a ella (a ellas).	*Her father gives it to her (them).*

b. The position of double object pronouns is the same as for single object pronouns.

Me lo da.	*He gives it to me.*
Desea dár**melo**. **Me lo** desea dar.	*He wants to give it to me.*
Está dándo**melo**. **Me lo** está dando.	*He is giving it to me.*
¡Dé**melo** (Ud.)!	*Give it to me.*
BUT	
¡No **me lo** dé (Ud.)!	*Don't give it to me.*

NOTE: **When both object pronouns are attached to the verb, an accent mark is placed on the stressed syllable.**

EXERCISE O. **Ricky is reviewing a unit on careers and wants to be sure that he understands them. His sister confirms his statements using double object pronouns. Express what she says.**

EXAMPLE: La enfermera les da medicina a los enfermos. Sí, la enfermera **se la** da.

1. El peluquero les corta el pelo a las personas.
____
2. La profesora les enseña la lección a los alumnos.
____
3. El banquero le presta dinero al público.
____
4. El dependiente les vende cosas a los compradores.
____
5. El cocinero nos prepara la comida.
____
6. El arquitecto nos muestra algunos diseños.
____
7. El camarero les sirve la comida a los clientes.
____
8. El fotógrafo les saca fotos a las personas.
____
9. El abogado les da consejos legales a los clientes.
____
10. El científico nos mejora la vida.
____

EXERCISE P. **You help a friend empty her locker at the end of the school year. She finds that many of the things in it belong to other friends. Express what you suggest she do.**

EXAMPLE: Este suéter es de Marisol.
Se lo debes devolver.
OR Debes **devolvérselo.**

1. Este diccionario es de la señorita Almeda. ______________________________
2. Esta raqueta de tenis es tuya. ______________________________
3. Estos aretes son de mi prima Adela. ______________________________
4. Estos bolígrafos son de Enrique y Tomás. ______________________________
5. Estas camisetas son de Nanette. ______________________________

6. Este cartel es del amigo de Francisco. ______________________

7. Esta calculadora es tuya también. ______________________

8. Estas cartas son de Isabel. ______________________

EXERCISE Q. **You don't mind lending some of your things to friends but your brother disapproves of this practice. Express what your friends ask and what your brother says.**

EXAMPLE: Rogelio va a participar en una competencia de tenis y te pide prestada tu raqueta de tenis.

ROGELIO: **Préstamela.**

TU HERMANO: No **se la** prestes.

1. Jerry va a la playa y quiere usar tus anteojos de sol.

JERRY: ______________________

TU HERMANO: ______________________

2. Alfredo y Gustavo van a una fiesta en casa de sus primos y buscan ciertos discos compactos.

ELLOS: ______________________

TU HERMANO: ______________________

3. Laura tiene que llevar a su abuela al aeropuerto, pero su carro está en la estación de servicio.

LAURA: ______________________

TU HERMANO: ______________________

4. El hermano de Felipe se inscribió en una carrera de bicicleta, pero no le ha llegado su bicicleta nueva.

FELIPE: ______________________

TU HERMANO: ______________________

5. Gregorio sabe que tú no puedes ir a esquiar con ellos este fin de semana y quiere usar tus esquís.

GREGORIO: ______________________

TU HERMANO: ______________________

[6] *GUSTAR* AND OTHER VERBS WITH INDIRECT OBJECT PRONOUNS

a. Gustar (to please) is used to express "to like."

Me gusta la película.	*I like the film.*
La película me gusta.	(Literally: *The film pleases me.*)
Te gustan los dibujos animados.	*You like the cartoons.*
Los dibujos animados te gustan.	(Literally: *The cartoons please you.*)
Nos gusta nadar.	*We like to swim (swimming).*
Nadar nos gusta.	*(Literally: To swim [swimming] pleases us.)*

NOTE: **While it is more common to place the thing that is liked (noun or verb) after the verb *gustar*, it may also precede the verb.**

b. ***Gustar*** **is preceded by an indirect object pronoun. The form of *gustar* agrees with the subject, which generally follows it.**

Te gusta la fiesta.	*You like the party.*
Te gust**an** las fiestas.	*You like the parties.*
Nos gusta la canción.	*We like the song.*
Nos gust**an** las canciones.	*We like the songs.*
Me gusta bailar.	*I like to dance.*

NOTE: **If the thing liked is not a noun but an action (expressed by a verb in the infinitive), *gustar* is used in the third person singular.**

Me gust**a** bailar y cantar. *I like to dance and sing.*

c. **To clarify the indirect object pronouns *le* and *les*, or to give emphasis, the indirect object normally precedes the indirect object pronoun.**

A Tina no **le** gusta volar.	*Tina doesn't like to fly.*
A los alumnos no **les** gustan los exámenes.	*The students don't like examinations.*
A Cándida **le** gusta el pastel.	*Candida likes the cake.*
A mí **me** gusta dormir.	*I like to sleep.*

d. **Other Verbs Like *Gustar***

encantar
fascinar } *to delight* (Used for things that someone likes a lot or loves.)

Me encantan los conciertos. *I love concerts.*

parecer *to seem*

La película nos pareció corta.	*The film seemed short to us.*
Los cuentos nos parecieron aburridos.	*The stories seemed boring to us.*

NOTE: **Since *parecer* is usually followed by an adjective, the adjective must agree in number and gender with the item described.**

doler *to be painful, to cause sorrow*

Me duele la cabeza. *I have a headache.*

faltar *to be lacking, to need*

Me faltan cinco dólares. *I lack five dollars.*

quedar (a uno) *to remain (to someone), to have left*

Le queda un día de vacaciones. *He has one day of vacation left.*

tocar (a uno) *to be one's turn*

A ti te toca sacar la basura. *It's your turn to take out the garbage.*

EXERCISE R. Express what some friends say about their likes and dislikes.

EXAMPLE: a ti / gustar / las tortillas A ti **te gustan** las tortillas.

1. a Luis / no gustar / las legumbres

____

2. a mí / gustar / el café

____

3. a ellos / no gustar / los tes naturales

____

4. a nosotros / gustar / conocer restaurantes nuevos

____

5. a Silvia / encantar / los dulces

____

6. a ti / fascinar / los postres de chocolate

____

7. a Rafael y a Clara / gusta / compartir la comida

____

8. a mí / no gustar / el servicio malo en un restaurante

____

9. a nosotros / no gustar / pedir solamente un plato

____

10. a Jackie / gustar / hablar y comer al mismo tiempo

____

EXERCISE S. **Hugo just returned from a trip to Peru and Macchu Picchu. Express what he describes about the trip he made with two friends.**

EXAMPLE: a mí / tocar / hablar de mi viaje A mí **me toca** hablar de mi viaje.

1. a nosotros / encantar / la familia con que vivimos

____

2. a Daniel / faltar / muchas conveniencias norteamericanas

____

3. a mí / parecer / una experiencia formidable

____

4. a Manolo y a mí / doler la cabeza / por la altura

____

5. a nosotros / fascinar / visitar las ruinas arqueológicas

____

6. a mí / encantar / las vistas desde los picos de las montañas

____

7. a Manolo / no quedar / ningún rollo de película

____

8. a ellos / faltar / dinero para comprar curiosidades peruanas

____

9. a mí / gustar / hablar español y conocer a nuevos amigos

____

10. a Uds. / faltar / visitar este país

____

MASTERY EXERCISES

EXERCISE T. **Ruth was absent from school today and Alicia is bringing her up-to-date about what happened there. Ruth can't believe what she hears. Express Ruth's reaction using as many pronouns as possible.**

EXAMPLE: Elena le prestó diez dólares a Carolina. ¿**Se los** prestó ella?

1. Gloria comió el almuerzo con Alfredo.

____

2. Jackie quería pedirle prestado el trabajo a Gustavo.

____

3. Yo invité a Felipe a ir al baile conmigo.

____

4. Mike y Luke le hicieron muchas preguntas al profesor.

____

5. Fred vino a la escuela sin el proyecto de arte.

____

6. Janice le devolvió los aretes a Nancy.

____

7. Tú y yo tenemos que planear la celebración del Día de los Muertos.

____

8. Los alumnos escogieron a Roberto para representarnos en el concurso.

____

9. El director del grupo teatral le dio el papel principal a Elvira.

____

10. Todos los muchachos te echaron de menos a ti hoy.

____

EXERCISE U. **Lisa and her family are having a garage sale. When she returns from a break, she wants to know what happened to different objects. Express in Spanish what she says.**

1. The chess set? How much did you charge for it?

____

2. The garden chairs? Why didn't she take them with her?

____

3. I love that lamp. Please don't sell it.

____

4. The letter opener? Don't leave it there. Someone could take it.

____

5. That's my tennis racket. Why do you want to see it?

____

6. The Barbie doll. Do they want to buy it? Show it to them.

____

7. That toy? I don't want to lose it. Put it under the table.

____

8. The football banner? Joe gave it to me last year. I want to hang it in my room.

____

9. The money? Who has it?

____

10. We are going to divide the money among ourselves.

____

Chapter 23
Prepositions

Prepositions relate two elements of a sentence: noun to noun, verb to noun or pronoun, or verb to infinitive.

una cadena **de** plata	*a silver chain*	Ellos trabajan **con**migo.	*They work with me.*
Entro **en** la tienda.	*I enter the store.*	La niña comenzó **a** llorar.	*The girl began to cry.*

[*1*] Prepositional Modifiers

a. **A preposition + noun modifying another noun is equivalent to an adjective.**

una taza **de** café	*a cup of coffee*	una copa **para** vino	*a wine glass*
un anillo **de** oro	*a gold ring*		

b. **A preposition + noun modifying a verb is equivalent to an adverb.**

El anciano camina **con** cuidado. *The old man walks carefully (with care).*

EXERCISE A. **You are in a gift shop. Tell what the objects you see are made of, or explain their purpose.**

EXAMPLE: un marco / plástico — Un marco **de** plástico.
un jarro / limonada — Un jarro **para** limonada.

1. figura / porcelana ____________________

2. un baúl / madera ____________________

3. platos / ensalada ____________________

4. aretes / plata ____________________

5. espejo / lata ____________________

6. flores / seda ____________________

7. copas / champaña ____________________

8. anillo / oro ____________________

9. camiseta / algodón ____________________

10. servilletas / papel ____________________

EXERCISE B. **Tell how these people do the actions described.**

EXAMPLE: Estela habla. (*rapidez*) Estela habla **con** rapidez.

1. Mi mamá recibe a los invitados. (*gusto*) ____________________

2. Mi hermana conduce el carro. (*cuidado*) ____________________

3. Yo bailo. (*entusiasmo*) ____________________

4. Victoria cuida a su hermanita. (*cariño*) ______________________

5. Gustavo abre la carta de la universidad. (*miedo*) ______________________

6. El cajero cuenta el dinero. (*exactitud*) ______________________

7. Pilar canta. (*dulzura*) ______________________

8. Mi papá arma el juguete. (*precisión*) ______________________

[2] USES OF THE PREPOSITION *A*

a. The preposition *a* is used to indicate direction or destination.

Ella dobla **a** la izquierda. — *She turns to the left.*
Vamos **al** estadio. — *We are going to the stadium.*
Ella llegó **a** la estación. — *She arrived at the station.*

NOTE:

1. **The preposition *a* (to) combines with *el* (the) to form the contraction *al* (to the).**

   Ellos van **al** concierto. — *They are going to the concert.*
   La mamá riñe **al** niño. — *The mother scolds the child.*

2. **The preposition *a* never forms a contraction with the other articles (*la, los, las*).**

   Marta va **a** la escuela. — *Marta goes to the school.*
   El dependiente les habla **a** los clientes. — *The salesperson speaks to the customers.*

3. **In some expressions, *a* plus the definite article is used where there is no equivalent in English.**

   Nosotros jugamos **al** golf. — *We play golf.*

EXERCISE C. **Based on the drawings below, tell where Joe is going.**

EXAMPLE: Joe va al aeropuerto.

1. Joe va al museo.

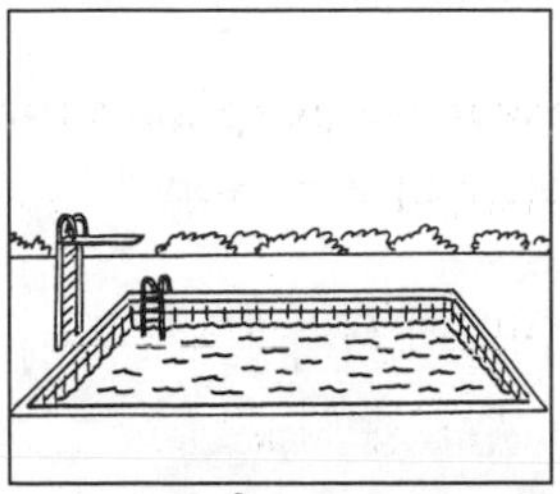

2. Joe va a la pisema.

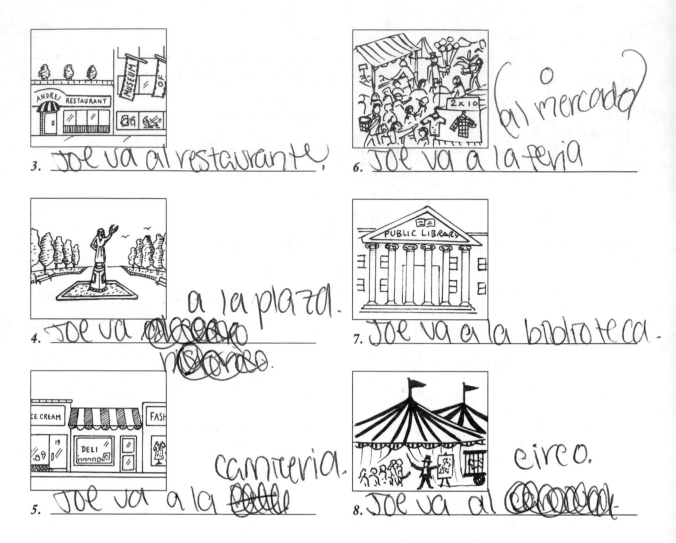

3. Joe va al restaurante,

6. Joe va a la feria (o al mercado)

4. Joe va a la plaza.

7. Joe va a la biblioteca.

5. Joe va a la cafeteria.

8. Joe va al circo.

b. **The preposition *a* is required before the direct object of a verb if the direct object is a person, a personalized group, a pet, or something personified.**

Juan visita **a** María.	*John visits Mary.*
Ella ve **al** cliente.	*She looks at the customer.*
Yo invito **a** mis primos.	*I invite my friends.*
Douglas saca **al** gato.	*Douglas takes the cat out.*

BUT

Ellos visitan la feria.	*They visit the fair.*
Joyce saca el papel.	*Joyce takes out the paper.*

c. **The preposition *a* is required before the pronouns *¿quién?, ¿quiénes?, nadie,* and *alguien,* when they refer to a person.**

No veo **a** nadie.	*I don't see anyone.*
Conocí **a** alguien en la fiesta.	*I met someone at the party.*
¿A quién buscamos?	*Whom do we look for?*

NOTE:

1. **When used before a direct object, the preposition *a* (personal *a*) has no equivalent in English. When used before an indirect object, it translates as "to."**

Vemos **a** nuestra tía.	*We see our aunt.*
Le hablamos **a** nuestra tía.	*We speak to our aunt.*

2. **The personal *a* is not used after the verb *tener* (to have).**

Tiene un hermano menor.	*He/she has a younger brother.*
Tengo muchos parientes.	*I have many relatives.*

EXERCISE D. Tell who saw or met whom at a company picnic.

EXAMPLE: yo / conocer / el dueño de la compañía — Yo conocí **al** dueño **de** la compañía.

1. Gladys / ver / su antiguo jefe ______________________
2. Felipe / conocer / la familia de su socio ______________________
3. nosotros / conocer / el esposo de la presidenta ______________________
4. la secretaria / conocer / los hijos de su jefe ______________________
5. el contador / conocer / todos los empleados El contador conoce todos los empleados.
6. mi madre / ver / la telefonista Mi madre ve la telefonista
7. mi hermano y yo / conocer / muchos niños Mi hermano y yo conocemos a muchos niños.
8. yo / ver / los colegas de mi papá Yo veo a los colegas de mi papá

EXERCISE E. Adam and his friends are discussing their plans for the evening. Tell what each one intends to do.

EXAMPLE: Adam / hablar / un amigo — Adam piensa hablar **a** un amigo.

1. Rogelio / jugar / los naipes ______________________
2. Jessie y yo / ver / una película ______________________
3. Gordon / escuchar / discos ______________________
4. Elvira / acompañar / sus hermanas ______________________
5. yo / llamar / Michael ______________________
6. Sharon / esperar / su novio ______________________

EXERCISE F. **A new Internet friend has sent you a series of questions to answer. Use complete sentences and the cues in parentheses to answer the questions.**

1. ¿A quiénes ves todos los días? (*los amigos*)

   ____

2. ¿Conoces a muchos jóvenes de tu edad? (*sí*)

   ____

3. ¿Tienes muchos amigos? (*sí*)

   ____

4. ¿A quién ayudas tú? (*mi abuelo*)

   ____

5. ¿A quién llamas tú al llegar a casa? (*nadie*)

   ____

6. ¿A quién admiras tú? (*un vecino*)

   ____

7. ¿Con qué frecuencia visitas al peluquero? (cada mes)

   ____

8. ¿A quién buscas para resolver un problema? (*mi padre*)

   ____

9. ¿Amas a tus hermanos? (*sí*)

   ____

10. ¿Escuchas a tus amigos atentamente? (*a veces*)

   ____

[3] USES OF THE PREPOSITION *DE*

a. The preposition *de* corresponds to *of, from,* or *about.*

¿De quién hablas?	*About whom are you speaking?*
Hablo del presidente.	*I'm speaking about the president.*
Recibí saludos de Elsa.	*I received regards from Elsa.*

NOTE:

1. **The preposition *de* (of, from) combines with *el* (the) to form *del* (of the, from the, about).**

Guy es el presidente **del** «Círculo Español».	*Guy is the president of the Spanish Club.*
Yo saqué dinero **del** banco.	*I took out money from the bank.*

2. **The preposition *de* never combines with the other articles (*la, los, las*) to form a single word.**

Recibí un paquete **de** las muchachas.	*I received a package from the girls.*

EXERCISE G. Tell what these people are talking about.

EXAMPLE: los padres / las vacaciones — Los padres hablan **de** las vacaciones.

1. yo / los deportes ____________________
2. el alcalde / la huelga de los taxistas ____________________
3. nosotros / el tiempo ____________________
4. tú / el examen de la clase de ciencia ____________________
5. los amigos / la fiesta ____________________
6. el profesor / las notas de los alumnos ____________________

b. In Spanish, possession is expressed as follows: noun (thing possessed) followed by *de* plus noun (possessor). This is equivalent to the English possessive expressed with *of.* In Spanish there is no apostrophe to indicate possession.

la camisa **de** Raúl	*the book of Raúl (Raúl's book)*
la muñeca **de** la niña	*the doll of the girl (the girl's doll)*
los juguetes **de** los niños	*the toys of the children (the children's toys)*

c. *¿De quién, -es?* (Whose?) is used to ask to whom something belongs.

¿De quién son las revistas?	*Whose (sing.) magazines are they?*
¿De quiénes son los tenis?	*To whom (pl.) do the sneakers belong?*

EXERCISE H. Tell to whom these objects belong.

EXAMPLE: la calculadora / el maestro — Es la calculadora **del** maestro.

1. el cuadro / pintor ____________________
2. la bandeja / mesera ____________________
3. el martillo / carpintero ____________________
4. los instrumentos musicales / músicos ____________________
5. la mochila / alumno ____________________
6. la estufa / cocinera ____________________
7. el edificio / dueño ____________________
8. las muñecas / niñas ____________________

[4] PREPOSITIONS WITH INFINITIVES

In Spanish, the infinitive is the only verb form that may immediately follow a preposition.

Ella salió **sin** cerrar la puerta.	*She went out without closing the door.*
Vamos **a** nadar en la piscina.	*We are going to swim in the pool.*
Ellos acaban **de** llegar.	*They have just arrived.*

a. Verbs Requiring *a* Before an Infinitive

Verbs expressing beginning, motion, teaching or learning, helping, and several others require the preposition *a* before an infinitive.

(1) Beginning

comenzar a + infinitive
empezar a + infinitive
ponerse a + infinitive
} *to begin to* + infinitive

El bebé se pone a llorar.	*The baby begins to cry.*
Empezamos a comer.	*We began to eat.*

(2) Motion

ir a + infinitive *to go to* + verb

Va a abrir la carta.	*He's going to open the letter.*
correr a + infinitive	*to run to* + infinitive
Corren a saludar a su papá.	*They run to greet their father.*

venir a + infinitive *to come to* + infinitive

Viene a disculparse.	*He / She is coming to ask for forgiveness.*

acercarse a + infinitive *to approach*

Se acerca a leer el anuncio.	*He/she approaches to read the announcement.*

apresurarse a + infinitive *to hurry to*

Me apresuro a hacer una llamada telefónica.	*I hurry to make a telephone call.*

(3) Teaching or Learning

enseñar a + infinitive *to teach to* + infinitive

Mi mamá me enseña a conducir.	*My mother teaches me to drive.*

aprender a + infinitive *to learn to* + infinitive

Aprendemos a bailar.	*We are learning to dance.*

(4) Helping

ayudar a + infinitive *to help (to)* + infinitive

Yo te ayudo a cocinar.	*I help you cook.*

(5) Other Verbs

acostumbrarse a + infinitive *to become accustomed to*
atreverse a + infinitive *to dare to*
convidar a + infinitive *to invite to*
decidirse a + infinitive *to decide to*
dedicarse a + infinitive *to devote oneself to*
invitar a + infinitive *to invite to*
llegar a + infinitive *to succeed in*
negarse a + infinitive *to refuse to*
obligar a + infinitive *to force, to compel to*

Se dedica a tocar el piano.	*He devotes himself to playing the piano.*

Te invité a cenar conmigo. *I invited you to have dinner with me.*
Ella llegó a ser doctora. *She succeeded in becoming a doctor.*
Se negaron a pagar la cuenta. *They refused to pay the bill.*

b. Verbs Requiring *de* Before an Infinitive

The following verbs require *de* before an infinitive:

acabar de *to have just*
acordarse de *to remember to*
alegrarse de *to be glad*
cesar de *to stop*
dejar de *to fail to, to stop*
encargarse de *to take charge of*
olvidarse de *to forget to*
tratar de *to try to*

Cesó de nevar. *It stopped snowing.*
La niña dejó de llorar. *The girl stopped crying.*
Me olvidé de echar la carta. *I forgot to mail the letter.*
Tratará de ir a la fiesta. *He / She will try to go to the party.*

c. Verbs Requiring *en* Before an Infinitive

The following verbs require the preposition *en* before an infinitive:

consentir (ie) en *to consent to*
consistir en *to consist of*
convenir en *to agree to*
insistir en *to insist on*
meterse en *to become involved in*
quedar en *to agree to*
tardar en *to be long in, to delay in*

Consiente en venir. *He / She consents to come.*
Tarda en llegar. *He / She delays in arriving.*

d. Other Common Prepositions

al (from **a** + **el**) + infinitive *on, upon*
antes de *before*
después de *after*
en vez de *instead of*
sin *without*

Al entrar en la casa, saludó a los invitados. *Upon entering the house, he/she greeted the guests.*
Antes de salir de la casa, cerré las ventanas. *Before going out, I closed the windows.*

e. Verbs Requiring No Preposition Before an Infinitive

deber *ought to, must*
dejar *to let, to allow*
desear *to desire*
esperar *to hope, to expect*
hacer *to make, to have (something done)*
lograr *to succeed in*
oír *to hear*
pensar (ie) *to intend*
poder (ue) *to be able, can*
querer (ie) *to want*
saber *to know (how)*
soler (ue) *to be in the habit of*
ver *to see*

Debe hacer el trabajo. *He/She ought to do the work.*
No me dejó entrar. *He/She did not let me enter.*
Me hace reír. *He/She makes me laugh.*
Hizo construir una casa. *He/She had a house built.*

Logró convencerle.	*He/She succeeded in convincing him.*
No lo oímos salir.	*We didn't hear him leave.*
Quiero comprar un traje.	*I want to buy a suit.*
¿Sabe Ud. tocar el piano?	*Do you know how to play the piano?*
Suele comer temprano.	*He/She is in the habit of eating early.*
Lo vi jugar.	*I saw him playing.*

EXERCISE I. Tell what the following people are doing.

EXAMPLE: mi hermana / enseñarme / bailar. Mi hermana **me enseña a** bailar.

1. el médico / apresurarse / cuidar al enfermo

____

2. la joven / aprender / conducir un carro

____

3. el niño / negarse / comer el cereal

____

4. mi amiga / convidar / cenar con ella

____

5. los padres / dedicarse / educar a los hijos

____

6. los alumnos / venir / estudiar juntos para el examen

____

7. la nieta / correr / saludar a los abuelos

____

8. el equipo / empezar / jugar el partido a las diez

____

9. todos los amigos / ayudar / colgar los adornos

____

10. el alumno tímido / no atreverse / hablar en la clase

____

EXERCISE J. Complete the message that Albert left on his friend's answering machine with the appropriate preposition.

Ya cesó ________ (*1.*) nevar. Acabo ________ (*2.*) entrar en la casa y me acordé ________ (*3.*) llamarte. Me alegro ________ (*4.*) recibir tu respuesta afirmative a mi invitación. No dejes ________ (*5.*) traer tus nuevos discos compactos. Yo me encargaré ________ (*6.*) comprar unos refrescos. No te olvides ________ (*7.*) tomar el autobús número 20 para llegar a mi casa. Trata ________ (*8.*) llegar antes de las cinco.

EXERCISE K. Tell what these people are planning to do. Use an expression from each column.

A	B
deber	nadar en una piscina
desear	comer en un restaurante
esperar	pasar las vacaciones en una isla tropical
hacer	asistir a un baile formal
pensar	visitar a los abuelos
poder	alquilar varios videos
preferir	encontrar un trabajo para el verano
querer	ir al centro comercial
soler	lavar la alfombra

EXAMPLE: Mi mamá **hace lavar la alfombra.**

1. Hugo ______________________________.

2. Luisa y Kyoko ______________________________.

3. Larry y yo ______________________________.

4. Jeffrey ______________________________.

5. Tú ______________________________.

6. Gloria ______________________________.

7. Yo ______________________________.

8. Nosotros ______________________________.

EXERCISE L. Complete each sentence with your own ideas using an infinitive.

EXAMPLE: Yo debo **empezar a** ahorrar dinero para **ir a** la universidad.

1. Yo puedo ______________________________.

2. Yo espero ______________________________.

3. Yo suelo ______________________________.

4. Yo pienso ______________________________.

5. Yo quiero ______________________________.

6. Yo debo ______________________________.

EXERCISE M. Complete the story Jack is telling a friend about his plans with some other friends with the appropriate preposition if one is needed.

Cada año, unos amigos del campamento de verano y yo solemos ________ (1.) reunirnos ________ (2.) pasar un fin de semana juntos. Este año, en vez vamos ________ (3.) ir a casa de uno de ellos, pensamos ________ (4.) ir a las montañas porque ellos desean ________ (5.) esquiar. Yo no sé ________ (6.) esquiar muy bien, pero yo consentí ________ (7.) acompañarlos porque tengo muchas ganas ________ (8.) verlos. Mis amigos

me dijeron que yo podría ________ alquilar los esquís allí. Debo ________ salir muy temprano el viernes
9. 10.
por la mañana. El autobús tarda tres horas ________ llegar a las montañas. Antes ________ ir, debo
11. 12.
________ comprar ropa gruesa porque ellos insisten ________ pasar mucho tiempo al aire libre y
13. 14.
va ________ hacer mucho frío allí. Ellos van ________ ayudarme a aprender ________ esquiar.
15. 16. 17
Trataré ________ aprender aunque no me gusta mucho practicar ________ los deportes de invierno.
18. 19.
Eddie se encarga ________ hacer las reservaciones porque él suele ________ pasar cada otro fin de
20. 21.
semana allí. El precio del fin de semana consiste ________ viajar en autobús y alojarse en una pensión
22.
con comidas cerca de la montaña donde vamos ________ esquiar. Ya comencé ________ hacer la
23. 24.
maleta. No debo ________ olvidarme ________ llevar una gorra y guantes. Trataré ________
25. 26. 27.
divertirme y acostumbrarme ________ pasar tiempo en el frío y la nieve. No dejaré ________ contarte
28. 29.
los acontecimientos del fin de semana después ________ volver a casa. Espero ________ lograr
30. 31.
________ aprender ________ esquiar mejor.
32. 33.

EXERCISE N. **Using the cues provided, answer the questions that an exchange student at school asks you.**

1. ¿Vas a llamar a tu amigo(-a) hoy? (*sí*)

____

2. ¿Qué deseas hacer esta tarde? (*ir a la librería*)

____

3. ¿Piensas hacer un viaje el año que viene? (*sí*)

____

4. ¿Te olvidaste de traer los anteojos de sol hoy? (*no*)

____

5. ¿Qué lengua aprendes a hablar? (*japonés*)

____

6. ¿Sabes conducir un carro? (*sí*)

____

7. ¿Sueles practicar la costumbre de pensar antes de hablar? (*a veces*)

____

8. ¿Tratas de conversar en japonés? (*sí*)

____

9. ¿Te alegras de vivir en esta ciudad? (*sí*)

____

10. ¿Te gusta divertirte en vez de trabajar? (*sí*)

[*5*] COMMON EXPRESSIONS WITH PREPOSITIONS

a causa de *because of*

No jugaron el partido a causa del mal tiempo. — *They didn't play the game because of the bad weather.*

a eso de *about* + time

Llegaré a eso de las siete. — *I'll arrive about seven o'clock.*

a fines de *at the end of*

Pago las cuentas a fines del mes. — *I pay the bills at the end of the month.*

a mediados de *in the middle of*

Las cuentas llegan a mediados del mes. — *The bills arrive in the middle of the month.*

a pesar de *in spite of*

A pesar de la herida, el atleta compitió en la carrera. — *In spite of the injury, the athlete competed in the race.*

a pie *on foot*

Voy al centro comercial a pie. — *I go to the mall on foot.*

a principios de *at the beginning of, early in*

Tenemos vacaciones a principios de junio. — *We have vacation at the beginning of June.*

a tiempo *on time*

Me gusta llegar a tiempo. — *I like to arrive on time.*

a través de *through, across*

Puedo ver el parque a través de la ventana. — *I can see the park through the window.*

al aire libre *outdoors, in the open air*

Prefieren comer al aire libre. — *They prefer eating outdoors.*

de hoy en adelante *from now on, henceforth*

De hoy en adelante, no voy a comer dulces. — *From now on I'm not going to eat candy.*

de otro modo *otherwise*

Termino la tarea ahora; de otro modo no podré ir al cine. — *I finish the assignment now; otherwise, I won't be able to go to the movies.*

de pie *standing*

En la clase debo estar de pie cuando contesto una pregunta. — *In class I have to be standing when I answer a question.*

de vez en cuando *from time to time*

De vez en cuando me gusta no hacer nada. — *From time to time I like to do nothing.*

desde luego *of course*

Desde luego, vimos el desfile.	*Of course we saw the parade.*

en cuanto a *as for, in regard to*

En cuanto a la deuda, te la pago pronto.	*As for the debt, I'll pay it to you soon.*

en efecto *in fact, really; yes, indeed* (as a response)

En efecto, te llamo más tarde.	*Yes, indeed, I'll call you later.*

en siete días *(in) seven days (a week)*

Tengo que entregar el trabajo en siete días.	*I have to hand in the work in seven days.*

en quince días *(in) fifteen days (two weeks)*

Regreso en quince días.	*I return in fifteen days (two weeks).*

en vez de *instead of*

Compré la blusa roja en vez de la negra.	*I bought the red blouse instead of the black one.*

EXERCISE O. Complete the response Lydia is writing to an e-mail message from a friend.

Anoche fuimos al cine _______________ (*1.* in spite of) pronóstico del tiempo. Dijeron que iba a empezar a nevar _______________ (*2.* about) las ocho de la noche y _______________ (*3.* in fact) tuvieron razón por primera vez. Llegamos al cine _______________ (*4.* on time) y _______________ (*5.* in the middle of) la película oí a un señor decir que se había asomado _______________ (*6.* through) de la puerta del cine y caía mucha nieve. Cuando salimos del cine había muchas personas _______________ (*7.* standing) en la parada del autobús, pero ningún autobús llegó y tuvimos que regresar a casa _______________ (*8.* on foot). No me gusta estar _______________ (*9.* out of doors) cuando nieva. _______________ (*10.* Because of) la nevada cancelaron las clases hasta _______________ (*11.* the beginning of) la semana que viene. _______________ (*12.* Of course), esta noticia me dio alegría pero si perdemos más días de clases, vamos a tener clases hasta _______________ (*13.* the end of) junio, _______________ (*14.* instead of) _______________ (*15.* the middle of) junio. _______________ (*16.* From now on), voy a prestar más atención al pronóstico del tiempo. _______________ (*17.* In regard to) la película, no me gustó nada.

[6] *PARA* AND *POR*

Both *para* and *por* have similar basic meanings in English. However, the use of *para* or *por* depends on the Spanish context. The meanings in English may vary with the context.

a. *Para*

(1) ***Para* expresses purpose or goal.**

Estudia para abogado.	*He studies to be a lawyer.*
Ahorré dinero para comprarlo.	*I saved money in order to buy it.*
Trabaja para ganar dinero.	*He works to earn money.*

(2) *Para* expresses the special use of an object.

Compré un cepillo para los dientes.	*I bought a toothbrush.*
Es una taza para café.	*It is a coffee cup.*

BUT

Es una taza de café.	*It is a cup of coffee.*

(3) *Para* expresses destination or direction.

Salieron para el centro.	*They left for downtown.*
Este regalo es para ellos.	*This gift is for them.*

(4) *Para* indicates a time or date in the future.

Necesito la camisa para mañana.	*I need the shirt for (by) tomorrow.*
Estarán aquí para las cinco.	*They will be here by five o'clock.*

(5) *Para* means *for* or *considering that,* when comparing a person, object, or situation with others of its kind.

Para niño, se porta bien.	*For a child, he behaves himself.*
Ella es alta para su edad.	*She is tall considering her age.*

(6) *Estar para* + infinitive means *to be about to.*

Estoy para salir.	*I am about to leave.*

EXERCISE P. Tell what you need these things for.

EXAMPLE: impermeable Necesito un impermeable **para** protegerme de la lluvia.

1. diccionario ______________________________
2. traje de baño ______________________________
3. peine ______________________________
4. champú ______________________________
5. toalla ______________________________
6. dinero ______________________________
7. cámara ______________________________

EXERCISE Q. Tell why these people are going to these destinations.

EXAMPLE: yo / tienda / suéter Yo voy a la tienda para comprar un suéter.

1. José / parque / fútbol ______________________________
2. Luis y Joan / cine / película ______________________________
3. Clara y yo / centro comercial / regalos ______________________________
4. mis amigos / montañas / esquiar ______________________________
5. Dennis / restaurante / sandwich ______________________________

6. mi papá / río / pescar ____________________

7. tú / casa de una amiga / televisión ____________________

EXERCISE R. Complete the statements you hear around the dinner table at a friend's house.

1. Deben estudiar mucho __________ asistir a la universidad.

2. __________ gozar de la buena salud, deben comer muchas frutas frescas.

3. Beber mucha agua es bueno __________ limpiar el cuerpo.

4. Dame un plato __________ ensalada, __________ favor.

5. __________ joven, eres muy listo.

6. Saldremos __________ el campo pasadomañana.

7. __________ alegrar a todo el mundo, debes sonreír mucho.

8. __________ ser un buen atleta, hay que practicar mucho.

9. Tendré el dinero __________ el sábado.

10. Estoy __________ ir al centro. Ven conmigo.

b. *Por*

(1) ***Por* introduces the agent (doer) in a passive construction.**

Esta novela fue escrita **por** Carlos Fuentes.	*This novel was written by Carlos Fuentes.*

(2) ***Por* expresses in exchange for.**

Pagamos diez dólares **por** la pluma.	*We paid ten dollars for the pen.*
Quiero cambiar estos dólares **por** pesetas.	*I want to exchange these dollars for pesetas.*

(3) ***Por* means along, through, by, and around after a verb of motion.**

Salieron **por** la puerta de atrás.	*They left through the back door.*
Caminé **por** el río.	*I walked along the river.*
Pasamos **por** allí ayer.	*We came by there yesterday.*

(4) ***Por* expresses the duration of an action.**

Fue a la escuela de verano **por** seis semanas.	*He went to summer school for six weeks.*
Estudió **por** dos horas.	*She studied for two hours.*

(5) ***Por* means for the sake of and on behalf of.**

Lo hago **por** ti.	*I am doing it for you.*
Habló **por** todo el mundo.	*He spoke on behalf of everyone.*

(6) ***Estar por* + infinitive means to be in favor of.**

Están **por** salir.	*They are in favor of leaving.*

(7) *Por* (meaning *for*) is used after *enviar* (to send), *ir* (to go), *luchar* (to fight), *mandar* (to send), *preguntar* (to ask).

Envía (Manda) **por** el médico.	*He sends for the doctor.*
Voy **por** leche.	*I am going for milk.*
Luchan **por** su patria.	*They fight for their country.*
Preguntó **por** mi mamá.	*He asked for (about) my mother.*

NOTE:

1. **_Por_ and _para_ are not used with the verbs _buscar_ (to look for, to seek), _esperar_ (to wait for, to await), and _pedir_ (to ask for, to request).**

Buscan un hotel.	*They are looking for a hotel.*
Esperé el tren.	*I waited for the train.*
Pidió un vaso de leche.	*She asked for a glass of milk.*

2. **_En_ is used instead of _por_ to mean by means of transportation.**

Mandé la carta por avión.	*I sent the letter by air.*
BUT	
Viajé por México en autobús.	*I traveled through Mexico by bus.*

EXERCISE S. Answer the questions a younger cousin asks you while you are visiting relatives.

1. ¿Te gusta dar un paseo por el centro comercial?

____

2. ¿A quién visitas para curar un dolor de muelas?

____

3. ¿Estás por ir conmigo al parque ahora mismo?

____

4. ¿Has estudiado la lección para el lunes?

____

5. ¿Tienes que correr a la escuela para llegar a tiempo?

____

6. ¿Has viajado alguna vez por el Canadá?

____

7. ¿Para qué es el jabón?

____

8. ¿Lucharías por la justicia?

____

9. ¿Envía tu mamá por el médico cuando tú tienes fiebre?

____

10. ¿Hay un estante para libros en tu cuarto?

____

EXERCISE T. **Complete the story that Rosa tells about a friend with *por* or *para*, if needed.**

Ayer ___por___ la tarde fui de compras con mi hermana. Yo quería comprar un regalo ___para___
1. _2._

un amigo que va a estudiar en México ~~por~~ ___por___ seis meses. Él sale ___para___ México el primero
 3. _4._

del próximo mes. Caminamos ___por___ el centro comercial buscando ___X___ un regalo
 5. _6._

apropiado ___para___ él. Es difícil comprar un regalo ___para___ él. La última vez que le di un
 7. _8._ exchange por

regalo le compré un suéter pero, él lo cambió ___por~~para~~___ otro. Era un suéter bonito que fue hecho
 9.

~~por~~ ~~para~~ recipient ___por~~para~~___ un diseñador famoso y pagué mucho ___para___ él. Me dijo que no era su talla.
 10. _11._

___para___ un joven, su gusto en ropa es muy conservativo. Otra amiga nos dijo que ella quería
12.

encontrarnos en el centro comercial ___para___ tomar un café. Esperamos ~~para~~ ___X~~por~~___ más de media
 13. _14._

hora pero nunca llegó. Quizás había problema en el metro porque ella viaja ~~para~~ ___por___ transporte
 15.

público. La buscamos ___~~XXX~~ por___ todas partes en el centro comercial pero no dimos con ella.
 16.

Buscamos ___X___ el regalo ~~para~~ ___por___ casi dos horas y mi hermana se ponía furiosa.
 17. _18._

___por___ fin caminamos ___para___ una librería y tomé la decisión de comprar un diccionario
19. _20._

inglés-español ___para___ él. Si no le gusta lo puede cambiar ___por___ otro libro. Compré papel
 21. _22._

de envoltura ___para___ regalo en otra tienda. Era tarde cuando fuimos al estacionamiento
 23.

___para___ recoger el carro y nos dimos cuenta de que no teníamos bastante dinero en efectivo
24.

___para___ pagar ___para___ la cuota.
25. _26._

M A S T E R Y E X E R C I S E S

EXERCISE U. **Express your feelings by completing each sentence with an infinitive and the necessary prepositions.**

EXAMPLE: Yo aprendí a conducir un carro y logré hacerlo en un mes.
 Yo espero **llegar a** ser médico y **curar a** los enfermos.

1. Yo pienso _____

2. Yo no me atrevo _____

3. Yo dejo _____

4. Yo insisto _____

5. Yo me niego _____

6. Yo consiento _____

7. Yo me acuerdo ______________________________

8. Yo me apresuro ______________________________

EXERCISE V. Complete this story with the appropriate prepositions.

El viaje ______ (1.) la carretera era larga y solitaria. Yo suelo ______ (2.) dormirme en los viajes ______ (3.) automóvil pero esta vez no podía ______ (4.) hacerlo. Nosotros íbamos ______ (5.) visitar varias universidades ______ (6.) mi hermana. ______ (7.) distraerme, traté ______ (8.) meterme ______ (9.) jugar ______ (10.) un juego. Contaría las placas de los carros que pasamos. Conté las placas ______ (11.) media hora y me decidí ______ (12.) dejar ______ (13.) hacerlo porque solamente conté diez. No me atrevía ______ (14.) decirles ______ (15.) mis papás que yo estaba aburrido. Me obligarían ______ (16.) empezar ______ (17.) leer una novela ______ (18.) la clase ______ (19.) inglés. ______ (20.) decirles algo, cerré los ojos y comencé ______ (21.) soñar. En el sueño, yo buscaba ______ (22.) un lugar donde había mucha gente y mucho ruido. Tardamos tres horas ______ (23.) llegar a la primera universidad. Yo insistí ______ (24.) ir a la cafetería ______ (25.) tomar un refresco. Quería caminar y estirarme las piernas ______ (26.) un rato. Mi hermana se negó ______ (27.) acompañarnos a la cafetería porque quería ______ (28.) caminar ______ (29.) los terrenos universitarios ______ (30.) conocer los diferentes edificios. Mis padres se decidieron ______ (31.) acompañarla. Yo me dediqué ______ (32.) buscar ______ (33.) el estadio y el gimnasio porque me interesan mucho los deportes. ______ (34.) media hora yo caminaba en círculos hasta ______ (35.) fin los encontré. Nos citamos ______ (36.) encontrarnos en la cafetería ______ (37.) las cinco. Cuando pasamos ______ (38.) el pueblo donde está la universidad, mi mamá dijo que quería ______ (39.) pasar la noche allí. Ella logró ______ (40.) convencer a mi papá y ______ (41.) visitar la universidad buscamos ______ (42.) hotel ______ (43.) pasar la noche. ______ (44.) la mañana, damos un paseo por el pueblo. ______ (45.) hacer esto, mi hermana insistió ______ (46.) volver ______ (47.) visitar la biblioteca de la universidad. ______ (48.) el mes que viene ella piensa ______ (49.) volver ______ (50.) visitar esta universidad.

EXERCISE W. Express in Spanish what Ruth tells a friend about her plans.

1. I hope to receive a scholarship in order to attend college.

____

2. In order to receive a scholarship, I should present outstanding grades.

____

3. In order to do this, I have decided to devote myself to studying a lot.

____

4. My parents intend to pay for my education, but my brother also attends college.

____

5. I want to become a civil engineer.

____

6. I must remember to speak to the college advisor at school.

____

7. She will be glad to help me look for the best college.

____

8. She is usually in her office after classes end each day in the afternoon.

____

9. I am going to make an appointment to see her at the end of the week.

____

10. I don't want to fail to investigate all the possibilities that exist.

____

11. I have already begun to look for a job for the summer.

____

12. I want to find a job that lasts for two months and save the money I earn in order to buy my college textbooks.

____

13. If I succeed in receiving a scholarship, my parents are going to be very proud.

____

14. In order to earn money, from time to time I babysit for my neighbor's children.

____

15. From now on, instead of going out with my friends, I am going to study and work hard in school.

____

ACTIVIDADES

1. Prepare a short story in Spanish in which you describe a day or afternoon you spent with a friend. Be sure to use as many verbs requiring prepositions in the story as you can.
2. Write your friend a letter in which you talk about your plans for the future and your reasons for deciding on those plans. Be sure to use as many verbs requiring prepositions in the letter as you can.
3. In celebration of good health and nutrition months, prepare a list of things people should do to improve their lives. Use *por* or *para* in as many of them as you can.

Part three

Adjectives / Adverbs and Related Structures

Chapter 24
Adjectives

[1] GENDER OF ADJECTIVES

Adjectives agree in gender (masculine or feminine) with the nouns they describe.

Adjectives ending in *-o* form the feminine by changing *-o* to *-a*. Most adjectives ending in a consonant form the feminine by adding *-a*.

ric**o**, ric**a** *rich*
delgad**o**, delgad**a** *thin*
cómic**o**, cómic**a** *funny*
español, español**a** *Spanish*
alemán, aleman**a** *German*
hablador, hablador**a** *talkative*
trabajador, trabajador**a** *hard-working*

Some adjectives, many of them ending in *-e*, have the same form for both the masculine and the feminine.

difícil, difícil *difficult*
fuerte *strong*
amable, amable *nice*
inteligente *intelligent*
grande, grande *large*
estable *stable*
agrícola, agrícola *agricultural*

[2] PLURAL OF ADJECTIVES

The plural of adjectives is formed by:

a. adding *-s* when the singular form ends in a vowel.

cómico**s**, alemana**s**, amable**s**

b. adding *-es* when the singular form ends in a consonant.

español**es**, hablador**es**, difícil**es**

NOTE:

1. **Adjectives with singular forms ending in *-z* change *z* to *c* in the plural.**
   feli**z**, feli**ces** *happy*

2. **Some adjectives add or drop an accent mark in order to keep the original stress.**
   joven, j**ó**venes *young*
   portugu**é**s, portuguesa, portugueses, portuguesas *Portuguese*
   ingl**é**s, inglesa, ingleses, inglesas *English*
   cort**é**s, corteses *polite*

EXERCISE A. **Manny is describing some of his friends. Express what he says.**

EXAMPLE: Jeanette / cómico   Jeanette **es** cómic**a**.

1. Andrés / fuerte ______________________________

2. Ruth / cortés ______________________________

3. Silvia y Estela / simpático ______________________________

4. Carlos / diligente ______________________________

5. Catherine / francés ______________________________

6. Douglas y Fernando / perezoso ______________________________

7. Jaime / tacaño ______________________________

8. Gina y Rosa / guapo ______________________________

9. Vicente y Pilar / antipático ______________________________

10. Laura / encantador ______________________________

11. Donald / responsable ______________________________

12. Harriet y Diana / hablador ______________________________

EXERCISE B. **How would you describe your teachers? Express how each one is by completing the statement with the appropriate form of one of the following adjectives.**

aburrido	divertido	inteligente	justo
bondadoso	estricto	interesante	olvidadizo
creativo	hablador	joven	severo

EXAMPLE: La profesora de historia es **interesante.**

1. El profesor / La profesora de música es ______________________________.

2. El profesor / La profesora de español es ______________________________.

3. El profesor / La profesora de historia es ______________________________.

4. El profesor / La profesora de educación física es ______________________________.

5. El profesor / La profesora de inglés es ______________________________.

6. El profesor / La profesora de ciencia es ______________________________.

7. El profesor / La profesora de matemáticas es ______________________________.

8. El profesor / La profesora de arte es ______________________________.

EXERCISE C. **Using the adjectives below, tell how you and the people indicated differ.**

alegre	cómico	hablador	tímido
amable	diligente	quieto	trabajador
antipático	generoso	serio	responsable

EXAMPLE: tu hermano Mi hermano es **responsable,** yo soy **cómico.**

1. tu mejor amigo(-a) ______________________________

2. tus padres ______________________________

3. tus hermanos(-as) ______________________________

4. tu primo(-a) ______________________________

EXERCISE D. **Adam and David rarely agree with each other. Express what David responds to Adam's statements.**

EXAMPLE: La película es **interesante.** La película es **aburrida.**

1. Es una pieza de música clásica. ______________________________

2. Los actores son conocidos. ______________________________

3. Es un cine antiguo. ______________________________

4. El argumento de la película se basa en un acontecimiento imaginario. ______________________________

5. La fotografía está borrada. ______________________________

6. El director recibió una reseña buena. ______________________________

7. Es un cine cómodo. ______________________________

8. El protagonista es viejo. ______________________________

9. Las palomitas son sabrosas. ______________________________

10. Las entradas son caras. ______________________________

[3] Position of Adjectives

a. Descriptive adjectives normally follow the nouns they describe.

una **película cómica** *a funny film* el **carro rojo** *the red car*

b. Descriptive adjectives may stand before the noun to emphasize the quality of the adjective or its inherent characteristic.

Vi los pájaros, con sus **coloridas plumas.** *I saw the birds, with their colorful feathers.*
El verano me trae **bonitos recuerdos.** *Summer brings me beautiful memories.*

NOTE:

1. Some adjectives have different meanings, depending on their position.

Lincoln fue un **gran hombre.** *Lincoln was a great man.*

BUT

Mi padre es un **hombre grande.** *My father is a big man.*

2. The following adjectives may change their meaning according to their position:

	AFTER THE NOUN	BEFORE THE NOUN
antiguo, -a	*old (ancient)*	*old (former, old-time)*
cierto, -a	*sure; true*	*a certain*
grande	*large, big*	*great*
mismo, -a	*him (her, it)-self*	*same*
nuevo, -a	*new*	*another, different*
pobre	*poor*	*unfortunate*
simple	*silly, simpleminded*	*simple, mere*

3. **Limiting adjectives (numbers, possessive and demonstrative adjectives, adjectives of quantity) usually precede the noun.**

tres lápices	*three pens*	**esa mujer**	*that woman*
ningún hombre	*no man*	**tal cosa**	*such a thing*
sus hermanos	*his brothers*	**más pan**	*more bread*

COMMON LIMITING ADJECTIVES	
algunos, -as *some*	**poco, -a, -os, -as** *little, few*
cada *each, every*	**tal** *such (a)*
cuanto, -a, -os, -as *as much*	**tanto, -a, -os, -as** *so much, so many*
más *more*	**todo, -a, -os, -as** *all, every*
menos *less*	**unos, -as** *some*
ningunos, -as no, not any	**unos, -as cuantos, -as** *a few*
numerosos, -as *numerous*	**varios, -as** *several*

[4] AGREEMENT OF ADJECTIVES

a. Adjectives agree in gender and number with the nouns they describe.

Elena es tímida.	*Elena is shy (timid).*
Los dueños son ricos.	*The owners are rich.*

b. An adjective modifying two or more nouns of different gender is masculine plural.

La rosa y el clavel son bonitos. *The rose and the carnation are pretty.*

EXERCISE E. Make a list of the things you saw on a recent trip to Costa Rica.

EXAMPLE: iglesia / mucho, antiguo **muchas** iglesias **antiguas**

1. selva / varios, tropical ______________________
2. mar / uno, tranquilo ______________________
3. montaña / uno, impresionante ______________________
4. flor / numeroso, exótico ______________________
5. hotel / alguno, elegante ______________________
6. vista / mucho, panorámico ______________________
7. insecto / varios, feo ______________________

8. persona / tanto, simpático ______________________________

9. animal / numeroso, salvaje ______________________________

10. planta / mucho, verde ______________________________

EXERCISE F. **Mr. Salinas is being relocated to another city. Complete the e-mail message he sends to his family with the appropriate forms of the adjectives given.**

Querida familia:

Yo ya encontré ______________ (*1.* el) casa ______________ (*2.* perfecto). Es ______________ (*3.* un) casa ______________ (*4.* grande) y ______________ (*5.* cómodo). ______________ (*6.* Este) casa es de dos pisos. Hay ______________ (*7.* ocho) cuartos ______________ (*8.* amplio) y ______________ (*9.* lleno) de sol. En la sala hay ______________ (*10.* un) chimenea ______________ (*11.* antiguo). Hay ______________ (*12.* un) jardín ______________ (*13.* extenso) con ______________ (*14.* mucho) árboles ______________ (*15.* viejo) y flores ______________ (*17.* bonito). También hay ______________ (*18.* un) piscina ______________ (*19.* amplio) pero tiene ______________ (*20.* un) forma ______________ (*21.* extraño). Parece ______________ (*22.* un) oreja ______________ (*23.* humano). Los dueños de la casa son ______________ (*24.* un) pareja ______________ (*25.* simpático). También conocí a ______________ (*26.* un) vecinos ______________ (*27.* amable). Creo que ______________ (*28.* este) ______________ (*29.* nuevo) casa les va a gustar a todos Uds. Nos veremos ______________ (*30.* el) semana ______________ (*31.* próximo) cuando Uds. vengan a conocer ______________ (*32.* este) ciudad ______________ (*33.* interesante) y ______________ (*34.* divertido) que pronto será su casa ______________ (*35.* nuevo).

Hasta pronto,

Papá

[5] SHORTENED FORMS OF ADJECTIVES

a. The following adjectives drop the final *-o* when used before a masculine singular noun:

uno	*one, a, an*	→	**un** pastel	*one (a) cake*
bueno	*good*	→	un **buen** jugador	*a good player*
malo	*bad*	→	un **mal** rato	*a bad time*
primero	*first*	→	el **primer** mes	*the first month*
tercero	*third*	→	el **tercer** día	*the third day*
alguno	*some*	→	**algún** año	*some year*
ninguno	*no, not any*	→	**ningún** pensamiento	*no thought*

NOTE:

1. The adjectives *alguno* and *ninguno* require an accent mark when the *-o* is dropped: *algún, ningún*

2. If a preposition comes between the adjective and the noun, the full form of the adjective is used.

el primero del mes	*the first of the month*
ninguno de los amigos	*none of the friends*

b. ***Santo*** **becomes** ***San*** **before the masculine name of a saint, except with names beginning with** ***To-*** **or** ***Do-*****.**

San Felipe	*Saint Philip*	**San Antonio**	*Saint Anthony*

BUT

Santo Tomás	*Saint Thomas*	**Santo Domingo**	*Saint Dominic*

c. ***Grande*** **becomes** ***gran*** **when used before a singular noun of either gender.**

un gran pintor
una gran pintora } *a great painter*

BUT

un río grande	*a large river*
una montaña grande	*a large mountain*

d. ***Ciento*** **becomes** ***cien*** **before a noun of either gender and before the numbers** ***mil*** **and** ***millones*****. This short form is not used with multiples of** ***ciento*** **(like** ***doscientos*** **and** ***trescientos*****) or in combination with any other number.**

cien hombres (mujeres)	*one (a) hundred men (women)*
cien mil dólares	*one (a) hundred thousand dollars*
cien millones de habitantes	*one (a) hundred million inhabitants*

BUT

seiscientos ganadores	*six hundred winners*
doscientas habitaciones	*two hundred rooms*
ciento treinta y dos comidas	*one (a) hundred thirty-two meals*

EXERCISE G. Jeremy wants to see how well you answer the trivia questions he asks you. Use a form of *bueno, malo, santo, primero, tercero, ninguno* or *alguno* in your responses.

EXAMPLE: ¿Qué dices al ver a tus padres por la mañana? **Buenos días.**

1. ¿Qué dices al describir el tiempo cuando llueve?

____

2. ¿Qué dices al describir el tiempo cuando hace un sol brillante?

____

3. ¿Qué dices cuando te preguntan el precio de estos zapatos? (*$100*)

____

4. ¿Qué dices al identificar la capital de la República Dominicana?

____

5. ¿Qué dices cuando te preguntan «¿Cuándo conocerás Madrid?»?

____

6. ¿Qué dices al identificar el nombre español de "Saint Andrew"?

____

7. ¿Qué dices al contestar la pregunta «¿Cuántos cuartos hay en ese hotel?»? (*191*)

____

8. ¿Qué dices al identificar la fecha de Año Nuevo?

____

9. ¿Qué dices al despedirte de tus padres por la noche?

____

10. ¿Qué dices cuando le deseas éxito a alguien?

____

11. ¿Qué le dices a alguien cuando se sienta a comer?

____

12. ¿Qué dices para completar el siguiente trío de islas: San Juan, Santa Cruz y . . . ?

____

13. ¿Qué dices cuando identificas las tres carabelas de Cristóbal Colón: la Niña, la Pinta y . . . ?

____

14. ¿Qué dices al identificar el equivalente del cuarto piso en un edificio en México?

____

15. ¿Qué dices al explicarle a un hombre que está libre de problemas?

____

MASTERY EXERCISES

EXERCISE H. **Describe some of the things you see as you walk through a flea market. Use the following adjectives.**

antiguo	feo	largo	pequeño	viejo
ciento	grande	nuevo	raro	

EXAMPLE: una espada larga

1. ______________________________

2. ______________________________

3. ______________________

4. ______________________

5. ______________________

6. ______________________

7. ______________________

8. ______________________

EXERCISE I. **Express your opinion about the following topics using two adjectives in each sentence.**

EXAMPLE: la natación (*un deporte*) La natación es un deporte **divertido** y **saludable.**

1. el invierno (*una estación*)

____

2. los juegos electrónicos y el ajedrez (*pasatiempos*)

____

3. la leche (*una bebida*)

____

4. la contaminación y las enfermedades (*problemas*)

____

5. el avión (*un modo de transporte*)

____

6. Puerto Rico (*una isla*)

____

7. los chícharos y las espinacas (*legumbres*)

____

8. el Día de la Raza y el Día de la Independencia de los Estados Unidos (*días festivos*)

____

EXERCISE J. **Express in Spanish what Greg tells about his summer plans.**

1. This is the third time that I am going to Spain.

____

2. I have heard interesting commentaries about the country and the Spanish people.

____

3. Spain is a large country and during the 16th and 17th centuries it was also a great European empire.

____

4. On my first trip I visited Madrid and Barcelona. They are large cosmopolitan Spanish cities.

____

5. The Spanish people are friendly, kind, and courteous.

____

6. Generally I am very timid and serious, but when I travel to Spain I am talkative and funny.

____

7. One special dream that I have is to visit the city of Pamplona during the famous festival of Saint Fermin.

____

8. A good friend went there last and took many colorful photographs.

____

9. It will be a great opportunity to practice Spanish again.

____

10. I intend to leave for Spain on July first.

____

11. Some good friends are going with me. We will stay in several new youth hostels.

____

12. We hope to visit several small cities in which there are good examples of ancient civilizations.

____

13. We plan to spend the entire month traveling in comfortable buses and trains.

____

14. Spain has very good roads and modern means of public transportation.

____

15. It is certain that we will have a good time.

____

ACTIVIDADES

1. Prepare a list of questions you would ask a new penpal to find out about his/her physical and personality traits.

2. Write a description of yourself that will help an Internet penpal identify you in a group of people. Then, describe your personality traits.

3. Write a short paragraph of six to ten sentences in which you describe two of the following:

your friends	your school and classes
your teachers	your favorite musical personality or group, entertainer, athlete, or team.

4. Write a short paragraph of six to ten sentences in which you describe your vision of the world and society twenty years from now.

Chapter 25
Demonstrative Adjectives and Pronouns

[1] DEMONSTRATIVE ADJECTIVES

Demonstrative adjectives precede the nouns they modify and agree with them in gender (masculine or feminine) and number (singular or plural).

MASCULINE	FEMININE	MEANING
este **estos**	**esta** **estas**	*this* *these*
ese **esos**	**esa** **esas**	*that* *those*
aquel **aquellos**	**aquella** **aquellas**	*that* *those*

este papel — *this paper*
esas ventanas — *those windows*

NOTE:

1. *Este* (this), *estos* (these), etc. refer to what is near or directly concerns the speaker. *Ese* (that), *esos* (these), etc. refer to what is not so near or directly concerns the person addressed. *Aquel* (that), *aquellos* (those), etc. refer to what is remote from both the speaker and the person addressed, or does not directly concern either.

   Esta novela es interesante. — *This novel is interesting.*
   Raúl, quiero **ese** libro que tienes en la mano. — *Raúl, I want that book that you have in your hand.*
   Raúl, prefiero **aquel** libro. — *Raúl, I prefer that book over there.*

2. The adverbs *aqul* (here), *ahl* (there), and *allí* ([over] there) correspond to the demonstratives *este, ese,* and *aquel,* respectively.

   Pon { esta silla **aquí.** / esa mesa **ahí.** / aquella lámpara **allí.** }
   Put { *this chair (here).* / *that table (there).* / *that lamp (over there).* }

EXERCISE A. **Paco received money for his birthday and wants to buy some sports equipment with it. Express what he asks the salesperson in the sports shop.**

EXAMPLE: raqueta de tenis — ¿Cuánto vale **esta raqueta de tenis?**

1. bicicleta ______________________________

2. guante de béisbol ______________________________

3. pelota de fútbol ______________________________

4. patines ______________________________

5. monopatín ______________________

6. pelotas de golf ______________________

7. zapatos de tenis ______________________

8. traje de baño ______________________

9. tienda de campaña ______________________

10. compás ______________________

EXERCISE B. **Lisa and a friend are visiting a museum. Express what they say about the things they see, using the proper form of *ese*.**

EXAMPLE: pintura / oscura **Esa** pintura es muy oscura.

1. estatuas / modernas ______________________

2. tapices / antiguos ______________________

3. templo / griego ______________________

4. muebles / incómodos ______________________

5. retrato / interesante ______________________

6. escalera / alta ______________________

7. paisaje / sereno ______________________

8. cuadros / feos ______________________

EXERCISE C. **Alfonso and a friend are walking around the perimeter of "El Parque del Buen Retiro" in Madrid. Express what they see as they look into the park. Use the proper form of aquel.**

EXAMPLE: árboles / viejos **Aquellos** árboles son muy viejos.

1. lago / grande ______________________

2. monumentos / interesantes ______________________

3. flores / bonitas ______________________

4. estatua / famosa ______________________

5. paseo / largo ______________________

6. barcos / divertidos ______________________

7. palmera / alta ______________________

EXERCISE D. **Hilda is in a souvenir shop in Mexico. Express what she would like to see. Use the proper demonstrative adjective.**

EXAMPLE: camiseta / ahí Quisiera ver **esa** camiseta.

1. llavero / allí ______________________

2. figura de barro / aquí ______________________

3. sarape / ahí ______________________

4. juego de ajedrez / aquí ______________________

5. huaraches / allí ______________________

6. muñeca / allí ______________________

7. canasta / ahí ______________________

8. acuarela / aquí ______________________

9. sombrero de charro / allí ______________________

10. aretes de plata / ahí ______________________

EXERCISE E. **Elsa just moved into a new neighborhood. Answer the questions she asks a neighbor about the area, using the appropriate demonstrative adjective.**

EXAMPLE: ¿Venden buen pan en la panadería de allí?
Sí, venden buen pan en **aquella** panadería.

1. ¿Venden periódicos en la librería de ahí?
____

2. ¿Hay un buen surtido de frutas en el supermercado de aquí?
____

3. ¿Juegan al tenis en el parque de allí?
____

4. ¿Es seguro caminar por las calles de ahí por la noche?
____

5. ¿Limpian bien la ropa en la tintorería de allí?
____

6. ¿Son buenos los cafés de ahí?
____

7. ¿Trabajan muchas personas en las fábricas de allí?
____

8. ¿Sirven buena comida en el restaurante de aquí?
____

9. ¿Pasan muchos taxis en la avenida de allí?
____

10. ¿Tienen buenas películas en el cine de aquí?
____

[2] Demonstrative Pronouns

MASCULINE	FEMININE	NEUTER	MEANING
éste **éstos**	**ésta** **éstas**	**esto**	*this (one)* *these*
ése **ésos**	**ésa** **ésas**	**eso**	*that (one)* *those*
aquél **aquéllos**	**aquélla** **aquéllas**	**aquello**	*that (one)* *those*

a. Demonstrative pronouns agree in number and gender with the nouns they replace.

este cuadro y aquél (cuadro) — *this painting and that (one)*

b. The neuter forms *esto, eso, aquello* refer to general statements, ideas, or an object of indeterminate gender. These forms do not vary in gender and number.

Es un hotel tranquilo, y eso les gusta a los huéspedes. — *It is a quiet hotel, and the guests like that.*

The question *¿Qué es esto (eso, aquello)?* uses the neuter form because the noun's gender is unknown. After the noun has been mentioned, the form of the demonstrative adjective or pronoun must correspond to the noun.

¿Qué es esto? —Es una piedra. — *What is this? –It is a stone.*

¿Es grande esta piedra? —Sí. — *Is this stone large? —Yes.*

NOTE: Demonstrative pronouns are distinguished from demonstrative adjectives by an accent mark. The neuter pronouns have no accent mark, since there are no corresponding neuter adjectives.

EXERCISE F. **Roberto and Emilio are buying school supplies for the new school year. They rarely agree on what to buy. Express what they say in the following dialogue using an appropriate demonstrative pronoun.**

EXAMPLE: ROBERTO: Me gustan **estas** plumas.
EMILIO: Yo prefiero **aquéllas** de allí.

1. ROBERTO: Debes comprar este libro.
   EMILIO: Voy a comprar ______________ de ahí.

2. ROBERTO: Esas gomas son muy buenas.
   EMILIO: Yo siempre uso ______________ de aquí.

3. ROBERTO: ¿Te sirven estos cuadernos?
   EMILIO: No, ______________ de allí son más útiles.

4. ROBERTO: Aquellas mochilas son muy baratas.
   EMILIO: Sí, pero ______________ de aquí son de mejor calidad.

5. ROBERTO: Esta revista es buena para la tarea de la clase de inglés.
   EMILIO: Prefiero ______________ de allí porque trata de los deportes.

6. ROBERTO: Estos bolígrafos son bonitos.

EMILIO: Voy a comprar dos de ____________ de ahí.

EXERCISE G. **Gladys is packing for a trip and is explaining why she chose the clothing she will take. Complete her statements with the appropriate demonstrative pronoun.**

EXAMPLE: Llevo esta blusa porque **ésa** de ahí no va bien con aquella falda.

1. No llevo ese chaleco porque ____________ de aquí es más bonito.

2. Estos zapatos son más cómodos que ____________ de allí.

3. Voy a llevar aquel traje de baño porque es más nuevo que ____________ de aquí.

4. Esos pantalones cortos son más prácticos que ____________ de allí.

5. Aquellas sandalias son más de moda que ____________ de ahí.

6. Estos suéteres son más ligeros que ____________ de allí.

7. Esa falda negra es más útil que ____________ de aquí de flores.

8. La única bolsa que voy a llevar es ____________ de ahí.

EXERCISE H. **Lucy is tired of listening to the comments her younger sister asks when they go out together. Complete her questions with the appropriate demonstrative pronoun based on the cue given.**

EXAMPLE: (*aquí*) ¿Qué quiere decir **esto?**

1. (*ahí*) ¿Qué es __________ ?

2. (*aquí / allí*) Yo quiero ver __________ y __________ .

3. (*ahí*) ¿Comprendes __________ ?

4. (*aquí*) ¿Viste __________ ?

5. (*aquí / ahí*) ¡Lee __________ , no leas __________ !

6. (*ahí*) Yo no recuerdo __________ .

7. (*aquí*) Yo sé __________ .

8. (*allí*) ¿Quién dijo __________ ?

9. (*ahí*) ¿Oíste __________ ?

10. (*allí*) ¿De quién es __________ ?

c. **The pronoun *éste* (*ésta, éstos, éstas*) also means *the latter* (*the latest, the most recently mentioned*); *aquél* (*aquélla, aquéllos, aquéllas*) also means *the former* (*the most remotely mentioned*).**

Ana y Susana: ésta es rubia, aquélla es morena.	*Ann and Susan: the former is brunette, the latter is blonde.*

NOTE: **In English, we usually say "the former and the latter." In Spanish, the order is reversed: *ésta* (the latter) comes first.**

EXERCISE I. Monty likes to comment on a variety of topics. Express what he says using the appropriate demonstrative pronouns.

EXAMPLE: Tengo dos cartas de Juan. En **ésta** escribe en español y en **aquélla** escribe en inglés.

1. Vicente es de la Argentina y Harry es de Inglaterra. ____________ es inglés y ____________ es argentino.
2. Carmen escribe poemas originales. A Daniel le gusta contar chistes. ____________ es muy cómico y ____________ es muy creativa.
3. Mis hermanos practican muchos deportes. Los hermanos de Berta leen muchas novelas. ____________ son serios y ____________ son activos.
4. El hermano menor de Julia siempre dice «por favor» y «gracias». Mi hermano menor nunca dice nada. ____________ es descortés y ____________ es cortés.
5. José mide seis pies. Arturo mide cuatro pies y siete pulgadas. ____________ es bajo y ____________ es alto.

EXERCISE J. Julio is usually at a loss for words and just repeats comments his friends make. Express what he says using the appropriate forms of *éste* and *aquél*.

EXAMPLE: La bicicleta roja es más ligera que la bicicleta negra.
Si, **ésta** pesa más que **aquélla.**

1. Nancy estudia más que Felipe.
   Sí, ____________ es menos diligente que ____________ .
2. La tortilla española es más sabrosa que los huevos fritos.
   Sí, ____________ son menos sabrosos que ____________ .
3. Los videojuegos son más divertidos que los juegos de mesa.
   Sí, ____________ son menos divertidos que ____________ .
4. Las películas de ciencia-ficción son emocionantes pero las películas policíacas son más emocionantes.
   Sí, ____________ son más emocionantes que ____________ .
5. El fútbol americano es divertido pero el fútbol es más divertido.
   Sí, ____________ es más divertido que ____________ .

d. **The definite article (*el, la, los, las*) followed by *de* (that of, the one of) or *que* (the one that) functions like a demonstrative pronoun.**

el (la) de Luis	*that of (the one of) Luis; Luis's*
los (las) de Luis	*those of (the ones of) Luis; Luis's*
el (la) que está aquí	*the one that is here*
los (las) que están aquí	*the ones that are here*
El profesor de Raúl es más estricto que el de Pedro.	*Raul's teacher is stricter than Peter's.*
El suéter de Nadia es muy parecido al que lleva Marta.	*Nadia's sweater is very similar to the one that Martha is wearing.*

EXERCISE K. **Mrs. Perales sent this e-mail message to one of her twin sons who are away at camp. Complete her message with the demonstrative pronoun, using the appropriate form of the article (*el, la, los, las*).**

Querido Hugo:

Hoy fui al centro para buscar las cosas que tú y tu hermano me pidieron. Pude encontrar _____________ (1.) que tú me pediste pero _____________ (2.) de tu hermano fueron más difíciles. En la tienda de deportes encontré la máscara de béisbol que me pediste pero no pude encontrar _____________ (3.) de bucear de tu hermano. Les mandaré las cosas en dos paquetes pero tengan cuidado al abrirlos porque tu paquete será muy parecido a _____________ (4.) de tu hermano. Todavía no encuentro la ropa que te falta ni _____________ (5.) de tu hermano. El sábado voy a otra tienda. Es una tienda nueva y el surtido es mejor que _____________ (6.) de la tienda donde siempre hago las compras. Será más fácil encontrar los pantalones que tú quieres, pero _____________ (7.) que quiere tu hermano ya no se ven en las tiendas. Si tengo suerte, podré terminar mis quehaceres y _____________ (8.) que Uds. me dejaron. Hasta luego.

Tu mamá

MASTERY EXERCISES

EXERCISE L. **You are on a sightseeing bus traveling through the countryside in Spain. You and the other passengers on the bus comment about what you see. Describe five things you see, using a demonstrative adjective in each.**

SUGGESTIONS:				
	aldea	iglesia	castillo	calle
	toros	montañas	paisaje	flores

EXAMPLE: **Esas** casas son de piedra.
Aquella torre es muy alta.

1. ____
2. ____
3. ____
4. ____
5. ____

EXERCISE M. **Armando usually agrees with what his friends say. Express what he says, using the appropriate form of *éste* and *aquél*.**

EXAMPLE: El italiano es un idioma bonito pero el español es más bonito.
Éste es un idioma más bonito que **aquél.**

1. El helado es un postre rico pero el flan es más rico.

____

2. Las novelas hacen regalos buenos pero los discos compactos hacen mejores regalos.

____

3. Un concurso de deletrear es emocionante pero una carrera es más emocionante.

____

4. La riqueza es una meta difícil a alcanzar pero la fama es una meta más difícil a alcanzar.

____

5. Los videojuegos son diversiones más divertidas que los juegos de mesa.

____

EXERCISE N. **Andrés and Beatriz are preparing for a picnic in the park to which they have invited their friends. Express what they say in Spanish.**

1. Those decorations are very nice.

____

2. Put this table under that tree over there.

____

3. You can put these things on those blankets over there.

____

4. Put these plates on this table and those on that one over there.

____

5. Which compact disks do you prefer, these or those?

____

6. Chairs? I didn't think about that.

____

7. What is that?

____

8. I brought this dish and and those of my mother.

____

9. Where can we hide these games?

____

10. That's a good idea.

____

ACTIVIDADES

A friend is helping you set up your room in the college dormitory. Prepare a list indicating where you will place each of your belongings illustrated in the picture. Use as many demonstrative adjectives and pronouns as you can.

Chapter 26
Possession

[*1*] Expressing Possession

a. Possession is normally expressed in Spanish by *de + the possessor.*

la camisa **de José**	*Jose's shirt*
los hijos **de los señores Ruiz**	*the Ruiz's children*
las muñecas **de la niña**	*the girl's dolls*
la bicicleta **de mi amigo**	*my friend's bicycle*

b. When the preposition *de* is followed by the definite article *el,* the contraction *del* is formed.

el babero **del** bebé	*the baby's bib*

c. When followed by a form of *ser, ¿De quién,-es . . . ?* is equivalent to the English interrogative "Whose . . . ?".

¿De quién es el carro?	*Whose car is it?*
¿De quién son los lápices?	*Whose pencils are they?*
¿De quiénes es la casa?	*Whose house is it?*
¿De quiénes son los patines?	*Whose skates are they?*

EXERCISE A. As you and your family go through customs in Mexico, the customs inspector wants to know to whom different items belong. Express the questions he asks.

EXAMPLE: muñeca **¿De quién es** la muñeca?

1. calculadora ______________________

2. teléfono celular ______________________

3. radio portátil ______________________

4. revistas ______________________

5. patines ______________________

6. anteojos ______________________

EXERCISE B. Using the questions you prepared in Exercise A, express how your father answers them according to the cues provided.

EXAMPLE: la muñeca / mi hija La muñeca es **de mi hija.**

1. la calculadora / Carlos ______________________

2. el teléfono celular / mi esposa ______________________

3. el radio portátil / el joven ______________________

4. las revistas / mis hijos ________________________________

5. los patines / mi sobrina ________________________________

6. los lentes de sol / los jóvenes ________________________________

EXERCISE C. **A friend is helping you clean the car after a family motor trip. Express the question your friend asks to find out to whom different items belong and then answer his questions.**

EXAMPLE: zapatos / Frank
¿De quién son estos zapatos? Estos zapatos **son de Frank.**

1. novelas / Grace y Emma

____

2. juego electrónico / mi hermano

____

3. dulces / mi mamá

____

4. refresco / mi abuelo

____

5. cartera / mi papá

____

6. sombrero / el señor Velasco

____

[2] POSSESSIVE ADJECTIVES

In Spanish there are two sets of possessive adjectives: a short form and a long form.

SHORT FORM	LONG FORM	MEANING
mi, mis	**mío, -a, -os, -as**	*my*
tu, tus	**tuyo, -a, -os, -as**	*your* (fam. sing.)
su, sus	**suyo, -a, -os, -as**	*his, her, its, their; your* (formal)
nuestro, -a, -os, -as	**nuestro, -a, -os, -as**	*our*
vuestro, -a, -os, -as	**vuestro, -a, -os, -as**	*your* (fam. pl.)

a. **The short forms of possessive adjectives precede the noun.**

mi casa	*my house*	**tus pañuelos**	*your handkerchiefs*
su fotografía	*his (her, its, your, their) photograph*	**nuestros juguetes**	*our toys*
nuestra escuela	*our school*		

b. **The long forms of possessive adjectives follow the noun.**

un libro **mío**	*a book of mine*	unos primos **nuestros**	*some cousins of ours*
una amiga **tuya**	*a friend of yours*		

NOTE:

1. **Possessive adjectives agree in gender (masculine or feminine) and number (singular or plural) with the person or thing possessed, not with the possessor.**

nuestra abuela	*our grandmother*
nuestras abuelas	*our grandmothers*
una cinta **tuya**	*a tape of yours (your tape)*
unas cintas **suyas**	*his / her/ its / their/ your (formal)/ your (pl.) tapes*

2. ***Nuestro* and *vuestro* have four forms. The other possessive adjectives have two forms.**

3. **To avoid ambiguity, *su* and *sus* may be replaced by the article plus de *Ud., de Uds., de él, de ella, de ellos,* or *de ellas.***

Yo vi a su mamá.	*I saw his (her, your, their) mother.*
Yo vi a la mamá de ella.	*I saw her mother.*

4. **The definite article is used instead of the possessive adjective with parts of the body or wearing apparel when the possessor is clear.**

El niño abrió **los** ojos.	*The boy opened his eyes.*
Yo me lavé **las** manos.	*I washed my hands.*
María se puso **los** lentes de sol.	*Mary put on her sunglasses.*
BUT	
María se puso **mis** lentes de sol.	*Mary put on my sunglasses.*

EXERCISE D. **Vivian is showing Frank a carton she found in the attic. He wants to know to whom these items belonged. Express what Vivian says.**

EXAMPLE: FRANK: ¿Eran **mis** botas?
VIVIAN Sí, eran **tus** botas.

1. FRANK: ¿Eran estos trenes eléctricos de Sergio y Luis?
VIVIAN: ________________________________

2. FRANK: ¿Era este reloj de Gloria?
VIVIAN: ________________________________

3. FRANK: ¿Eran estos sombreros de mi abuela?
VIVIAN: ________________________________

4. FRANK: ¿Eran estas camisetas de nuestros padres?
VIVIAN: ________________________________

5. FRANK: ¿Era mi camión?
VIVIAN: ________________________________

6. FRANK: ¿Era tu cadena de plata?

VIVIAN: ______________________________

7. FRANK: ¿Era la máscara de Luis?

VIVIAN: ______________________________

EXERCISE E. **Jean and Alice are trying to have a conversation while the stereo blasts in the background. Complete their conversation.**

EXAMPLE: JEAN: El gato de Vicki está enfermo y debe llevarlo al veterinario.
ALICE: ¿Qué debe llevar al veterinario?
JEAN: Su gato.

1. JEAN: Tengo unos discos compactos nuevos. Vamos a escucharlos.
ALICE: ¿Qué vamos a escuchar?
JEAN: ______________________________

2. JEAN: Yo tengo una bicicleta nueva. Mi hermana siempre quiere usarla.
ALICE: ¿Qué quiere usar?
JEAN: ______________________________

3. JEAN: Debemos empezar a trabajar en el proyecto que vamos a hacer juntas para la clase de ciencia.
ALICE: ¿Qué debemos hacer?
JEAN: ______________________________

4. JEAN: Elvira pidió prestadas las botas de Nora. Debe devolvérselas.
ALICE: ¿Qué debe devolver?
JEAN: ______________________________

5. JEAN: Tú nunca sigues las instrucciones que te da la maestra.
ALICE: ¿Qué nunca sigo?
JEAN: ______________________________

6. JEAN: Felipe tiene unos amigos muy simpáticos.
ALICE: ¿Quiénes son simpáticos?
JEAN: ______________________________

7. JEAN: Paula siempre tiene buenas sugerencias para divertirse.
ALICE: ¿Qué son buenas?
JEAN: ______________________________

8. JEAN: Yo le presté una llave a Berta pero ella la perdió.
ALICE: ¿Qué perdió?
JEAN: ______________________________

EXERCISE F. **Martin is telling his mother what happened in kindergarten today. Express what he says.**

EXAMPLE: Morgan se quitó los zapatos en la clase.

1. Kevin se cayó en el patio y se lastimó ________ rodilla.

2. Jorge levantó ________ mano para hacer una pregunta.

3. Yo me lavé ________ manos antes de comer.

4. Grace se cortó ________ el dedo con las tijeras.

5. Ralph no quiso leer porque olvidó ________ anteojos.

6. Mimi no quiso quitarse ________ suéter en la clase.

7. La maestra le dijo a otra maestra que le dolía ________ cabeza.

EXERCISE G. Mrs. Pacheco borrowed several items to make everything look nice for an anniversary dinner for her parents. Answer the questions her sister-in-law asks about different items.

EXAMPLE: ¿Son tus platos? Sí, son **los platos míos.**

1. ¿Es el mantel de tu mamá? ________________________

2. ¿Son mis servilletas? ________________________

3. ¿Son los candeleros de Sofía? ________________________

4. ¿Son las copas de Hilda? ________________________

5. ¿Es el florero de la señora Álvarez? ________________________

6. ¿Son los cubiertos de Uds.? ________________________

7. ¿Es el tocacintas de Pablo? ________________________

8. ¿Son los adornos de la tía Anita? ________________________

EXERCISE H. Renee and Celia are college roommates. Celia likes to compare her things with those of their friends. Answer the questions she asks.

EXAMPLE: Mi anillo es de plata. ¿Y tu anillo?
El anillo mío es de plata también.

1. Todas mis faldas son largas. ¿Y las faldas de Vivian?

____

2. Mis guantes son de piel. ¿Y tus guantes?

____

3. Todos mis zapatos son nuevos. ¿Y los zapatos de Carol y Elena?

____

4. Mi suéter es de casimir. ¿Y el suéter de Berta?

____

5. Mi computadora tiene muchísima memoria. ¿Y la computadora de Pedro?

____

6. Mi televisor mide veintisiete pulgadas. ¿Y el televisor de Uds.?

____

7. Mi calendario es electrónico. ¿Y tu calendario?

____

8. Todas las notas que recibo son sobresalientes. ¿Y tus notas?

____

EXERCISE I. There is a lot of commotion in the student dormitory on the last day of school. They realize that many of the things they have do not belong to them. React to the statements that your roommate Sandy makes.

EXAMPLE: SANDY: Enrique tiene los discos compactos de Beto.
USTED: Tienes razón, no son los discos compactos suyos; son los de Beto.

1. SANDY: Javier tiene el traje de baño de Chuck.
USTED: ____

2. SANDY: Lee tiene los libros de Marisa y Linda.
USTED: ____

3. SANDY: Fred y yo tenemos las llaves de Adam.
USTED: ____

4. SANDY: Tú tienes mi gorra.
USTED: ____

5. SANDY: Esteban tiene el diccionario de Rocío.
USTED: ____

6. SANDY: Nilda tiene los zapatos de Raquel.
USTED: ____

7. SANDY: Blanca y Sarita tienen los exámenes de Teresa.
USTED: ____

[*3*] POSSESSIVE PRONOUNS

el mío, la mía, los míos, las mías *mine*
el tuyo, la tuya, los tuyos, las tuyas *yours* (fam. sing.)
el suyo, la suya, los suyos, las suyas *his, hers, its, theirs; yours*
el nuestro, la nuestra, los nuestros, las nuestras *ours*
el vuestro, la vuestra, los vuestros, las vuestras *yours* (fam. pl.)

a. **Possessive pronouns consist of the definite article + the long form of the possessive adjective.**

b. The possessive pronoun agrees in number and gender with the noun it replaces, not with the possessor.

Mi bicicleta es más nueva que **la** (bicicleta) **suya.**	*My bicycle is newer than his.*
Esos papeles y **los** (papeles) **tuyos** son importantes.	*These papers and yours are important.*

NOTE:

1. The specific meaning of *el suyo* (*la suya, los suyos, las suyas*) may be made clear by replacing the possessive with the expressions de *Ud.* (*Uds.*), *de él* (*ella*), or *de ellos* (*ellas*) after the article.

sus discos y los **de ella**	*his records and hers*
mis monedas y las **de Uds.**	*my coins and yours*

2. After forms of *ser*, the article preceding the possessive pronoun is usually omitted.

Este cinturón **es mío.**	*This belt is mine.*
Aquellas bufandas **son suyas.**	*Those scarves are hers.*

EXERCISE J. **Jerry likes to compare his possessions with those of his friends. Express what he says using the appropriate possessive pronouns.**

EXAMPLE: Mi casa es más grande que la casa de Federico.
La mía es más grande que **la suya (la de él).**

1. Mi computadora es más moderna que la computadora de Esteban.

___

2. Mi equipo de fútbol gana más juegos que el equipo de mis primos.

___

3. Hay más libros en español en mi biblioteca que en tu biblioteca.

___

4. Mi mochila es más amplia que tus mochilas.

___

5. Nuestra tienda de campaña es más grande que la tienda de campaña de ellos.

___

6. Las uñas de mi hermana son más largas que las uñas de mi abuela.

___

7. Mi cartera es de piel pero la cartera de Alberto es de plástico.

___

8. Las bromas que yo hago son más divertidas que las bromas que hace José.

___

EXERCISE K. **Gina can never find what she is looking for. Using the cues provided, help her locate the items she needs.**

EXAMPLE: No encuentro las fotografías de mis abuelos (*en el álbum*)
Las suyas están en el álbum.

1. ¿Dónde está mi toalla? (*detrás de la puerta del baño*)

____

2. Necesito una camiseta blanca. ¿Me prestas la tuya? (*en el armario*)

____

3. Aquí está el llavero de mi hermana. ¿Dónde está mi llavero? (*en tu mochila*)

____

4. ¿Dónde están los aretes de mi mamá? (*en el estuche*)

____

5. El carro de mi mamá está delante de la casa. ¿Y el carro de mi papá? (*en la gasolinera*)

____

6. Tengo todos los regalos menos uno para ti. (*en la tienda*)

____

7. ¿No tienes tu cartera? Ni yo tampoco. (*en la mesa de la cocina*)

____

EXERCISE L. **Neil always has to borrow things when he travels with his friends. Help him obtain what he needs.**

EXAMPLE: ¿Pasta de dientes? Felipe puede prestarte **la suya.**

1. ¿Un peine? Yo puedo prestarte ______________ .
2. ¿Calcetines? Vicente puede prestarte ______________ .
3. ¿Champú? Carlos dejó ______________ en la ducha. Allí está ______________ .
4. ¿Aspirinas? Jacques dejó ______________ en el baño.
5. ¿El secador de pelo? Solamente hay uno que nosotros usamos. Puedes usar ______________ .
6. ¿Lentes de sol? Arturo tiene dos pares. Puedes usar ______________ .

MASTERY EXERCISES

EXERCISE M. **Tommy likes to tell his friends what belongs to him, to his older brother, and what is theirs. Use the long form adjective to tell to whom each item belongs.**

EXAMPLE: ¿De quién es el diccionario?
El diccionario **es suyo.**

1. ¿De quién es el perro? ________________
2. ¿De quién es la calculadora? ________________
3. ¿De quién son los juegos electrónicos? ________________
4. ¿De quién es la casa? ________________
5. ¿De quién es la raqueta de tenis? ________________
6. ¿De quién es la pelota? ________________
7. ¿De quién son los discos compactos? ________________
8. ¿De quién es el guante de béisbol? ________________
9. ¿De quién es el tocacintas? ________________
10. ¿De quién es la tienda de campaña? ________________

EXERCISE N. Jan likes to compare her things with those of her friends. Using the cues provided, complete the sentences with the appropriate possessive.

EXAMPLE: Los pantalones ______ son de algodón. ______ son de lana. ______ son de seda. (*Sarita / Gabi y Luz / yo*)

Los pantalones **de Sarita** son de algodón. **Los de ellas (los suyos)** son de lana. **Los míos** son de seda.

1. La camiseta de talla mediana es ____________ . ____________ es talla pequeña. La talla grande es ____________ . (*yo / tú / Rodolfo*)

2. ____________ carro es negro. ¿De qué color es ____________ ? ____________ es azul. (*yo / Ud. / nosotros*)

3. Flor perdió las llaves ____________ . ¿Tienes ____________ ? Yo no encuentro ____________ . (*Flor / ella / yo*)

4. ____________ mochila es negra. ____________ es azul. ¿De qué color es ____________ ? (*tú / yo / Ana*)

5. El reloj ____________ es elegante. ____________ es para uso diario. ____________ es modelo deportivo. (*Linda / Tere / yo*)

EXERCISE O.

1. My house is large and spacious.

   ____

2. I live there with my parents and my brothers and sisters.

   ____

3. My mother's brother lives in a house on the same street.

   ____

4. His house is not as large as ours.

   ____

5. Our house is older than theirs.

   ____

6. My uncle and his family like to swim in our pool when theirs isn't working.

   ____

7. My cousins have their friends and I have mine.

   ____

8. Our relatives confuse our addresses frequently.

   ____

9. They don't remember that my uncle's house is green and ours is white.

   ____

10. I share my bicycle with my cousin and he shares his with me.

   ____

ACTIVIDADES

You have just gotten a new gadget (piece of sports equipment, computer, computer program, etc.) that you believe is superior to the one your friend has. Write ten statements in which you describe and compare yours and your friend's. Use as many possessive adjectives and pronouns as you can in each statement.

Chapter 27.
Comparisons

[1] Comparisons of Equality

a. *Tan* + adjective (or adverb) + *como* = as . . . as

Jorge es **tan fuerte como** tú.	*Jorge is as strong as you.*
Ellos son **tan alegres como** yo.	*They are as happy as I.*
Ella baila **tan bien como** su hermana.	*She dances as well as her sister.*

EXERCISE A. **Grace is comparing herself to her friends and finds that they have many similarities. Express what she says.**

EXAMPLE: Yo soy muy lista. Alicia es muy lista también.
Yo soy **tan lista como** Alicia.

1. Imelda es muy cortés. Yo soy muy cortés también.
____

2. Ruthie y Beatriz son simpáticas. Yo soy simpática también.
____

3. Jeanne y yo somos atléticas. Tawny es atlética también.
____

4. Silvia es delgada. Yo soy delgada también.
____

5. Yo soy popular. María e Inés son populares también.
____

6. Rosa es cómica. Sandra y yo somos cómicas también.
____

7. Pedro es serio. Yo soy seria también.
____

EXERCISE B. **Jimmy is always comparing how well (sometimes how badly) he does things to his older brother and his friends. Express what he says.**

EXAMPLE: correr rápidamente / mi hermano — Yo corro **tan rápidamente como** mi hermano.

1. jugar bien al béisbol / sus amigos ______________________________
2. reírse alegremente / mi hermano ______________________________
3. salir mal en los exámenes / mi hermano ______________________________

4. cantar fuertemente / sus amigos ______________________

5. caminar lentamente / mi hermano ______________________

b. *Tanto* (*tanta, tantos, tantas*) + noun + *como* = as much (as many) . . . as

Tengo **tanto dinero como** tú.	*I have as much money as you.*
Él lee **tantos libros como** su amigo.	*He reads as many books as his friend.*

c. *Tanto* (tanta, tantos, tantas) + como = *as much (as many) . . . as*

¿Cuántas manzanas comió? Comió **tantas como** Juan.	*How many apples did he eat?* *He ate as many as John.*
Ella no hace **tanto como** yo.	*She doesn't do as much as I.*

EXERCISE C. **Rogelio believes that he has to keep up with his cousin. Express what he says.**

EXAMPLE: discos compactos Yo tengo **tantos** discos compactos **como** mi primo.

1. amigos ______________________
2. juegos electrónicos ______________________
3. experiencia ______________________
4. suerte ______________________
5. dinero ______________________
6. fe ______________________
7. gorras ______________________

EXERCISE D. **Janet is very competitive with her friends. Express what she did.**

EXAMPLE: correr millas Ella corrió **tantas** millas **como** sus amigas.

1. comprar ropa ______________________
2. gastar dinero ______________________
3. leer novelas ______________________
4. tener notas buenas ______________________
5. ganar trofeos ______________________
6. visitar museos ______________________
7. dar fiestas ______________________

[2] COMPARISONS OF INEQUALITY

a. Adjectives are compared as follows:

POSITIVE	**alto (alta, altos, altas)**	*tall*
COMPARATIVE	**más (menos) alto (alta, altos, altas)**	*taller*
SUPERLATIVE	**el (la, los, las) ... más (menos) alto (alta, altos, altas)**	*the tallest*

Pedro es alto. — *Pedro is tall.*
Pedro **es más (menos) alto** que Andrés. — *Pedro is taller (less tall) than Andrés.*
Pedro **es el más (menos) alto de** la clase. — *Pedro is the tallest (least tall) in the class.*

NOTE:

1. Generally, *than* is equivalent to *que.*

   Juan es más cómico **que** Adán. — *Juan is funnier than Adán.*

2. When *than* precedes a number, it is expressed by *de*, except when the sentence is negative.

   Él gastó más **de** diez dólares. — *He spent more than ten dollars.*
   Cuesta menos **de** treinta centavos. — *It costs less than thirty cents.*

   BUT

   Él no gastó más **que** diez dólares. — *He spent only ten dollars. (He did not spend more than ten dollars.)*

3. In the superlative, the nouns stands between the article (*el, la, los, las*) and the adjective.

   Él es el profesor **más** popular. — *He is the most popular teacher.*
   Es la revista **menos** interesante. — *It's the least interesting magazine.*

4. After a superlative, *de* means *in.*

   Él es el alumno más inteligente **de** la clase. — *He is the most intelligent pupil in the class.*

EXERCISE E. **Express your opinion about the following things, using *más* or *menos* and the adjective in parentheses.**

EXAMPLE: una biografía / un drama (*interesante*)
Una biografía es **más (menos) interesante** que un drama.

1. la televisión / la radio (*divertido*) ______________________
2. los discos compactos / las cintas (*práctico*) ______________________
3. un carro / un avión (*rápido*) ______________________
4. una bicicleta / una motocicleta (*peligroso*) ______________________
5. un diccionario / una revista (*útil*) ______________________
6. el helado / el pastel (*delicioso*) ______________________

EXERCISE F. **Compare the following pairs of people.**

EXAMPLE: Miguel es diligente. (– / *Felipe*)
Miguel es **menos diligente que** Felipe.

Sarita es bondadosa. (+ / *Flor*)
Sarita es **más bondadosa que** Flor.

1. Stan es atlético. (+ / *Vinny*) ____________________
2. Estela es ambiciosa. (– / *Tomás*) ____________________
3. Larry es cómico. (+ / *Fred*) ____________________
4. Hugo es descortés. (+ / *Anita*) ____________________
5. Nilda es habladora. (– / *Carmen*) ____________________
6. Ari es nervioso. (– / *Greg*) ____________________
7. Sonia es orgullosa. (+ / *Norma*) ____________________

EXERCISE G. **Use the following adjectives to describe your teachers.**

simpático	justo	aburrido	bondadoso
paciente	cómico	interesante	exigente

EXAMPLES: Mi profesor de inglés es el más **estricto.**
Mi profesora de historia es la más **generosa.**

1. ____________________
2. ____________________
3. ____________________
4. ____________________
5. ____________________
6. ____________________

EXERCISE H. **Express your opinion of the importance of the elements in each category.**

EXAMPLE: una persona famosa (*el Papa, el presidente, la reina*)
El presidente **es una persona** famosa.
La reina **es una persona más** famosa.
El Papa **es la persona más** famosa.

1. un deporte peligroso (el motociclismo, montar a caballo, el fútbol americano)

____

____

____

2. un animal feroz (el león, el lobo, el zorro)

____

____

____

3. una profesión noble (ser médico, ser profesor, ser policía)

____

____

____

4. una materia interesante (la química, la sicología, las matemáticas)

____

____

____

5. un sueño alcanzable (visitar otros países, viajar a la luna, graduarse de la universidad)

____

____

____

b. **Adverbs are compared as follows:**

POSITIVE	**lentamente**	*slowly*
COMPARATIVE	**más (menos) lentamente**	*more (less) slowly*
SUPERLATIVE	**más (menos) lentamente**	*more (less) slowly than*

NOTE: **The superlative of adverbs is not distinguished from the comparative.**

EXERCISE I. **Tell how these people do different things.**

EXAMPLE: estudiar diligentemente / Gabriel (+) / Beto (-)
Gabriel estudia más diligentemente.
Beto estudia menos diligentemente.

1. cantar dulcemente / Carmen (–) / Clara (+)

____

2. gritar fuertemente / el niño (+) / la niña (–)

____

3. hablar claramente / Jorge (+) / Esteban (–)

____

4. correr rápidamente / Neil (–) / Pablo (+)

____

5. cocinar hábilmente / mi mamá (+) / mi tía (–)

____

EXERCISE J. **Celia is telling a new aide at the daycare center about the children. Express what she says. Alternate the use of *más* and *menos.***

EXAMPLE: Felipe / dormir profundamente / Arturo
Felipe duerme **más** (**menos**) **profundamente** que Arturo.

1. Leticia / llorar fácilmente / Susana y Heather

____

2. Janet / comer lentamente / su hermano

____

3. Amanda / actuar respetuosamente / Rebecca

____

4. Brian / colorear cuidadosamente / ese niño

____

5. Jennifer / reírse fácilmente / Nina

____

[3] IRREGULAR COMPARATIVES

POSITIVE	COMPARATIVE	SUPERLATIVE
bueno, -a, -os, -as *good*	**mejor, -es** *better*	**el / la mejor; los / las mejores** *the best*
malo, -a, -os, -as *bad*	**peor, -es** *worse*	**el / la peor; los / las peores** *the worst*
grande, -es *large (great)*	**mayor, -es** *greater, older*	**el / la mayor; los / las mayores** *greatest, oldest*
pequeño, -a, -os, -as *small*	**menor, -es** *lesser, younger*	**el / la menor; los / las menores** *least, youngest*

NOTE:

1. *Mejor* and *peor* generally precede the nouns they modify.

   el mejor libro *the best book* la peor película *the worst film*

2. *Mayor* and *menor* usually follow the nouns they modify.

   el hijo mayor *the oldest son* mi hermana menor *my youngest sister*

3. The regular and irregular comparative forms of *grande* and *pequeño* have different meanings. *Más grande* and *más pequeño* compare differences in size or height (physical meaning); *mayor* and *menor* compare differences in age or status (figurative meaning).

   el hijo más pequeño *the smaller (smallest) son*
   el hijo menor *the younger (youngest) son*
   de mayor (menor) importancia *of greater (lesser) importance*

EXERCISE K. **Tell who does these things better or worse than you.**

EXAMPLE: bailar — Mi hermano baila **mejor** (**peor**) que yo.

1. nadar — Mi amiga nada mejor que yo.
2. jugar al tenis — Mi mamá juega al tenis peor que yo.
3. esquiar — Mi amiga esquia mejor que yo.
4. correr — Mis padres corren peor que yo.
5. cocinar — Mi hermano cocina peor que yo.
6. conducir un carro — Mi hermana conduce un carro mejor que yo
7. hablar español — Señorita Waddell habla español mejor que yo.

EXERCISE L. **You and a friend are discussing different things. For each one, give your opinion about which is the best and which is the worst.**

EXAMPLE: equipo de fútbol — El equipo de fútbol de la Argentina es **el mejor** equipo.
El equipo de fútbol de los Estados Unidos es **el peor** equipo.

1. película ______________________
2. disco compacto ______________________
3. carro ______________________
4. canción ______________________
5. grupo musical ______________________
6. atleta profesional ______________________
7. programa de televisión ______________________

[4] The Absolute Superlative

To express an absolute superlative (when no comparison is involved), *-ísimo, ísima, ísimos, -ísimas* is often added to the adjective. The meaning is the same as *muy* + adjective.

un libro muy popular
un libro popularísimo } *a very popular book*

una casa **muy grande** una casa **grandísima**	*an extremely large house*

NOTE:

1. Adjectives ending in a vowel drop that vowel before adding *-ísimo.*

2. *Muchísimo* = very much.

   Juan quiere muchísimo a su novia. *Juan loves his girlfriend very much.*

3. Before adding *-ísimo,* adjectives ending in *co* change to *qu;* those ending in *go* change to *gu;* and those ending in *z* change to *c.*

rico	→	**riquísimo**	*very rich*
largo	→	**larguísimo**	*very long*
feliz	→	**felicísimo**	*very happy*

EXERCISE M. **Mrs. Soto is telling a friend about her family. Express what she says by adding -ísimo (-a, -os, -as) to the adjective given.**

EXAMPLE: (*grande*) Mi hijo tiene un apetito **grandísimo.**

1. (*largo*) Yo paso horas larguísimas en la cocina.
2. (*caro*) La comida es carísima.
3. (*temprano*) Él siempre llega a casa tempranísimo.
4. (*poco*) Mis otros hijos comen poquísimo.
5. (*mucho / flaco*) Aunque él come muchísimo, él es flaquísimo.
6. (*dulce*) Él prefiere los postres dulcísimos.
7. (*gordo*) Si yo comiera como él, yo estaría gordísimo.
8. (*feliz*) Somos una familia felicisima.

MASTERY EXERCISES

EXERCISE N. **Answer the questions a new student asks you.**

1. ¿Eres más alto / alta que tus compañeros?
2. ¿Quién es el / la más inteligente de la clase de español?
3. ¿Eres mayor que tu hermano(-a)?

4. ¿Quién es el menor de tu familia?

____

5. ¿Cómo se llama tu mejor amigo(-a)?

____

6. ¿Tienes más de cincuenta dólares en el banco?

____

7. ¿Cuál es el peor grupo de música en tu opinión?

____

8. ¿Eres más aplicado / aplicada que los otros alumnos?

____

9. ¿Cuál es la mejor estación del año?

____

10. ¿Quién es el muchacho / la muchacha más popular de la escuela?

____

EXERCISE O. **Mrs. Sosa received a card from a long lost friend. In her response, she describes her family. Complete her letter with the following comparatives.**

grandísima	más... de	más... que	más de
mayor	menor	menos... que	muchísimo
tan... como	tantas	tantos	tantos... como

Querida Antonia,

Me dio ____________ (1.) gusto recibir tu tarjeta. Han pasado ____________ (2.) años y ____________ (3.) cosas desde la última vez que nos vimos. ¡Hace ____________ (4.) veinticinco años! Estábamos en la universidad y teníamos ____________ (5.) años ____________ (6.) mis hijos tienen ahora.

Tengo tres hijos: Elvira, Alfredo y Sarita. Elvira tiene treinta años, es la ____________ (7.), Alfredo tiene veintiocho y Sarita, la ____________ (8.), tiene veinticuatro. Elvira y Alfredo están casados y cada uno tiene dos hijos. Yo tengo ____________ (9.) nietos ____________ (10.) tú, cuatro. Los hijos de Elvira son ____________ (11.) simpáticos ____________ (12.) los de Alfredo. Elvira y su familia viven en una casa ____________ (13.) en el campo. Alfredo y su familia viven cerca de aquí en un apartamento que es ____________ (14.) grande ____________ (15.) la casa de Elvira: hay doce cuartos. Sarita sigue estudiando porque quiere llegar a ser médico. Ella es la ____________ (16.) inteligente ____________ (17.) mis hijos. Ella siempre ha trabajado ____________ (18.) para lograr sus metas. Escríbeme pronto. Recibe ____________ (19.) besos ____________ (20.) abrazos de mi parte.

Tu amiga,

Dolores

EXERCISE P. **Jack is describing his best friend. Express in Spanish what he says.**

1. Peter is my best friend.
____

2. He is older than I.
____

3. He has as many brothers as sisters.
____

4. He and his family live in a very large house.
____

5. He is the youngest child in his family.
____

6. He is the most generous of my friends.
____

7. He laughs a great deal.
____

8. He is as funny as I.
____

9. His worst trait is that he talks a lot.
____

10. He spends as much time in my house as I do in his.
____

ACTIVIDADES

You are preparing a "show and tell" presentation for your Spanish class. Select an object that you can bring to class (sports equipment, compact disc of your favorite music group, a picture or photo of a larger object, etc.) and explain how it compares to a similar object. Use as many comparative expressions as possible.

EXAMPLE: una bicicleta
Esta bicicleta **es mejor que las otras.**
Es tan bonita como las otras pero no cuesta **tanto dinero como ésas.**
Yo creo que **es la mejor bicicleta de todas.**

Chapter 28
Numbers

[1] Cardinal Numbers

0	cero	28	veintiocho (veinte y ocho)
1	uno	29	veintinueve (veinte y nueve)
2	dos	30	treinta
3	tres	31	treinta y uno
4	cuatro	40	cuarenta
5	cinco	50	cincuenta
6	seis	60	sesenta
7	siete	70	setenta
8	ocho	80	ochenta
9	nueve	90	noventa
10	diez	100	cien
11	once	101	ciento uno
12	doce	115	ciento quince
13	trece	116	ciento dieciséis
14	catorce	200	doscientos, -as
15	quince	300	trescientos, -as
16	dieciséis (diez y seis)	400	cuatrocientos, -as
17	diecisiete (diez y siete)	500	quinientos, -as
18	dieciocho (diez y ocho)	600	seiscientos, -as
19	diecinueve (diez y nueve)	700	setecientos, -as
20	veinte	800	ochocientos, -as
21	veintiuno (veinte y uno)	900	novecientos, -as
22	veintidós (veinte y dos)	1.000	mil
23	veintitrés (veinte y tres)	2.000	dos mil
24	veinticuatro (veinte y cuatro)	100.000	cien mil
25	veinticinco (veinte y cinco)	1.000.000	un millón (de)
26	veintiséis (veinte y seis)	2.000.000	dos millones (de)
27	veintisiete (veinte y siete)	100.000.000	cien millones (de)

NOTE:

1. Compound numbers 16 to 99 are connected by *y*.

2. Although numbers 16 to 19 and 21 to 29 may be connected by *y*, they are usually written as one word. Note the spelling changes that occur when these numbers are written as one word.

   diez y seis → dieciséis   veinte y dos → veintidós

3. *Uno* and combinations of *uno* (like *veintiuno* and *treinta y uno*) become *un* before masculine nouns and *una* before feminine nouns.

un periódico	*one (a) newspaper*	**una** silla	*one (a) chair*
veinti**ún** lápices	*twenty-one pencils*	veinti**una** blusas	*twenty-one blouses*
treinta y **un** alumnos	*thirty-one students*	treinta y **una** plumas	*thirty-one pens*

4. The only numerals that vary with gender are *uno* (*una, un*) and the compounds of *ciento* (*doscientos, -as; trescientos, -as*), and so on.

un alumno	*one (a) student*	quinientas mujeres	*five hundred women*
una alumna	*one (a) student*	veintiún centavos	*twenty-one cents*
trescientos hombres	*three hundred men*	cuarenta y una mesas	*forty-one tables*

5. *Cien* becomes *ciento* when it's followed by another number from one to ninety-nine.

cien bolívares　　cien mil habitantes

BUT

ciento veinticinco dólares

6. *Un* is not used before *cien* or *mil*. *Un* is used before the noun *millón*. If another noun follows *millón*, *de* is placed between *millón* and the other noun.

ciento diez personas　　mil cuatrocientos años　　un millón de dólares

7. Spanish usually uses periods rather than commas to separate digits.

2.568.953 (Spanish)　　2,568,953 (English)

8. Spanish usually uses a comma in decimals where English uses a period.

$8,95 (Spanish)　　$8.95 (English)

EXERCISE A. **Use the chart below to answer the questions based on it. Write out the numbers in Spanish.**

BUENOS AIRES, ARGENTINA			
Población			
Ciudad	3.036.891	Suburbios	13.711.746
Clima en noviembre			
Temperatura	alta		76°
	baja		56°
Días con lluvia			9
Hotel (tarifa diaria)			
Cuarto para uno (con impuesto)			$319,00
Cena para uno			
Con impuesto y propina			$28,00
Taxi			
Al subir			$1,20
Cada kilómetro adicional			$0,85
Del aeropuerto			$47,00
Alquiler de carro por un día			
Tamaño mediano, no automático con 150 o 200 kilómetros gratis			$86,00

1. ¿Cual es la población de la ciudad de Buenos Aires?

____

2. ¿Cuál es la población de los suburbios de Buenos Aires?

____

3. ¿Cuál es la temperatura alta en noviembre?

____

4. ¿Cuál es la temperatura baja en noviembre?

____

5. Cuántos días de lluvia hay en el mes de noviembre?

____

6. ¿Cuánto cuesta al día un cuarto en un hotel para una persona?

____

7. ¿Cuánto cuesta una cena para una persona con propina?

____

8. ¿Cuánto marca el taximetro al subir?

____

9. ¿Cuánto cuesta cada kilómetro adicional en el taxi?

____

10. ¿Cuánto cuesta un taxi del aeropuerto al centro?

____

11. ¿Cuánto cobran para alquilar un carro por un día?

____

12. Por lo general, ¿cuántos kilómetros gratis dan al alquilar un carro?

____

EXERCISE B. **As Norma prepares to apply to colleges, her parents want to know how many students attend each of the institutions she is considering. Tell the number of students that attend each one; the number of male students, and the number of female students.**

UNIVERSIDAD	HOMBRES	MUJERES	TOTAL
Boston College	4,183	4,785	8,968
Brown	2,597	3,028	5,625
Columbia	1,884	1,845	3,729
Emory	2,558	3,231	5,789
Harvard	3,683	2,917	6,600
Northwestern	3,701	3,908	7,609
Notre Dame	4,250	3,450	7,700
Ohio State	15,845	14,434	30,279
Pennsylvania State	17,103	14,006	31,109
University of Maryland	10,744	10,251	20,995
University of Miami	3,556	3,816	7,372
University of Michigan	13,088	14,674	27,762

1. seis ~~cientos~~ mil seis cientos estudiantes.
2. tres cientos setenta y dos estudiantes.
3. setecientos sesenta y dos estudiantes.
5. veinte mil novecientos noventa y cinco estudientes
6. novecientos sesenta y ocho estudiantes

EXAMPLE: Brown — dos mil quinientos noventa y siete hombres; tres mil veintiocho mujeres; cinco mil seiscientos veinticinco estudiantes

1. Harvard — tres mil seiscientos ochenta y tres hombres; dos mil novecientos diecisiete mujeres;
2. University of Miami — tres mil quinientos cincuenta y seis hombres; tres mil ocho cientos dieciseis mujeres; siete mil
3. University of Michigan — trece mil ochenta y ocho hombres; catorce mil seis cientos setenta y cuatro mujeres; veintisiete mil
4. Pennsylvania State — diecisiete mil cien tres hombres; catorce mil seis mujeres; treinte y uno cien nueve estudientes.
5. University of Maryland — diez mil setecientos cuarenta y cuatro hombres; diez mil dos cientos ~~cin~~ conquenta y uno mujeres;
6. Boston College — cuatro mil cien ochenta y tres hombres; cuatro mil setecientos ochenta y cinco mujeres; ocho mil
7. Ohio State — quince mil ochocientos cuarenta y cinco hombres; catorce mil cuatro cientos treinta y cuatro
8. Northwestern — tres mil setecientos uno hombres; tres mil novecientos ocho mujeres; siete mil seis cientos nueve estudiantes
9. Columbia — mil ochocientos ochenta y cuatro hombres; mil ochocientos cuarenta y cinco mujeres;
10. Notre Dame — cuatro mil dos cientos cincuenta hombres; tres mil cuatro cientos cincuenta mujeres; siete setecientos estudientes.

EXERCISE C. **You are helping your younger sister prepare for a test. Help her answer the following questions.**

1. ¿Cuántos zapatos hay en un par de zapatos? ______
2. ¿Cuántos jugadores hay en un equipo de béisbol? ______
3. ¿Cuántas letras hay en el alfabeto inglés? ______
4. ¿Cuántos centavos hay en un dólar? ______
5. ¿Cuántos estados hay en los Estados Unidos? ______
6. ¿Cuántos días hay en un año? ______
7. ¿Cuántos días hay en mes de marzo? ______
8. ¿Cuántos días hay en el mes de febrero? ______

7. mujeres; treinta mil dos cientos setecientos nueve estudiantes
9. tres mil setecientos veintinueve estudiantes.

9. ¿Cuántas preguntas hay en este ejercicio? ____________________

10. ¿En qué capítulo está este ejercicio? ____________________

11. ¿Cuántos años hay en un siglo? ____________________

12. ¿Cuántos dedos tiene una persona en cada mano? ____________________

13. ¿Cuántas naranjas hay en una docena? ____________________

14. ¿Cuántas horas hay en un día? ____________________

15. ¿Cuántas estaciones hay en un año? ____________________

EXERCISE D. **Angelo is very interested in the maximum and minimum temperatures in different cities in Spanish America. Tell what the maximum and minimum temperatures are and help him calculate the difference between them. Write the numbers in Spanish.**

CUIDAD	TEMPERATURA MÁXIMA	TEMPERATURA MÍNIMA	GRADOS DE DIFERENCIA
Asunción	68	54	
Bogotá	66	49	
Caracas	88	75	
Chihuahua	95	64	
Guayaquil	89	66	
Montevideo	56	38	
Quito	76	44	
San Salvador	91	67	
Tegucigalpa	89	49	
Tierra del Fuego	39	30	

1. Asunción

Máxima ____________________

Mínima ____________________

Diferencia ____________________

2. Bogotá

Máxima ____________________

Mínima ____________________

Diferencia ____________________

3. Caracas

Máxima ____________________

Mínima ____________________

Diferencia ____________________

4. Chihuahua

Máxima ____________________

Mínima ____________________

Diferencia ____________________

5. Guayaquil
Máxima ______
Mínima ______
Diferencia ______

6. Montevideo
Máxima ______
Mínima ______
Diferencia ______

7. Quito
Máxima ______
Mínima ______
Diferencia ______

8. San Salvador
Máxima ______
Mínima ______
Diferencia ______

9. Tegucigalpa
Máxima ______
Mínima ______
Diferencia ______

10. Tierra del Fuego
Máxima ______
Mínima ______
Diferencia ______

[2] Arithmetic Expressions

The following expressions are used in arithmetic problems in Spanish:

y, más	*plus* (+)	**dividido por**	*divided by* (÷)
menos	*minus* (−)	**son, es igual a**	*equals* (=)
por	*(multiplied) by, "times"* (×)		

EXERCISE E. Express the following in Spanish.

1. 7,632 + 895 = 8,527 ______

2. 27 + 83 = 110 ______

3. 800,000 − 300,000 = 500,000 ______

4. 729 − 208 = 521 ______

5. 910 × 45 = 40,950 ______________________________

6. 763 × 22 = 16,786 ______________________________

7. 9,000 ÷ 90 = 100 ______________________________

8. 195 ÷ 13 = 15 ______________________________

9. 1,000,000 ÷ 50 = 20,000 ______________________________

10. 10,081 + 7,629 = 17,710 ______________________________

11. 2,700,000 + 300,000 = 3,000,000 ______________________________

12. 26 × 36 = 936 ______________________________

13. 9,389 − 5,018 = 4,371 ______________________________

14. 863 − 175 = 688 ______________________________

15. 4,020 ÷ 12 = 335 ______________________________

16. 280 + 21 = 301 ______________________________

17. 1,100 − 82 = 1,018 ______________________________

18. 777 × 20 = 15,540 ______________________________

19. 64 × 80 = 5,120 ______________________________

20. 1,250 ÷ 25 = 50 ______________________________

EXERCISE F. **While the family is taking a car trip, the children are assigning a numerical value to everything they see. Tell what they say:**

EXAMPLE: 100 cien dólares

1. 500 ______________________________

2. 41 ______________________________

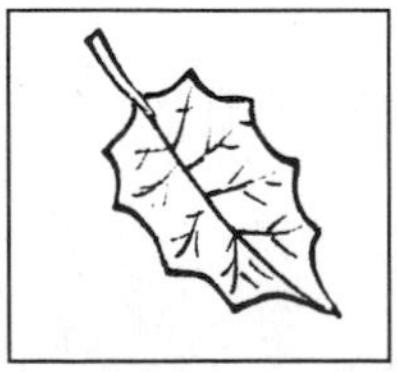

3. 1,000,000 ______________________________

4. 101 ______________________________

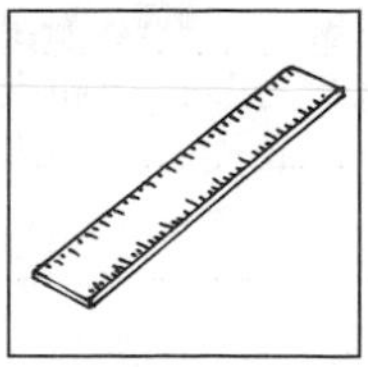

5. 700 ______________________

6. 81 ______________________

7. 92 ______________________

8. 109 ______________________

9. 2,331 ______________________

10. 230 ______________________

[3] ORDINAL NUMBERS

1°	primero, -a; primer	*1st, first*	6°	sexto, -a	*6th, sixth*
2°	segundo, -a	*2nd, second*	7°	séptimo, -a	*7th, seventh*
3°	tercero, -a; tercer	*3rd, third*	8°	octavo, -a	*8th, eighth*
4°	cuarto, -a	*4th, fourth*	9°	noveno, -a	*9th, ninth*
5°	quinto, -a	*5th, fifth*	10°	décimo, -a	*10th, tenth*

NOTE:

1. All ordinal numbers agree in gender (m./f.) and number (sing./pl.) with the nouns to which they refer.

   el octavo día *the eighth day* la quinta semana *the fifth week*

2. The numbers *primero* and *tercero* drop the final *-o* when they come before a masculine singular noun.

   el primer mes *the first month* el tercer piso *the third floor*

   BUT

   la primera semana *the first week* la tercera estación *the third season*

3. If a preposition comes between *primero* or *tercero* and the noun, the full form is used.

   el primero de septiembre *September 1*

4. Ordinal numbers are generally used to express rank order only from the first to the tenth in a series. Numbers above ten also have ordinal forms, but they are seldom used. Instead, a cardinal number is placed after the noun, and the word *número* is understood.

la quinta página	*the fifth page*
Carlos V (Carlos Quinto)	*Charles the Fifth*
BUT	
la lección quince	*the fifteenth lesson or lesson (number) fifteen*
Alfonso XII (Alfonso Doce)	*Alfonso the Twelfth*

EXERCISE G. **You are looking at the directory in the hospital lobby. Tell to which floor you would go to do the various activities.**

(Note: In most Spanish-speaking countries, the ground floor or first floor is called *la planta baja (PB)*; the second floor, *primer piso*, and so forth.)

SERVICIO / DEPARTAMENTO	PISO
Cafetería	11
Caja	4
Cirugía	10
Consultorios de doctores	7
Farmacia	1
Información	PB
Maternidad	5
Oficina ejecutivas	4
Ortopedía	3
Pediatría	2
Sala de Emergencia	PB
Tienda / Florería	PB

EXAMPLE: hablar con el director del hospital **el cuarto piso**

1. para visitar a un niño enfermo ______________________
2. para comer ______________________
3. para pedir información ______________________
4. para pagar una cuenta ______________________
5. para ver a un médico ______________________
6. para obtener medicina ______________________
7. en caso de accidente ______________________
8. para hablar con el director de las enfermeras ______________________
9. para visitar a un bebé recién nacido y a su mamá ______________________

10. para ver a un amigo que se ha roto una pierna ______________________

11. para ver a una persona a quien han operado ______________________

12. para comprar un regalo o flores ______________________

EXERCISE H. **Pete has just learned that a Spanish calendar begins with Monday. Identify which day of the week each day is according to a Spanish calendar.**

EXAMPLE: domingo **el séptimo día**

1. miércoles ______________ *4.* lunes ______________

2. sábado ______________ *5.* jueves ______________

3. viernes ______________ *6.* martes ______________

EXERCISE I. **Write each number in parentheses as a Spanish word.**

1. Juan Carlos (1°) es un rey moderno. primero

2. Estamos en la (5°) ciudad de la excursión. quinta

3. Tu dormitorio está en el (1°) piso de la casa. primero

4. Yo era la (9°) persona en la cola. novena

5. Este es el (3°) carro que compra mi papá este año. tercero

6. Debo bajarme en la (2°) parada del autobús. segunda

7. Es el (4°) verano que trabajo con mi hermano. cuarto

8. Celebro mi cumpleaños en el (8°) mes del año: agosto. octavo

9. Esos señores acaban de celebrar su aniversario (47°). cuarenta y séptimo

10. Contesta la (1°) pregunta al final del examen. primera

[4] FRACTIONS

$^1/_2$	**un medio, medio, -a, una mitad de**	*a/one) half, half of*
$^1/_3$	**un tercio, una tercera parte de**	*(a/one) third, the third part of*
$^1/_4$	**un cuarto, una cuarta parte de**	*(a/one) fourth, a quarter of*
$^2/_3$	**dos tercios, dos terceras partes de**	*two-thirds, two-thirds of*
$^3/_4$	**tres cuartos, tres cuartas partes de**	*three-fourths, three quarters of*
$^4/_5$	**cuatro quintos, cuatro quintas partes de**	*four -fifths of*
$^1/_{10}$	**un décimo, una décima parte de**	*(a/one) tenth, a tenth of*

NOTE:

1. **Except for *medio* and *tercio*, noun fractions are formed with ordinal numbers up through *décimo* (tenth). Thereafter, the ending *-avo* is usually added to the cardinal number to express fractions smaller than a tenth.**

   $^1/_{12}$ **un doceavo, una doceava parte de** *(a / one) twelfth of*

2. **Fractions are masculine nouns.**

$3\,^1/_3$	tres y un tercio	*three and one-third*

When the fraction precedes the thing divided, it may be used with the feminine noun *parte*, unless a unit of measure is expressed.

una tercera parte (un tercio) del pan	*a third of the bread*
BUT	
un tercio de libra	*a third of a pound*

3. **The adjective *medio, -a* means "half," while the noun *mitad* means "half (of)."**

media docena de huevos	*half a dozen eggs*
la mitad del público	*half of the audience*

EXERCISE J. **You and some friends are going to spend the day at a picnic and you have to buy the food. Copy the following list, writing out the fractions as words in Spanish.**

1. ______________________ *5.* ______________________

2. ______________________ *6.* ______________________

3. ______________________ *7.* ______________________

4. ______________________ *8.* ______________________

[5] MULTIPLES

Terms that indicate that one quantity is a multiple of another are used in the same manner as their English equivalents.

una vez	*once*	simple	*single, simple*
dos veces	*twice*	doble	*double*
tres veces	*thrice, three times*	triple	*triple*

Me habló una vez.	*He spoke to me once.*
Nos visitaron dos veces.	*They visited us twice.*
Leí el doble de lo que leíste tú.	*I read twice as much as you.*

NOTE:

1. **Adverbial phrases explaining the number of times that an event occurs are formed by a cardinal number and the feminine noun *vez* (a time).**

   Lavé la ropa cuatro veces. — *I washed the clothes four times.*

2. **Multiples like *doble, triple* may be either adjectives or nouns.**

   Es una máquina de doble motor. — *It's a double-motor machine.*

   Este carro cuesta hoy el doble. — *This car costs twice as much today.*

EXERCISE K. **Nick is telling some friends how many times he has done these things. Tell what he says using the cues in parentheses.**

EXAMPLE: comer en un restaurante japonés (*2*)
Es la **segunda vez** que como en un restaurante japonés.

1. viajar en avión (*10*) ______________________

2. estudiar la literatura española (*1*) ______________________

3. trabajar después de las clases (*3*) ______________________

4. remar en el lago (*4*) ______________________

5. tocar el violín en un concierto (*8*) ______________________

6. ir a una fiesta de disfraces (*6*) ______________________

EXERCISE L. **You and a friend are trying to decide what to do. Your friend is giving you a hard time because for every suggestion you make, your friend tells you how many times she has done that. Tell what he says using the cues in parentheses.**

EXAMPLE: ver la película «The Lion King» (*5*)
Vi la película «The Lion King» **cinco veces.**

1. patinar en hielo (*10*) ______________________

2. correr en un maratón (*3*) ______________________

3. ir de compras (*100*) ______________________

4. ver la obra de teatro «Gatos» (*15*) ______________________

5. visitar el museo de ciencia y tecnología (*1*) ______________________

6. escuchar los discos compactos (*1,000*) ______________________

MASTERY EXERCISES

EXERCISE M. Solve these word problems in Spanish. Write out the numbers in Spanish.

1. Alex tiene que leer una novela en quince días. La novela contiene 600 páginas. ¿Cuántas páginas debe leer Alex cada día para terminar a tiempo?

___

2. Mi mamá tiene 3 cheques: uno por $ 1,000.00; el segundo por $ 750.00, y el tercero por $ 2,500.00. ¿Cuántos dólares tiene en total?

___

3. José tiene $ 350.00. Va a la tienda y compra un suéter por $ 79.00, pantalones por $ 85.00 y zapatos por $60.00. ¿Cuánto gasta José en las compras y cuánto dinero le queda?

___

4. Gloria quiere comprar una pulsera de oro que cuesta $ 270.00. Si ella ahorra $ 15.00 a la semana, ¿en cuántas semanas podrá Gloria comprar la pulsera?

___

5. Mi familia piensa visitar a mis abuelos que viven en otro estado. Vamos a viajar en carro. Si tenemos que viajar 360 millas y seguimos una velocidad de 60 millas por hora, ¿en cuántas horas llegaremos? (Use la fórmula: distancia = velocidad x tiempo)

___

6. Aníbal está trabajando en un almacén. Recibe una comisión de 10 por ciento en todo lo que vende. Si trabaja 5 días y vende $ 810.00 de mercancía cada día, ¿cuánta comisión recibirá al fin de la semana?

___

EXERCISE N. Express the following in Spanish.

1. No one answered the first time I called Julie.

___

2. The second time I called, a machine answered.

___

3. A voice said: "This is 34-72-89. Please leave a message."

___

4. I said: "It's Fred. My telephone number is 96-61-45. Please call me."

___

5. She called in 2 1/2 hours but it seemed like 100 hours.

___

6. She said that there were 21 messages on the machine.

____

7. She understood half the message.

____

8. She told me that we had to read pages 267 to 331 for our English class.

____

9. I said: "That's 65 pages! Why didn't he ask for 1,000 pages?"

____

10. She heard that 1,000,000 people watched the marathon on television.

____

11. Her cousin won sixth place in the race.

____

12. One third of the people didn't complete the race.

____

ACTIVIDADES

1. Select six of your favorite family members and write in Spanish the year in which each one was born. Then tell how old each person is.

2. Do the following word problem. Write the numbers in Spanish.

Un promedio de 4.7 personas vive en cada una de los 66 apartamentos de este edificio. ¿Cuántas personas viven en el edificio?

Now create a word problem in Spanish and solve it.

3. You and your parents are planning to drive to several college campuses during a school vacation. Select three colleges that you will drive to and tell in Spanish how many miles each one is from the city in which you live. Then tell the total number of miles you travelled during this vacation.

Chapter 29
Time and Dates

[1] Expressing Time

a. *¿Qué hora es?* is equivalent to *What time is it?*

b. In expressing time, *it is* is equivalent to *es la* (for one o'clock) and *son las* for other hours (two o'clock, three o'clock, and so on.)

Es la una.	*It's one o'clock.*
Son las diez (once, . . .)	*It's ten (eleven, . . .) o'clock.*

c. Time after or past the hour (up to half past) is expressed by the hour + *y,* followed by the number of minutes. Half past is expressed by *y media;* a quarter past is expressed by *y cuarto.*

Es la una **y** veinte.	*It's twenty (minutes) after one. It's 1:20.*
Son las ocho **y media.**	*It's half past eight. It's 8:30.*
Son las dos **y cuarto.**	*It's a quarter after two. It's 2:15.*

d. After half past, the time is expressed in terms of the following hour minus (*menos*) the minutes.

Son las cuatro **menos** diez.	*It's ten minutes to four. (It's 3:50.)*
Son las once **menos** cuarto.	*It's a quarter to eleven. (It's 10:45.)*

e. The expression *de la mañana* corresponds to English A.M. (in the morning). *De la tarde* (in the afternoon) and *de la noche* (in the night) correspond to English P.M. *En punto* means "sharp" or "on the dot."

f. The twenty-four hour clock is used in many Spanish-speaking countries, especially in the announcement of television and theater presentations.

9.00	las nueve **de la mañana**	*nine in the morning*
12.00	el mediodía	*noon*
13.15	la una y quince de la tarde	*one fifteen in the afternoon*
19.00	las siete **de la noche**	*seven in the evening*
21.45	las diez menos cuarto **de la noche**	*nine forty-five in the night*
24.00	la medianoche en punto	*midnight sharp*

NOTE:

1. Instead of *media* and *cuarto*, the number of minutes may be used (*treinta, quince*).

Son las tres y **treinta.**	*It's three-thirty. It's half past three.*
Es la una y **quince.**	*It's one-fifteen. It's a quarter past one.*

2. It is not uncommon to hear times like 12:45 and 12:50 expressed with *y.*

Son las siete y cuarenta.	*It's seven forty.*
Son las siete y cincuenta y cinco.	*It's seven-fifty-five.*

g. Common Time Expressions

¿Qué hora es?	*What time is it?*	**a eso de las siete**	*at about seven o'clock*
¿A qué hora?	*At what time?*	**Es mediodía.**	*It's noon.*
a las dos (tres, etc.)	*at two (three, etc.) o'clock*	**a mediodía**	*at noon*
de la mañana	*in the morning, A.M.*	**Es medianoche.**	*It's midnight.*
de la tarde	*in the afternoon, P.M.*	**a medianoche**	*at midnight*
de la noche	*in the evening, P.M.*	**Es temprano.**	*It's early.*
en punto	*sharp, exactly*	**Es tarde.**	*It's late.*
a tiempo	*on time*		

EXERCISE A. **You are in a clock store at the mall. Every clock shows a different time. Tell what time it is on each clock.**

EXAMPLE: Son las **ocho menos veinticinco.**

1. ______________________________

2. ______________________________

3. ______________________________

4. ______________________________

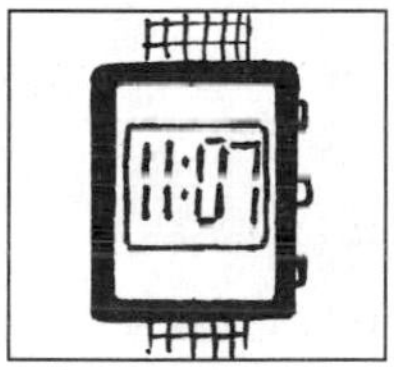

5. ______________________________

6. ______________________________

7. ______________________________

8. ______________________________

9. ______________________________

10. ______________________________

11. ______________________________

12. ______________________________

13. ______________________________

14. ______________________________

15. ______________________________

16. ______________________________

17. ______________________________

18. ______________________________

19. ______________________________

20. ______________________________

EXERCISE B. **Answer the questions a new friend asks you.**

1. ¿A qué hora te levantas? ______________________
2. ¿A qué hora te desayunas? ______________________
3. ¿Cuándo llegas a la escuela? ______________________
4. ¿A qué hora comienzan las clases? ______________________
5. ¿A qué hora almuerzan tus amigos y tú? ______________________
6. ¿Cuándo sales de la escuela? ______________________
7. ¿A qué hora cena tu familia? ______________________
8. ¿Cuándo estudias tus lecciones? ______________________
9. ¿A qué hora terminan las clases? ______________________
10. ¿A qué hora te acuestas? ______________________

EXERCISE C. **You are looking at a schedule of movies. Answer the questions based on the schedule.**

• Comodidad • Sonido Stereo	• Pantallas Gigantes de Alta Definición • Las Mejores Salas de Cine	
GRAN REX	**EMPERATRIZ**	**LAMONTE**
Cenizas del paraiso	*Máxima velocidad*	*Hércules*
17:10 / 19:40 / 22:20	16:10 / 18:20 / 20:30 / 22:40	14:30 / 16:15 / 18:20

1. ¿A qué hora es la primera función del Cine Lamonte?

____

2. ¿A qué hora es la última función en el Cine Emperatriz?

____

3. ¿A qué hora es la tercera función de «Máxima velocidad»?

____

4. Si yo quiero ver la película «Cenizas del paraiso» pero quiero llegar a casa antes de las nueve de la noche, ¿a qué función debo ir?

____

5. Si voy a la última función de «Máxima velocidad» y la película dura dos horas, ¿a qué hora saldré del cine?

____

[2] Expressing Dates

a. Days of the Week (*Los días de la semana*)

lunes	*Monday*	viernes	*Friday*
martes	*Tuesday*	sábado	*Saturday*
miércoles	*Wednesday*	domingo	*Sunday*
jueves	*Thursday*		

NOTE:

1. "On" before a day of the week is expressed by *el* for the singular and *los* for the plural.

el lunes	*on Monday*	los lunes	*on Mondays*
el martes	*on Tuesday*	los martes	*on Tuesdays*
el miércoles	*on Wednesday*	los miércoles	*on Wednesdays*
el sábado	*on Saturday*	los sábados	*on Saturdays*
el domingo	*on Sunday*	los domingos	*on Sundays*

2. Days of the week whose names en in *-s* do not change their form in the plural.

3. The days of the week are not capitalized in Spanish.

b. Months (*los meses*)

enero	*January*	mayo	*May*	septiembre	*September*
febrero	*February*	junio	*June*	octubre	*October*
marzo	*March*	julio	*July*	noviembre	*November*
abril	*April*	agosto	*August*	diciembre	*December*

NOTE: Like the days of the week, the months are not capitalized in Spanish.

c. Dates

¿Cuál es la fecha de hoy? ¿A cuántos estamos hoy?	*What is today's date?*
Es el primero de abril. Estamos a primero de abril.	*It's April 1.*
Es el dos de marzo.	*It's March 2.*
Es el cinco (seis) de mayo.	*It's May 5 (6)*
mil novecientos noventa y siete	*1997*
el cuatro de julio de mil setecientos setenta y seis	*July 4, 1776*

NOTE:

1. Cardinal numbers are used for all dates except for *primero* (first).

el **primero** de enero	*January 1*
el dos (tres, cuatro) de enero	*January 2 (3, 4)*

2. The year is expressed in Spanish by thousands and hundreds, not by hundreds alone as in English.

mil ochocientos doce	*eighteen hundred twelve*

3. The date and month are connected by the preposition *de.* The month and the year are also connected by *de.*

   el veinte **de** agosto **de mil novecientos diez** ***(on) August 20, 1910***

4. With dates, *el* corresponds to *on.*

EXERCISE D. **Look at the excerpt from Julia's calendar and tell on which days she does the different activities.**

EXAMPLE: clase de piano **Los lunes** Julia tiene clase de piano.

LUNES	MARTES	MIÉRCOLES	JUEVES
clase de piano	el gimnasio	cuidar al hermanito	clase de natación

VIERNES	SÁBADO	DOMINGO
libre	ayudar en casa	ir al cine

1. ir al cine ______
2. practicar el gimnasio ______
3. ayudar en casa ______
4. no hacer nada ______
5. cuidar al hermanito ______
6. ir a la piscina ______

EXERCISE E. **Tell on which date these holidays are celebrated in the United States.**

EXAMPLE: Veteran's Day Se celebra el **once de noviembre.**

1. Valentine's Day ______
2. Christmas ______
3. Independence Day ______
4. Columbus Day ______
5. Halloween ______
6. Lincoln's birthday ______
7. Washington's birthday ______
8. April Fools Day ______
9. New Year's Day ______

EXERCISE F. **The dates listed below are of holidays that are usually celebrated in most Spanish-speaking countries. Express the dates in Spanish.**

EXAMPLE: December 25 el **veinticinco de diciembre**

1. November 2 ______________________
2. January 1 ______________________
3. October 12 ______________________
4. January 6 ______________________
5. May 1 ______________________

EXERCISE G. **Express the following dates in Spanish.**

1. December 7, 1942 ______________________
2. August 25, 1910 ______________________
3. February 1, 1458 ______________________
4. March 15, 1212 ______________________
5. May 5, 1808 ______________________
6. January 1, 2001 ______________________
7. September 20, 1647 ______________________
8. June 3, 1555 ______________________
9. April 23, 1616 ______________________
10. November 11, 1779 ______________________

EXERCISE H. **You are preparing a family tree that is based on the birth date of your family members. Tell the date of birth (including the year) of these members of your family.**

EXAMPLE: tu padre Mi padre nació el **ocho de julio de mil novecientos sesenta y dos.**

1. tu abuela materna ______________________
2. tu hermano / hermana ______________________
3. tú ______________________
4. tu abuelo paterno ______________________
5. un /una tío(-a) ______________________
6. un / una primo(-a) ______________________
7. tu madre ______________________

MASTERY EXERCISES

EXERCISE I. **Your mother left her daily calendar near the telephone. She calls from her cellular telephone. Answer the questions she asks about her schedule for the day.**

18 MARTES noviembre

9:00		Sr. Mateo -- Marcas Finas
10:00		Banco Internacional
11:00	11:30	--- Reunión de vendedores
12:00		
1:00	1:15	Jack/Rosa - Restaurante del Lago
2:00		
3:00	3:45	llamada internacional --- Sr. Rupert
4:00		
5:00		Gimnasio
6:00	6:30	Cena y teatro

1. ¿A qué hora es la reunión de vendedores? ______________________
2. ¿Cuándo debo estar en el «Restaurante del Lago?» ______________________
3. ¿A qué hora tengo cita con el Sr. Mateo? ______________________
4. ¿A qué hora iré al gimnasio? ______________________
5. ¿A qué hora me llamará el señor Rupert? ______________________
6. ¿Cuándo debo estar en el «Banco Internacional»? ______________________
7. ¿A qué hora es la cena y el teatro? ______________________

EXERCISE J. **You are preparing a birthday bulletin board for your Spanish class. Tell when these classmates celebrate their birthday. Include yourself at the end.**

EXAMPLE: Rosalía / November 20 Rosalía celebra su cumpleaños el **veinte de noviembre.**

1. Abe y Peter / September 3 ______________________
2. Francisco / January 1 ______________________
3. Lucy / April 18 ______________________
4. Ricky / December 12 ______________________
5. Andrea / October 31 ______________________

6. Justino / August 27 ______________________

7. Emma / March 9 ______________________

8. Brian / November 15 ______________________

9. Carmen / July 21 ______________________

10. yo / ______________________

EXERCISE K. You are studying for a Spanish test. Answer the questions that may appear on the test.

1. ¿Cuáles son los días del fin de la semana? ______________________

2. ¿Qué meses del año tienen treinta y un días? ______________________

3. Si hoy es jueves, ¿qué día fue ayer ? ______________________

4. ¿En qué días asistes a la escuela? ______________________

5. ¿En qué días no vas a la escuela? ______________________

6. ¿Cuál es el décimo mes del año? ______________________

7. ¿En qué meses suele hacer mucho calor? ______________________

8. ¿Cuál es el cuarto mes del año? ______________________

9. ¿En qué mes celebras tu cumpleaños? ______________________

10. ¿En qué mes terminan las clases? ______________________

11. Si hoy es viernes, ¿qué día será mañana? ______________________

12. ¿Cuál es el primer mes del año? ______________________

13. ¿En qué meses hay treinta días? ______________________

14. ¿En qué fecha celebramos el «Día de la Raza»? ______________________

15. ¿Cuál es la fecha de hoy? ______________________

EXERCISE L. Help a friend write a letter in Spanish to his Bolivian pen pal.

1. The concert is on Saturday, January 5th.

____

2. I bought the tickets in July.

____

3. It begins at four o'clock in the afternoon.

____

4. We have to be there on time.

____

5. The doors open at 3:15 sharp.

____

6. At what time do you intend to arrive?

____

7. On Saturdays, there is a train that arrives at 2:50 P.M.

____

8. I will meet you at the station at 3:00 P.M.

____

9. The concert should end at about 7:00 P.M.

____

10. There is a second concert at 10:00 P.M.

____

11. We can eat dinner at about 7:30 P.M.

____

12. We should arrive home at midnight.

____

ACTIVIDADES

1. Prepare a journal entry in which you describe all of the activities that you did today. Be sure to include the time you began and ended each activity.
2. Select a month and prepare a calendar for it. Label the days of the week in Spanish and write out each day's date in numbers. Then list different activities for the month. Include special events, parties, sports activities, birthdays, holidays, etc.
3. It's time to move the clock forward (spring) or back (fall). Write a paragraph in Spanish in which you explain this concept and how it affects your activities, for example, "Now I can play ball in the park at 7:00 P.M. on Tuesdays." Refer to as many different times as you can.

Chapter 30

Adverbs and Adverbial Phrases

Adverbs describe the action expressed by a verb. They explain how, when, where, why, or in what way the action takes place. Adverbs also modify adjectives and other adverbs. They don't change form according to gender or number. An adverbial phrase is a group of words that together function as an adverb.

[1] Adverbs and Adverbial Phrases of Mode

a. Adverbs of mode (those answering the question how? or in what way?) are generally formed by adding *-mente* to the feminine singular form of an adjective.

ADJECTIVE	ADVERB
clara *clear*	**claramente** *clearly*
cortés *polite, courteous*	**cortésmente** *politely, courteously*
inteligente *intelligent*	**inteligentemente** *intelligently*

NOTE:

1. Adjectives that have an accent mark keep the accent mark when they are changed to adverbs.

   rápida → rápidamente   fácil → fácilmente

2. In a series of two or more adverbs, the ending *-mente* is added only to the last one.

   Ella cantó clara y divinamente. — *She sang clearly and divinely.*

3. The adjectives *bueno* and *malo* have irregular adverb forms.

bueno	*good*	bien	*well*
malo	*bad*	mal	*badly*

   Juan es un atleta **bueno,** pero hoy jugó **mal.** — *Juan is a good athlete, but today he played badly.*

4. Some adverbs have special forms:

   aprisa *quickly*   despacio *slowly*

b. Adverbial phrases of mode are usually formed as follows:

de manera + adjective
Ella canta **de manera cómica.** — *She sings in a funny way.*

de modo + adjective
Ella canta **de modo cómico.** — *She sings in a funny way.*

c. Adverbial phrases may be formed by using *con* + noun.

El joven corrió **con rapidez** (rápidamente). — *The young man ran with rapidity (rapidly).*

El poeta escogió las palabras **con cuidado** (cuidadosamente).	*The poet chose the words with care (carefully).*
Salimos con nuestros amigos **con frecuencia** (frecuentemente).	*We go out with our friends with frequency (frequently).*

EXERCISE A. **When Jack returned from a homestay in Venezuela, his parents wanted to know about the family with whom he stayed. Using the cues given in parentheses, answer his family's questions.**

EXAMPLE: ¿Cómo hablan ellos? (*rápido*) Ellos hablan **rápidamente.**

1. ¿Cómo juegan al fútbol? (*hábil*) ______________________________
2. ¿Cómo comen ellos? (*lento*) ______________________________
3. ¿Cómo hablan inglés? (*mal*) ______________________________
4. ¿Cómo tratan a los huéspedes? (*cortés*) ______________________________
5. ¿Cómo te recibieron a ti? (*alegre*) ______________________________
6. ¿Cómo se despidieron de ti? (*triste*) ______________________________
7. ¿Piensan ellos visitarnos? (*probable*) ______________________________

EXERCISE B. **A group of friends took their driving test on the same day. Express what Sam tells about each one's performance.**

EXAMPLE: Yo conduje ______________. (*cuidadoso*) Yo conduje **cuidadosamente.**

1. Felipe contestó las preguntas ______________. (*claro*)
2. Sarita sacó la licencia ______________. (*fácil*)
3. Esteban y Arturo condujeron ______________. (*lento*)
4. Félix frenó ______________. (*impulsivo*)
5. Josh y Laura aplaudieron ______________. (*fuerte*)
6. El inspector se portó ______________. (*profesional*)

EXERCISE C. **Victor repeats, with a slight change, what his friend Jared says about the sports event they attended. Tell what Victor says using an adverbial phrase composed of *con* + noun.**

EXAMPLE: El equipo jugó el partido seriamente.
Sí, el equipo jugó el partido **con seriedad.**

1. El equipo jugó enérgicamente.

____

2. Los otros miembros del equipo esperaron su turno a jugar pacientemente.

____

3. Los árbitros trabajaron profesionalmente.

____

4. Los aficionados aplaudieron al equipo locamente.

____

5. Los locutores anunciaron el partido alegremente.

____

6. Los ganadores salieron entusiásticamente del campo de juego.

____

7. Los oponentes dejaron el campo de juego tristemente.

____

d. The words *más, menos, mucho, poco, mejor, peor,* and *demasiado* may be used either as adjectives or adverbs.

ADJECTIVE	ADVERB
Alicia tiene *menos* dinero que yo. *Alice has less money than I do.*	**Ella es *más* pobre.** *She is poorer.*
La Sra. Goya tiene *demasiadas* joyas. *Mrs. Goya has too many jewels.*	**Ella es *demasiado* rica.** *She is too rich.*
Tu pintura es *peor* que la mía. *Your painting is worse than mine.*	**Yo pinto *mejor* que tú.** *I paint better than you.*

NOTE: **As adjectives, *mucho, poco*, and *demasiado* vary in gender and number; as adverbs, they do not change.**

EXERCISE D. Express Martin's comments using the adverb and the appropriate form of the adjective in parentheses.

1. Roberto tiene _______________ amigos que yo porque yo soy _______________ amistoso. (*más, menos*)
2. Freddy cree _______________ supersticiones. Él es _______________ supersticioso. (*demasiado, demasiado*)
3. La comida de mi mamá es _______________ que la de mi abuela. Mi abuela cocina _______________ que mi mamá. (*mejor, peor*)
4. Mi hermana tiene _______________ ositos de peluche. Ella colecciona _______________ . (*mucho, demasiado*)
5. Alex toca _______________ el piano pero él va a dar _______________ recitales. (*poco, demasiado*)
6. Jack y Berta no pelean _______________ pero tienen _______________ desacuerdos. (*mucho, demasiado*)
7. En el calendario hay _______________ días festivos pero las personas los celebran _______________ . (*mucho, poco*)

[2] Adverbs and Adverbial Phrases of Time or Frequency

a. Adverbs of Time or Frequency (answering the question when?)

ahora	*now*	**hoy**	*today*	**siempre**	*always*
anoche	*last night*	**luego**	*then*	**tarde**	*late*
ayer	*yesterday*	**nunca**	*never*	**temprano**	*early*
entonces	*then*	**pronto**	*soon*	**todavía**	*still, yet*

b. Adverbial Phrases of Time or Frequency

algún día	*some day*	**muchas veces**	*often*
a veces	*sometimes*	**pocas veces**	*seldom*
esta noche	*tonight*	**primero**	*first*
este fin de semana	*this weekend*	**todos los días**	*every day*
más tarde	*later*		

EXERCISE E. **Using the suggested adverb or adverbial phrase, tell when, or how frequently, you do, did, or will do the following things.**

EXAMPLE: preparar la tarea / más tarde **Yo prepararé la tarea más tarde.**

1. cantar en la calle / pocas veces ____________________
2. ayudar a los padres / siempre ____________________
3. hacer el esquiar acuático / algún día ____________________
4. montar a caballo / este fin de semana ____________________
5. jugar al tenis / todos los días ____________________
6. volver a ver una película / anoche ____________________
7. entrar en el cine sin pagar / nunca ____________________
8. usar la ropa del mejor amigo / muchas veces ____________________
9. dejar la llave en casa / ayer ____________________
10. faltar a una clase / a veces ____________________

EXERCISE F. **Tell when or how frequently these people do these activities. Use the expressions given.**

a veces	nunca	siempre	tarde
muchas veces	pocas veces	temprano	todos los días

EXAMPLE: A Paco le gusta ver la salida del sol. Él se levanta **temprano.**

1. Rosa lee más de cien libros en un año. Ella lee ________________ .
2. Alberto es un niño cortés. Él ________________ dice «por favor» y «gracias».

3. A Ken le gusta estudiar las estrellas. Él se acuesta ________________ .

4. Victoria no es partidaria de los deportes. Ella ________________ practica ningún deporte.

5. Ricardo es tímido y no le gusta mucho bailar. Él baila ________________ .

6. Cuando Elsa va de compras nunca tiene bastante dinero con ella. ________________ ella pide dinero prestado a sus amigas.

7. A Gladys no le gustan los dulces pero ________________ se le antoja un chocolate.

8. El señor Prado es muy puntual. Le gusta llegar ________________ a sus citas.

[*3*] ADVERBS AND ADVERBIAL PHRASES OF PLACE

a. Common Adverbs of Place (answering the question where?)

abajo	*below, downstairs*	**dentro**	*inside*
¿adónde?	*(to) where?*	**derecho**	*straight ahead*
allí	*there*	**detrás**	*behind*
aquí	*here*	**¿dónde?**	*where?*
arriba	*above, upstairs*	**enfrente**	*in front of, opposite*

b. Common Adverbial Phrases of Place

a la derecha	*to the right*	**delante de**	*in front of, ahead of*
a la izquierda	*to the left*	**detrás de**	*behind*
al lado de	*next to, alongside*	**encima de**	*on top of*
debajo de	*beneath*	**frente a**	*facing, in front of*

EXERCISE G. Tell the location of each one of the following.

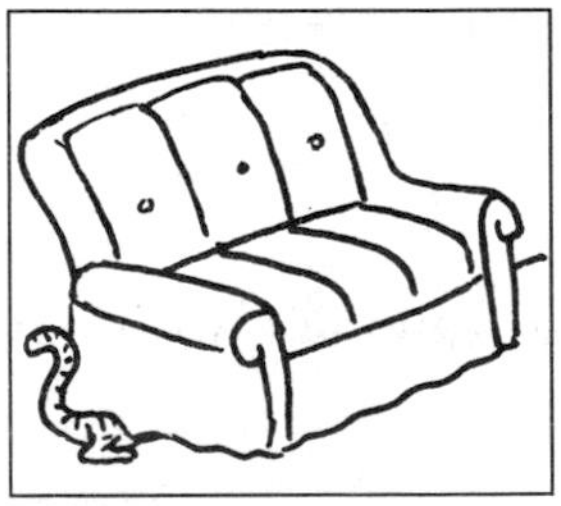

EXAMPLE: El gato está debajo del sofá.

1. Las llaves están encima de la mesa.

2. La pelota está detrás de la silla.

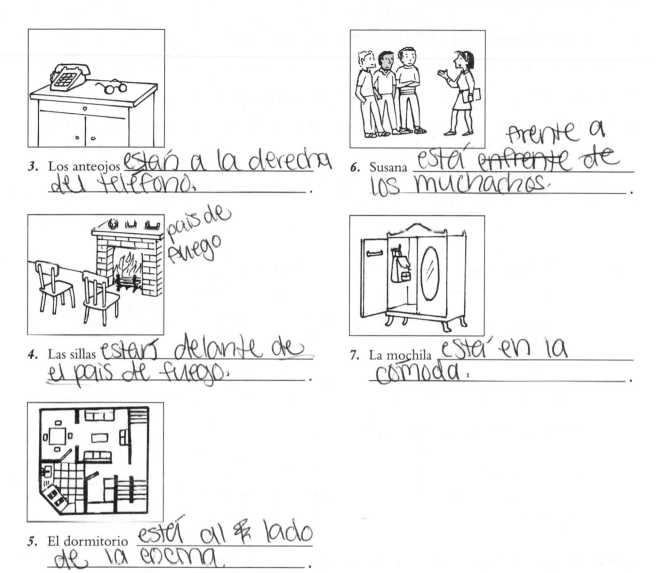

3. Los anteojos están a la derecha del teléfono.

pais de fuego

4. Las sillas están delante de el pais de fuego.

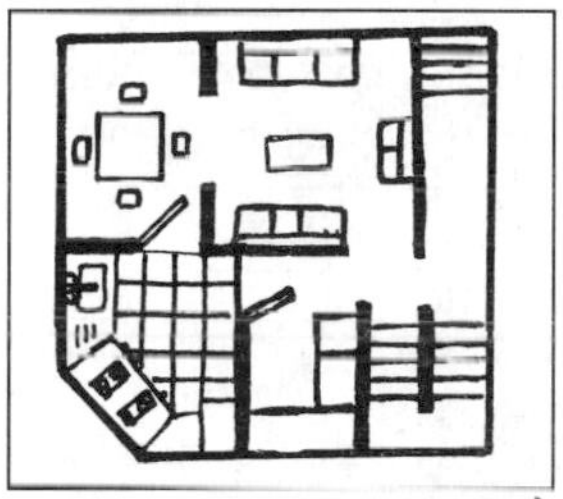

5. El dormitorio está al lado de la cocina.

6. Susana está ~~enfrente de~~ frente a los muchachos.

7. La mochila está en la cómoda.

[4] Other Adverbial Expressions

a. Some adverbial expressions are formed by combining prepositions with other words:

(1) Preposition + noun

a la vez	*at the same time*	**de veras**	*really, truly*
al fin	*finally*	**en seguida**	*immediately, at once*
de día	*by day*	**por desgracia**	*unfortunately*
de memoria	*by heart*	**sin duda**	*undoubtedly*
de noche	*by night*	**sin embargo**	*nevertheless*
de repente	*suddenly*		

(2) Preposition + adjective

a menudo	*often*	**en general, por lo general**	*generally*
de nuevo	*again*	**por consiguiente**	*consequently*
de pronto	*suddenly*	**por supuesto**	*of course*

(3) **Preposition + adverb**

al (a lo) menos	*at least*	**en cuanto**	*as soon as*

(4) **Preposition + verb form**

al amanecer	*at daybreak*	**por escrito**	*in writing*
al anochecer	*at nightfall*	**por lo visto**	*apparently, evidently*

(5) **Preposition + adjective + noun**

de buena (mala) gana	*(un)willingly*	**en otra parte**	*elsewhere*
en ninguna parte	*not anywhere, nowhere*	**en todas partes**	*everywhere*

b. The following are common adverbial expressions formed with several words:

ahora mismo	*right now*	**hoy mismo**	*this very day*
a pesar de	*in spite of*	**junto a**	*beside*
cada vez más	*more and more*	**mientras tanto**	*meanwhile*
cuanto antes	*as soon as possible*	**rara vez**	*seldom*
de cuando en cuando	*from time to time*	**tal vez**	*perhaps*
dentro de poco	*shortly*	**tan pronto como**	*as soon as*
hoy (en) día	*nowadays*	**ya no**	*no longer*

EXERCISE H. **Michael likes to comment about everyone and everything. Complete his comments using the following adverbial expressions.**

a la vez	de cuando en cuando	de repente	por lo visto
al amanecer	de día	en seguida	sin duda
al anochecer	de memoria	hoy mismo	sin embargo
al fin	de noche	por escrito	tal vez

1. ______________ Marta viaja en autobús, pero ______________ ella prefiere viajar en taxi.

2. Pilar se despierta ______________ porque los pájaros comienzan a cantar.

3. A mi abuela le fascinan los colores que se ven en el cielo ______________ .

4. Verónica nunca tarda en contestar cuando alguien le hace una pregunta. Ella responde ______________ .

5. Los dos carros chocaron en la carretera porque el primer carro frenó ______________ .

6. Enrique toca todas las canciones populares en la guitarra y no tiene que leer la música. Él las sabe ______________ .

7. Tomás y David tenían un partido de fútbol ayer pero estaba lloviendo. ______________ , ellos fueron al estadio listos para jugar.

8. Lina hace muchas cosas en un día porque tiene la habilidad de hacer dos cosas ______________ .

9. Nina gasta mucho dinero cuando va de compras. ______________ , sus padres son ricos.

10. El profesor no aceptó el perdón oral de Rodolfo. Rodolfo tiene que pedírselo ______________ .

11. Estela y Marco andan juntos ____________ . ____________, ellos son novios.

12. Me olvidé del cumpleaños de Antonia que fue ayer. ____________ yo voy a llamarle para felicitarla.

13. Yo no soy gran partidario de las películas de la ciencia-ficción. Pero, ____________ yo veo una.

14. El cielo está muy nublado hoy. ____________ va a llover.

15. ____________ ayer terminaron la construcción en la escuela.

EXERCISE I. **Complete the story that Linda wrote about her father with the correct expression that corresponds to the word given in parentheses.**

Yo no visito ____________ (*1.* never) a mi padre donde él trabaja. ____________ (*2.* Now) él es el gerente de una tienda grande de ropa. El dueño de la tienda dijo que mi papá aprendió ____________ (*3.* by heart) los nombres de todos los empleados en media hora. ____________ (*4.* In general), él trabaja ____________ (*5.* too much) y nosotros no podemos pasar tiempo ____________ (*6.* together) en la tienda. ____________ (*7.* Consequently), cuando yo quiero hablar con él, le llamo por teléfono. Su oficina está ____________ (*8.* upstairs), en el segundo piso. ____________ (*9.* seldom) lo encuentro ____________ (*10.* there). Él ____________ (*11.* always) está ____________ (*12.* downstairs) trabajando ____________ (*13.* next to) los dependientes. Según su secretaria, él está ____________ (*14.* everywhere). Él cree que los empleados trabajan ____________ (*15.* better) al verlo ayudándolos. Él trata a todo el mundo ____________ (*16.* politely), aun a los clientes que ____________ (*17.* often) le gritan ____________ (*18.* furiously). ____________ (*19.* In spite of) las horas largas y los problemas que se presentan ____________ (*20.* daily), le fascina su trabajo.

MASTERY EXERCISES

EXERCISE J. **Using adverbs in your responses, answer the questions a friend asks.**

1. ¿A qué hora te levantas en general? ____________

2. ¿Qué haces ahora mismo? ____________

3. ¿Cómo patinas en hielo? ____________

4. ¿Qué cosas haces de mala gana? ____________

5. ¿Cómo tratas a tus hermanos? ____________

6. ¿Siempre preparas la tarea con cuidado? ______________________________

7. ¿Eres hábil cuando juegas a un deporte? ______________________________

8. ¿Dónde estacionas tu carro? ______________________________

9. ¿Todavía piensas estudiar en México en el verano? ______________________________

10. ¿Cúando vas a esquiar? ______________________________

EXERCISE K. Complete the statements with an appropriate adverb.

1. A mi mamá le fascina ir al teatro. Ella va allí ______________ .

2. Yo traté de llamar a Juan por teléfono pero ______________ tiene el mismo número.

3. ______________ se ven menos expresiones de la cortesía.

4. Larry no supo dónde buscar un libro en la biblioteca. ______________ , él va allí ______________ .

5. ______________ , diez alumnos van a participar en el concurso.

6. A Tere no le gustaba el tenis pero ahora parece que le gusta ______________ .

7. Al ver la gravedad de la herida, el médico atendió al señor ______________ .

8. El señor Molina ha viajado mucho y dice que ______________ se habla español ______________ .

9. Tengo muchísima hambre. Tengo que comer ______________ .

10. Van a tardar ______________ menos dos días en revelar las fotografías.

EXERCISE L. José is describing a meeting he had with his boss. Express in Spanish what he says.

1. Today the manager spoke to me again, but in a courteous manner.

____

2. Evidently, sometimes I don't arrive at the office early.

____

3. I work well, carefully and diligently but too slowly.

____

4. Many employees are in the office at daybreak and are still there at nightfall.

____

5. I do my work willingly and each day I show him that I learn easily.

____

6. Nevertheless, I often spend too much time talking to my colleagues.

____

7. Suddenly, he turned to the right and began to speak quickly.

____

8. Perhaps I would prefer to be in another department.

____

9. Meanwhile, another employee wanted to see him at the same time.

____

10. Finally, I returned to my desk and of course I began to work more quickly.

____

ACTIVIDADES

1. Write ten sentences in which you describe the manner in which you do different things.

2. Write a paragraph of six to ten sentences in which you describe your favorite activities. Tell how you do them and when.

3. Write a short sketch of ten to twelve sentences in which you describe an event or incident you witnessed recently. Include as many adverbs as possible in the description.

Chapter 31
Interrogative and Exclamatory Words

[1] INTERROGATIVES

a. Common interrogative expressions

¿qué?	what?	¿cuánto, -a?	*how much?*
¿quién, -es?	*who?*	¿cuántos, -as?	*how many?*
¿a quién, -es	*whom?, to whom?*	¿cómo?	*how?*
¿de quién?	*whose?, of whom?*	¿por qué?	*why?*
¿con quién, -es?	*with whom?*	¿dónde?	*where?*
¿cuál, -es?	*which?, which one(s)?*	¿de dónde?	*(from) where?*
¿cuándo?	*when?*	¿a dónde?	*(to) where?*

NOTE:

1. All interrogative words have a written accent.
2. In Spanish, questions have an inverted question mark (*¿*) at the beginning and a standard one (*?*) at the end.
3. When interrogatives words such as *¿qué?*, *¿cuándo?*, and *¿dónde?* are used in a question, the subject-verb order is reversed from the order in statements.

¿**Qué** hacen ellos?	*What are they doing?*
Ellos comen.	*They are eating.*
¿**Dónde** está Enrique?	*Where is Henry?*
Él está aquí.	*He is here.*

4. Both *¿qué?* and *¿cuál?* are equivalent to English *what?* and *which?*, but the two words are not usually interchangeable in Spanish.

(a) *¿Qué?* seeks a description, definition, or explanation. It is used instead of *¿cuál?* before a noun.

¿**Qué** es esto?	*What is this?*
¿**Qué** vestido prefiere Ud.?	*Which dress do you prefer?*

(b) *¿Cuál?* implies a choice or selection.

¿**Cuál** es la capital de México?	*What is the capital of Mexico?*
¿**Cuáles** son los productos importantes de la Argentina?	*What are the important products of Argentina?*
¿**Cuál** de los vestidos prefiere Ud.?	*Which of the dresses do you prefer?*

5. *¿Adónde?* is used instead of *¿dónde?* to indicate motion to a place (to where).

¿**Adónde** va Ud.?	*Where are you going?*

EXERCISE A. **Ricardo doesn't listen carefully to his friends when they are talking and always has to ask about whom they are speaking. Express the questions he asks to find out who does the following.**

EXAMPLE: Arturo y Vicki van al cine esta noche. **¿Quiénes** van al cine esta noche?

1. Mario es miembro del equipo de béisbol. ____________________
2. Sarita trabaja de salvavidas. ____________________
3. Ali recibió un carro nuevo para su cumpleaños. ____________________
4. Nosotros pensamos ir al parque de diversiones. ____________________
5. Jacques piensa visitar a su familia en Francia. ____________________
6. Yo tengo que cuidar a mi hermanito. ____________________
7. Eliot y Víctor están en el estadio. ____________________

EXERCISE B. **Your mother is telling you why she couldn't sleep last night. You ask her to repeat what she said.**

EXAMPLE: Una sirena no dejó de sonar. **¿Qué** no dejó de sonar?

1. Un teléfono sonó varias veces. ____________________
2. Muchos carros tocaron la bocina. ____________________
3. Entró mucha luz en el cuarto. ____________________
4. Un farol se encendía y se apagaba. ____________________
5. Los vecinos tocaron discos toda la noche. ____________________
6. Cayó un relámpago. ____________________
7. Oí muchos ruidos en la casa. ____________________

EXERCISE C. **Alex was absent from school today. Complete the questions he asks with *¿qué?* or *¿quién / quiénes?***

1. ¿ ______________ enseñó la clase de química?
2. ¿ ______________ tarea dio el señor Vargas?
3. ¿ ______________ más faltó a las clases hoy?
4. ¿ ______________ hará el experimento pasadomañana?

5. ¿ __________ ayudaron al profesor?

6. ¿ __________ te acompañó durante el recreo?

7. ¿ __________ deporte jugaste en la clase de educación física?

8. ¿ __________ jugaron contigo?

9. ¿ __________ necesito llevar a la escuela mañana?

10. ¿ __________ fue elegido presidente del club?

EXERCISE D. **Your younger brother is looking through a book. He asks you to explain the words he doesn't understand. According to the answers given, express his questions.**

EXAMPLE: Un incendio es un fuego. **¿Qué** es un incendio?

1. Una violeta es una flor. __________
2. Una excursión es un viaje. __________
3. Un ciprés es un árbol. __________
4. Una ciruela es una fruta. __________
5. Una enciclopedia es un libro. __________

EXERCISE E. **Your teacher has asked you to prepare a series of questions to ask the class. Complete the following questions with *¿qué?* or *¿cuál /cuáles?*.**

1. ¿ __________ día es hoy?

2. ¿ __________ son los días de la semana?

3. ¿ __________ tiempo hace hoy?

4. ¿ __________ haces cuando llueve?

5. ¿ __________ es tu estación favorita?

6. ¿ __________ quieres recibir de regalo para tu cumpleaños?

7. ¿ __________ es el mejor equipo de fútbol?

8. ¿ __________ mes del año tiene sólo 28 días?

9. ¿ __________ deporte prefieres?

10. ¿ __________ de los grupos musicales es tu predilecto?

EXERCISE F. **You are helping your teacher clean the classroom on the last day of school. As she begins to put things in a box for the lost and found she wants to know to whom they belong. Express the question that she asks for each item.**

EXAMPLE: llaves **¿De quién** son las llaves?

1. anteojos __________

2. paraguas ______________________

3. tarjetas de béisbol ______________________

4. mochila ______________________

5. patines ______________________

EXERCISE G. Based on the answers given, express the questions Jenny asks a new exchange student.

EXAMPLE: Les escribo a mis amigos por el correo electrónico.
¿A quiénes les escribes por el correo electrónico?

1. Llamo a mis padres por larga distancia. ______________________

2. Extraño más a mis hermanos. ______________________

3. Aquí llamo a mi amiga Lola. ______________________

4. Le mando una carta a diario a mi novio, Gerardo. ______________________

5. Visito a mis tíos a menudo. ______________________

EXERCISE H. Ricky is corresponding with a penpal. From the paragraph below, express the questions Ricky asked him in his last correspondence.

EXAMPLE: **¿Dónde** está la escuela a la que asistes?

La escuela a la que asisto no está lejos de la casa. Mi mejor amigo, Hugo, vive a una cuadra de mi casa. Los cines están en el centro. Hay un parque cerca de la escuela. Mi restaurante favorito, un restaurante chino, está en el centro comercial. Mis amigos y yo nos reunimos en el centro comercial.

1. ______________________

2. ______________________

3. ______________________

4. ______________________

5. ______________________

EXERCISE I. A classmate wants to know where you and some of your friends went during the summer vacation. Express the questions she asks.

EXAMPLE: Lucinda **¿Adónde** fue Lucinda durante las vacaciones?

1. Gregorio y Ralph ______________________

2. tú ______________________

3. Kamal ______________________

4. Jimmy y su familia ______________________

5. las gemelas Ortega ______________________

EXERCISE J. **Denise is visiting her aunt who just returned from a trip around the world. She wants to know where everything is from. Express her questions.**

EXAMPLE: esta pintura **¿De dónde** es esta pintura?

1. el calendario azteca ____________________
2. las muñecas ____________________
3. esta estatua ____________________
4. el florero ____________________
5. la caja de música ____________________
6. los grabados en madera ____________________

EXERCISE K. **Mr. Arenas is speaking to a travel agent about a proposed trip. Complete the questions he is asked by the travel agent with the appropriate question words.**

1. ¿ ____________ se llama Ud.?
2. ¿ ____________ vive Ud.?
3. ¿ ____________ es su número de teléfono?
4. ¿ ____________ personas harán el viaje?
5. ¿ ____________ piensan ir?
6. ¿ ____________ es el propósito del viaje?
7. ¿ ____________ días piensan estar allí?
8. ¿ ____________ dinero quieren gastar?
9. ¿ ____________ clase de viaje quieren hacer?
10. ¿ ____________ ciudades quieren visitar?
11. ¿ ____________ quieren conocer en cada ciudad?
12. ¿ ____________ van a visitar en la última ciudad?
13. ¿ ____________ no quieren pasar más días allí?
14. ¿ ____________ piensan regresar?
15. ¿ ____________ van a pagar el viaje?

[2] EXCLAMATIONS

Exclamatory words, like interrogative words, have written accents. The most common exclamatory words are:

¡Qué... !	*What ... !, What a ... !, How ... !*	**¡Qué grande es!**	*How large it is!*
¡Qué película!	*What a film!*	**¡Qué rica es la sopa!**	*How delicious the soup is!*

¡Cuánto, -a... !	*How much . . . !*	**¡Cuánta** comida!	*How much food!*
¡Cuántos, -as... !	*How many . . . !*	**¡Cuántos** carros tienen!	*How many cars they have!*

NOTE:

1. Exclamatory sentences have an inverted exclamation mark (*¡*) at the beginning and a standard one (*!*) at the end.
2. If there is an adjective next to a noun, the exclamation is made more intense by placing *tan* or *más* before the adjective.

   ¡Qué tren **más (tan)** rápido! *What a fast train!*

EXERCISE L. **Alfredo and some friends are on a camping trip. Express what they exclaim upon seeing the following.**

EXAMPLE: oso / grande **¡Qué** oso **tan (más)** grande!

1. árbol / antiguo ______________________
2. flores / bonitas ______________________
3. arroyo / ancho ______________________
4. ardillas / graciosas ______________________
5. caverna / oscura ______________________
6. pájaros / ruidosos ______________________
7. choza / rústica ______________________
8. tienda de campo / pequeña ______________________

EXERCISE M. **You and several friends have mixed opinions about a musical comedy that you just saw. Express the comments you make as you leave the theater using *¡qué!*, *¡cuánto!*, or *¡cuántos!***

EXAMPLE: música / viva **¡Qué** música **tan (más)** viva!

1. vestuario / original ______________________
2. bailarines / torpes ______________________
3. argumento / ridículo ______________________
4. cantantes / talentosos ______________________
5. músicos / tocar / la orquesta ______________________
6. intermedios / largos ______________________
7. producción / aburrida ______________________

MASTERY EXERCISES

EXERCISE N. Prepare as many questions as you can based on the following paragraphs.

EXAMPLE: El sábado por la tarde, mientras Jorge estaba en la playa, conoció a Elena, una joven guatemalteca. Ella habla inglés muy bien y por eso no hablaron español.

¿A quién conoció Jorge? *¿Qué lengua hablaron?*
¿Dónde estaba Jorge? *¿Cómo habla Elena el inglés?*
¿Cuándo conoció Jorge a Elena? *¿Por qué no hablaron español?*

1. Cada año Felipe espera con muchísimas ganas el día de su cumpleaños. Su familia suele darle un regalo colectivo que representa uno de sus pasatiempos favoritos. Este año Felipe recibió varios juegos electrónicos que puede usar en la computadora.

____

____

____

____

2. Los padres de Elisa están contentos porque Elisa tiene la costumbre de acostarse temprano. A ella le gusta leer en la cama antes de dormirse. Ahora ella lee una novela muy interesante y divertida. Su mamá se sorprendió porque Elisa no apagó la luz de su dormitorio hasta la medianoche.

____

____

____

____

EXERCISE O. You and several friends are spending the weekend in the country. Express what someone says when he/she hears the different comments.

EXAMPLE: Es un día hermoso. **¡Qué** día **más** hermoso!

1. Había muchas estrellas en el cielo. ______________________________
2. El cielo es muy azul. ______________________________
3. El paisaje es muy verde. ______________________________
4. El ambiente es tranquilo. ______________________________
5. El agua está muy fría. ______________________________
6. Hay muchas montañas altas. ______________________________
7. Hay poca gente aquí. ______________________________
8. Es un lugar ideal. ______________________________

EXERCISE P. **The Spanish Club in your school is going to review short stories and novels in Spanish. You have been put in charge of this event. Prepare a list of questions that each reviewer will have to answer in his/her presentation. Express the following in Spanish.**

1. What is the title of the novel (short story)?

___

2. What is the author's name?

___

3. Where is the author from?

___

4. Where does the action of the story (novel) take place?

___

5. How many characters are there?

___

6. Who are the main characters?

___

7. Which of the characters is the most realistic?

___

8. When does the story (novel) take place?

___

9. What did you like most (least) about the story (novel)?

___

10. Why did you like (dislike) the story (novel)?

___

11. How does the story (novel) end?

___

12. What type of message does the story (novel) give?

___

13. Which literary techniques does the author employ?

___

14. To whom would you recommend the story (novel)?

___

15. Why would you recommend or not recommend it?

___

ACTIVIDADES

1. Prepare a list of ten questions you would ask in each of the following situations:

  a. You are working in a department store for the summer. What would you ask a customer who wants to buy an article of clothing?
  b. You are interviewing an alumnus /alumna of your school to learn about their impressions of the school now that they have been graduated.
  c. You are going to spend the summer in a Spanish-speaking country. What questions will you ask to learn about the host family with whom you will live?

2. Prepare a list of positive comments (exclamatory expressions) you can use while living with the host family.

Part four

Word Study

Chapter 32
Word Building

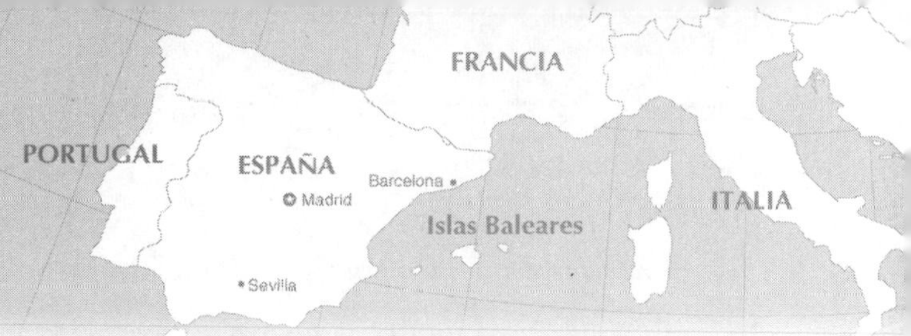

One way to increase your Spanish vocabulary is to think of words as roots or word families. Learning specific patterns can help you to expand your Spanish vocabulary and read more effectively.

A. Some nouns drop their final vowel and add *-ero, -era* to indicate the person associated with the noun.

la aventura	*the adventure*	la cocina	*the kitchen*
el aventurero / la aventurera	*the adventurer*	el cocinero / la cocinera	*the cook*

EXERCISE A. **Mr. Whitman is talking to a colleague in his company's office in Mexico. Complete the dialogue with the word that comes from the word in boldface.**

EXAMPLE: SR. WHITMAN: Espero **una carta** importante.
EL COLEGA: **El cartero** llega a las diez.

1. SR. WHITMAN: No he recibido ningún **mensaje.**
   EL COLEGA: ____________________ no ha venido hoy.

2. SR. WHITMAN: ¿Cuándo van a terminar **la obra** de reparación?
   EL COLEGA: ____________________ la terminarán esta tarde.

3. SR. WHITMAN: Tuve un problema en **la aduana.**
   EL COLEGA: ____________________ son muy estrictos.

4. SR. WHITMAN: ¿Dónde puedo mandar arreglar **los zapatos?**
   EL COLEGA: ____________________ de la esquina hace buen trabajo.

5. SR. WHITMAN: ¿Cómo viajaré por la ciudad? Yo no tengo **coche.**
   EL COLEGA: ____________________ de la compañía lo llevará.

6. SR. WHITMAN: Fue **un viaje** largo y pesado.
   EL COLEGA: ____________________ se cansan fácilmente.

B. Some nouns ending in *-ero* change to *-ería* to indicate the shop or store in which the person works.

el barbero	*the barber*	el librero	*the book seller*
la barbería	*the barber shop*	la librería	*the bookstore*

EXERCISE B. **Mrs. Andrade is telling a new neighbor where she can do her shopping. Write the name of the store based on the word in italics.**

EXAMPLE: Nuestro vecino, el señor Vega, es **carnicero.** Su **carnicería** está en la Calle Londres.

1. Mi marido es *joyero* y trabaja en la ____________________ «Princesa».

2. *El lechero* ya no hace entrega a domicilio pero hay una buena____________ en la Calle Reforma.

3. El mejor *panadero* del vecindario es Humberto Flores. Su____________ está al lado de la carnicería.

4. Mi *peluquero* se llama Antonio y voy a su____________ mañana, si Ud. me quiere acompañar.

5. Hay *un zapatero* fabuloso muy cerca de aquí. Su____________ está en la esquina. También vende zapatos nuevos de última moda.

6. Yo soy una buena *repostera* pero prefiero comprar los pasteles en la____________ «La Francesa».

7. Venden *flores* frescas y bonitas en la____________ «El Jardín».

8. Si necesita reparar un reloj, el mejor *relojero* del barrio está en la____________ de la Calle Mayor.

C. Some nouns are derived from the past participle of the verb.

resultar *to result*	**oír** *to hear*	**decir** *to say*
el resultado *the result*	**el oído** *hearing*	**el dicho** *the saying*

EXERCISE C. Estela often talks incessantly when she is with her friends. Complete her statements with the appropriate word from the suggestions provided.

SUGGESTIONS:

asado	contenido	oído	vestido
cocido	dichos	pescado	
conocidos	empleados	resultado	

1. La explosión les afectó el ____________ .

2. En la cocina de mi abuela hay muchos imanes con ____________ chistosos.

3. Prefiero la carne y el pollo; no me gusta el ____________ para nada.

4. Los ____________ de esa tienda son muy amables. Siempre tratan bien a los clientes.

5. Para la boda de su hija, la señora Lozano piensa comprar un ____________ carísimo.

6. Echaron a perder el ____________ porque nadie lo cuidó en el horno.

7. Muchos ____________ míos han recomendado esa película. Creo que nos gustará.

8. Antes de ordenar en un restaurante, mi mamá quiere saber el ____________ de todos los platos, especialmente del ____________ .

9. El ____________ del partido de hoy fue un empate.

D. Some feminine nouns are formed from past participles by changing the *-o* ending to *-a*.

entrar *to enter*	**beber** *to drink*	**ver** *to see*
la entrada *the entrance*	**la bebida** *the drink, beverage*	**la vista** *the sight, view*

EXERCISE D. **You are watching the nightly news. Complete the statements the news reporter makes basing your response on the word in italics.**

EXAMPLE: **Nevó** toda la noche al norte y tuvieron **una nevada** de doce pulgadas.

1. Es más económico *ir* a Roma si compramos un boleto de__________ y vuelta.
2. Muchas personas *comen* en el Restaurante Real porque la__________ es muy sabrosa y fresca.
3. Un niño fue *herido* en el accidente pero los médicos dicen que la__________ es superficial.
4. A la hora de *salir* del cine, los acomodadores abrieron todas las__________ .
5. El rey de España *llega* mañana. Todo el mundo espera su__________ con entusiasmo.
6. Los carros no deben *parar* en esa esquina porque es una__________ de autobús.
7. La maestra *miró* a los alumnos con seriedad. Es decir, ella tiene una__________ seria.
8. En muchos casos, cuando una persona se *cae,* la__________ es más embarazosa que dolorosa.

E. Some stem-changing verbs have a corresponding noun with a stem-change.

almorzar	*to (eat) lunch*	**llover**	*to rain*
el almuerzo	*the lunch*	**la lluvia**	*the rain*

EXERCISE E. **Michael keeps a journal in his Spanish class. Complete the entry he made using the words provided.**

cuentos	vuelo	recuerdos	encuentro	prueba
sueño	gobierno	nieve	juegos	comienzo

Anoche tuve un __________ (1.) muy bonito. Tuve un __________ (2.) con unos amigos de mi niñez. Viajé en avión al Canadá y el __________ (3.) fue corto y agradable. Aunque era el __________ (4.) del invierno, la __________ (5.) blanca ya cubría las calles. Tuve que pasar por inmigración en el aeropuerto y el __________ (6.) exige una __________ (7.) de la nacionalidad de los viajeros. Afortunadamente tenía mi pasaporte. Mis amigos y yo contamos muchos __________ (8.) de la niñez: de los __________ (9.) infantiles que jugábamos y las bromas que hacíamos. Me desperté con muchos __________ (10.) bonitos.

F. Some nouns are formed from verbs by dropping the *-ar* ending of the verb and adding *-amiento,* or dropping the *-er* or *-ir* ending of the verb and adding *-imiento.*

casar	*to marry*	**establecer**	*to establish*
el casamiento	*the marriage*	**el establecimiento**	*the establishment*

EXERCISE F. **Luke is preparing some statements to ask his classmates in his Spanish class. Complete each statement with a noun formed from the following verbs.**

casar	consentir	nombrar	ofrecer
conocer	mover	nacer	descubrir

EXAMPLE: Cristóbal Colón es muy famoso por razón de su **descubrimiento** del Nuevo Mundo.

1. Rodolfo y su novia piensan casarse. ____________ tendrá lugar el año próximo.
2. El romanticismo y el naturalismo son dos ____________ literarios.
3. Un adorno tradicional de Navidad es el ____________ .
4. El ____________ de los ganadores del Premio Nobel siempre atrae mucha atención de la prensa.
5. Para quedar bien con sus dioses, los aztecas les hacían muchos ____________ .
6. Un cirujano necesita el ____________ del enfermo antes de operarlo.
7. Muchas personas mayores no tienen ningún ____________ de computadoras.

G. **Some nouns are derived from verbs by dropping the *-r* of the infinitive and adding *-ador* to the stem of *-ar* verbs, *-edor* to the stems of *-er*, and *-idor* to those of *-ir* verbs.**

trabajar *to work*	**comer** *to eat*	**servir** *to serve*
el trabajador *the worker*	**el comedor** *the dining room*	**el servidor** *the servant*

EXERCISE G. **Using the verbs *conquistar, descubrir, explorar, fundar, pensar,* and *vencer,* form nouns and complete the statements.**

EXAMPLE: (*gobernar*) En muchas de las repúblicas que se dividen en estados, cada estado elige a su propio **gobernador.**

1. En la batalla entre moros y cristianos en España en el siglo XI, el Cid fue el ____________ .
2. De Soto y Ponce de León fueron dos ____________ españoles.
3. Miguel de Unamuno fue uno de los gran ____________ de la «Generación del '98».
4. Thomas Edison fue el ____________ de la electricidad.
5. Henry Ford fue el ____________ de una empresa que fabrica automóviles.
6. Francisco Pizarro fue el ____________ de los incas.

H. **Some nouns are formed from adjectives by dropping the final vowel of the adjective and adding *-eza.***

bello *beautiful*	**limpio** *clean*
la belleza *the beauty*	**la limpieza** *the cleanliness*

EXERCISE H. **Jim is helping a friend study for a vocabulary test. For each of the adjectives given, express the noun that comes from that adjective.**

EXAMPLE: agudo → **agudeza**

1. ligero ______________
2. noble ______________
3. triste ______________
4. puro ______________
5. grande ______________
6. rico ______________
7. franco ______________
8. pobre ______________

I. Some English nouns ending in *-ty* are expressed in Spanish by changing the *-ty* to *-dad.*

brutality **la brutalidad** *capacity* **la capacidad**

EXERCISE I. **Giselle tells a friend some of the things she learned when she visited her sister at school. Complete her statements with the Spanish equivalent of the following words.**

activity	curiosity	humanity	society	university
brutality	generosity	prosperity	unity	

EXAMPLE: Visité la **universidad** donde mi hermana estudia medicina.

1. Las guerras muestran la ______________ en contra de la ______________ .
2. La ______________ intelectual es una característica buena.
3. Una persona tacaña no practica la ______________ .
4. Para ganar una elección, muchos políticos prometen la ______________ a los ciudadanos.
5. Ha habido muchos cambios en la ______________ actual porque las costumbres han cambiado.
6. La ______________ de una comunidad es un concepto básico e importante del ser humano.
7. Prefiero una ______________ donde me ejercite activamente.

J. Some English nouns ending in *-tion* are expressed in Spanish by changing *-tion* to *-ción.*

invention **la invención** *section* **la sección**

EXERCISE J. **Based on the English words given below, complete each of the following statements with the appropriate Spanish word.**

construction	description	formation	invitation	operation
conversation	direction	intention	nation	

EXAMPLE: Ésta es una **operación** difícil en la computadora.

1. Cada noche hay noticias sobre la ______________ en el noticiero de las seis.

2. Para saber cómo era Carlos, Rita le pidió una ______________ de sí mismo.

3. Recibí una ______________ a la quinceañera de mi prima.

4. Mi mamá tuvo una ______________ con mi maestra de matemáticas y ahora no puedo salir con mis amigos.

5. Yo no tengo ninguna ______________ de trabajar durante las vacaciones de verano.

6. Se han vendido muchas casas en esta calle y ahora hay mucha ______________ .

7. Ralph y Edward nunca caminan juntos. Edward siempre camina en ______________ opuesta.

8. Los romanos contribuyeron mucho a la ______________ de la cultura hispana.

K. A number of adjectives are formed from nouns by adding *-oso* to the stem of the noun.

número *the number* **religión** *the religion*
numeroso *numerous* **religioso** *religious*

EXERCISE K. Complete the following statements using the italicized word to form an adjective.

EXAMPLE: Dicen que una persona que muestra mucho **amor** es una persona **amorosa.**

1. El viento sopla afuera con mucha *furia*. Es un viento ______________ .

2. Este actor tiene *fama* mundial. Es decir, es muy ______________ .

3. Cuando hay hielo en la calle hay mucho *peligro.* Es ______________ caminar allí.

4. La paella es una *delicia* de la cocina española. Me gusta porque es ______________ .

5. El partido político que tiene más *poder* que el otro es el más ______________ .

6. Hay mucho *silencio* en el jardín porque el vecino está dentro de la casa. Por fin es una tarde ______________ .

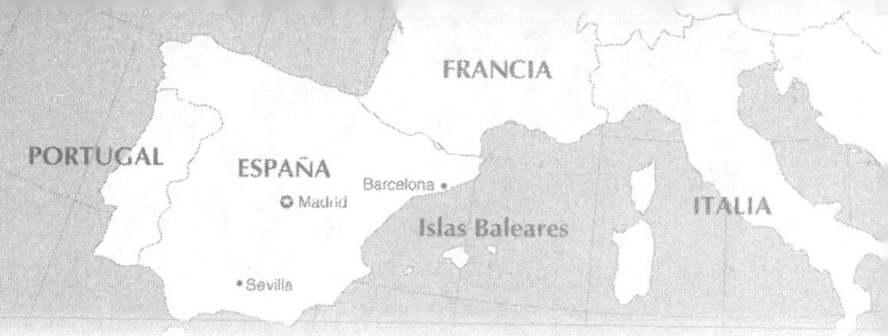

Chapter 33
Synonyms and Antonyms

[1] SYNONYMS

a. Nouns

afecto, cariño, amor *affection, love*
alumno, estudiante *student, pupil*
amo, dueño, propietario *master, owner, boss*
batalla, combate, lucha *battle, fight, struggle*
broma, chiste *joke, trick*
buque, barco, vapor *ship, boat*
cabello, pelo *hair*
cara, rostro *face*
cuarto, habitación *room*
cura, sacerdote *priest*
demonio, diablo *devil*
error, falta *error, mistake*
esposo, marido *husband*
idioma, lengua *language*
lugar, sitio *place*
maestro, profesor *teacher*
miedo, temor *fear*
país, nación *country, nation*
pájaro, ave *bird*

b. Adjectives

alegre, feliz, contento *happy, merry, content*
antiguo, viejo *old, ancient*
aplicado, diligente, trabajador *industrious, diligent, hard-working*
bastante, suficiente *enough, sufficient*
bello, hermoso *beautiful*
bonito, lindo *pretty*
célebre, famoso, ilustre *famous*
corto, breve *short*
delgado, flaco *thin, slender*
diferente, distinto *different*
grave, serio *serious*
igual, semejante *similar, alike*
tonto, necio *foolish, stupid*

c. Verbs

acabar, terminar, concluir (y) *to finish, to end, to conclude*
acordarse (ue) de, recordar (ue) *to remember*
aguardar, esperar *to wait (for)*
alzar (c), elevar, levantar *to raise*
andar, caminar *to walk*
asustar, espantar *to frighten, to scare*
atravesar (ie), cruzar (c) *to cross*
colocar (qu), poner (g) *to put, to place*
comprender, entender (ie) *to understand*
conseguir (i, gu), obtener (ie, g) *to get, to obtain*
contestar, responder *to answer, to reply*
dejar, permitir *to let, to allow, to permit*
desear, querer (ie) *to want, to wish*
detenerse (ie, g), pararse *to stop*
echar, arrojar, lanzar (c), tirar *to throw*
empezar (ie), principiar, comenzar (ie) *to begin*
enfadarse, enojarse *to become angry*
enviar (í), mandar *to send*
hallar, encontrar (ue) *to find*
invitar, convidar to *invite*
irse, marcharse *to go away*
mostrar (ue), enseñar *to show*
quedarse, permanecer (zc) *to remain*
rogar (ue, gu), suplicar (qu) *to beg, to implore*
romper, quebrar (ie) *to break*
seguir (i, gu), continuar (ú) *to continue*
sorprender, asombrar *to surprise*
suceder, ocurrir *to happen, to occur*
sufrir, padecer (zc) *to suffer*
volver (ue), regresar *to return*

d. Adverbs

aún, todavía *still, yet* | **jamás, nunca** *never*
despacio, lentamente *slowly* | **sólo, solamente** *only*

EXERCISE A. **Susan and her family are on a cruise. Rewrite the note she sends to a friend with synonyms for the words in italic.**

Querida amiga:

Te *envío* esta carta del *barco* en que viajo en el Mar Caribe. *Quiero* compartir contigo algunas de mis observaciones. Estoy muy *alegre* porque estoy divirtiéndome mucho. Hemos visitado tres islas *hermosas*. Cada isla es muy *diferente*. En una isla vi muchas *aves* exóticas. La tripulación del crucero es muy amable y todos hablan varios *idiomas*. Hay un novelista *célebre* en el crucero pero él prefiere *permanecer* en su *cuarto*. Cada mañana mi mamá y yo *andamos* lo largo del barco. Conocí a un joven *delgado* de *cabello* rubio. Es el hijo del *propietario* de una tienda del barco. Mis padres me *permiten* participar en muchas de las actividades a bordo. *Aún* faltan tres días en el mar. El tiempo en el crucero pasa *despacio*. El crucero *termina* el sábado.

Con *afecto*,

Susan

EXERCISE B. **Joey is preparing a word game for his Spanish class. Complete the choices he will offer his classmates by writing the appropriate synonym for the initial words given.**

EXAMPLE: *trabajador:* alegre, **diligente,** bello

1. *aguardar:* terminar, ____________________, dejar
2. *broma:* barco, sacerdote, ____________________
3. *alzar:* cruzar, ____________________, caminar
4. *lucha:* ____________________, vapor, amor
5. *bastante:* antiguo, ____________________, grave
6. *concluir:* atravesar, recordar, ____________________
7. *corto:* feliz, ____________________, aplicado
8. *obtener:* ____________________, comprender, principiar
9. *asustar:* lanzar, padecer, ____________________
10. *poner:* ____________________, desear, rogar
11. *sorprender:* suceder, volver, ____________________
12. *jamás:* ____________________, sólo, todavía
13. *romper:* sufrir, mostrar, ____________________

14. *país:* demonio, ________________ , dueño

15. *falta:* lengua, sitio, ________________

EXERCISE C. Describe this bullfighter, giving a synonym for the words in italic.

1. Conocí a un torero muy *famoso.*

____

2. También es *dueño* de una estancia en la que crían toros.

____

3. Los toros no lo *asustan.*

____

4. Los toros no son ni *delgados* ni *bellos.*

____

5. Los toros no le dan *temor* a él.

____

6. Él ya no lidia; es *maestro* de la tauromaquia.

____

7. Él *comprende* bien el inglés.

____

8. Él habla cuatro *lenguas.*

____

9. *Todavía* pasa cada domingo en la plaza de toros.

____

10. Siempre hablaba con un *cura* antes de lidiar en una corrida de toros.

____

11. La plaza de toros es un *lugar* de mucho espectáculo y valentía.

____

[2] ANTONYMS

a. Nouns

algo *something*	**nada** *nothing*
alguien *someone, somebody*	**nadie** *no one, nobody*
amigo *friend*	**enemigo** *enemy*
amo *master*	**esclavo** *slave*
amor *love*	**odio** *hate*
caballero *gentleman*	**dama** *lady*

cielo *heaven, sky*	**tierra** *earth, ground*
día *day*	**noche** *night*
entrada *entrance*	**salida** *exit*
este *east*	**oeste** *west*
éxito *success*	**fracaso** *failure*
fin *end*	**principio** *beginning*
guerra *war*	**paz** *peace*
héroe *hero*	**heroína** *heroine*
hombre *man*	**mujer** *woman*
madre *mother*	**padre** *father*
marido *husband*	**esposa** *wife*
muerte *death*	**vida** *life*
norte *north*	**sur** *south*
príncipe *prince*	**princesa** *princess*
respuesta *answer*	**pregunta** *question*
rey *king*	**reina** *queen*
ruido *noise*	**silencio** *silence*
verano *summer*	**invierno** *winter*
verdad *truth*	**mentira** *lie*
vicio *vice*	**virtud** *virtue*

b. Adjectives

alegre *happy*	**triste** *sad*
alguno *some*	**ninguno** *none*
alto *high, tall*	**bajo** *low, short*
amargo *bitter*	**dulce** *sweet*
ancho *wide*	**estrecho** *narrow*
antiguo *old, ancient*	**moderno** *modern*
barato *cheap*	**caro** *dear, expensive*
blanco *white*	**negro** *black*
común *common*	**raro** *rare*
corto *short*	**largo** *long*
débil *weak*	**fuerte** *strong*
difícil *difficult*	**fácil** *easy*
duro *hard*	**blando** *soft*
feliz *happy*	**triste** *sad*
flaco *thin*	**gordo** *fat*
frío *cold*	**caliente** *hot*
grande *large*	**pequeño** *small*
hermoso *beautiful*	**feo** *ugly*
inteligente *intelligent*	**estúpido** *stupid*
ligero *light*	**pesado** *heavy*
limpio *clean*	**sucio** *dirty*
lleno *full*	**vacío** *empty*
mayor *older*	**menor** *younger*

mejor *better*	**peor** *worse*
mismo *same*	**diferente** *different*
mucho, -s *much (many)*	**poco, -s** *little (few)*
oscuro *dark*	**claro** *light*
perezoso *lazy*	**trabajador, aplicado** *hard-working*
pobre *poor*	**rico** *rich*
posible *possible*	**imposible** *impossible*
primero *first*	**último** *last*
rubio *blond*	**moreno** *brunette*
sabio *wise*	**tonto** *foolish*
tarde *late*	**temprano** *early*
todo *everything*	**nada** *nothing*
valiente *brave*	**cobarde** *cowardly*
viejo *old*	**joven** *young* **nuevo** *new*
vivo *alive*	**muerto** *dead*

c. Verbs

acercarse (qu) (a) *to approach*	**alejarse (de)** *to move away (from)*
acordarse (ue) de *to remember*	**olvidarse de** *to forget*
aparecer (zc) *to appear*	**desaparecer (za)** *to disappear*
bajar *to go down*	**subir** *to go up*
callarse *to keep quiet*	**hablar** *to speak*
comprar *to buy*	**vender** *to sell*
contestar *to answer*	**preguntar** *to ask*
dar *to give*	**tomar** *to take* **recibir** *to receive*
despertarse (ie) *to wake up*	**dormirse (ue, u)** *to fall asleep*
empezar (ie, c) *to begin*	**acabar, terminar** *to end*
encender (ie) *to light, to ignite*	**apagar (gu)** *to put out, to extinguish*
ir *to go*	**venir (ie, g)** *to come*
levantarse *to get up*	**sentarse (ie)** *to sit down* **acostarse (ue)** *to go to bed*
llorar *to cry*	**reír (i)** *to laugh*
mentir (ie, i) *to lie*	**decir (i, g) la verdad** *to tell the truth*
meter *to put (in)*	**sacar (qu)** *to take out*
morir (ue, u) *to die*	**vivir** *to live*
perder (ie) *to lose*	**ganar** *to win* **hallar** *to find*
permitir *to permit*	**prohibir** *to prohibit*
ponerse (g) *to put on*	**quitarse** *to take off*
prestar *to lend*	**pedir prestado** *to borrow*
recoger (j) *to pick up*	**dejar caer** *to drop*
salir (g) (de) *to leave*	**entrar (en)** *to enter*

d. Adverbs

abajo *below, downstairs*	**arriba** *above, upstairs*
allí *there*	**aquí** *here*
anoche *last night*	**esta noche** *tonight*
antes (de) *before*	**después (de)** *after*
aprisa *quickly*	**despacio** *slowly*
ausente *absent*	**presente** *present*
bien *well*	**mal** *badly, poorly*
cerca de *near*	**lejos de** *far from*
debajo (de) *under*	**encima (de)** *on top*
delante de *in front of*	**detrás de** *in back of, behind*
fuera *outside*	**dentro** *inside*
hoy *today*	**mañana** *tomorrow* **ayer** *yesterday*
más *more*	**menos** *less*
no *no*	**sí** *yes*
siempre *always*	**nunca** *never*
tarde *late*	**temprano** *early*

e. Prepositions

con *with*	**sin** *without* **contra** *against*

EXERCISE D. **Ruth is preparing a crossword puzzle to help her improve her Spanish vocabulary. Complete the crossword puzzle with the appropriate antonym for the words given.**

HORIZONTAL	VERTICAL
2. tarde	1. fuera
4. ir	3. hoy
7. sabio	5. dar
8. valiente	6. contestar
9. posible	7. empezar
12. siempre	10. rubio
13. ganar	11. peor
15. último	14. delante
16. entrada	15. madre
17. diligente	16. limpio

EXERCISE E. **You like to annoy your brother by saying the opposite of what he says. Express what you tell him using an antonym for the word in italic.**

EXAMPLE: Hay mucho **ruido** aquí. No, hay mucho **silencio** aquí.

1. Víctor *tomó* noventa dólares por la bicicleta.

____

2. El plato está *lleno.*

____

3. Hay *más* nieve hoy que había el año pasado.

____

4. Luis *se acuesta* temprano.

____

5. Es *fácil* entrar al estadio cuando hay un partido.

____

6. El lago está ochenta millas al *oeste.*

____

7. La mujer *ríe* sin cesar.

____

8. El perro *se despierta.*

____

9. *Algo* extraordinario ocurrió *hoy.*

____

10. *Apagaron* la luz.

____

11. Los zapatos están *debajo* de la mesa.

____

12. No me gustan los panecillos *calientes.*

____

13. Todas las calles del centro son *anchas.*

____

14. Nunca escuchas *la respuesta.*

____

15. El carro está *sucio.*

____

EXERCISE F.

Alex answers negatively each question his mother asks him. Express his responses by replacing the word in italic with an antonym.

EXAMPLE: ¿Es **pequeña** la casa de Enrique?
No, la casa de Enrique es **grande.**

¿Siempre **te olvidas de** traer tus libros?
No, siempre **me acuerdo de** traer mis libros.

1. ¿Es *amargo* el jugo de naranja? ________________________
2. ¿Contestas *siempre* en voz *alta*? ________________________
3. ¿Te gustan las películas *antiguas?* ________________________
4. ¿Te lavas las manos *con* jabón? ________________________
5. ¿Estuvo *ausente* el profesor el jueves pasado? ________________________
6. ¿Son *cortas* las vacaciones de invierno? ________________________
7. ¿Son *baratos* los patines? ________________________
8. ¿Es *blanco* el carbón? ________________________
9. ¿Tienes muchos *amigos?* ________________________
10. ¿ *Subes* la escalera para llegar al piso bajo? ________________________

EXERCISE G.

Correct the statements a younger cousin tells you by providing the antonym of the word in italic.

1. España está al *oeste* de Portugal. ________________________
2. Yo soy *mayor* que mi hermano. ________________________
3. Dar limosna a los pobres es *un vicio.* ________________________
4. Generalmente los héroes son *cobardes.* ________________________
5. Hoy día *se permite* fumar en los restaurantes. ________________________
6. La última novela del autor fue *un fracaso;* sólo se vendieron tres millones de ejemplares. ________________________
7. Una mujer de cien años de edad es *joven.* ________________________
8. Cuando dos naciones tienen conflictos grandes, están en estado de *paz.* ________________________
9. Hace frío en *el verano.* ________________________
10. Un rascacielos es un edificio *bajo.* ________________________

11. El sótano está *encima* de la casa. ______________________

12. Las piedras son *blandas.* ______________________

13. Las aguas de los ríos son *calientes.* ______________________

14. Una persona se siente *fuerte* cuando tiene un resfriado. ______________________

15. Las estrellas se distinguen por *el día.* ______________________

MASTERY EXERCISES

EXERCISE H. Complete each analogy with the word that is missing:

EXAMPLES: pequeño : grande :: ancho : estrecho
buque : barco :: batalla : lucha

1. esposo : marido :: maestro : ______________
2. antiguo : viejo :: corto : ______________
3. andar : caminar :: dejar : ______________
4. dar : recibir :: comprar : ______________
5. ligero : pesado :: flaco : ______________
6. permitir : prohibir :: ganar : ______________
7. sabio : tonto :: rico : ______________
8. cielo : tierra :: vida : ______________
9. colocar : poner :: arrojar : ______________
10. limpio : sucio :: vacío : ______________
11. sufrir : padecer :: mostrar : ______________
12. alegre : contento :: bonito : ______________
13. hoy : ayer :: esta noche : ______________
14. aún : todavía :: nunca : ______________
15. tarde : temprano :: bien : ______________
16. cura : sacerdote :: ave : ______________
17. dulce : amargo :: alegre : ______________
18. fuera : dentro :: cerca : ______________
19. pelo : cabello : rostro : ______________
20. afecto : amor :: broma : ______________

EXERCISE I. **Express the synonyms or antonyms for each set of drawings.**

EXAMPLE: caminar ; correr

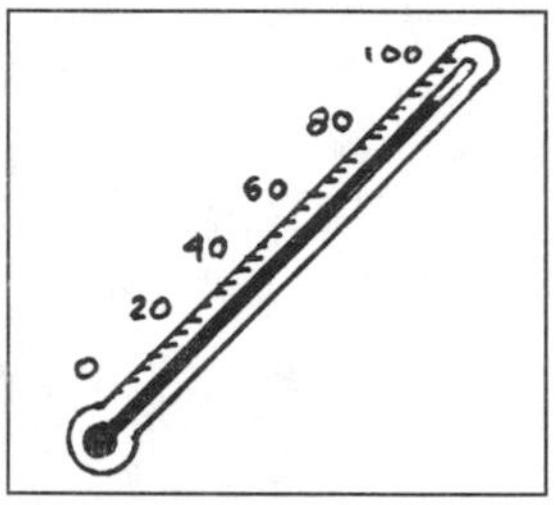

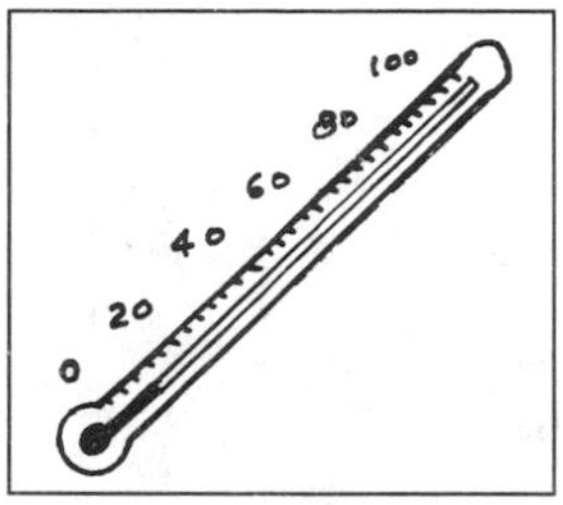

1. ____________________ ; ____________________

2. ____________________ ; ____________________

3. ____________________ ; ____________________

4. ____________________ ; ____________________

5. ____________________ ; ____________________

6. ____________________ ; ____________________

7. ____________________ ; ____________________

8. ____________________ ; ____________________

9. ____________________ ; ____________________

10. ______________________ ; ______________________

EXERCISE J. **Express what Raquel says about herself and her family.**

1. My mother is short and blond. My father is tall and brunette.

____

2. Her first language is English but his first language is Italian.

____

3. Someone asked something but no one responded.

____

4. I am happy at the end of spring but I am sad at the beginning of autumn.

____

5. I like cold soups in the summer and warm soups in the winter.

____

6. My parents believe that everything is possible and that nothing is impossible.

____

7. They also believe that children should know when to keep quiet and when they should speak.

____

8. I like to get up late but I don't like to go to bed early.

____

9. I love to give gifts but I also like to receive gifts.

____

10. I have many friends but my sister has few friends.

____

ACTIVIDADES

1. Write a brief description of yourself and a description of a friend who is very similar. Use as many synonyms as you can.

2. Describe an acquaintance or relative and explain how he/she differs from you. Use as many antonyms as you can.

3. Your family is planning to relocate from the city to the country or vice versa. Prepare a list of arguments you can use to explain why the country or the city is better using synonyms and antonyms.

Chapter 34
Thematic Vocabulary

[1] LA IDENTIFICACIÓN PERSONAL / *Personal Identification*

a. La información biográfica / *Biographical information*

(1) La nacionalidad / *Nationality*

alemán *German*
argentino *Argentinean*
asiático *Asian*
boliviano *Bolivian*
brasileño *Brazilian*
canadiense *Canadian*
centroamericano *Central American*
chileno *Chilean*
chino *Chinese*
colombiano *Colombian*
coreano *Korean*
costarricense *Costa Rican*
cubano *Cuban*
dominicano *Dominican*
ecuatoriano *Ecuadorean*
español *Spanish*
europeo *European*
francés *French*
griego *Greek*
guatemalteco *Guatemalan*
guyanés *Guianan*
haitiano *Haitian*
hondureño *Hondurean*
indio *Indian*
inglés *English*
italiano *Italian*
jamaiquino *Jamaican*
japonés *Japanese*
mexicano *Mexican*
nicaragüense *Nicaraguan*
norteamericano *North American*
panameño *Panamanian*
paraguayo *Paraguayan*
peruano *Peruvian*
puertorriqueño *Puerto Rican*
salvadoreño *El Salvadorian*
sudamericano *South American*
uruguayo *Uruguayan*
venezolano *Venezuelan*
vietnamita *Vietnamese*

(2) La familia / *Family*

la abuela *grandmother*
el abuelo *grandfather*
los abuelos *grandfathers, grandparents (grandfather and grandmother)*
el cuñado *brother-in-law*
la cuñada *sister-in-law*
la esposa *wife*
el esposo *husband*
la familia *family*
la hermana *sister*
el hermano *brother*
los hermanos *brothers, brothers and sisters*
la hija *daughter*
el hijo *son*
los hijos *children, sons and daughters*
la madrastra *stepmother*
la madre *mother*
la madrina *godmother*
la mamá *mom, mother*
la nieta *granddaughter*
el nieto *grandson*
la niña *girl*
el niño *boy*
la nuera *daughter-in-law*
el padrastro *stepfather*
el padre *father*
los padres *fathers, parents (father and mother)*
el padrino *godfather*

los padrinos *godparents*
los papás *fathers, parents (father and mother)*
el pariente *relative*
la prima *cousin*
el primo *cousin*
la sobrina *niece*
el sobrino *nephew*
la suegra *mother-in-law*
el suegro *father-in-law*
los suegros *fathers-in-law; in-laws (father-in-law and mother-in-law)*
la tía *aunt*
el tío *uncle*
los tíos *uncles, aunts and uncles*
el yerno *son-in-law*

b. Las características fisicas / *Physical characteristics*

alto *tall*
bajo *short*
bonito *pretty, beautiful*
calvo *bald*
ciego *blind, visually-impaired*
débil *weak*
delgado *thin*
feo *ugly*
flaco *skinny*
fuerte *strong*
gordo *fat*
hermoso *handsome, beautiful*
joven *young*
minusválido *handicapped*
sordo *deaf, hearing-impaired*
viejo *old*

tener . . . años *to be . . . years old*
tener los ojos azules *to have blue eyes*
tener los ojos cafés *to have brown eyes*
tener los ojos negros *to have black eyes*
tener los ojos verdes *to have green eyes*
tener el pelo rubio *to have blond hair*
tener el pelo moreno *to have dark hair*
tener el pelo castaño *to have brown hair*
tener el pelo negro *to have black hair*
tener el pelo rojo *to have red hair*
tener el pelo risado *to have curly hair*
tener el pelo ondulado *to have wavy hair*
tener el pelo lacio *to have straight hair*

c. Las características sicológicas / *Psychological characteristics*

activo *active*
alegre *happy*
amable *friendly*
ambicioso *ambitious*
antipático *unpleasant*
atlético *athletic*
bondadoso *kind*
cómico *funny*
contento *happy*
cortés *polite*
cruel *cruel*
curioso *curious*
descontento *unhappy*
divertido *fun*
egoísta *selfish*
franco *frank*
furioso *furious*
generoso *generous*
honesto *honest*
imaginativo *imaginative*
impulsivo *impulsive*
ingenuo *naive*
inteligente *intelligent*
interesante *interesting*
orgulloso *proud*
perezoso *lazy*
serio *serious*
simpático *nice, congenial*
supersticioso *superstitious*
triste *sad*
valiente *brave*

d. **Las emociones y los sentimientos** / *Emotions and feelings*

la alegría *joy*
el amor *love*
la envidia *envy*
la felicidad *happiness*
el gusto *pleasure*
la lealtad *loyalty*
el miedo *fear*
el odio *hate*
el orgullo *pride*
la pasión *passion*
la piedad *pity*
la tristeza *sadness*
la valentía *bravery*
la vergüenza *shame*

EXERCISE A. **Write a letter to a new Spanish-speaking pen pal, in which you introduce yourself and your family and describe your physical and psychological characteristics.**

¡Hola amiga! Me llamo Lauren. Tengo 15 años y vivo en California con mi familia. ~~Tengo~~ Son seis personas en mi familia. Tengo una hermana, Ariel, y dos hermanos, Ben y Austin. Soy rubia y ~~alta~~ soy baja. Tengo ojos verdes como mi mamá. Juego al voleibol y basquétbol. Me gusta los deportes mucho. También toco la guitarra y el piano. ¡Me encanta la música! Soy amable y simpática.

y ~~[illegible]~~ tengo el pelo lacio.

[2] LA CASA Y EL HOGAR / *House and Home*

a. **Las casa y los cuartos** / *House and rooms*

el alquiler *rent*
el apartamento *apartment*
el armario *wardrobe, closet*
el ascensor *elevator*
el balcón *balcony*
la casa *house*
el césped *lawn*
la chimenea *fireplace*
la cocina *kitchen*
el comedor *dining room*
el contrato *lease*
el cuarto *room*
el cuarto de baño *bathroom*
el desván *attic*
el dormitorio *bedroom*
el edificio de apartamentos *apartment house*
la escalera *stairs*
el estudio *study, den*
el fregadero *kitchen sink*
el garaje *garage*
la habitación *room*
el inquilino *tenant*
el jardín *garden*
la pared *wall*
el pasillo *hall*
el patio *patio*
el piso *floor, story*
la planta baja *ground floor*
el propietario *owner*
la puerta *door*
la sala *living room*
el sótano *basement*
el techo *ceiling, roof*
la terraza *terrace*
la ventana *window*

b. **Los muebles y los aparatos domésticos** / *Furniture and appliances*

la alfombra *rug, carpet*
la almohada *pillow*
el armario *wardrobe, closet*
la aspiradora *vacuum cleaner*
el buró *night stand*
la butaca *armchair (upolstered)*
la cama *bed*
la cómoda *dresser*
la computadora *computer*
el congelador *freezer*
la cortina *curtain*
el cuadro *painting*
el espejo *mirror*
el estéreo *stereo*
la estufa *stove*
el horno *oven*
  de microondas *microwave oven*
la lámpara *lamp*
la lavadora *washing machine*
el lavaplatos *dishwasher*
el librero *bookcase*
la mesa *table*
el mueble *piece of furniture*
el ordenador *computer*
el piano *piano*
la pintura *painting*
el refrigerador *refrigerator*
el reloj *clock*
  despertador *alarm clock*
la secadora *clothes dryer*
la silla *chair*
el sillón *armchair*
el sofá *sofa*
el televisor *television set*
el tocador *dresser*
la videocasetera *VCR*

c. **Los quehaceres del hogar** / *Housework*

cocinar *to cook*
cortar el césped *to mow the lawn*
cuidar a los niños *to babysit*
ir de compras *to go shopping*
lavar los platos *to wash dishes*
limpiar la casa *to clean the house*
pasar la aspiradora *to vacuum*
planchar la ropa *to iron the clothing*
poner la mesa *to set the table*
quitar la mesa *to clear the table*
sacar la basura *to throw out the garbage*
sacudir los muebles *to dust the furniture*

EXERCISE B. **Describe what you see in each room.**

1. Yo veo un dormitorio grande. Hay una alfombra en la pisa, y los muebles. El librero tiene muchos libros y un estereo. Hay un ordenador en el escritorio. También hay un luz. Yo veo una cama con las almohadas y un tocador. Detrás de el tocador hay un espejo. Hay los cuadros en las paredes también. Yo veo un sillón en el cuarto. Hay las cortinas en la ventana.

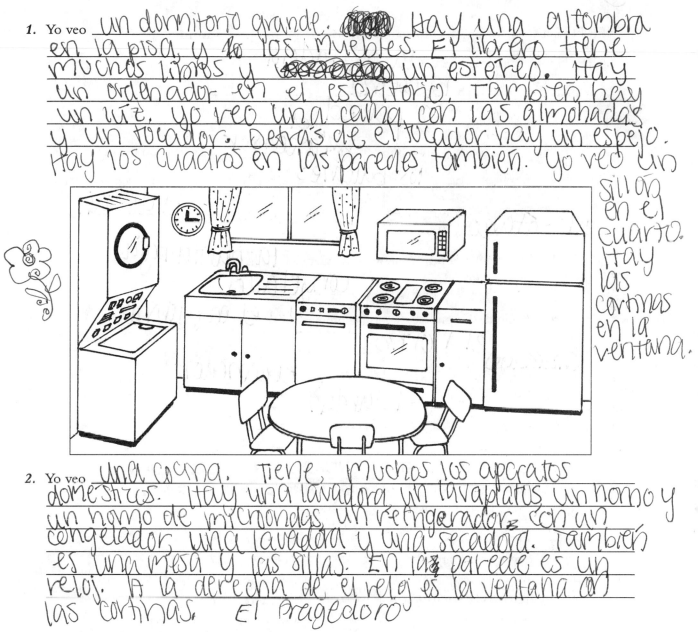

2. Yo veo una cocina. Tiene muchos los aparatos domestricos. Hay una lavadora, un lavaplatos, un horno y un horno de microondas, un refrigerador con un congelador, una lavadora y una secadora. También es una mesa y las sillas. En la pared es un reloj. A la derecha de el relog es la ventana con las cortinas. El fregedoro

EXERCISE C. **Express what household chore each person does.**

EXAMPLE: Felipe / lavar platos — Felipe **lava los platos.**

1. mi abuela / cocinar — Mi abuela cocinas.
2. Papá / pasar la aspiradora — Papá pasas la aspiradora.
3. tú / poner la mesa — Tú pones la mesa.
4. nosotros / sacar la basura — Nosotros sacamos la basura.
5. Mamá / sacudir los muebles — Mamá sacudes los muebles.
6. Uds. / quitar la mesa — Uds. quitan la mesa.
7. Papá / ir de compras — Papá vas de compras.
8. Laura / cuidar a los niños — Laura cuidas a los niños.

EXERCISE D. Complete each statement with the appropriate word.

1. Para limpiar la alfombra se usa la aspiradora.
2. Se prepara la comida en la cocina.
3. Se cuelgan los cuadros en la pared.
4. En un edificio alto de apartamentos se usa el ascensor para ir de un piso a otro.
5. Muchos apartamentos tienen los balcónes donde las personas pueden sentarse al aire libre.
6. En una casa particular se guardan las cosas que no se usan a menudo en el desván o en el sótano.
7. En los Estados Unidos, el primer piso es equivalente a la planta baja en España.
8. La parte más fría del refrigerador es el congelador.
9. El contrato es un documento legal entre el propietario y el inquilino.
10. Se asa un pavo en el horno.
11. En los días feriados (holidays) se sirve una comida elegante en el comedor de la casa.
12. Se cultivan plantas y flores en el jardín.

[3] LA COMUNIDAD; EL VECINDARIO; LOS ALREDEDORES / *Community; Neighborhood; Physical Environment*

a. La ciudad / *city*

la acera *sidewalk*
el aeropuerto *airport*
la aldea *village*
el almacén *department store*
la avenida *avenue*
el ayuntamiento *town hall*
el banco *bank*
el barrio *neighborhood*
la biblioteca *library*
la bodega *grocery store*
el café *cafe*
la calle *street*
la carnicería *butcher shop*
la catedral *cathedral*
el centro *commercial mall*
el centro juvenil *youth center*
el cine *movies (movie theater)*
el cuartel de policía *police precinct*
el correo *post office*
la corte *court (house)*
el edificio *building*
la escuela *school*
la estación *(train) station*
el estadio *stadium*
la fábrica *factory*
la farmacia *drugstore, pharmacy*
la ferretería *hardware store*
la florería *florist*
la frutería *fruit store*
la gasolinera *gas station*
el hospital *hospital*
el hotel *hotel*
la iglesia *church*
el jardín *garden*
la joyería *jewelry store*
la lavandería *laundry*

la librería *bookstore*
el mercado *market*
el monumento *monument*
el museo *museum*
la panadería *bakery*
el parque *park*
el parque de bomberos *fire station*
la pastelería *pastry shop*
la perfumería *perfume shop*
la piscina *swimming pool*
la plaza *square*
el pueblo *town*
el puente *bridge*
el rascacielos *skyscraper*
el restaurante *restaurant*
la sinagoga *synagogue*
el suburbio *suburbs*
el supermercado *supermarket*
el teatro *theater*
el templo *temple*
la terminal de autobuses *bus terminal*
la tienda *store*
la tienda de ropa *clothing store*
la tintorería *dry cleaners*
la universidad *university*
el vecindario *neighborhood*
la zapatería *shoe store*

EXERCISE E. **Tell what you can buy in the following stores.**

EXAMPLE: Se compran medicinas en una **farmacia.**

1. ______________________________
______________________________.

3. ______________________________
______________________________.

2. ______________________________
______________________________.

4. ______________________________
______________________________.

5. ______________________________
______________________________.

6. ______________________________
______________________________.

7. ______________________________
______________________________.

8. ______________________________
______________________________.

b. Materiales de construcción / *Building materials*

el acero	*steel*	la madera	*wood*	el hierro	*iron*	el vidrio	*glass*
el cemento	*cement*	el ladrillo	*brick*	la piedra	*stone*		

EXERCISE F. Tell what each of the things shown is made of.

EXAMPLE: La casa es **de piedra.**

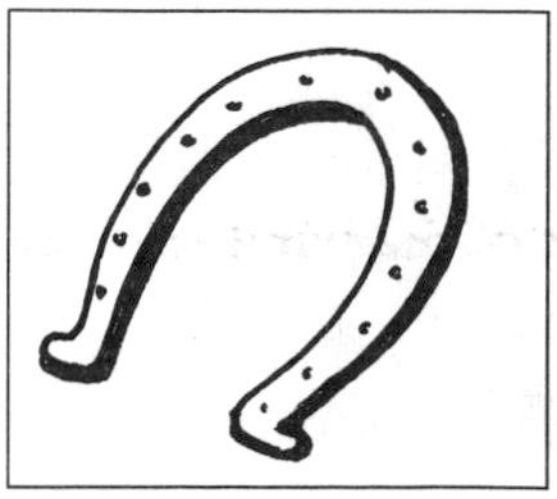

1. ______________________________
______________________________.

2. ______________________________
______________________________.

3. ______________________________
______________________________.

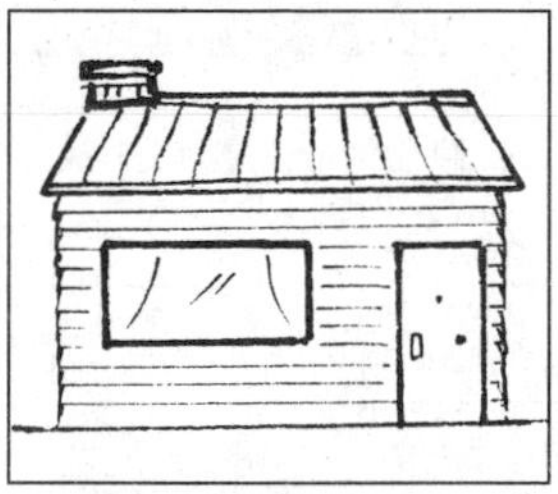

5. ______________________________
______________________________.

4. ______________________________
______________________________.

c. La naturaleza / *Nature*

el árbol *tree*
la arena *sand*
el arroyo *stream*
el bosque *woods*
el campo *country, field*
el cielo *sky*
la colina *hill*
la costa *coast*
el desierto *desert*
la estrella *star*
la flor *flower*
la hierba *grass*
la hoja *leaf*
la isla *island*
el lago *lake*
la laguna *lagoon*
la lluvia *rain*
la luna *moon*
el / la mar *sea*
la montaña *mountain*
el mundo *world*
la niebla *fog*
la nieve *snow*
la nube *cloud*
el océano *ocean*
el paisaje *landscape*
el planeta *planet*
la planta *plant*
la playa *beach*
la ribera *shore, bank (of a river)*
el río *river*
la selva *forest*
el sol *sun*
la tierra *earth*
el viento *wind*
el volcán *volcano*

EXERCISE G. You are traveling cross-country by train. As you look out of the window at the changing landscape, make a list of ten things you see.

EXAMPLE: un río, una colina, etc.

1. ______________________________

2. ______________________________

3. ____________________

4. ____________________

5. ____________________

6. ____________________

7. ____________________

8. ____________________

9. ____________________

10. ____________________

d. Los animales / *Animals*

la abeja	*bee*	**el conejo**	*rabbit*	**el pájaro**	*bird*
la araña	*spider*	**el elefante**	*elephant*	**la pantera**	*panther*
la ardilla	*squirrel*	**la gallina**	*hen*	**el pavo**	*turkey*
la ballena	*whale*	**el gallo**	*rooster*	**el perro**	*dog*
el buey	*ox*	**el gato**	*cat*	**el pez**	*fish*
el burro	*donkey*	**la jirafa**	*giraffe*	**el pollo**	*chicken*
el caballo	*horse*	**el león**	*lion*	**la serpiente**	*snake*
la cabra	*goat*	**el leopardo**	*leopard*	**el tigre**	*tiger*
el canguro	*kangaroo*	**el lobo**	*wolf*	**el tiburón**	*shark*
la cebra	*zebra*	**el mono**	*monkey*	**la tortuga**	*turtle*
el cisne	*swan*	**el murciélago**	*bat*	**la vaca**	*cow*
el cochino	*pig*	**el oso**	*bear*	**la zorra**	*fox*
el cocodrilo	*crocodile*	**la oveja**	*sheep*		

EXERCISE H. Name five animals you see in each of these sites.

1. En el campo: la ardilla, la vaca, la oveja, el caball
2. En la jungla: el pájaro, el leopardo, el mono, el murci
3. Cerca del mar: ~~el elefante~~, la ballena, el pez,
4. En el parque zoológico: el elefante, el león, el tigre, la pantera, la cebra.

[4] LAS COMIDAS; LA COMIDA; LAS BEBIDAS / *Meals; Food; Drinks*

a. Las comidas / *Meals*

el almuerzo	*lunch*	**la cena**	*dinner, supper*	**el desayuno**	*breakfast*
el apetito	*appetite*	**la comida**	*meal, food*	**el menú**	*menu*
la botella	*bottle*	**la cuenta**	*check*	**la propina**	*tip*

b. Los cubiertos / *Utensils (Cutlery)*

la cuchara *spoon*	el mantel *tablecloth*	la taza *cup*
la cucharita *teaspoon*	el plato *plate, dish*	el tenedor *fork*
el cuchillo *knife*	la servilleta *napkin*	el vaso *glass*

c. La comida / *Food*

el agua mineral *mineral water*	el jamón *ham*	la papa *potato*
el arroz *rice*	las judías verdes *green beans*	las papas fritas *French fries*
el azúcar *sugar*	el jugo *juice*	el pastel *cake*
el biftec *steak*	el ketchup *ketchup*	la pera *pear*
el café *coffee*	la leche *milk*	el pescado *fish*
la carne *meat*	la lechuga *lettuce*	la pimienta *pepper*
la carne de res *beef*	las legumbres *vegetables*	la pizza *pizza*
el cereal *cereal*	el limón *lemon*	el plátano *plantain*
la cereza *cherry*	la limonada *lemonade*	el pollo *chicken*
el chícharo *pea*	la mantequilla *butter*	el queso *cheese*
el chocolate *chocolate*	la manzana *apple*	la sal *salt*
el cordero *lamb*	los mariscos *seafood*	la salchicha *sausage*
los dulces *candies*	la mayonesa *mayonnaise*	el sándwich *sandwich*
el elote *green bean*	el melocotón *peach*	la sopa *soup*
la ensalada *salad*	la mermelada *jam, marmalade*	el té *tea*
la espinaca *spinach*	la mostaza *mustard*	la ternera *veal*
la fresa *strawberry*	el pan *bread*	el tomate *tomato*
la fruta *fruit*	el pan tostado *toast*	la uva *grape*
la hamburguesa *hamburger*	el panecillo *roll*	las verduras *greens, vegetables*
el helado *ice cream*		la zanahoria *carrot*
el huevo *egg*		

el venado

EXERCISE 1. A friend has invited you to spend a weekend at his house. He wants to be a good host and asks you to list the foods you like and those you dislike. Prepare the list for him.

el lago, la serpiente

el tiburón, la tortuga,

ME GUSTA(N):	NO ME GUSTA(N):
la pizza	los tamales
el helado	la mostaza
el pan	el agua mineral
la ensalada	el cordero
las papas	la ternera
el queso	el huevo
el melocotón	
el chocolate	
el pastel

EXERCISE J. **You are celebrating your birthday at an elegant restaurant. Describe what you see on the table.**

yo veo la ~~...~~ servilleta con el plato y los cubiertos: dos tenedors, los cuchillos, y una cuchara. Hay pan delicioso con la mantequilla. Hay una taza ~~de agua mineral. También yo veo~~ y la botella de ~~...~~ agua mineral. También yo veo un menú y el vaso. Hay el azúcar y el sal.

[5] LA SALUD Y EL BIENESTAR / *Health and Well-being*

a. El cuerpo / *The body*

la barba *beard*	**el dedo del pie** *toe*	**el ojo** *eye*
la barbilla *chin*	**el diente** *tooth*	**la oreja** *(outer) ear*
el bigote *moustache*	**la espalda** *back*	**la pantorrilla** *calf*
la boca *mouth*	**el estómago** *stomach*	**el párpado** *eyelid*
el brazo *arm*	**la frente** *forehead*	**el pecho** *chest*
el cabello *hair*	**la garganta** *throat*	**el pelo** *hair*
la cabeza *head*	**el hombro** *shoulder*	**las pestañas** *eyelashes*
la cara *face*	**el labio** *lip*	**el pie** *foot*
las cejas *eyebrows*	**la lengua** *tongue*	**la piel** *skin*
el codo *elbow*	**la mano** *hand*	**la pierna** *leg*
el corazón *heart*	**la mejilla** *cheek*	**la rodilla** *knee*
el cuello *neck*	**la muela** *molar*	**el rostro** *face*
el cuerpo *body*	**la nariz** *nose*	**la sangre** *blood*
el dedo *finger*	**el oído** *(inner) ear*	**el tobillo** *ankle*

b. **Las enfermedades** / *Illnesses*

tener dolor de cabeza *to have a headache*
tener dolor de estómago *to have a stomachache*
tener dolor de garganta *to have a sore throat*
tener dolor de pie *to have foot pain*

la apendicitis *appendicitis*
el asma (f.) *asthma*
el dolor *pain*
la energía *energy*
la fiebre *fever*
la fractura *fracture*
la fuerza *strength*
el gripe *flu*
la infección *infection*
la neumonía *pneumonia*
las paperas *mumps*
la pulmonía *pneumonia*
la quemadura *burn*
el resfriado *cold (illness)*
la rotura *fracture*
el sarampión *measles*
la tos *cough*
la urgencia *emergency*
la varicela *chicken pox*

c. **Palabras relacionadas** / *Related words*

el accidente *accident*
la ambulancia *ambulance*
la aspirina *aspirin*
el cuidado *care*
la cura *cure*
la enfermera *nurse*
el enfermo *patient*
la medicina *medicine*
la pomada *salve*
el reposo *rest*
la salud *health*
el sudor *sweat*
la temperatura *temperature*
el tratamiento *treatment*
la vacuna *vaccine*

EXERCISE K. **Complete the drawing by labeling the different parts of the body.**

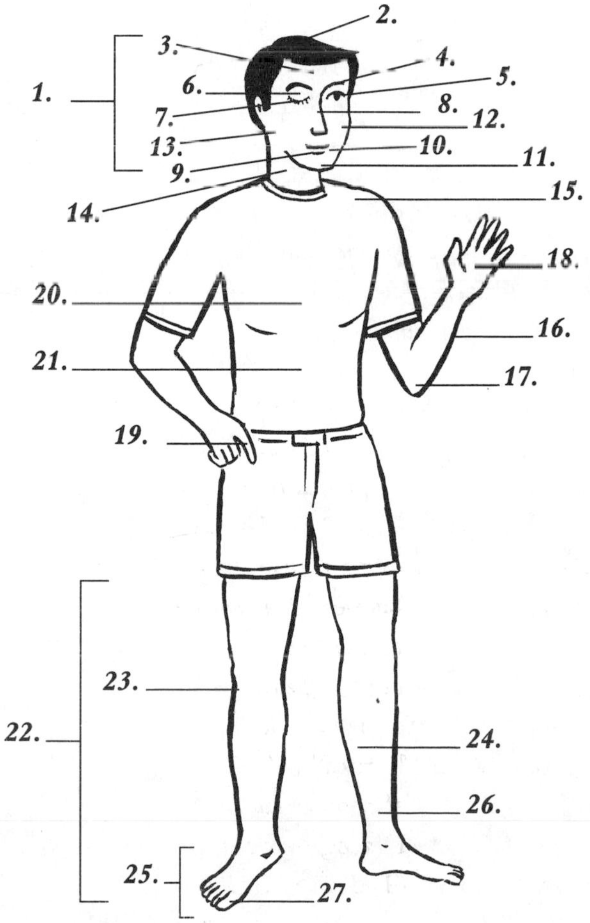

1. la cabeza
2. el pelo
3. la frente
4. la ceja
5. el ojo
6. el párpado
7. las pestañas
8. la nariz
9. la boca
10. el labio
11. la barbilla
12. la mejilla
13. la cara
14. el cuello
15. el hombro
16. el brazo
17. el codo
18. el mano
19. el dedo
20. el pecho
21. el estómago
22. la pierna
23. la rodilla
24. la pantorrilla
25. el pie
26. el tobillo
27. el dedo del pie

EXERCISE L. **A new pen pal has asked you to describe yourself. Write a detailed description of yourself.**

____

____

____

____

____

____

EXERCISE M. **You are completing the application for a summer internship program. List the illnesses you have had.**

____

____

____

____

____

____

[6] EDUCACIÓN / *Education*

a. La escuela / *School*

el alumno *pupil*
la aula *classroom*
el banco *bench*
el bolígrafo *ballpoint pen*
la calculadora *calculator*
el calendario *calendar*
la clase *class*
el colegio *school, academy*
el consejero *counselor*
el cuaderno *notebook*
el diccionario *dictionary*
el dictado *dictation*
el director *principal*
el ejercicio *exercise*
el error *error*
la escuela *school*
la escuela primaria *elementary school*
la escuela secundaria *high school*
el estudiante *student, pupil*
el estudio *study*
el examen *test*
la explicación *explanation*
la falta *error*
la fila *line (of people)*
la frase *sentence*
la goma *eraser*
la gramática *grammar*
el horario de clases *class schedule*
el lápiz *pencil*
la lección *lesson*
la lectura *reading*
el libro *book*

el maestro *teacher*
el mapa *map*
la materia *subject*
la mochila *knapsack, backpack, bookbag*
la nota *grade*
la oración *sentence*
la página *page*
la palabra *word*
el papel *paper*
el patio *patio; schoolyard*
la pizarra *chalkboard*
la pluma *pen*
la poesía *poetry*
la pregunta *question*
el profesor *teacher*
el pupitre *(student) desk*
la regla *ruler*
la respuesta *answer*
el resumen *summary*
la sala de clases *classroom*
la tarea *homework*
las tijeras *scissors*
el timbre *bell*
la tiza *chalk*
el trabajo *work*
los útiles *school supplies*
el vocabulario *vocabulary*

b. Las materias / *School subjects*

el álgebra *algebra*
las artes industriales *shop*
la artesanía *arts and crafts*
el inglés *English*
la biología *biology*
la química *chemistry*
el diseño *drawing*
la educación física *gym*
el español *Spanish*
la geografía *geography*
la historia *history*
la informática *computer science*
el latín *Latin*
las matemáticas *math*
la física *physics*
la ciencia *science*
la technología *technology*

c. Las actividades escolares / *School activities*

la banda *band*
el círculo *club*
el círculo de matemáticas *math club*
el círculo dramático *drama club*
el círculo español *Spanish club*
el círculo internacional *international club*
el coro *chorus*
el equipo *team*
el equipo de béisbol *baseball team*
el equipo de fútbol *soccer team*
la excursión *field trip*
la orquesta *orchestra*

EXERCISE N. **Prepare a list of the school supplies you will need to purchase for the new school year.**

____

____

____

____

____

____

EXERCISE O. **You are sending a pen-pal photographs you took in your school. Label each photograph so that your pen pal knows the subject of the picture.**

EXAMPLE: Es el equipo de fútbol.

1. ______________________________

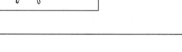

2. ______________________________

3. ______________________________

4. ______________________________

5. ______________________________

6. ______________________________

7. ______________________________

8. ______________________________

[7] OFICIOS Y PROFESIONES / *Trades and Professions*

el /la abogado(-a) *lawyer*
el actor *actor*
la actriz *actress*
el /la atleta *athlete*
el/la artista *artist, performer*
el /la bombero(-a) *firefighter*
el /la campesino(-a) *farmer*
el /la carnicero(-a) *butcher*
el /la cartero(-a) *mail carrier*
el /la científico(-a) *scientist*
el /la cocinero(-a) *chef*
el /la comerciante *merchant*
el /la dentista *dentist*
el /la dependiente *salesperson*
el /la director(-ora) *manager, principal*
el /la diseñador(-ora) *designer*
el /la enfermero(-a) *nurse*
el /la escritor(-ora) *writer*
el /la farmaceútico(-a) *pharmacist*
el /la gerente *manager*
el /la ingeniero(-a) *engineer*
el investigador *researcher*
el /la juez(-a) *judge*
el /la médico(-a) *doctor*
el /la mesero(-a) *waiter*
el /la mozo(-a) *waiter, server*
el /la músico *musician*
el /la obrero(-a) *laborer, worker*
el /la panadero(-a) *baker*
el /la peluquero(-a) *barber, hair stylist*
el /la piloto(-a) *pilot*
el /la pintor(-ora) *painter*
el poeta *poet*
la poetisa *poet*
el /la policía *police officer*
el /la presidente(-a) *president*
la profesión *profession*
el /la profesor(-ora) *teacher*
el /la programador(-ora) *programmer*
el /la secretario(-a) *secretary*
el /la soldado(-a) *soldier*

EXERCISE P. **Use the clues below to identify the profession described.**

1. Soy muy creativa. Mis dibujos cambian el estilo de ropa de cada estación.

____

2. Reparo las sandalias y los zapatos de las personas.

____

3. Creo nuevos programas para la computadora.

____

4. Me gusta escribir cuentos y publicarlos en forma de libro.

____

5. Para mí los dientes son una parte muy importante de la buena salud.

____

6. Sigo las instrucciones de los médicos cuando cuido a los enfermos.

____

7. Reparto la correspondencia que las personas y las compañías reciben cada día.

____

8. Apago los incendios y trato de salvar la vida y las propiedades de las personas.

____

9. Siempre busco nuevas maneras de preparar la comida. Todo el mundo quiere mis recetas.

____

10. Defiendo a mis clientes en la corte.

____

11. Ayudo a las personas cuando van de compras a un almacén.

____

12. Me gusta hacer el papel de otras personas. Así me divierto y también divierto al público.

____

13. Trabajo en la corte y dirijo los juicios. Estudié leyes. Llevo una túnica negra.

____

14. Me gusta trabajar a solas en un laboratorio y descubrir nuevas cosas.

____

15. Paso mucho tiempo corrigiendo exámenes. Uso la tinta roja pero no es mi color favorito.

____

[*8*] EL TIEMPO LIBRE / *Leisure*

a. Los pasatiempos / *Hobbies; leisure activities*

el baile *dance*
el campo *country*
el centro comercial *mall*
el cine *movies*
el concierto *concert*
el deporte *sport*
el día feriado *legal holiday*
el día libre *day off*
la discoteca *discotheque*
el estadio *stadium*
la exposición *exhibit, show*
la feria *fair*
la fiesta *holiday, celebration, party*
la isla tropical *tropical island*
la montaña *mountain*
el museo *museum*
los naipes *cards*
la ópera *opera*
el parque nacional *national park*
el parque zoológico *zoo*
el partido *game, match*
el paseo *walk*
la pelota *ball*
la playa *beach*
el teatro *theater*
la televisión *television*
las vacaciones (pl.) *vacation*

b Los deportes / *Sports*

el alpinismo *mountain climbing*
el atletismo *athletics*
el barco de vela *sailboat*
el béisbol *baseball*
los bolos *bowling*
el buceo *diving*
la carrera *track*
el esquí *skiing*

el esquí acuático *waterskiing*
el fútbol *soccer*
el fútbol americano *football*
el golf *golf*
el hockey *hockey*
la natación *swimming*
la pesca *fishing*
el tenis *tennis*
el voleibol *volleyball*

EXERCISE Q. **You will be visiting a friend in another city for a long weekend. In preparation for your visit, write a note in which you remind him / her of the leisure activities you like to do and those you dislike doing.**

EXAMPLE: **Me gusta ir al cine. Visitar un museo es aburrido.**

____

____

____

____

____

____

EXERCISE R. **Identify the pastimes these people describe.**

1. Las montañas me llaman la atención. Me gusta caminar y cuando el terreno es duro y la montaña es alta, tanto mejor.

   ____

2. Me gusta el mar, especialmente cuando el agua está muy clara y hay mucha profundidad.

   ____

3. Me gusta moverme al compás de la música. Es divertido ir a las discotecas con mis amigos.

   ____

4. El único juego que no me gusta es el Solitario. Prefiero jugar con mis amigos.

   ____

5. Mi abuelo es muy partidario de este deporte. Desde niño me ha gustado acompañarlo en su barco. Si tenemos suerte comemos bien en la noche.

   ____

6. Estoy aprendiendo a ser un buen jugador porque mi equipo participa en una competencia. Es difícil lanzar la pelota y derribar todos los bolos.

   ____

7. Correr es una buena actividad y un buen ejercicio. Cada día corro más rápidamente

   ____

8. A mi papá le gusta este deporte porque hay que caminar. A veces voy con él, pero quisiera que alquilara un carrito para ir de un hoyo en otro.

   ____

9. Me gusta este deporte porque hay que saltar para pegarle a la pelota con las manos y pasarla por encima de una red alta.

____

10. No sé tocar ningún instrumento musical pero me gusta sentarme en un teatro y escuchar mientras una orquesta toca una obra sinfónica.

____

[9] SERVICIOS PÚBLICOS Y PRIVADOS / *Public and Private Services*

a. El teléfono / *Telephone*

la cabina telefónica *telephone booth*
el carnet telefónico *calling card*
colgar (ue, gu) *to hang up*
descolgar *to pick up (the phone)*
la guía telefónica *telephone book*
larga distancia *long distance*
la llamada *call*
la máquina de contestar *answering machine*
marcar (qu) *to dial*
el número equivocado *wrong number*
ocupado *busy*
la operadora *operator*
el receptor *receiver*

b. El correo / *Post Office*

el apartado postal *post office box*
el buzón *mailbox*
la carta *letter*
el cartero *mail carrier*
el código postal *Zip Code*
el correo *mail*
la dirección *address*
la estampilla *stamp*
el giro *money order*
el paquete *package*
por avión *air mail*
el sobre *envelope*
la tarjeta postal *postcard*
el telegrama *telegram*
la ventanilla *(service) window*

c. El banco / *Bank*

el billete *bill*
la caja *cash register, teller's window*
el / la cajero(-a) *cashier, teller*
la caja fuerte *safe*
el cambio *exchange rate*
el cheque de viajero *traveler's check*
la cuenta de ahorros *saving account*
la cuenta de cheques *checking account*
depositar *to deposit*
el depósito *deposit*
el dinero *money*
el efectivo *cash*
el giro *money order*
la moneda *coin, currency*
retirar *to withdraw*
el retiro *withdrawal*

d. Otros servicios / *Other services*

la aduana *customs*
el aduanero *customs official*
el Seguro Social *Social Security*

EXERCISE S. **Express what Jamie says about his grandfather.**

Mi abuelo prefiere hacer todo a la antigua. Cada mes él recibe su ____________ (*1.* check) de ____________ (*2.* Social Security) por ____________ (*3.* mail). No le gusta el ____________ (*4.* deposit) directo. Él prefiere llevarlo al ____________ (*5.* bank) para depositarlo en su ____________ (*6.* checking account). También tiene que hacer ____________ (*7.* withdrawal) de su ____________ (*8.* savings account) porque necesita dinero en ____________ (*9.* cash). Los ____________ (*10.* tellers) ya lo conocen y siempre lo saludan muy cordialmente.

EXERCISE T. **In each group, select the word that is not related to the other three.**

1. buzón, carta, paquete, llamada ____________
2. marcar, colgar, retirar, descolgar ____________
3. cuenta, correo, caja, retiro ____________
4. caja fuerte, cabina telefónica, guía telefónica, número equivocado ____________
5. apartado postal, operadora, código postal, estampillas ____________
6. efectivo, moneda, cambio, telegrama ____________
7. ahorros, receptor, cheques, cajero ____________

[*10*] LAS COMPRAS / SHOPPING

a. La ropa / Clothing

el abrigo *overcoat*
la blusa *blouse*
el bolsillo *pocket*
las botas *boots*
la bufanda *scarf*
el calcetín *sock*
la camisa *shirt*
la camiseta *T-shirt*
el chaleco *vest*
la chaqueta *jacket*
el cinturón *belt*
la corbata *tie*
la falda *skirt*
la gorra *cap*
los guantes *gloves*
el impermeable *raincoat*
el pantalón *pants*
el pantalón corto *shorts*
las pantimedias *pantyhose*
el pañuelo *handkerchief*
la ropa *clothing*
el saco *jacket*
las sandalias *sandals*
el sombrero *hat*
el suéter *sweater*
los tenis *sneakers*
los tirantes *suspenders*
el traje *suit*
el traje de baño *bathing suit*
el vestido *dress*
el zapato *shoe*

b. Los colores / *Colors*

amarillo *yellow*
anaranjado *orange*
azul *blue*
blanco *white*
café *brown*
gris *gray*
marrón *brown*
morado *purple*
negro *black*

rojo *red*	**verde** *green*
rosado *pink*	**violeta** *purple*

c. Las telas y los materiales / *Fabrics and materials*

el algodón *cotton*	**la lana** *wool*	**el poliéster** *polyester*
el encaje *lace*	**el lino** *linen*	**el raso** *satin*
el fieltro *felt*	**el nilón** *nylon*	**la seda** *silk*
la franela *flannel*	**la piel** *leather, fur*	**el terciopelo** *velvet*
la gamusa *suede*		

d. La joyería / *Jewelry*

el anillo *ring*	**la cadena** *chain*	**la pulsera** *bracelet*
el arete *earring*	**el collar** *necklace*	**el reloj** *watch*
la argolla *wedding band*	**el prendedor** *pin*	**la sortija** *ring*
el broche *brooch, pin*		

e. Piedras preciosas y metales / *Gems and metals*

el brillante *diamond*	**el rubí** *ruby*	**el oro** *gold*
el diamante *diamond*	**el safiro** *sapphire*	**la plata** *silver*
la esmeralda *emerald*	**el topacio** *topaz*	**el platino** *platinum*
la perla *pearl*		

EXERCISE U. **Describe what you and your date will wear in the following circumstances. Include the articles of clothing, accessories, colors, and materials of each item.**

EXAMPLE: ir a la escuela
YO: una blusa verde de algodón, pantalones blancos de algodón, tenis blanco de piel
ÉL / ELLA: una camisa azul de algodón, pantalones azules de lana, zapatos negros de piel

1. ir a la playa
YO: ______________________________
ÉL/ELLA: ______________________________

2. ir a una fiesta
YO: ______________________________
ÉL/ELLA: ______________________________

3. ir a trabajar en una oficina
YO: ______________________________
ÉL/ELLA: ______________________________

4. descansar en casa
YO: ______________________________
ÉL/ELLA: ______________________________

5. ir a una boda
YO: ______________________________
ÉL/ELLA: ______________________________

[11] El viaje y la transportación / *Travel and Transportation*

el aeropuerto *airport*
el alojamiento *lodging*
el asiento *seat*
el aterrizaje *landing*
el autobús *bus*
el automóvil *car*
la autopista *highway*
el avión *airplane*
el barco *boat*
el baúl *trunk*
la bicicleta *bicycle*
el billete *ticket*
el boleto *ticket*
la brújula *compass*
la calle *street*
el camarote *cabin*
el camino *road*
el camión *truck*
la camioneta *van*
la carretera *road*
el carro *car*
el compartamento *compartment*
el despegue *takeoff*
el equipaje *luggage*
la escala *stop (air travel)*
la estación *train station*
el ferrocarril *railroad*
el guía *guide*
el horario *schedule*
el huésped *guest*
el itinerario *itinerary*
la llegada *arrival*
la maleta *suitcase*
el medio de transporte *means of transportation*
el metro *subway*
la motocicleta (la moto) *motorcycle*
el muelle *pier*
el peaje *toll*
la parada *stop, bus stop*
el pasajero *passenger*
la posada *inn*
la puerta *gate*
la ruta *route*
la salida *departure*
la tarifa *rate, price*
el taxi *taxi*
la terminal de autobuses *bus terminal*
el tranvía *streetcar*
el tren *train*
el vapor *steamship*
la ventanilla *ticket window*
el viaje *trip*
el viajero *traveler*
el vuelo *flight*

EXERCISE V. **Complete each statement with the appropriate word.**

1. Un instrumento importante para los pilotos es ____________.
2. Las posadas y los hoteles son dos formas de ____________.
3. Por lo general, a los choferes no les importa pagar un peaje para conducir en ____________ porque es más rápida y segura.
4. Para saber la hora de salida o llegada de un avión o un tren, debo consultar ____________.
5. Hay muchas personas que temen ____________ y ____________ de los aviones.
6. Prefiero un vuelo directo sin ____________.
7. Los barcos embarcan y desembarcan en ____________.
8. Puesto que mi papá no es muy aficionado a conducir mucho, él prefiere siempre tomar ____________ más directa y corta.
9. Cuando hay una demora o una huelga en el aeropuerto, ____________ se ponen furiosos.
10. El tren, el autobús y el taxi son tres ____________ públicos de una ciudad grande.

[12] EVENTOS DE ACTUALIDAD / *Current Events*

a. La política / *Politics*

el / la alcalde (-esa) *mayor*
la asamblea *assembly*
el / la ayudante militar *military aide*
el ayuntamiento *town hall*
la cámara de diputados *house of representatives*
el / la candidato(-a) *candidate*
la conferencia *conference*
el congreso *congress*
la democracia *democracy*
los derechos *rights*
el desempleo *unemployment*
el / la dictador(-ora) *dictator*
la dictadura *dictatorship*
el / la diputado(-a) *representative*
la economía *economy*
el ejército *army*
la embajada *embassy*
el / la embajador(-ora) *ambassador*
la entrevista *interview*
la frontera *border*
el gabinete *cabinet*
el gobierno *government*
el / la gobernador(-ora) *governor*
la guerra *war*
el / la guerrillero(-a) *guerrilla fighter*
la inflación *inflation*
la insurrección *rebellion*
el / la jefe(-a) de estado *head of state*
la mayoría *majority*
el / la ministro(-a) *minister*
la minoría *minority*
las noticias *news*
el noticiero *news broadcast*
el parlamento *parliament*
el partido *party*
el periódico *newspaper*
el / la periodista *journalist*
el plazo *term*
el poder ejecutivo *executive power*
el / la político(-a) *politician*
el / la presidente(-a) *president*
el / la primer(-a) ministro(-a) *Prime Minister*
la primera dama *the first lady*
el programa *program, platform*
la rebeldía *rebellion, revolt*
la recesión *recession*
la reina *queen*
la república *republic*
la revista *magazine*
la revolución *revolution*
el rey *king*
el senado *senate*
el / la senador(-ora) *senator*
los titulares *headlines*
el tratado *treaty*
el / la vice-presidente(-a) *vice president*

EXERCISE W. **You are explaining the United States government to a new pen pal. Complete each statement with the appropriate word.**

En los Estados Unidos hay dos ______________ (*1.* parties) políticos: los demócratas y los republicanos. El ______________ (*2.* term) de ______________ (*3.* politicians) elegidos es de cuatro años. El ______________ (*4.* government) federal se divide en dos secciones: ______________ (*5.* the senate) y ______________ (*6.* house of representatives). ______________ (*7.* The president) nombra a los miembros de su ______________ (*8.* cabinet). También nombra a ______________ (*9.* ambassadors), pero su nombramiento tiene que ser aprobado por ______________ (*10.* Congress). ______________ (*11.* The First Lady) es importante porque ella se interesa en las causas sociales como ______________ (*12.* rights) humanos. Casi todos los días se puede ver el nombre del presidente en ________ (*13.* (headlines)) de los periódicos o en ________ (*14.* (news broadcast)) de radio o televisión. Cada ________ (*15.* (state)) tiene su propio ________ (*16.* (governor)) y cada ciudad o pueblo tiene su propio ________ (*17.* (mayor)). Todos tienen interés en mantener ________ (*18.* (economy)) próspera y estable mientras trabajan para disminuir ________ (*19.* (inflation)) y ________ (*20.* (unemployment)).

b. La vida cultural / *Cultural life*

el /la acomodador(-ora) *usher*
el acto *act*
las artes *arts*
el/la artista *artist, performer*
el auditorio *auditorium*
el ballet *ballet*
la cola *line (of people)*
la comedia *comedy*
el / la compositor(-ora) *composer*
el concierto *concert*
la cultura *culture*
el / la dramaturgo(-a) *playwright*
la escena *scene*
el / la escultor(-ora) *sculptor*
la escultura *sculpture*
el espectáculo *show*
la estrella *star*
la exposición *exhibit, exposition*
la fila *row*
la función *performance, showing (movie)*
la música *music*
el músico *musician*
la obra de teatro *play*
la ópera *opera*
la orquesta *orchestra*
el personaje *character*
el / la pintor(-ora) *painter*
la pintura *painting*
la poesía *poetry*
el poeta *poet*
la poetisa *poet*
el reparto *cast (theater, film)*
la taquilla *box office*
el teatro *theater*

EXERCISE X. Complete each statement with the appropriate word.

1. Generalmente una obra de teatro se divide en dos o tres ________ .
2. Para comprar boletos para el cine, hay que hacer ________ en ________ .
3. En un teatro ________ conduce a las personas a sus asientos.
4. Cuando una persona va a ________ espera escuchar música.
5. La persona que escribe obras de teatro es ________ .
6. En una ópera los ________ cantan.
7. Los actores en una película u obra de teatro forman ________ .
8. Una persona que escribe frases cortas sin o con rima es ________ .
9. En el arte, una forma tridimensional es ________ .
10. Las personas inventadas por el autor de una novela o un drama son ________ .

MASTERY EXERCISES

EXERCISE Y. **Complete each statement with an appropriate word.**

1. Las personas usan ______________ para respirar y oler.

2. Mi padre es ______________ de mi madre.

3. En una pastelería se venden ______________ .

4. Antes de la cena, la madre ______________ la mesa.

5. Muchos hombres llevan ______________ entre la nariz y el labio superior.

6. ______________ gobierna sin el apoyo del pueblo e impone muchas restricciones a los derechos de los ciudadanos.

7. Hoy día ______________ son muy populares porque hay un surtido de tiendas en un solo lugar.

8. En una oficina ______________ contesta el teléfono y escribe las cartas de su jefe en la computadora.

9. Se exhiben obras de arte valiosas en ______________ .

10. Una persona a quien no le gusta trabajar es ______________ .

11. Lo contrario del amor es ______________ .

12. Para ir de un piso a otro en una casa particular se usa ______________ .

13. Muchas madres se ponen furiosas cuando sus hijos dejan los vasos sucios en ______________ sin lavarlos.

14. Se guarda la ropa en ______________ .

15. Para verse, una persona usa ______________ .

16. Para quitar las arrugas a una prenda de ropa, hay que ______________ la prenda.

17. La parte central de muchos pueblos y ciudades hispanos es ______________ .

18. La nubes, el sol, la luna y las estrellas están en ______________ .

19. En el otoño ______________ caen de los árboles.

20. Un terreno árido con arena y muy pocas plantas es ______________ .

21. Los magos siempre sacan ______________ de su sombrero.

22. ______________ es un animal que camina muy despacio.

23. Se encuentra el significado de las palabras en ______________ .

24. Para cortar papel se usan ______________ .

25. Muchos vestidos de novia son de ______________ fino y bonito.

EXERCISE Z. **Express in Spanish what this young woman told a friend.**

1. I read an article in a Spanish magazine about the king and queen of Spain.

 ____

2. They visited a large city in the eastern part of the United States.

 ____

3. They are a serious, friendly, kind, and handsome couple.

 ____

4. They arrived by airplane and traveled by car from the airport to the center of the city.

 ____

5. They visited schools and hospitals in the city and in the suburbs, where they spoke to students, teachers, doctors, nurses, and sick people.

 ____

6. They dedicated a monument to Spain in the park.

 ____

7. Many politicians and business people were present.

 ____

8. In the schools, the girls wore blue skirts and white blouses. The boys wore blue pants, white shirts, and ties. No one wore sneakers.

 ____

9. In the evening they attended a formal dinner, where the king discussed the economy, commerce, unemployment, and inflation. The mayor and governor were present.

 ____

10. There were so many people in the photos. I think that no one went to work that day because everyone wanted to see a king and queen with their own eyes.

 ____

ACTIVIDADES

1. Prepare a food pyramid in Spanish for display in your classroom.
2. Prepare the school's breakfast and lunch menus in Spanish for a week.
3. Prepare a description of the club or extracurricular program in your school for a group of Spanish-speaking visitors.
4. Your school is planning a week to celebrate the arts. Prepare several flyers that highlight the activities the Spanish Club will organize for this event.
5. Research the Spanish-speaking nations and prepare a report that includes such things as the type of government, name of the head of state, election term, voting age, etc.
6. Prepare a mini-handbook about your school for new Spanish-speaking students.

Part five

Spanish and Spanish-American Civilizations

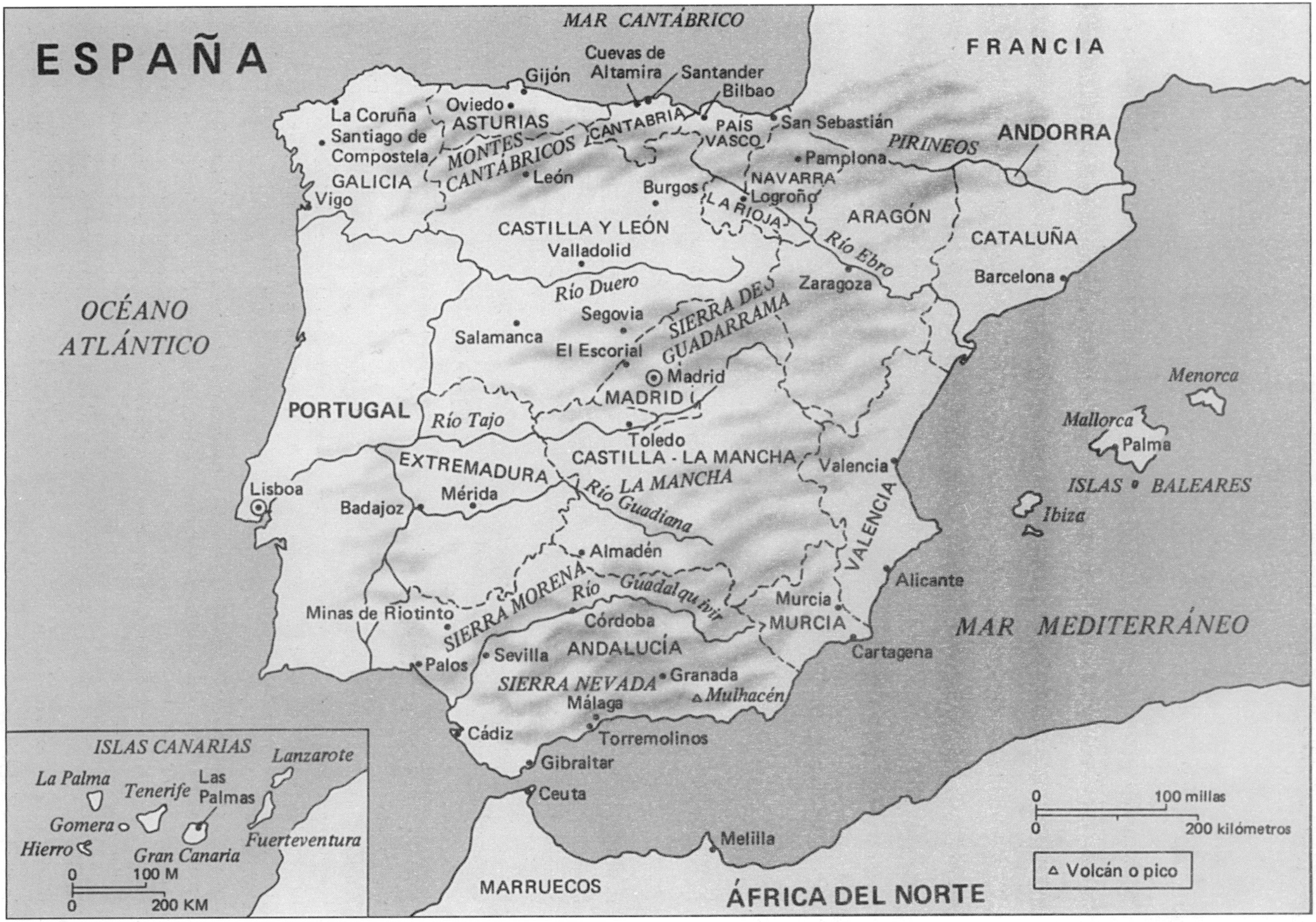
ESPAÑA
MAR CANTÁBRICO
FRANCIA
OCÉANO
ATLÁNTICO
La Coruña
Santiago de
Compostela
GALICIA
Vigo
Oviedo
ASTURIAS
Gijón
Cuevas de
Altamira
Santander
Bilbao
MONTES
CANTÁBRICOS
CANTABRIA
León
PAÍS
VASCO
San Sebastián
PIRINEOS
ANDORRA
Pamplona
NAVARRA
Logroño
LA RIOJA
Burgos
ARAGÓN
CATALUÑA
Barcelona
CASTILLA Y LEÓN
Valladolid
Río Duero
Río Ebro
Zaragoza
Segovia
SIERRA DE
GUADARRAMA
Salamanca
El Escorial
Madrid
MADRID
PORTUGAL
Río Tajo
Toledo
CASTILLA - LA MANCHA
LA MANCHA
Valencia
EXTREMADURA
Lisboa
Badajoz
Mérida
Río Guadiana
VALENCIA
Almadén
Alicante
SIERRA MORENA
Río
Guadalquivir
Murcia
MURCIA
Minas de Riotinto
Córdoba
Cartagena
Sevilla
ANDALUCÍA
Palos
Granada
SIERRA NEVADA
Mulhacén
Málaga
Cádiz
Torremolinos
Gibraltar
Ceuta
Melilla
MARRUECOS
ÁFRICA DEL NORTE
Menorca
Mallorca
Palma
ISLAS
BALEARES
Ibiza
MAR MEDITERRÁNEO
ISLAS CANARIAS
La Palma
Tenerife
Las
Palmas
Lanzarote
Gomera
Hierro
Gran Canaria
Fuerteventura
0
100 M
0
200 KM
0
100 millas
0
200 kilómetros
Volcán o pico

Chapter 35
La geografía de España

LOCALIZACIÓN DE ESPAÑA

España está situada en el sudoeste de Europa. Ocupa el 80 por ciento de la Península Ibérica, que comparte con Portugal.

EXTENSIÓN Y POBLACIÓN

Su extensión es de unas 200 millas cuadradas, (cuatro veces más grande que la del estado de Nueva York). Tiene una población de unos 40.000.000 de habitantes.

MONTAÑAS

España es un país muy montañoso.

1. Los Montes Pirineos están en el nordeste y marcan la frontera entre España y Francia.
2. La Cordillera Cantábrica está en el noroeste.
3. La Sierra de Guadarrama está en el centro, cerca de Madrid.
4. La Sierra Nevada y la Sierra Morena están en el sur.

RÍOS

1. El Ebro, en el nordeste, desemboca en el Mar Mediterráneo.
2. El Tajo, en la región central, es el río más largo. Pasa por la ciudad de Toledo.
3. El Guadalquivir, en el sur, es el río más profundo y navegable de España. Pasa por las ciudades de Sevilla y Córdoba.

INDUSTRIAS Y PRODUCTOS PRINCIPALES

1. España es un país agrícola e industrial.
2. Los productos principales agrícolas son aceitunas, naranjas, uvas, trigo, limones y corcho.
3. España ocupa el tercer lugar mundial en la producción de vinos de Europa. Los centros principales de la producción de vinos son Málaga y Jerez.
4. España es uno de los productores principales del aceite de oliva del mundo.
5. Sus recursos minerales incluyen carbón, hierro, mercurio, plomo y cobre.

REGIONES

España está dividida en quince regiones:

Cantabria, en el norte.

Galicia, en el noroeste.

Asturias, en el norte al este de Galicia.

el País Vasco, en el norte, con frontera en los Pirineos.

Navarra, en el norte.

Aragón, en el nordeste, al este de Navarra.

Cataluña, en el nordeste.

La Rioja, en el centro al sur de Navarra.

Castilla y León, en el noroeste-centro.

Castilla-La Mancha, en el centro, al sur de Castilla y León.

Madrid, en el centro, al norte de Castilla-La Mancha.

Valencia, en el este.

Extremadura, en el norte, entre Portugal y Castilla-La Mancha.

Murcia, en el sudeste.

Andalucía, en el sur.

POSESIONES ULTRAMARINAS

1. **Las Islas Baleares** están en el Mar Mediterráneo. Mallorca es la isla más grande del grupo.
2. **Las Islas Canarias** están en el Océano Atlántico, cerca de la costa noroeste de Africa.
3. **Ceuta y Melilla** son dos puertos de Marruecos, África.

IDIOMAS

1. El **español** (también llamado el castellano) es el idioma principal de España.
2. El **gallego** es un dialecto que se habla en Galicia.
3. El **catalán** es la lengua de Cataluña.
4. El **vascuence** es la lengua de los vascos, que viven en el País Vasco.

CIUDADES IMPORTANTES

Madrid es la capital y la ciudad más grande de España. Tiene una población de unos 4.500.000 de habitantes. Entre los lugares de mayor interés de Madrid y sus alrededores se encuentran:

1. **El Retiro** es un parque famoso.
2. **La Puerta del Sol** es la plaza principal de Madrid. De allí se extienden muchas calles que conducen a todas partes de la ciudad.

3. **El Museo del Prado** es un museo de bellas artes de fama mundial.
4. **El Escorial** está situado cerca de Madrid. Es un edificio enorme que tiene un monasterio, un palacio, una biblioteca y un mausoleo para reyes españoles. Fue construído por orden del rey Felipe II entre 1563 y 1584.
5. **El Valle de los Caídos** también está situado cerca de Madrid. Es un monumento grandísimo dedicado a la memoria de los soldados que murieron en la Guerra Civil española (1936-1939). El dictador Francisco Franco está enterrado allí.

Barcelona, en la región de Cataluña, es el puerto principal y la ciudad más industrial de España. Tiene unos 4.000.000 de habitantes. Cerca de la ciudad está el famoso Monasterio de Montserrat.

Sevilla, en la región de Andalucía, es la ciudad más pintoresca y romántica. Está situada a orillas del río Guadalquivir. Entre sus lugares de interés se encuentran:

a. **La Catedral de Sevilla,** la catedral más grande de España.
b. **La Giralda,** una torre de la catedral, es un admirable ejemplo de la arquitectura árabe.
c. **El Alcázar** que es un famoso palacio moro.

Valencia es la ciudad principal de la región del mismo nombre. Esta región se llama «la huerta de España» y es famosa por las naranjas que produce.

Bilbao, en el norte, es famosa por su producción de hierro y acero. Tiene el apodo de «el Pittsburgh de España».

Toledo es una antigua ciudad situada en el Río Tajo. Es famosa por sus productos de acero y de metales preciosos. También es conocida por ser la casa del pintor famoso El Greco. Muchas de sus pinturas se exhiben allí.

Granada, en la región de Andalucía, tiene la famosa Alhambra, y también otro palacio moro, el Generalife. Granada fue la última posesión de los moros en España. La volvieron a ganar los cristianos en 1492.

Córdoba, también en Andalucía y situada en el Río Guadalquivir, tiene la famosa **Mezquita** (Mosque), un antiguo templo de la época de los moros, que fue convertido en una catedral católica en 1238. Durante los siglos X y XI Córdoba fue la capital mora de España y uno de los centros culturales de Europa.

Burgos, que se encuentra en Castilla y León, es la ciudad natal del Cid, el héroe nacional de España. Su tumba está en la Catedral de Burgos.

Salamanca es famosa por su universidad. Establecida en el siglo XIII, la **Universidad de Salamanca** es la más antigua de España y una de las más prestigiosas de Europa.

Segovia es una antigua ciudad situada en la parte central de España. Es famosa por el acueducto romano, construido bajo el emperador romano Trajano (A.D. 53-117). El acueducto funciona aun hoy en día.

EXERCISE A. A la izquierda de cada expresión de la columna A, escriba la letra de la expresión correspondiente de la lista B.

A

______ *1.* la Península Ibérica
______ *2.* la Sierra de Guadarrama
______ *3.* la Puerta del Sol
______ *4.* el Tajo
______ *5.* Córdoba
______ *6.* el catalán
______ *7.* Málaga
______ *8.* El Escorial
______ *9.* los Pirineos
______ *10.* el Guadalquivir
______ *11.* Andalucía
______ *12.* Burgos
______ *13.* Mallorca
______ *14.* Cueta
______ *15.* La Giralda

B

a. lengua hablada en Cataluña
b. río más navegable
c. construido por orden de Felipe II
d. las Islas Baleares
e. el Cid
f. España y Portugal
g. región situada en el sur
h. Sevilla
i. el río más largo
j. centro de la producción de vinos
k. plaza principal de Madrid
l. cerca de Madrid
m. puerto de Marruecos
n la Mezquita
o. frontera entre España y Francia

EXERCISE B. Escoja las frases que completen correctamente las oraciones.

1. La frontera que separa a España de Francia es (la Sierra de Guadarrama, la Sierra Nevada, los Pirineos).

____

2. España está situada en la parte (sudoeste, nordeste, central) de Europa.

____

3. Una región del norte de España es (Valencia, Extremadura, Galicia).

____

4. En (Madrid, Segovia, Valencia) se encuentra un acueducto romano.

____

5. Andalucía es (una ciudad, un río, una región) de España.

____

6. Las ciudades de Jerez y Málaga son famosas por sus (aceitunas, vinos, naranjas).

____

7. (El Generalife, El Escorial, La Mezquita) es un palacio moro.

____

8. Mallorca es una de (las Islas Baleares, las Islas Canarias, los Cantábricos).

____

9. La población de España es aproximadamente (40.000.000, 25.000.000, 37.000.000) de habitantes.

____

10. La catedral más grande de España se encuentra en (Madrid, Burgos, Sevilla).

____

11. Un dialecto que se habla en Galicia es el (vascuence, catalán, gallego).

____

12. Salamanca es famosa por su (catedral, universidad, acueducto).

____

13. Los recursos minerales de España incluyen el (estaño, mercurio, oro).

____

14. El río más navegable de España es el (Guadalquivir, Tajo, Ebro).

____

15. El Greco se relaciona con la ciudad de (Burgos, Córdoba, Toledo).

____

EXERCISE C. **Indique si cada frase es cierta o falsa. Si es falsa, cámbiela para hacerla cierta.**

1. El río Tajo desemboca en el Mar Mediterráneo.

____

2. La Cordillera Cantábrica marca la frontera entre España y Francia.

____

3. El Cid, el héroe nacional, nació en la ciudad de Toledo.

____

4. España tiene una población de más de cuarenta millones de habitantes.

____

5. El tabaco es un producto principal agrícola de España.

____

6. La Universidad de Salamanca se estableció en el siglo XIII.

____

7. Jerez y Málaga son los centros de la producción de vinos.

____

8. Galicia está en el noroeste del país.

____

9. Barcelona es el puerto principal de España.

____

10. Hay veinte regiones tradicionales en España.

____

11. El vascuence es el idioma principal de España.

____

12. La Giralda era un templo antiguo de la época de los moros.

____

13. Las Islas Canarias están en el Mar Mediterráneo.

____

14. España es un productor principal de jugo de naranja del mundo.

____

15. Bilbao es la ciudad conocida por su producción de hierro y acero.

____

EXERCISE D. **Complete las frases siguientes.**

1. El gallego es el idioma de ______________ .

2. En ______________ , hay dos ciudades españolas en la costa de Marruecos.

3. Los vascos hablan ______________ además del español.

4. Los Pirineos separan a España de ______________ .

5. El río más navegable de España es el

6. Un famoso palacio moro de Sevilla es ______________ .

7. El monasterio de Montserrat se encuentra cerca de la ciudad de ______________ .

8. La región central de España se llama ______________ .

9. El río más grande de España es el ______________ .

10. España ocupa la mayor parte de la ______________ .

11. La última posesión de los moros en España fue ______________ .

12. Durante los siglos X y XI ______________ fue la capital mora de España.

13. Dos posesiones ultramarinas de España son ______________ y ______________ .

14. Dos riquezas mineras de España son ______________ y ______________ .

15. El museo famoso de Madrid es ______________ .

Chapter 36
La historia de España

HABITANTES PRIMITIVOS

1. Los **iberos** y los **celtas** fueron los primeros habitantes de España. De la unión de iberos y celtas se formó la raza celtíbera, precursor de los españoles de hoy.
2. Los **fenicios** fueron una nación de marineros. Fundaron la ciudad de Cádiz. Los griegos fundaron colonias en la costa oriental de España. Estos dos grupos estaban en España del siglo once al siglo ocho, antes de Cristo, aproximadamente.
3. Los **cartagineses** invadieron a España en el siglo III antes de Cristo. Una nación guerrera, vencieron a los celtíberos en la batalla de Sagunto.
4. Los **romanos** vencieron a los cartagineses alrededor del año 200 antes de Cristo y reinaron en España durante seis siglos (hasta el año 400 después de Cristo, aproximadamente). Dejaron mucha influencia en España: dieron a España la religión cristiana, las leyes romanas, y su lengua (el castellano se deriva del latín). También construyeron puentes, acueductos y caminos.
5. Los **visigodos,** una tribu germánica, vencieron a los romanos e invadieron a España por el año 409 después de Cristo. Reinaron hasta la invasión de los moros.
6. Los **moros** invadieron a España y vencieron a los visigodos en 711. Se quedaron en España por siete siglos, hasta 1492, y dominaron el país durante gran parte del tiempo. Dejaron mucha influencia en la vida española. Esta influencia morisca incluye la introducción de la noria para regar los campos, la introducción de las ciencias (matemáticas, medicina, astronomía, filosofía, etc.), la construcción de palacios, alcázares y mezquitas, y la introducción de nuevas palabras en el idioma español, sobre todo palabras que comienzan con *al-* (algodón, alcalde, álgebra, etc.).

RECONQUISTA DE ESPAÑA

1. **Pelayo** venció a los moros en la batalla de Covadonga en 718.
2. **El Cid** (Rodrigo Díaz de Vivar), el héroe nacional de España, capturó la ciudad de Valencia de los moros en 1094.
3. En 1492, después de más de siete siglos de lucha, los españoles, bajo **Fernando** e **Isabel** (los Reyes Católicos), vencieron finalmente a los últimos moros, en Granada. Así terminó la Reconquista.

ESPAÑA, UN PAÍS PODEROSO

Los Reyes Católicos —Fernando, el rey de Aragón, e Isabel, la reina de Castilla—terminaron la Reconquista de España y empezaron su unificación. Bajo su reinado, España llegó a ser la primera nación de Europa. Ayudaron al navegante genovés Cristóbal Colón a realizar su empresa y le dieron tres carabelas, la Niña, la Pinta y la Santa María. Colón y sus marineros pisaron tierra el 12 de octubre en una isla que llamaron San Salvador. Con el descubrimiento del Nuevo Mundo empezó el gran imperio español.

Carlos V (1516-1556), nieto de Fernando e Isabel, fue uno de los reyes más poderosos de España. Durante su reinado, la época de los grandes descubrimientos y conquistas, España llegó a tener posesiones en Europa y en el Nuevo Mundo.

Felipe II fue hijo de Carlos V. Durante su reinado España tomó parte en muchas guerras. Venció a los turcos en la batalla de Lepanto (1571). Su «Armada Invencible» fue vencida por Inglaterra en 1588.

DECADENCIA DE ESPAÑA (SIGLO XVIII)

La decadencia de España se debió, entre muchas cosas, a las guerras, los altos impuestos y a los reyes débiles que gobernaron al país durante esa época.

LOS SIGLOS XIX Y XX

1. La **Guerra de Independencia** (1808-1814), comenzó el 2 de mayo de 1808 con una rebelión contra los franceses (Napoleón). Esta fecha se convirtió en la fiesta nacional del país. Lograron expulsar a las fuerzas francesas en 1814.
2. Las **Guerras Carlistas** (1833-39; 1872-76) fueron largas guerras civiles en las cuales Carlos, hermano de Fernando VII, trató de quitarle el trono del país a Isabel, hija de Fernando VII.
3. La **Guerra Hispanoamericana** entre España y los Estados Unidos tuvo lugar en 1898. España fue vencida y perdió sus posesiones ultramari-

nas de Cuba, Guam, Puerto Rico, y las Islas Filipinas.

4. La Primera República fue establecida en 1873, y duró solamente un año. Alfonso XII estableció otra vez la monarquía. Su hijo, Alfonso XIII, fue rey de España hasta 1931. Durante su reinado, estableció una dictadura bajo Primo de Rivera. La segunda república fue establecida el 14 de abril de 1931.

5. En 1936 estalló una guerra civil que duró hasta 1939. El general Francisco Franco venció a las fuerzas de la república y estableció una dictadura. Franco rigió (*ruled*) el país hasta su muerte en 1975. El gobierno actual es una monarquía constitucional. En 1975, Juan Carlos I fue proclamado rey por las Cortes. En 1982, Felipe González Márquez llegó a ser presidente del Gobierno. A partir de 1985, España es miembro de la Comunidad Económica Europea (C.E.E.).

EXERCISE A. **A la izquierda de cada expresión de la lista A, escriba la letra de la expresión correspondiente de la lista B.**

	A	B
________	*1.* Pelayo	*a.* el Cid
________	*2.* los Reyes Católicos	*b.* Napoleón
________	*3.* Rodrigo Díaz de Vivar	*c.* rey de España hasta 1931
________	*4.* Felipe II	*d.* los Estados Unidos
________	*5.* Dos de Mayo	*e.* Fernando e Isabel
________	*6.* Alfonso XIII	*f.* Armada Invencible
________	*7.* guerra que ocurrió al fin del siglo XIX	*g.* monumento romano
________	*8.* puente de Alcántara	*h.* 14 de abril de 1931
________	*9.* la segunda república	*i.* dictador español
________	*10.* Francisco Franco	*j.* principió la Reconquista

EXERCISE B. **Escoja y subraye la palabra o expresión que complete correctamente cada frase.**

1. Los primeros habitantes de España fueron los (iberos, moros, romanos).

____

2. La segunda república española se estableció en el año (718, 1931, 1808).

____

3. El acueducto de Segovia fue construido por los (fenicios, romanos, moros).

____

4. Muchas palabras españolas que principian con "al-" son de origen (romano, árabe, ibero).

____

5. Las guerras entre los moros y los españoles se llamaron (las Guerras Civiles, las Guerras Carlistas, la Reconquista).

____

6. España perdió a Cuba, Puerto Rico, y las Filipinas en (la guerra civil, la guerra con los Estados Unidos, la guerra de independencia).

____

7. Pelayo venció a los moros en la batalla de (Covadonga, Lepanto, Sagunto).

____

8. Los visigodos vencieron a los (moros, romanos, fenicios).

____

9. El dictador de España bajo Alfonso XIII fue (Francisco Franco, Primo de Rivera, Pelayo).

____

10. El hijo de Carlos V fue (Fernando VII, Felipe II, Alfonso XIII).

____

EXERCISE C. Indique si cada frase es cierta o falsa. Si es falsa, cámbiela para hacerla cierta.

1. Los romanos reinaron hasta la invasión de los moros.

____

2. Se debe la introducción de la noria a los cartagineses.

____

3. Pelayo venció a los moros en la batalla de Sagunto.

____

4. Los españoles vencieron a los turcos en la batalla de Lepanto.

____

5. España llegó a tener muchas posesiones ultramarinas durante el reinado de Fernando e Isabel.

____

6. La «Armada Invencible» fue vencida por los ingleses en 1588.

____

7. La primera república española duró cinco años.

____

8. La decadencia de España se debió a muchas guerras, reyes débiles, y la expulsión de los judíos y los moros.

____

9. La Guerra Civil comenzó en 1936 y no terminó hasta 1941.

____

10. Hoy día el gobierno de España es una monarquía constitucional.

____

EXERCISE D. Complete las frases siguientes.

1. El español se deriva del ______________________ .
2. El día de la independencia española se celebra ______________________ .
3. Los cartagineses vencieron a los celtíberos en la batalla de ______________________ .
4. La Reconquista fue terminada por ______________________ .
5. Los moros introdujeron ______________________ en España.
6. España sufrió una decadencia completa en el siglo ______________________ .
7. Los fenicios fundaron la ciudad de ______________________ .
8. Los españoles vencieron a los turcos en la batalla de ______________________ .
9. El héroe nacional de España es ______________________ .
10. Las guerras entre la reina Isabel y Carlos se llaman ______________________ .

Chapter 37
La vida y las costumbres de España

Hoy día la vida diaria de España es muy semejante a la vida diaria de los Estados Unidos. Sin embargo, cada país tiene algo de particular. En España existen muchas costumbres y tradiciones interesantes.

LA CASA Y LA FAMILIA

Las casas de las ciudades grandes se parecen a las de las otras ciudades del mundo. Hay edificios de apartamentos y casas particulares. Muchos españoles viven en su condominio o piso que forma parte de un edificio alto.

En los pueblos pequeños, las ciudades antiguas y en las partes antiguas de las ciudades grandes las casas están en calles estrechas. Generalmente, estas casas son de un solo piso, con balcones, ventanas con rejas y pintorescos patios interiores. En muchas casas, las paredes están cubiertas de azulejos.

LOS NOMBRES Y LOS APELLIDOS

Los nombres españoles son diferentes a los de los anglosajones, y esta costumbre de los nombres se extiende a todos los países hispanos. Además del nombre de pila, los españoles e hispanos llevan dos apellidos (el apellido del padre seguido del apellido de la madre): por ejemplo, Rafael *Hernández Silva*. Este nombre se archiva bajo «H» porque se considera más importante el apellido del padre.

Cuando una mujer se casa, ella retiene el apellido de su padre y añade el «de» seguido por el apellido de su esposo. Por ejemplo, si Rafael se casa con Marisa Trujillo Rodríguez, su nombre sería Marisa Trujillo de Hernández. Ella no usa ninguno de los apellidos maternos.

Por lo general, el nombre de pila de la mayoría de los españoles (y de los hispanoamericanos) es el nombre de un santo. Además de su propio cumpleaños, celebran el día del santo.

TIPOS PINTORESCOS

La tuna es un grupo de músicos ambulantes que ha sido parte de la vida estudiantil universitaria desde el siglo XVI. Los tunos usan un traje tradicional de color negro y una capa. Tocan música romántica y alegre. Sus instrumentos incluyen el laúd, la bandurria, el requinto, la guitarra y la pandereta.

Los gitanos viven en el sur de España, principalmente cerca de las ciudades de Sevilla y Granada. Conservan muchas de sus tradiciones dentro de las que la música y el baile son muy importantes. Hablan un idioma llamado romani.

COSTUMBRES

La vida social es muy importante para los españoles. Son muy sociales y amigables. Les gusta pasar mucho tiempo charlando con los amigos en los cafés y en los bares. Cenan mucho más tarde que en nuestro país, y por consiguiente, se acuestan más tarde.

En muchas ciudades hay un **ateneo,** un club intelectual donde se reúnen grupos literarios y científicos.

La tertulia es una reunión informal con el propósito de charlar y divertirse. Muchas veces no termina hasta después de la medianoche.

La siesta es la tradición de acostarse por la tarde durante las horas de mayor calor. Las tiendas y las oficinas se cierran, y los trabajadores regresan a sus casas para comer, descansar o dormir la siesta. Después de la siesta, las tiendas y oficinas vuelven a abrir y quedan abiertas hasta muy tarde. La tradición de la siesta ha ido desapareciendo en las ciudades grandes.

La lotería está dirigida por el gobierno y es muy popular. Se usan las ganancias de la lotería para el beneficio de las personas pobres y los niños huérfanos. El sorteo tiene lugar tres veces al mes y hay muchos premios. El premio mayor se llama «el premio gordo».

«Pelar la pava» es una tradición antigua que se usaba cuando el novio cortejaba a la novia. El novio le hablaba a la novia por medio de la reja. El estaba de pie afuera y la mujer estaba sentada dentro de la casa al otro lado de la reja. Hoy día muchas de las costumbres de cortejar a las mujeres están desapareciendo, especialmente en las ciudades grandes.

COMIDAS Y BEBIDAS

La tradición de comer tres comidas al día existe tanto en España como en los Estados Unidos. Principalmente, la diferencia está en el horario. En España existe la costumbre de comer más tarde. Se toma el desayuno a eso de las ocho de la mañana y generalmente consiste en café con leche o chocolate y pan con mantequilla y mermelada o bollos. Se toma la comida a eso de las dos de la tarde y no se toma la cena hasta después de las ocho o nueve de la noche. Estas dos comidas son comidas completas. Pueden consistir en sopa, ensalada, carne con arroz o verduras y postre. Alrededor de las seis de la tarde los españoles toman la merienda, algo ligero como un sándwich. Se acostumbra comer bocados que llaman «tapas» cuando toman el aperitivo antes de la cena.

España tiene una gastronomía variada, interesante y deliciosa. Entre los platos tradicionales está el **puchero** que es considerado quizás el plato nacional de España. Es un guisado que se sirve casi a diario, especialmente entre los campesinos. Se llama también olla o cocido.

El plato más conocido de España es el **arroz con pollo.** En Valencia añaden mariscos y otros ingredientes al arroz con pollo y lo llaman paella.

Las bebidas que toman los españoles incluyen el **café,** el **té,** la **leche** y los **refrescos.** La **horchata** es una bebida tradicional hecha de almendras, agua y azúcar. La horchata se toma fría en el verano como refresco. El **chocolate caliente** es una bebida popular del desayuno y de la merienda. Lo preparan muy espeso y lo toman muy caliente con **panecillos, bizcochos** o **churros.**

LA ROPA

La ropa de los españoles se parece a la del resto de Europa. Sin embargo, existen prendas tradicionales. La **mantilla** es un pañuelo grande de seda y encajes que la mujer lleva en la cabeza. Debajo de la **mantilla** se usa un peine alto, ricamente adornado, que se llama **peineta.** El **mantón** es un chal grande, ricamente bordado. Sirve de adorno o de abrigo. La **boina** es una gorra de lana redonda parecida al «beret» francés. Las **alpargatas** son una especie de sandalia hecha de lona. Son comunes entre los trabajadores en muchas partes de España.

FIESTAS RELIGIOSAS

Puesto que la mayoría de los españoles practican la religión católica, las fiestas religiosas son muy importantes en el país.

1. La **Navidad** se celebra el 25 de diciembre y es la fiesta más importante del año. Desde principios de diciembre en cada casa se preparan los **Nacimientos** (grupos de figuras que representan el nacimiento de Jesucristo). La **Nochebuena** (Christmas Eve) la gente asiste a la **misa del gallo** (midnight mass) en las iglesias. Grupos de personas caminan por las calles cantando villancicos (Christmas carols). También se acostumbra dar regalos, llamados aguinaldos, a las personas que han servido a la familia durante el año (el cartero, los criados y otros). Los niños reciben sus regalos el 6 de enero, que se llama el **Día de los Reyes Magos.** Los Reyes Magos corresponden a nuestro Santa Claus.
2. El **Carnaval** es un período de tres días de diversión antes del Miércoles de Ceniza, que comienza la **Cuaresma** (Lent). La Cuaresma son los cuarenta días que siguen. Termina el domingo de Resurrección, la **Pascua Florida.** La **Semana Santa,** que precede a la Pascua Florida, se celebra con mucha solemnidad y devoción, sobre todo en Sevilla. El **Viernes Santo** hay procesiones religiosas en muchos pueblos y ciudades.

   Cada pueblo tiene su santo patrón, cuyo día se celebra con una fiesta. La noche anterior se celebra una **verbena** (evening festival). El día del santo hay **romerías** (religious picnics) a la tumba del santo.
3. El **Día de los Difuntos o Muertos** (All Souls' Day) se celebra el 2 de noviembre, en memoria de los muertos.

FIESTAS NACIONALES

1. El **dos de mayo** es la fiesta nacional de España. Conmemora un suceso patriótico, el comienzo de la resistencia contra los franceses en 1808.
2. El **Día de la Raza,** que se celebra el 12 de octubre, corresponde a nuestro «Columbus Day». Se celebra esta fiesta en todo el mundo hispano.

DEPORTES Y DIVERSIONES

1. La **corrida de toros** es un espectáculo muy típico de España. Generalmente hay corridas los domingos por la tarde y los días de fiesta. Tiene lugar en la plaza de toros. La corrida comienza con un desfile de todos los participantes por la arena, mientras se escucha la música de pasadobles.

   La corrida tiene tres partes o lo que llaman suertes. Los picadores entran, montados a caballo en la primera suerte. Llevan picas largas. Los banderilleros entran a pie en la segunda suerte. Ellos llevan banderillas. En la tercera suerte el matador (el torero final), armado de una espada de acero muy fina, y llevando una pequeña muleta roja, exhibe su arte y su valor. Ejecuta varios pases con la muleta, hasta que el momento ideal llega para matar al toro.
2. El **jai-alai** es un juego de pelota de origen vasco que se juega con una pelota dura en un

gran frontón de tres paredes. Es semejante al «handball» pero el jugador usa una cesta larga y estrecha, que está atada a la muñeca, para tirar y coger la pelota.

3. El **fútbol** es muy popular no sólo en España, sino también en el resto de Europa y en Latinoamérica. Se puede decir que es el deporte nacional de la mayoría de esos países.

EXERCISE A. **Identifique cada una de las siguientes palabras como alimento, bebida, prenda de vestir, fiesta religiosa, o costumbre social.**

1. boina ______________________

2. verbena ______________________

3. paella ______________________

4. tertulia ______________________

5. cocido ______________________

6. romería ______________________

7. horchata ______________________

8. el Día de los Difuntos ______________________

9. alpargatas ______________________

10. arroz con pollo ______________________

11. mantilla ______________________

12. Carnaval ______________________

13. merienda ______________________

14. peineta ______________________

15. chocolate ______________________

EXERCISE B. **A la izquierda de cada expresión de la lista A, escriba la letra de la palabra o expresión de la lista B que tenga relación con ella.**

	A	B
________	*1.* apellido	*a.* premio gordo
________	*2.* pelar la pava	*b.* frontón
________	*3.* lotería	*c.* sandalias
________	*4.* Nochebuena	*d.* músicos ambulantes
________	*5.* banderillero	*e.* reja
________	*6.* jai-alai	*f.* nombre
________	*7.* día del santo patrón	*g.* alimento
________	*8.* puchero	*h.* Navidad
________	*9.* tuna	*i.* corrida de toros
________	*10.* alpargatas	*j.* verbena

EXERCISE C. Complete las frases siguientes.

1. Antonio Moreno y Villa está casado con Luisa Gómez y Vega, y tienen un hijo, Juan. El nombre completo del hijo es Juan ______________ .
2. Un alimento popular en Valencia, hecho de arroz, pollo y mariscos se llama ______________ .
3. La fiesta nacional de España se celebra ______________ .
4. Los niños españoles reciben regalos el 6 de enero, el Día de los ______________ .
5. El torero que va montado a caballo se llama el ______________ .
6. El 12 de octubre se celebra ______________ .
7. En vez de celebrar su cumpleaños, los niños españoles celebran su ______________ .
8. ______________ es el nombre que se da a un club científico y literario.
9. La horchata es una bebida fría que se hace de ______________ .
10. El jai-alai es un deporte que se juega en un ______________ .

EXERCISE D. Explique cada uno de los siguientes.

1. Día de los Muertos ______________________________
2. matador ______________________________
3. Semana Santa ______________________________
4. azulejos ______________________________
5. verbena ______________________________
6. Pascua Florida ______________________________
7. romería ______________________________
8. villancicos ______________________________
9. nacimiento ______________________________
10. Misa del Gallo ______________________________

Chapter 38

La contribución española a la literatura, las artes, la música y las ciencias

LITERATURA

España siempre ha tenido una presencia en la literatura mundial.

La Edad Media

El más antiguo poema épico y la primera obra importante de la literatura española, es el **«Poema (Cantar) del Mío Cid».** De escritor anónimo, fue compuesto hacia el año 1140. Celebra la vida y las hazañas de Rodrigo Díaz de Vivar, el héroe nacional de España. **Alfonso X,** El Sabio (1221-1284), hizo mucho para adelantar la literatura de España. Compiló una colección de leyes y costumbres de la época, **«Las siete partidas»** y escribió varias obras de poesía. Además, reunió en su corte a los hombres más cultos de la época para estudiar, traducir y escribir textos en distintas áreas.

En el siglo XV, el **Renacimiento** comenzó una renovación de la poesía en España. Los romances, poemas narrativos épico-líricos que se cantan, tuvieron su origen en este siglo. Un autor que se destacó en la poesía lírica fue Jorge Manrique, quien escribió **«Las Coplas»,** una bella poesía escrita en memoria de la muerte de su padre. Esta poesía fue traducida al inglés por el poeta norteamericano Henry Wadsworth Longfellow.

Antonio de Nebrija fue el autor del primer libro de gramática española, escrito en 1492.

El Siglo de Oro (1535-1680)

En el siglo XVI aparece un género literario narrativo de tipo realista y satírico, conocido como «la novela picaresca». Describe la vida de un pícaro, una persona que trata de vivir sin trabajar. Es una sátira de la vida y de la sociedad de la época. La primera y la más famosa de las novelas picarescas es **«El Lazarillo de Tormes»,** escrita por un autor anónimo.

1. **Miguel de Cervantes** (1547-1616) fue el novelista principal de España y es quizás el más conocido. Su obra más famosa es **«Don Quijote de la Mancha»,** uno de los libros más leídos en todos los idiomas. Los personajes principales son don Quijote y Sancho Panza, su escudero y criado. Cervantes también escribió una colección de cuentos, las «Novelas ejemplares». Su obra literaria también incluye poesías y obras de teatro.
2. **Lope de Vega** (1562-1635) fue el dramaturgo más importante del Siglo de Oro. Escribió centenares de obras de teatro. Se le considera el padre del teatro español. Dos de sus obras teatrales más famosas son «Fuenteovejuna» y «Peribáñez y el Comendador de Ocaña».
3. **Tirso de Molina** (1584-1648) es famoso por haber creado el personaje de don Juan en su drama «El burlador de Sevilla».
4. **Pedro Calderón de la Barca** (1600-1681) fue el último de los grandes dramaturgos del Siglo de Oro. Fue autor de «La vida es sueño». Con su muerte se considera terminado el Siglo de Oro.

Siglos XVIII y XIX

Durante este período hubo poca producción literaria de valor en España. El estilo más popular imitaba en español a los escritores franceses. Al regresar a España muchos de los escritores que habían salido del país durante el reinado de Fernando VII, comenzó en España el **«Romanticismo».**

José Zorrilla (1817-1893) escribió obras de teatro inspiradas en las leyendas de España. Su obra principal, **«Don Juan Tenorio»,** se representa anualmente en los teatros de todo el mundo hispano el 2 de noviembre, el Día de los Muertos.

Otro movimiento literario, el realismo, siguió al romanticismo. El realismo pretendía representar la realidad sin idealizarla.

Benito Pérez Galdós (1843-1920), fue el novelista principal del siglo XIX. Fue gran enemigo de la intolerancia religiosa y de la injusticia social. Una de sus mejores novelas, **«Doña Perfecta»,** ataca el fanatismo.

Armando Palacio Valdés (1853-1938) fue un novelista muy popular. Entre sus obras debe mencionarse **«José»** que trata de los pescadores de Asturias.

Vicente Blasco Ibáñez (1867-1928) escribió novelas sobre los campesinos de Valencia. Su obra principal es **«La barraca».** También escribió **«Los cuatro jinetes del Apocalipsis»** (*The Four Horsemen of the Apocalypse*), sobre la primera Guerra Mundial, y **«Sangre y arena»,** (*Blood and Sand*), sobre la corrida de toros.

La «Generación del 98»

La guerra contra los Estados Unidos en 1898 resultó un desastre para España. Como resultado de la guerra, muchos escritores y filósofos se dedicaron a examinar y modernizar la cultura del país. Estos escritores, que representan todos los géneros literarios, se conocen hoy con el título de la «Generación del 98».

1. **Miguel de Unamuno** (1864-1936) es la figura más dominante de la Generación del 98. Fue filósofo y ensayista. Su ensayo más conocido es **«Del sentimiento trágico de la vida».**
2. **Jacinto Benavente** (1866-1954) fue un dramaturgo ganador del Premio Nobel de Literatura en 1922. Sus obras más importantes son **«La malquerida»** y **«Los intereses creados».**
3. **Ramón Menéndez Pidal** (1869-1968) fue un erudito famoso. Hizo estudios profundos sobre la lengua y la literatura medievales de España.
4. **Pío Baroja** (1872-1956) fue un novelista. Entre sus obras más importantes se destacan **«El árbol de la ciencia»** y **«Camino de perfección».**
5. **José Martínez Ruiz** (1873-1967), llamado Azorín, fue un gran ensayista y novelista. Entre sus obras principales deben mencionarse **«La voluntad»** y **«Los valores literarios».**
6. **Antonio Machado** (1875-1939) fue uno de los mejores poetas de este siglo. Su obra **«Campos de Castilla»** es muy conocida y tiene por tema el paisaje austero de su país.

Otros autores modernos

1. **José Ortega y Gasset** (1883-1955) fue un filósofo y ensayista. Dos de sus obras principales son **«La rebelión de las masas»** y **«Meditaciones del Quijote».**

   La época de la Guerra Civil de España (1936-1939) afectó la literatura. Muchos escritores se opusieron a la dictadura que Franco estableció al terminar la guerra y salieron del país para vivir en el extranjero. Otros fueron encarcelados o condenados a muerte.
2. **Juan Ramón Jiménez** (1881-1958) además de ser poeta, escribió libros en prosa. El más conocido de sus libros en prosa es **«Platero y yo».** Ganó el Premio Nobel de Literatura en 1956.
3. **Gregorio Martínez Sierra** (1881-1947) fue un dramaturgo que logró crear notables personajes femeninos en sus obras dramáticas. Escribió **«Canción de cuna».**
4. **Federico García Lorca** (1898-1936) fue un notable poeta y dramaturgo. Escribió los dramas **«Bodas de sangre»** y **«La casa de Bernarda Alba»** que se representan mucho en los teatros hoy. Murió en circunstancias trágicas durante la Guerra Civil.
5. **Vicente Aleixandre** (1898-1984) fue ensayista y poeta. Escribió **«Pasión de la tierra».** Ganó el Premio Nobel de Literatura en 1977.
6. **Camilo José Cela** (1916-) es novelista. Escribió **«La familia de Pascual Duarte».** Ganó el Premio Nobel de Literatura en 1989.
7. **Carmen Laforet** (1920-) es una escritora que trata el tema de la España de la posguerra. Recibió un premio por su novela **«Nada»** que se publicó en 1946.
8. **Ana María Matute** (1926-) es una escritora contemporánea cuyas novelas han recibido muchos premios nacionales. Su obra incluye **«Fiesta al noroeste», «Los hijos muertos»** y **«Primera memoria».**

EXERCISE A. **Identifique cada escritor como novelista, dramaturgo, poeta, o ensayista.**

1. Miguel de Cervantes ______________________

2. Jacinto Benavente ______________________

3. José Ortega y Gasset ______________________

4. Pío Baroja ______________________

5. Antonio Machado ______________________

6. Lope de Vega ______________________________

7. José Martínez Ruiz ______________________________

8. Miguel de Unamuno ______________________________

9. Pedro Calderón de la Barca ______________________________

10. Juan Ramón Jiménez ______________________________

EXERCISE B. Combine cada escritor en la columna A con su respectiva obra en la columna B.

A

________ *1.* Federico García Lorca

________ *2.* Vicente Blasco Ibáñez

________ *3.* Tirso de Molina

________ *4.* Alfonso X

________ *5.* Miguel de Cervantes

________ *6.* José Zorrilla

________ *7.* Jorge Manrique

________ *8.* Pedro Calderón de la Barca

________ *9.* Antonio de Nebrija

________ *10.* Benito Pérez Galdós

B

a. Don Quijote de la Mancha
b. El burlador de Sevilla
c. Bodas de sangre
d. Doña Perfecta
e. Sangre y arena
f. La vida es sueño
g. Las siete partidas
h. Don Juan Tenorio
i. gramática de la lengua castellana
j. Coplas

EXERCISE C. Complete las frases siguientes:

1. El escudero de don Quijote se llamaba ________________.

2. La novela «José» fue escrita por ________________.

3. Un dramaturgo que ganó el Premio Nobel fue ________________.

4. La más famosa de las novelas picarescas es ________________.

5. El fundador del drama nacional español fue ________________.

6. La primera obra importante de la literatura española fue un poema épico, ________________.

7. El último de los grandes escritores del Siglo de Oro fue ________________.

8. ________________ fue un rey español que complió una colección de leyes.

9. ________________ creó el personaje de don Juan.

10. Un drama que se representa en el Día de los Difuntos en todos los países hispanos es ________________.

PINTURA

España tiene una tradición amplia y rica en la pintura. Hay cuadros de famosos pintores españoles en casi todos los museos importantes del mundo. El museo principal de España es el Prado en Madrid. Entre los pintores españoles más distinguidos y conocidos están los siguientes:

1. **Doménico Theotocopulos** (1541-1614), llamado **el Greco,** era de origen griego pero vivió en Toledo en el siglo XVI. Sus obras tienen un profundo tono religioso. Su obra maestra es «El entierro del conde de Orgaz».
2. **Diego Velázquez** (1599-1660) es considerado el más importante de los pintores españoles. Fue pintor de cámara del Rey Felipe IV, y pintó muchos retratos de la familia real. Su obra maestra es «Las meninas». También pintó «La rendición de Bredá», llamada también «Las lanzas».
3. **Francisco Goya** (1746-1828) fue el pintor más importante de los siglos XVIII y XIX. Fue pintor de cámara del rey Carlos IV. En sus obras ataca la decadencia social y política de España. Entre sus obras principales deben mencionarse «Los fusilamientos del dos de mayo», y «Los caprichos».
4. **Joaquín Sorolla** (1863-1923) es el pintor de "sol y color." Pintó las costumbres y los trajes de las varias regiones de España. Muchos de sus cuadros se encuentran en el Museo de la Sociedad Hispánica, en Nueva York.
5. **José María Sert** (1876-1945) es pintor de murales, muchos de los cuales se encuentran en el Rockefeller Center y en el Salón Sert del Hotel Waldorf-Astoria, en Nueva York.
6. **Pablo Picasso** (1881-1973) tiene fama de ser el fundador del cubismo, estilo de pintura en que figuras geométricas representan figuras humanas.
7. **Joan Miró** (1893-1983) fue uno de los mejores pintores del arte abstracto unido a la fantasía surrealista.
8. **Salvador Dalí** (1904-1989) fue uno de los fundadores del surrealismo en la pintura. El artista trató de pintar los pensamientos y los sueños.

MÚSICOS Y COMPOSITORES

1. **Isaac Albéniz** (1860-1909) compuso música para el piano. Entre sus composiciones están **«Iberia»** y **«El Albaicín».**
2. **Enrique Granados** (1867-1916) también compuso música para el piano. Escribió la ópera «Goyescas», basada en las obras de Goya.
3. **Manuel de Falla** (1876-1946) fue el más importante de los compositores españoles. Compuso «La vida breve» y «El amor brujo».
4. **José Iturbi** (1896-1980) fue un pianista y compositor famoso.
5. **Andrés Segovia** (1893-1987) fue uno de los guitarristas más famosos del mundo.
6. **Pablo Casals** (1876-1973) fue uno de los mejores violoncelistas del mundo.

Entre los cantantes del género operático que se han destacado por todo el mundo son las sopranos **Victoria de los Angeles** y **Monserrat Caballé,** y los tenores **Plácido Domingo, Alfredo Krauss** y **José Carreras.**

Muchos cantantes españoles de la música popular han logrado fama mundial por su interpretación de la última onda. Entre ellos se encuentran **Sarita Montiel, Julio Iglesias, Raphael, Camilo Sexto, Rocío Jurado, Lolita, Joan Manuel Serrat** y **Rocío Dúrcal.**

EL BAILE

Casi cada región de España tiene sus propios bailes. De Andalucía viene un gran número de bailes, tales como el **bolero,** el **fandango,** el **jaleo,** y el **flamenco.** De Aragón viene la **jota,** de Cataluña la **sardana** y de Galicia la **muñeira.**

Muchos intérpretes del baile flamenco han logrado fama mundial. Entre ellos se hallan **Vicente Escudero, Carmen Amaya,** la pareja **Antonio** y **Rosario** y **Antonio Gades.**

INSTRUMENTOS

El instrumento típico de España es la guitarra. Además, en Galicia se emplea la gaita. La pandereta y las castañuelas son instrumentos de percusión que se emplean para acompañar la música y el baile.

CIENTÍFICOS

Varios científicos de fama mundial han venido de España. **Santiago Ramón y Cajal** (1852-1934) recibió el Premio Nobel de Medicina en 1906 por sus estudios sobre las funciones del sistema nervioso. **Juan de la Cierva** (1895-1936) inventó el autogiro, el precursor del helicóptero. **Severo Ochoa** (1905-1993) ganó el Premio Nobel de Medicina en 1959 por sus estudios sobre la herencia.

EXERCISE D. **Identifique las siguientes personas como bailarín, pintor, científico, o músico.**

1. El Greco ______
2. Santiago Ramón y Cajal ______
3. Severo Ochoa ______
4. Vicente Escudero ______
5. José Iturbi ______
6. Manuel de Falla ______
7. Juan de la Cierva ______
8. Francisco Goya ______
9. Pablo Casals ______
10. Isaac Albéniz ______
11. Joaquín Sorolla ______
12. Andrés Segovia ______
13. Salvador Dalí ______
14. Enrique Granados ______
15. Diego Velázquez ______

EXERCISE E. **Combine cada uno de los artistas con sus respectivas obras o definiciones.**

	A	B
______	1. Francisco Goya	a. pintor de «Las meninas»
______	2. El Greco	b. pintor de murales
______	3. Diego Velázquez	c. Doménico Theotocopulos
______	4. Juan de la Cierva	d. guitarrista
______	5. Manuel de Falla	e. violoncelista
______	6. Isaac Albéniz	f. «La vida breve»
______	7. Pablo Picasso	g. autogiro
______	8. Pablo Casals	h. Iberia
______	9. Andrés Segovia	i. cubismo
______	10. José María Sert	j. «Los fusilamientos del dos de mayo»

EXERCISE F. **Complete Ud. cada frase con un nombre o una palabra.**

1. Diego Velázquez fue el pintor de cámara de ____________________ .
2. El ____________________ es un baile de Andalucía.
3. Santiago Ramón y Cajal fue un gran ____________________ español.
4. «La rendición de Bredá» se llama también ____________________ .
5. ____________________ compuso música basada en las obras de un gran pintor.
6. Para acompañar la música se emplean las ____________________ .
7. ____________________ fue un gran compositor español.
8. ____________________ pintó «El entierro del conde de Orgaz».
9. El baile regional de Cataluña es la ____________________ .
10. ____________________ fue el pintor de cámara de Carlos IV.
11. Muchas de las obras de ____________________ se hallan en el Waldorf-Astoria y el Rockefeller Center.
12. Los aragoneses bailan mucho la ____________________ .
13. ____________________ fue un famoso pintor surrealista.
14. ____________________ pintor el «sol y color» de España.
15. En Galicia se oye mucha música producida en la ____________________ .

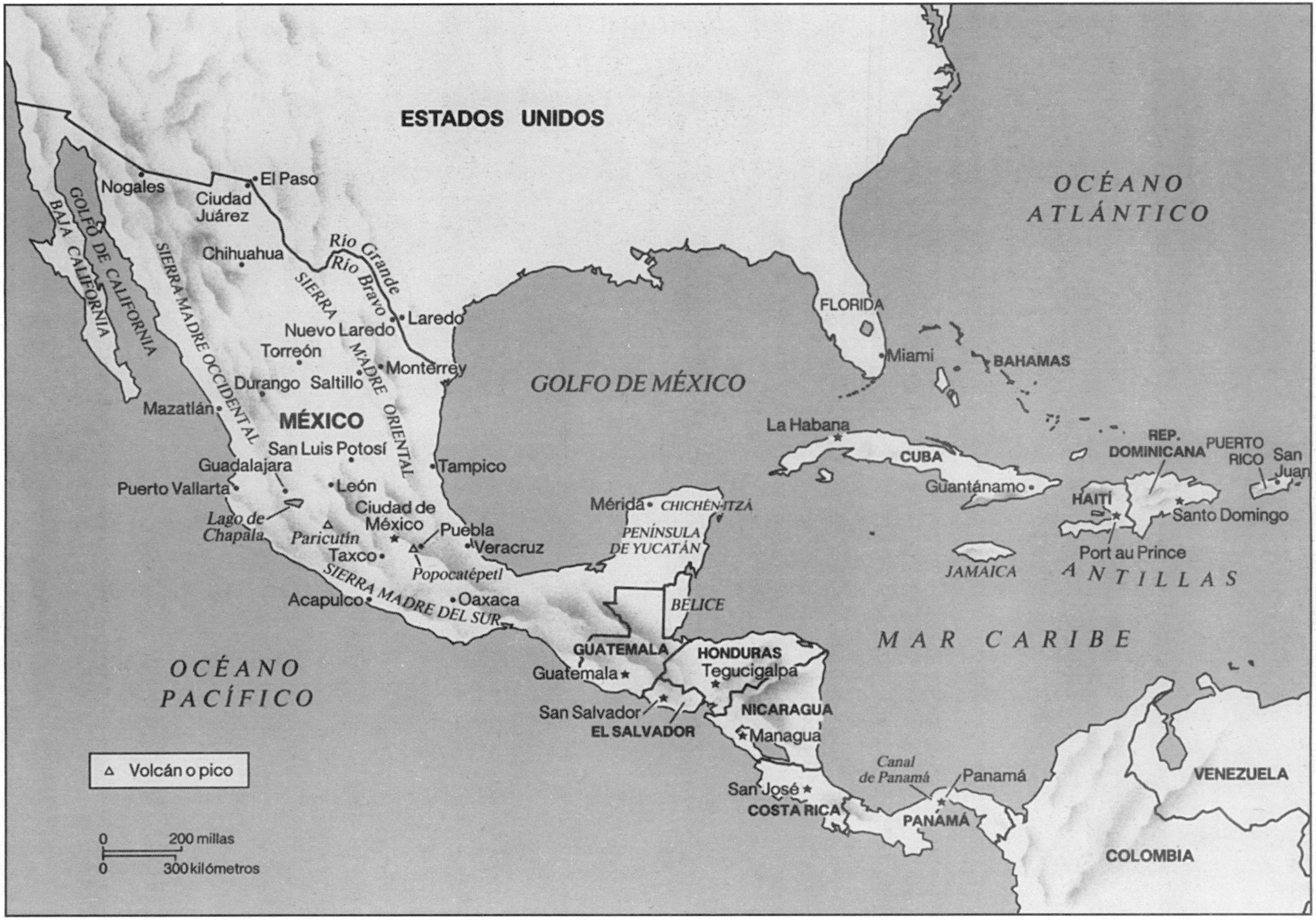
ESTADOS UNIDOS
OCÉANO ATLÁNTICO
GOLFO DE MÉXICO
OCÉANO PACÍFICO
MAR CARIBE
ANTILLAS
MÉXICO
BAJA CALIFORNIA
GOLFO DE CALIFORNIA
SIERRA MADRE OCCIDENTAL
SIERRA MADRE ORIENTAL
SIERRA MADRE DEL SUR
Río Grande
Río Bravo
Nogales
Ciudad Juárez
El Paso
Chihuahua
Laredo
Nuevo Laredo
Torreón
Monterrey
Durango
Saltillo
Mazatlán
San Luis Potosí
Tampico
Guadalajara
Puerto Vallarta
León
Ciudad de México
Lago de Chapala
Paricutín
Puebla
Veracruz
Taxco
Popocatépetl
Acapulco
Oaxaca
Mérida
CHICHÉN-ITZÁ
PENÍNSULA DE YUCATÁN
BELICE
GUATEMALA
Guatemala
HONDURAS
Tegucigalpa
San Salvador
EL SALVADOR
NICARAGUA
Managua
San José
COSTA RICA
Canal de Panamá
Panamá
PANAMÁ
FLORIDA
Miami
BAHAMAS
La Habana
CUBA
Guantánamo
JAMAICA
HAITÍ
Port au Prince
REP. DOMINICANA
Santo Domingo
PUERTO RICO
San Juan
VENEZUELA
COLOMBIA
Volcán o pico
0 200 millas
0 300 kilómetros

Chapter 39

La geografía de Hispanoamérica

Al sur de los Estados Unidos, viven alrededor de doscientos cuarenta millones de personas que constituyen la llamada América Española, o sea lugares donde el idioma oficial es el español. La América Española consta de diecinueve países, situados en tres regiones distintas: (1) la América del Norte, (2) la América Central y las Antillas y (3) la América del Sur.

AMÉRICA DEL NORTE

a. Extensión y población

México está al sur de los Estados Unidos en la parte sur de la América del Norte. Los límites de México son: al norte el **Río Bravo** (nosotros lo llamamos el Río Grande), que separa a México del estado de Texas, al oeste el **Océano Pacífico,** al este el **Golfo de México,** y al sur **Guatemala** y **Belice.**

Su extensión territorial es la cuarta parte de la de los Estados Unidos. México tiene más de 76 millones de habitantes.

b. Montañas y volcanes

Hay dos cadenas de montañas que cruzan a México de norte a sur: la **Sierra Madre Oriental** y la **Sierra Madre Occidental.** También hay varios volcanes, tales como el **Orizaba,** el **Popocatépetl,** el **Ixtaccíhuatl,** y el **Paracutín.**

c. Productos

La agricultura y la industria minera son importantes. Los minerales principales son la plata y el petróleo. Los productos agrícolas principales son el trigo, el maíz, y el ganado.

d. Ciudades principales

La Ciudad de México (el Distrito Federal) es la capital y está situada en una meseta a unos 7.000 pies de altura. Fue la antigua capital de los aztecas, quienes la llamaban Tenochtitlán. Entre los puntos de interés principales de la capital se encuentran:

el **Castillo de Chapultepec,** actualmente un museo de historia colonial.

el **Palacio de Bellas Artes,** el teatro más grande del país, es también un museo con una colección impresionante de pinturas mexicanas.

la **Basílica de Guadalupe,** una iglesia fundada en honor de la Virgen de la Guadalupe, santa patrona del país.

el **Zócalo,** la plaza principal de la ciudad de México. A un lado de la plaza esta la Catedral de México, la catedral más grande y más antigua del continente.

el **Museo de Antropología,** donde se puede aprender la historia y admirar la cultura y el arte de las tribus indias de la región.

los **jardines flotantes de Xochimilco** y los templos y **pirámides de Teotihuacán,** situados a poca distancia de la capital.

Guadalajara, la segunda ciudad de México y el centro principal de la agricultura y la ganadería.

Tampico y Veracruz, puertos del Golfo de México. Tampico es el centro de la industria petrolera.

Acapulco y Puerto Vallarta, puertos en el Océano Pacífico. Son famosos por sus playas hermosas.

Taxco, una ciudad antigua que hoy día es un monumento nacional a la arquitectura colonial y es el centro de la industria de la plata.

Chichén-Itzá, la antigua ciudad maya en el norte de la península de Yucatán donde hay notables ruinas mayas y toltecas.

EXERCISE A. Complete las frases siguientes.

1. La capital de México fue fundada sobre la antigua ciudad azteca de ____________________ .

2. ____________________ es un producto importante de México.

3. ____________________ es una sierra del este de México.

4. El Orizaba y el Paricutín son ________________.

5. La segunda ciudad de México es ________________.

6. ________________ y ________________ son dos puertos del Golfo de México.

7. En los Estados Unidos el Río Bravo es conocido como el ________________.

8. ________________ es una ciudad industrial de México.

9. El ________________ es un hermoso teatro y museo en la Ciudad de México.

10. La santa patrona de México es ________________.

EXERCISE B. **Combine cada punto geográfico en la columna A con su palabra correspondiente en la columna B.**

	A	B
________	*1.* Zócalo	*a.* museo histórico
________	*2.* Taxco	*b.* petróleo
________	*3.* Xochimilco	*c.* ruinas
________	*4.* Popocatépetl	*d.* plaza principal
________	*5.* Chapultepec	*e.* Santa Patrona
________	*6.* Tenochtitlán	*f.* ciudad pintoresca
________	*7.* Acapulco	*g.* jardines flotantes
________	*8.* Chichén-Itzá	*h.* capital azteca
________	*9.* Tampico	*i.* playa
________	*10.* Basílica de Guadalupe	*j.* volcán

La América Central y las Antillas

La América Central

1. **Guatemala** está situada al sur de México y es un país de montañas y de lagos. Su topografía variada le proporciona un clima variado que le ha permitido desarrollar una agricultura también muy variada. Sus productos principales incluyen las bananas, el café, las maderas finas y el chicle que se usa para fabricar la goma de mascar (*chewing gum*). Guatemala es el país de mayor población de la América Central y el que tiene el mayor porcentaje de indígenas puros (54% de la población). Guatemala fue la sede de los mayas, la civilización precolombina más avanzada. Su capital es la **Ciudad de Guatemala.**
2. **Honduras** es el país más montañoso de Centroamérica. Tiene un clima muy variado. También es un país agrícola. Sus productos principales son las bananas, el café, el tabaco, la caña de azúcar y las maderas finas. La capital es **Tegucigalpa.**
3. **El Salvador** es la nación más pequeña de Centroamérica y es el único país que no está limitado por el Océano Atlántico. Tiene más de 350 ríos, muchos lagos y lagunas. Su producto más importante es el café. También produce algodón y caña de azúcar. La capital es **San Salvador.**
4. **Nicaragua** es la república más grande de Centroamérica. Es también un país agrícola y produce maíz, algodón, café, plátano, caucho y maderas finas. Es el país de mayor producción

ganadera de Centroamérica. Su capital es **Managua.**

5. **Costa Rica** es el único país de América que no tiene ejército. Ha sido tradicionalmente un país democrático y ha fomentado la educación pública. Sus principales productos de exportación son el café y los plátanos, aunque produce también cacao, caña de azúcar, papas y una gran variedad de frutas. Su capital es **San José.**
6. **Panamá** es un istmo que conecta las dos Américas. El famoso **Canal de Panamá** atraviesa el país. Su producto principal es el plátano. La capital del país es la **Ciudad de Panamá** y el puerto principal es **Balboa** en la Zona del Canal.

Las Antillas

Las Antillas son un grupo de islas en el Mar Caribe que incluyen a Cuba, la República Dominicana y Puerto Rico.

1. **Cuba** es la isla más grande de las Antillas. Se conoce como «la perla de las Antillas». Produce mucha caña de azúcar y tabaco. Su capital es **La Habana.**
2. **La República Dominicana** comparte la isla de La Española con Haití, una república de habla francesa. Su capital es **Santo Domingo,** la ciudad más antigua de América, fundada en 1496. Es un país agrícola y sus productos principales incluyen la caña de azúcar, el cacao, el café, el plátano y el maíz.
3. **Puerto Rico** es hoy día un Estado Libre Asociado (*Commonwealth*) de los Estados Unidos. La isla, llamada Borinquén por los indígenas, fue descubierta por Cristóbal Colón en 1493 y nombrada **San Juan Bautista.** Su capital, **San Juan,** fue fundada en 1508 por Ponce de León, el primer gobernador de la isla. Es un puerto comercial muy activo. La ciudad de San Juan conserva aún fortificaciones y hermosos edificios de la época colonial española.

EXERCISE C. **Combine cada uno de los países en la columna A con su respectiva capital en la columna B.**

	A	B
________	*1.* Nicaragua	*a.* San José
________	*2.* Puerto Rico	*b.* Ciudad de Panamá
________	*3.* Guatemala	*c.* Santo Domingo
________	*4.* Costa Rica	*d.* Tegucigalpa
________	*5.* El Salvador	*e.* La Habana
________	*6.* Panamá	*f.* San Salvador
________	*7.* Honduras	*g.* San Juan
________	*8.* República Dominicana	*h.* Managua
________	*9.* Cuba	*i.* Ciudad de Guatemala

EXERCISE D. **Complete las frases siguientes.**

1. La república más grande de la América Central es ________________.

2. La república más pequeña de la América Central es ________________.

3. Un producto importante de Guatemala es ________________.

4. «La perla de las Antillas» es un nombre que se da a ________________ .

5. El plátano es un producto importante de ________________ .

6. El ________________ es el país que conecta a la América del Norte con la América del Sur.

7. La Española es una isla compartida por dos naciones: Haití y ________________ .

8. Una isla de las Antillas que mantiene un estado libre asociado con los Estados Unidos es ________________ .

9. Para fabricar la goma de mascar se usa el ________________ .

10. El azúcar y el tabaco son productos importantes de ________________ .

La América del Sur

a. Montañas y picos

Los Andes cruzan el continente de norte a sur, a lo largo de la costa occidental. El **Chimborazo** y el **Cotopaxi** son dos volcanes localizados en los Andes, en el territorio del Ecuador. El **Aconcagua,** el pico más alto de los Andes y de toda la América del Sur, está situado en la Argentina.

b. Ríos y lagos

El **Amazonas,** que atraviesa el Brasil, es el segundo río del mundo en longitud. En los países de habla española los ríos principales son el **Magdalena** (en Colombia), el **Orinoco** (en Venezuela) y el **Plata** (en la Argentina). Entre la Argentina y el Brasil se encuentra la famosa **catarata** (waterfalls) del **Iguazú.** Entre Bolivia y el Perú está el lago **Titicaca,** el lago navegable más alto del mundo.

c. Llanuras (*Plains*)

Las **pampas** son grandes llanuras en la Argentina, donde se producen trigo y ganado. Aquí se halla el ombú, árbol típico de la pampa. Aquí también vive el gaucho. En Venezuela las llanuras se llaman llanos. En Colombia y el Brasil se encuentran las selvas, densos bosques de gran extensión.

d. Clima

En la América del Sur las estaciones ocurren en orden opuesto a las nuestras. Cuando nosotros tenemos el verano aquí, allí tienen el invierno, y viceversa.

e. Población

La población de los países hispanos de América del Sur consiste en varias razas, que se originan en Europa, África y las tribus indígenas.

f. Países del Este

1. **La Argentina** se extiende desde el **Chaco,** en el norte, hasta el extremo sur del continente. Está separada de Chile por los Andes. En la frontera entre Chile y la Argentina hay una gran estatua, llamada «el **Cristo de los Andes**», que conmemora el arreglo pacífico de una disputa entre los dos países. Los productos principales de la Argentina son la carne, la lana y el trigo. Su capital, **Buenos Aires,** es la ciudad hispana más grande de Sudamérica. Los habitantes de Buenos Aires se llaman «porteños».
2. **El Uruguay** es el país hispano más pequeño de Sudamérica. Como la Argentina, sus productos principales son la carne, la lana y los cereales. Su capital es **Montevideo.**
3. **El Paraguay** no tiene puerto de mar, pero puede comunicarse con la costa por medio del río Paraná. Produce yerba mate, un té que se usa mucho allí, y quebracho, una madera muy dura que se usa para curtir el cuero. Su capital es **Asunción.**

g. Países de los Andes

1. **Chile** se encuentra entre los Andes y el Océano Pacífico. De norte a sur se extiende unas 3.000 millas. Es el país más largo y más estrecho del continente. Sus productos principales son el cobre y el salitre (*nitrates*). Las ciudades principales son **Santiago,** la capital, y **Valparaíso,** el puerto principal.

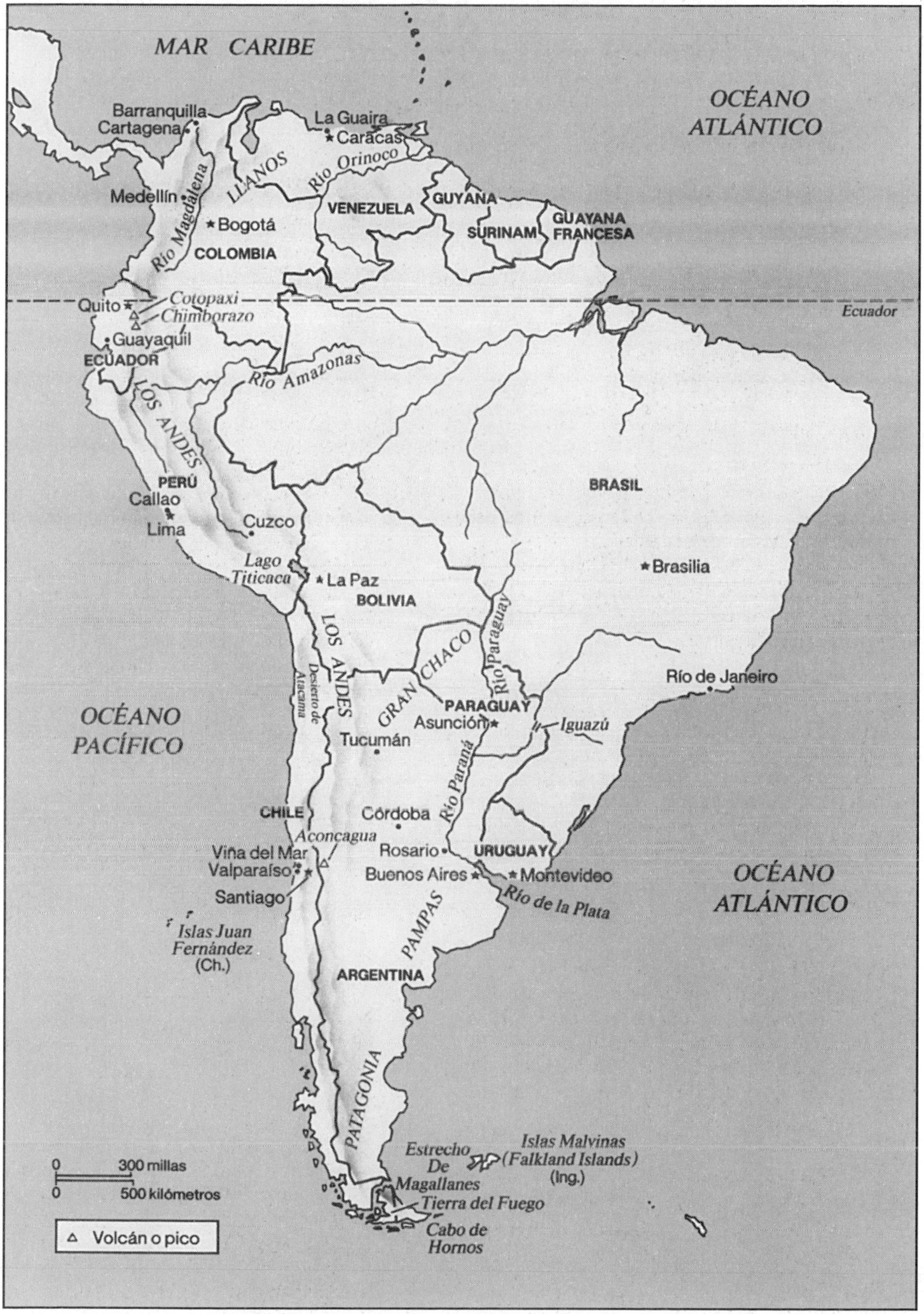
MAR CARIBE
OCÉANO ATLÁNTICO
Barranquilla
Cartagena
La Guaira
Caracas
LLANOS
Río Orinoco
Río Magdalena
Medellín
VENEZUELA
GUYANA
SURINAM
GUAYANA FRANCESA
Bogotá
COLOMBIA
Quito
Cotopaxi
Chimborazo
Ecuador
Guayaquil
ECUADOR
Río Amazonas
LOS ANDES
BRASIL
PERÚ
Callao
Lima
Cuzco
Lago Titicaca
La Paz
BOLIVIA
Brasilia
LOS ANDES
GRAN CHACO
Río Paraguay
Desierto de Atacama
Río de Janeiro
PARAGUAY
Asunción
Iguazú
OCÉANO PACÍFICO
Tucumán
Río Paraná
CHILE
Córdoba
Aconcagua
Viña del Mar
Valparaíso
Rosario
URUGUAY
Buenos Aires
Montevideo
OCÉANO ATLÁNTICO
Santiago
Río de la Plata
PAMPAS
Islas Juan Fernández (Ch.)
ARGENTINA
PATAGONIA
Estrecho De Magallanes
Islas Malvinas (Falkland Islands) (Ing.)
Tierra del Fuego
Cabo de Hornos
0 300 millas
0 500 kilómetros
Volcán o pico

2. **Bolivia** es el único país de Sudamérica que no tiene contacto con el mar. Para exportar sus productos depende de los países vecinos. Produce mucho estaño (*tin*). Su capital, **La Paz,** es la capital más alta del mundo (a más de 2 millas sobre el nivel del mar).
3. **El Perú** fue el centro del gobierno de los incas, que establecieron su capital en **Cuzco.** Hoy día, la capital y ciudad principal es **Lima.** En Lima se encuentra la universidad más antigua de la América del Sur, la **Universidad de San Marcos,** fundada en 1551. **El Callao,** cerca de Lima, es el puerto principal. El Perú tiene mucha riqueza minera. También exporta lana (de alpaca) y guano, un fertilizante, que se usa en la agricultura.
4. **El Ecuador** está en el centro de la **Zona Tórrida.** La línea geográfica llamada «el ecuador» cruza el país. Aquí se producen los sombreros de jipijapa, que nosotros llamamos «Panama hats». También se produce mucho cacao, del cual se hace chocolate. Las ciudades principales son **Quito,** la capital, y **Guayaquil,** el puerto principal.
5. **Colombia** está en el noroeste del continente. Tiene puertos en los dos mares: el mar Caribe y el Océano Pacífico. Su capital es **Bogotá. Medellín** es el centro de la industria del café. Los productos principales del país son el café, el petróleo, el platino (platinum) y las esmeraldas.
6. **Venezuela** está en el norte. Es la patria del Libertador, **Simón Bolívar.** Exporta mucho petróleo. Su capital es **Caracas,** y su puerto principal es **La Guaira.**

EXERCISE E. **Combine cada uno de los países en la columna A con su respectiva capital en la columna B.**

	A	B
________	*1.* Chile	*a.* La Paz
________	*2.* Venezuela	*b.* Bogotá
________	*3.* El Perú	*c.* Quito
________	*4.* El Ecuador	*d.* Asunción
________	*5.* Colombia	*e.* Santiago
________	*6.* Bolivia	*f.* Lima
________	*7.* El Uruguay	*g.* Buenos Aires
________	*8.* El Paraguay	*h.* Montevideo
________	*9.* la Argentina	*i.* Caracas

EXERCISE F. **Combine cada uno de los países en la columna A con sus respectivos productos en la columna B.**

A	B
______ *1.* Venezuela	*a.* salitre, cobre
______ *2.* Bolivia	*b.* petróleo
______ *3.* el Ecuador	*c.* esmeraldas, platino, café
______ *4.* Chile	*d.* sombreros de jipijapa
______ *5.* el Paraguay	*e.* estaño
______ *6.* Colombia	*f.* carne, trigo, lana
______ 7. la Argentina	*g.* yerba mate

EXERCISE G. **Complete las frases siguientes.**

1. Los habitantes de Buenos Aires se llaman ______________.

2. ______________ es un país sudamericano con puertos en dos mares.

3. La ciudad más grande de Sudamérica es ______________.

4. Cuzco fue la capital antigua de los ______________.

5. El país más estrecho de la América del Sur es ______________.

6. ______________ es una estatua en los Andes entre Chile y la Argentina.

7. El país hispano más pequeño de Sudamérica es ______________.

8. San Marcos es el nombre de una ______________ antigua del Perú.

9. Del cacao se hace ______________.

10. El único país sudamericano que no tiene contacto con el mar es ______________.

Chapter 40
La historia de Hispanoamérica

CIVILIZACIONES INDÍGENAS

Antes de la llegada de los españoles al «Nuevo Mundo», varias civilizaciones indígenas ya existían allí. La civilización de los **mayas** era la más avanzada. Su civilización floreció del siglo III a mediados del siglo XVI. Ocupaban un territorio bastante extenso que hoy incluye la península de Yucatán, Belice, Guatemala y partes de Honduras y El Salvador. Los mayas lograron un desarrollo increíble en la arquitectura, la astronomía y las matemáticas. Tenían su calendario y podían calcular con mucha precisión la duración de un año solar. Fueron la única cultura indígena que desarrolló una forma avanzada de escritura.

Los **aztecas** desarrollaron su imperio en México durante el siglo XV. Construyeron su capital, Tenochtitlán, en lo que hoy es la Ciudad de México. Sus ciudades eran tan grandes como las ciudades europeas de la época. La religión dominaba todos los aspectos de su vida. Edificaron enormes templos en forma de pirámides donde celebraban ceremonias religiosas que incluían sacrificios humanos. Las esculturas aztecas son muy detalladas. La más famosa es La Piedra del Sol, un calendario circular que representa la superficie del sol.

Los **incas** desarrollaron su imperio en los Andes. Se extendió desde lo que es hoy el Ecuador hasta el centro de Chile, incluyendo partes de Bolivia y la Argentina. El centro de la civilización inca estaba en el Perú. Tenían un fuerte y estructurado sistema político y social. Su ejército estaba muy bien organizado y tenían un sistema de caminos que comunicaba todos los puntos del imperio con la capital, Cuzco. En la capital construyeron grandes palacios, templos y edificios del gobierno. Según una leyenda, el emperador de los incas descendía de los dioses. Todas las tierras pertenecían al gobierno. Aunque no desarrollaron la escritura, tenían un sistema especial para escribir y contar: hacían nudos en cuerdas de varios colores y tamaños. Esto era llamado un quipú. Usaban la llama y la alpaca para el transporte y también les servían de alimento y proveían lana para la ropa. Hablaban el quechua, una lengua que se habla aún hoy en el Perú y algunas zonas de Bolivia, el Ecuador y el norte de Chile.

Otras de las civilizaciones indígenas que existían antes de la llegada de los españoles fueron los **caribes,** en las Antillas, los **chibchas** en la región andina de Colombia, los **guaraníes** en Paraguay, y los **araucanos** que vivían en la costa de Chile pero emigraron a la Argentina cuando llegaron los españoles.

DESCUBRIMIENTO, EXPLORACIÓN Y CONQUISTA

1. **Cristóbal Colón** salió de España con tres barcos, la Niña, la Pinta y la Santa María. El 12 de octubre de 1492 descubrió la isla de San Salvador (que hoy se llama Watlings Island). La fecha de este descubrimiento se celebra en todo el mundo hispano como el Día de la Raza.
2. **Vasco Núñez de Balboa** cruzó el istmo de Panamá y en 1513 descubrió el Océano Pacífico, que él llamó Mar del Sur.
3. **Hernando de Soto** descubrió el río Misisipí en 1541.
4. **Juan Ponce de León** descubrió la Florida en 1513.
5. **Francisco Vázquez de Coronado** exploró el sudoeste de los Estados Unidos, y descubrió el Gran Cañón en 1540.
6. **Álvar Núñez Cabeza de Vaca** exploró Nuevo México, Texas y parte de Kansas de 1528 a 1536.
7. **Fernando de Magallanes** fue un navegante portugués que trató de dar la vuelta al mundo. En 1520, descubrió y pasó por el Estrecho que lleva su nombre. Murió durante el viaje y Juan Sebastián Elcano, un español, completó el viaje.
8. **Hernán Cortés** conquistó a México, venciendo a los aztecas y a su emperador, Cuauhtémoc en 1521.
9. **Francisco Pizarro** conquistó al Perú. Venció a los incas y a su rey, Atahualpa. Fundó la ciudad de Lima, que él llamó «Ciudad de los Reyes».
10. **Pedro de Valdivia** conquistó a Chile (1541), luchando con los araucanos, una tribu de indígenas muy feroces.

GOBIERNO DE LAS COLONIAS

Las colonias eran gobernadas por el Consejo (Council) de Indias, un grupo de hombres nombrados por el rey. La Casa de Contratación dirigía el comercio colonial. Las colonias estaban divididas en cuatro virreinatos (viceroyalties), cada uno gobernado por un virrey (viceroy). Los virreinatos eran:

La Nueva España (México, Antillas, y la América Central).

La Nueva Granada (territorio que ocupan actualmente Colombia, Panamá, Venezuela, y el Ecuador).

El Perú (territorio que ocupan actualmente el Perú, Bolivia, y Chile).

La Plata (la Argentina, el Uruguay, y el Paraguay).

LOS MISIONEROS

1. **Fray Junípero Serra** (1713-1784) estableció varias misiones en California.
2. **Fray Bartolomé de las Casas** (1474-1566), el apóstol de los indios, luchó en favor de los indios.

LA INDEPENDENCIA (REVOLUCIÓN CONTRA ESPAÑA)

1. **Francisco Miranda** (1750-1816), de Venezuela, fue el primero de los revolucionarios.
2. **Simón Bolívar** (1783-1830), llamado «El Libertador», es la figura principal de la revolución hispanoamericana. Ganó la libertad de Venezuela, Colombia y el Ecuador.
3. **José de San Martín** (1778-1850) ganó la libertad de la Argentina, Chile y el Perú.
4. **Bernardo O'Higgins** (1778-1842), un general chileno, ayudó a San Martín en la lucha en Chile.
5. **Antonio José de Sucre** (1795-1830) venció a los españoles en la batalla de Ayacucho, en 1824, la última batalla de la revolución.
6. **El padre Miguel Hidalgo** (1753-1811), cura del pueblo mexicano de Dolores, inició el movimiento por la independencia en México con el «Grito de Dolores.»
7. **El padre José Morelos** (1765-1815), también sacerdote, continuó el trabajo comenzado en México por Hidalgo.
8. **José Martí** (1853-1895) fue un patriota y poeta cubano que luchó por la independencia de Cuba.

DICTADORES

En muchos países las guerras de independencia fueron seguidas de una época de dictaduras. Unos ejemplos incluyen:

1. **Agustín de Iturbide** se declaró Emperador de México (Agustín I) en 1822. La monarquía fue derribada (overthrown) un año después, en 1823.
2. **Maximiliano de Austria** (1864-1867), fue enviado por Napoleón III a ser emperador de México. Fue ejecutado por las fuerzas republicanas de Benito Juárez, un patriota mexicano. Los mexicanos consideran a Juárez el «Abraham Lincoln de México».
3. **Porfirio Díaz** fue dictador de México en dos ocasiones: de 1877 a 1880 y de 1884 a 1911.

También había dictaduras en otros países en distintas épocas. Entre los dictadores se encuentran a:

4. **Juan Manuel de Rosas,** la Argentina de 1829 a 1852.
5. **Juan Perón,** la Argentina de 1943 a 1955.
6. **José Gaspar** de Francia, el Paraguay de 1814 a 1840.
7. **Vicente Gómez,** Venezuela de 1908 a 1935.
8. **Marcos Pérez Jiménez,** Venezuela de 1953 a 1958.
9. **Fulgencio Batista,** Cuba en dos ocasiones: 1934 a 1944 y 1952 a 1958.
10. **Fidel Castro,** de Cuba en 1959 y sigue en poder.

RELACIONES INTERNACIONALES

El Panamericanismo es un movimiento que trata de fomentar (promote) la paz, el comercio, y la ayuda mutua entre los Estados Unidos y las repúblicas de la América Latina. Con este propósito se fundó la Unión Panamericana en 1910. En 1948 se cambió el nombre a la Organización de Estados Americanos (O.E.A.; en inglés, O.A.S.). Se celebra el Día Panamericano cada año el 14 de abril.

La Política (Policy) del Buen Vecino es una política de amistad hacia los otros países americanos. Fue iniciada por el presidente Franklin D. Roosevelt.

El Cuerpo de Paz (Peace Corps) y la Alianza Para el Progreso (Alliance for Progress) fueron iniciados por el presidente John F. Kennedy. El Cuerpo de la Paz manda maestros y técnicos a otros países para ayudar a los habitantes a mejorar su condición. La Alianza Para el Progreso ofrecía dinero y ayuda técnica a los países latinoamericanos que querían hacer más democrático su gobierno. El programa no tuvo el éxito esperado y ha sido reemplazado por otros métodos de ayuda económica.

En 1994 entró en vigor el Tratado de libre comercio de la América del Norte (TLC; en inglés, North American Free Trade Agreement-NAFTA). Este acuerdo estableció una sola zona comercial y una fuerza laboral entre el Canadá, los Estados Unidos y México.

EXERCISE A. Subraye Ud. la palabra o expresión que correctamente complete cada frase.

1. Atahualpa fue el rey de los (incas, mayas, aztecas, araucanos).

____

2. Colombia formaba parte del virreinato de (Nueva España, Nueva Granada, Perú, La Plata).

____

3. Ciudad de los Reyes es el nombre que Pizarro dio a la ciudad de (México, Buenos Aires, Caracas, Lima).

____

4. El Libertador de la Argentina, de Chile y del Perú fue (Miranda, Martí, San Martín, Morelos).

____

5. El jefe de las fuerzas que vencieron a Maximiliano fue (Benito Juárez, Porfirio Díaz, Miguel Hidalgo, Bernardo O'Higgins).

____

6. El Día Panamericano se celebra (el dos de mayo, el catorce de abril, el doce de octubre, el cinco de mayo).

____

7. «La Política del Buen Vecino» fue iniciada por (Perón, Roosevelt, Castro, Batista).

____

8. El patriota que luchó por la independencia de Cuba fue (Martí, Batista, O'Higgins, Sucre).

____

9. Una libre zona comercial fue establecida por (la Organización de Estados Americanos, la Política del Buen Vencino, el Cuerpo de Paz, el Tratado de libre comercio de la América del Norte).

____

10. La Florida fue descubierta por (Hernando de Soto, Juan Ponce de León, Vasco Núñez de Balboa, Francisco Vásquez de Coronado).

____

EXERCISE B. Combine cada lugar en la columna A con su respectivo descubridor, explorador o conquistador en la columna B.

	A	B
________	*1.* Chile	*a.* Vasco Núñez de Balboa
________	*2.* San Salvador	*b.* Hernando de Soto
________	*3.* el Perú	*c.* Juan Ponce de León
________	*4.* México	*d.* Francisco Vásquez de Coronado
________	*5.* la Florida	*e.* Álvar Núñez Cabeza de Vaca
________	*6.* Estrecho de Magallanes	*f.* Hernán Cortés
________	*7.* Nuevo México, Texas y Kansas	*g.* Pedro de Valdivia
________	*8.* Océano Pacífico	*h.* Fernando de Magallanes
________	*9.* río Misisipí	*i.* Cristóbal Colón
________	*10.* el Gran Cañón	*j.* Francisco Pizarro

EXERCISE C. **A la izquierda de cada nombre de la lista A, escriba Ud. la letra de la expresión de la lista B que tenga relación con él.**

	A	B
________	*1.* Bartolomé de las Casas	*a.* «el Libertador»
________	*2.* Simón Bolívar	*b.* Maximiliano de Austria
________	*3.* Miguel Hidalgo	*c.* dictador mexicano
________	*4.* Napoleón III	*d.* «apóstol de los indios»
________	*5.* Juan Manuel de Rosas	*e.* dictador cubano
________	*6.* Fray Junípero Serra	*f.* batalla de Ayacucho
________	*7.* Cristóbal Colón	*g.* fundó misiones en California
________	*8.* Fidel Castro	*h.* la Pinta
________	*9.* Porfirio Díaz	*i.* dictador argentino
________	*10.* Antonio José de Sucre	*j.* Grito de Dolores

EXERCISE D. **Lea cada frase e indique si es cierta o falsa. Si es falsa, cámbiela para que sea cierta.**

1. Las colonias españolas estaban divididas en cinco virreinatos.

____

2. El Gran Cañón fue descubierto por Juan Ponce de León.

____

3. El quechua es una tribu india.

____

4. Cuzco era la capital de los incas.

___

5. Chichén-Itzá fue la ciudad principal de los aztecas.

___

6. La gran época de la colonización española fue el siglo XIV.

___

7. Fulgencio Batista fue dictador de la Argentina.

___

8. La civilización indígena más avanzada fue la de los araucanos.

___

9. Los aztecas celebraban ceremonias religiosas en las pirámides.

___

10. El emperador azteca derrotado por Cortés se llamaba Atahualpa.

___

11. Moctezuma fue el último rey de los incas.

___

12. La Piedra del Sol es el calendario de los mayas.

___

13. El famoso «Grito de Dolores» fue dado por José Morelos.

___

14. El misionero que luchó más que ningún otro en favor de los indios se llamaba Fray Junípero Serra.

___

15. Tenochtitlán fue la capital de los aztecas.

___

EXERCISE E. **Identifique Ud. cada nombre, clasificándolo como conquistador, descubridor, dictador o patriota.**

1. José Anotnio de Sucre ___
2. Hernán Cortés ___
3. Vasco Núñez de Balboa ___
4. Francisco Pizarro ___
5. Juan Manuel de Rosas ___
6. Cristóbal Colón ___

7. Benito Juárez ______________________

8. Bernardo O'Higgins ______________________

9. Fidel Castro ______________________

10. José Martí ______________________

11. Miguel Hidalgo ______________________

12. Fernando Magallanes ______________________

13. José de San Martín ______________________

14. Simón Bolívar ______________________

15. Francisco Vásquez de Coronado ______________________

Chapter 41
La vida y las costumbres de Hispanoamérica

Las costumbres y tradiciones hispanoamericanas representan la mezcla de la influencia española e indígena. En las Antillas y en los países del Caribe se nota también la influencia africana, especialmente en la música y los bailes.

TIPOS PINTORESCOS

Todavía se ven tipos tradicionales en varias regiones de Hispanoamérica. Es más notable en las regiones donde se cría el ganado y el caballo es el medio de transporte principal. Allí se encuentran los vaqueros que tienen nombres distintos en diferentes países. En Venezuela y Colombia se llaman llaneros, y en la Argentina y el Uruguay se llaman gauchos.

El charro es el vaquero de México. Vestido de su traje tradicional es el jinete típico mexicano. La china poblana es su compañera. Su vestido típico representa los colores de la bandera mexicana: una falda ancha y larga de color rojo y verde y una blusa de color blanco.

Los mariachis son grupos de músicos y cantantes ambulantes que tocan la música mariachi del estado de Jalisco.

ROPA TÍPICA

1. El **poncho** es una capa que usan los gauchos para protegerse del frío y de la lluvia.
2. El **sarape** es una especie de manta de colores vivos, hecha de lana o de algodón. Es muy popular en México y los países centroamericanos.
3. El **rebozo** es un chal (shawl) muy popular entre las mujeres mexicanas y centroamericanas.
4. Los **huaraches** son sandalias populares en México.
5. El famoso **sombrero** de jipijapa (Panama hats) no se fabrica en Panamá, sino en el Ecuador.

COMIDAS Y BEBIDAS

Por lo general, las comidas reflejan una mezcla de las culturas española, indígena y africana. Sus ingredientes principales son el maíz, el frijol, el plátano, la carne y la papa. El tamal es un plato muy popular y casi todos los países tienen su propia versión. Es una masa de maíz fresco molido o de harina de maíz que se cuece al vapor dentro de una hoja de maíz o de plátano. Puede rellenarse con pollo, cerdo, carne de res, legumbres, garbanzos, etc. En México se hace la tortilla de maíz y sirve de base en la preparación de los tacos y las enchiladas.

Los frijoles son otro plato popular. Se llaman habichuelas en Puerto Rico. Se comen en diversos platos típicos. Los frijoles negros son muy populares en el Caribe y en Venezuela. Cuando se preparan con arroz, en Cuba se llaman moros y cristianos. Los frijoles pintos o colorados se preparan refritos en México y en potajes con jamón o carne y papas en otros países.

Además del café, que se bebe en todas partes, en la Argentina y el Paraguay también se bebe mate, que se hace de la yerba mate. Se bebe de una calabaza (gourd) por medio de un tubo llamado bombilla.

DÍAS DE FIESTA

La religión católica ha tenido un papel muy importante en la historia y en la vida diaria de los países hispanamericanos. Las Navidades se celebran de una forma u otra en todas partes. En México empiezan con las «posadas», que consisten en visitas a los vecinos durante los nueve días anteriores a la Nochebuena. En la fiesta que sigue a las posadas, la gente baila alrededor de una piñata (una figura de barro vivamente decorado, que contiene dulces y regalos). Después rompen la piñata y cogen los dulces. Otras fiestas religiosas católicas como la Semana Santa y el Día de Todos los Santos (el primero de noviembre) se celebran en casi todos los países.

Cada país tiene su fiesta nacional que conmemora la fecha en que comenzó la lucha por su independencia de España. Por ejemplo, en México el 16 de septiembre es la fecha de la fiesta nacional que conmemora el principio de la rebelión contra España y el 5 de mayo conmemora la lucha contra Francia y Maximiliano.

Dos días de fiesta que se celebran en toda la América Hispana son el Día de la Raza que corresponde a Columbus Day (el 12 de octubre) y el Día Panamericano, que se celebra el 14 de abril.

EXERCISE A. Complete las frases siguientes.

1. Un alimento mexicano es ______________ .
2. Los sombreros de jipijapa se fabrican en ______________ .
3. La calabaza y la bombilla se usan para beber ______________ .
4. Las mujeres mexicanas llevan en los hombros un ______________ .
5. Las ______________ y las ______________ son dos platos que se hacen de maíz.
6. El plato cubano que se prepara con arroz y frijoles se concoce como ______________ .
7. En Venezuela el «cowboy» se llama ______________ .
8. Las ______________ son sandalias populares en México.
9. Los mexicanos celebran el 5 de mayo para conmemorar su independencia de ______________ .
10. Para protegerse de la lluvia, el gaucho lleva un ______________ .

EXERCISE B. Combine las expresiones en las dos columnas.

	A	B
______	1. taco	*a.* cantante
______	2. 16 de septiembre	*b.* manta
______	3. mariachi	*c.* Columbus Day
______	4. sarape	*d.* alimento mexicano
______	5. china poblana	*e.* bebida
______	6. 14 de abril	*f.* Día Panamericano
______	7. Día de la Raza	*g.* pintos
______	8. yerba mate	*h.* Panama hat
______	9. sombrero de jipijapa	*i.* charro
______	10. una clase de frijol	*j.* día de la independencia mexicana

EXERCISE C. Lea cada frase e indique si es cierta o falsa. Si es falsa, cámbiela para que sea cierta.

1. Los gauchos son los vaqueros de Venezuela y Colombia.

____

2. Se celebran las posadas en todos los países de la América Latina.

____

3. La china poblana es la compañera del charro.

____

4. El sarape es una manta usada por los chilenos.

____

5. Se usan una calabaza y una bombilla para beber la yerba mate.

____

6. Una piñata es una figura de barro.

____

7. Se celebran las posadas en todos los países de Hispanoamérica.

____

8. El mariachi lleva un rebozo.

____

9. El 16 de septiembre es el Día de la Independencia de Colombia.

____

10. El tamal se cuece al vapor.

____

EXERCISE D. Identifique Ud. cada palabra, clasificándola como bebida, comida, tipo, traje o fiesta.

1. taco _______________
2. rebozo _______________
3. llanero _______________
4. tamal _______________
5. posada _______________
6. huaraches _______________
7. mariachi _______________
8. mate _______________
9. frijol _______________
10. china poblana _______________

Chapter 42

La contribución de Hispanoamérica a la literatura, el arte y la música

LA LITERATURA

Hispanoamérica tiene una literatura rica y abundante cuyos orígenes se encuentran desde los tiempos de la conquista. Los cronistas de Indias fueron historiadores españoles que vinieron al Nuevo Mundo y registraron los sucesos de la conquista. Uno de los grandes soldados y cronistas fue **Bernal Díaz del Castillo** (1492-1581). Acompañó a Hernán Cortés y describió la conquista de México en su famosa **«Historia verdadera de los sucesos de la conquista de la Nueva España».**

1. **Alonso de Ercilla** (1533-1594) escribió **«La araucana»,** un poema épico acerca de las luchas entre los conquistadores españoles y los indios araucanos de Chile. Fue la primera obra literaria importante escrita en el Nuevo Mundo.
2. **Sor Juana Inés de la Cruz** (1651-1695), de México, escribió la mejor poesía de la época colonial. Los temas de la obra de esta monja son el pesimismo, la angustia y la vanidad de la vida.
3. **Andrés Bello** (1781-1865) de Venezuela, fue poeta, crítico y erudito. Su **«Gramática castellana»** fue escrita hace más de cien años y aún se considera una de las mejores y más completas.
4. **Domingo Faustino Sarmiento** (1811-1888), de la Argentina, fue profesor y también presidente de su país. Escribió **«Facundo»,** biografía de un jefe gaucho.
5. **José Hernández** (1834-1886) escribió **«Martín Fierro»,** un poema épico que describe la vida del gaucho. Es el mejor ejemplo de la literatura gauchesca.
6. **Jorge Isaacs** (1837-1895), de Colombia, escribió la novela romántica **«María».**
7. **José Martí** (1853-1895) fue un poeta y patriota cubano. Sus **«Versos Sencillos»** son muy famosos.
8. **Rubén Darío** (1867-1916), de Nicaragua, fue uno de los mejores poetas de la América Hispana. Fundó un nuevo movimiento de poesía llamado **«el Modernismo».** Sus obras principales son **«Prosas profanas»** y **«Cantos de vida y esperanza».**
9. **Ricardo Palma** (1833-1919), del Perú, fue el autor de **«Tradiciones peruanas»,** cuentos de la época colonial.
10. **José Enrique Rodó** (1872-1917), del Uruguay, fue el ensayista más famoso de Hispanoamérica. Su obra maestra es **«Ariel»,** un libro de ensayos.
11. **Gabriela Mistral** (1889-1957), poetisa de Chile, ganó el Premio Nobel de Literatura en 1945.
12. **Ricardo Güiraldes** (1886-1927), de la Argentina, escribió **«Don Segundo Sombra»,** una novela gauchesca.
13. **Rómulo Gallegos** (1873-1952), de Venezuela, escribió **«Doña Bárbara»,** una novela que se desarrolla en los llanos de Venezuela.
14. **Mariano Azuela** (1873-1952), de México, escribió una novela acerca de la revolución mexicana, **«Los de abajo».**
15. **Ciro Alegría** (1909-1967), del Perú, escribió de los indios de su país en su novela **«El mundo es ancho y ajeno».**
16. **Jorge Luis Borges** (1899-1986), de la Argentina, fue uno de los poetas más importantes de Hispanoamérica.
17. **Pablo Neruda** (1904-1973), de Chile, ganó el Premio Nobel de Literatura en 1971.
18. **Octavio Paz** (1914-1998), poeta de México, ganó el Premio Nobel de Literatura en 1990.
19. **Gabriel García Márquez** (1928-), de Colombia, escribió la novela **«Cien años de soledad»,** que cuenta la historia de un pueblo colombiano ficticio. García Márquez ganó el Premio Nobel de Literatura en 1982.
20. **Julio Cortázar** (1914-1984), de la Argentina, revela una intensa preocupación por la relación entre la realidad y la fantasía y por la condición absurda del hombre moderno. Su obra más famosa es **«Rayuela».**
21. **Juan Rulfo** (1918-1986), de México, presenta en su obra literaria una voz y una visión muy profundas de su país. Es muy conocido por su novela **«Pedro Páramo».**
22. **José Donoso** (1924-1996), de Chile, es un autor que ha contribuido a la renovación de la novela hispanoamericana. Sus novelas **«Este domingo»** y **«El lugar sin límites»** son muy conocidas.
23. **Carlos Fuentes** (1929-), de México tiene mucha fama internacional. Una de sus obras más conocidas es **«Cambio de piel».**

24. El cubano **Guillermo Cabrera Infante** (1929-),que vive en el exilio en Inglaterra, es conocido como un gran innovador de la novela. Su obra «Tres tristes tigres» ha merecido varios premios literarios internacionales.
25. **Manuel Puig** (1932-1990), de la Argentina, tiene mucha fama internacional. Entre sus novelas más importantes están «Boquitas pintadas» y «El beso de la mujer araña».
26. **Mario Vargas Llosa** (1936-), del Perú, es un novelista que ha logrado mucha fama internacional. Muestra preocupación social y humana en todas sus obras. Entre sus novelas más famosas están «La ciudad y los perros» y «La casa verde».

EL ARTE

En el siglo XX se produjeron pintores hispanoamericanos de fama internacional. Representan en su obra sus raíces indígenas y lo histórico, político y social de su país. Los más importantes son los pintores y muralistas mexicanos. Ellos rechazaron la dominación cultural europea y cultivaron sus rasgos característicos y utilizaron la pintura como instrumento de protesta social.

1. **Diego Rivera** (1886-1957), es el más conocido de los pintores mexicanos. En sus murales que adornan muchos edificios públicos por toda la república mexicana tratan temas sociales, políticos e históricos.
2. **José Clemente Orozco** (1883-1949), es otro muralista mexicano que defendió la causa de la revolución mexicana. Durante los años que vivió en los Estados Unidos pintó una serie de frescos importantes en Dartmouth College.
3. **David Alfaro Siqueiros** (1896-1974), fue uno de los defensores más prominentes del arte como expresión de ideología política en la segunda mitad del siglo XX.
4. **Rufino Tamayo** (1899-1992), es uno de los pintores contemporáneos más famosos. Por medio del uso de colores vivos y formas semi-abstractas ha captado las alegrías y tragedias de su país.
5. **Miguel Covarrubias** (1904-1957), de México, fue famoso por sus caricaturas de personas famosas.
6. **Cesáreo Bernaldo de Quirós** (1879-1969), de la Argentina, captó lo pintoresco de la vida gauchesca en sus obras.
7. **José Sabogal** (1888-1956), del Perú, representó la cultura indígena en sus cuadros.
8. **Wifredo Lam** (1902-1982), de Cuba, fue influido por el surrealismo. Uno de sus cuadros más famosos «La jungla» está en la entrada del Museo de Arte Moderno de la ciudad de Nueva York.
9. **Frida Kahlo** (1907-1954), de México, fue la esposa de Diego Rivera. Su obra artística fue influida por el dolor que sufrió durante su vida. En su juventud tuvo polio y también fue víctima de un accidente de tránsito. Su obra incluye varios autorretratos.
10. **Roberto Matta** (1911-), de Chile, es un pintor contemporáneo de tendencia abstracta y surrealista.
11. **Oswaldo Guayasamín** (1919-1999), del Ecuador, es un pintor de tendencia cubista.
12. **Alejandro Obregón** (1920-1992) de Colombia, es un pintor de tendencia abstracta.
13. **Rómulo Macció** (1931-), de la Argentina, es un pintor vanguardista.
14. **Fernando Botero** (1932-), de Colombia, es un pintor de tendencia expresionista figurativa.
15. **Gerardo Chávez** (1937-), del Perú, es un pintor de tendencia surrealista.

LA MÚSICA

Mucha de la música hispanoamericana tiene sus raíces en temas folklóricos y sociales. Hay mucha variedad en la música tradicional y popular de los diversos países y de las distintas regiones dentro de un país. La música alegre, con influencia de ritmos africanos se halla en la región del Caribe, que incluye a Puerto Rico, Cuba, la República Dominicana y las costas de Honduras, Panamá, Venezuela y Colombia. El Perú también muestra influencias africanas en su música. Por otra parte, las canciones indígenas de los Andes son casi siempre lentas y tristes. En medio de estos dos extremos se halla una gran variedad de ritmos que incluye el **corrido mexicano,** el **candombre uruguayo,** el **joropo venezolano** (música de los llaneros), los **valses peruanos, ecuatorianos** y **argentinos, las canciones guaraníes del Paraguay** y **el tango argentino.**

INSTRUMENTOS MUSICALES

La **guitarra** española es muy popular en Hispanoamérica. Además hay otros instrumentos musicales de ascendencia indígena o africana. Estos incluyen el cuatro (una especie de guitarra venezolana con sólo **cuatro** cuerdas), la **marimba** (semejante al xilofono), el **bongó** (un tambor de origen africano), el **güiro** (hecho de un fruto seco parecido a la calabaza y que se toca con un palito), la quena (una flauta de los incas), las maracas (calabazas secas con piedritas o granos de maíz adentro) y las claves (dos palitos de madera dura que se usan para marcar el ritmo). También se usa una versión del arpa europea del siglo XVI.

EL BAILE

Los bailes tradicionales hispanoamericanos son tan ricos y variados como su música. Muchos de los ritmos como el **corrido,** el **tango** y el **joropo** son también bailes. Otros bailes tradicionales incluyen el **bambuco** colombiano, la **cueca** chilena, la **milonga** argentina y uruguaya, la **plena** puertorriqueña y el **jarabe tapatío** mexicano.

De la música bailable popular, hay ritmos como la **conga,** la **rumba,** el **mambo** y el **chachachá** cubanos, la **guaracha** puertorriqueña y cubana, el **merengue** dominicano y la **cumbia** colombiana. Se conocen estos bailes por todo el mundo.

COMPOSITORES

Dos compositores hispanoamericanos se destacan internacionalmente en la música clásica. **Carlos Chávez** (1899-1978), de México, fundó las orquestas Sinfónica de México y la Sinfónica Nacional. Entre sus obras más conocidas están el ballet **«El fuego nuevo»** y la **«Sinfonía india». Alberto Ginastera** (1916-1983), de la Argentina, fue compositor moderno de óperas, ballets, sinfonías y conciertos. Compuso la ópera **«Bomarzo».**

En el campo de la música popular se distinguen varios compisitores. **Manuel Ponce** (1882-1948), de México, debe su fama a canciones popularísimas como **«Estrellita».** El compositor y director de orquesta **Gonzalo Roig** (1890-1972) compuso muchas zarzuelas y canciones muy populares como **«Quiéreme mucho».** Otro cubano, **Ernesto Lecuona** (1896-1963) compuso canciones muy famosas como **«Siboney»** y **«Malagueña». Agustín Lara** (1897-1970), de México, debe su fama a canciones muy conocidas como **«María Bonita»** y **«Granada».**

ARTISTAS

Muchos cantantes y músicos han llegado a tener mucha fama en el extranjero. Entre ellos están el tenor de ópera chileno **Ramón Vinay,** el barítono puertorriqueño **Justino Díaz** y la gran cantante peruana **Yma Sumac. Claudio Arrau** es un famoso pianista chileno que interpreta la música clásica.

El venezolano **José Luis Rodríguez (El Puma),** los mexicanos **José José, Emmanuel, Marco Antonio Muñiz** y **Rocío Banquels,** el argentino **José Luis Perales,** y las puertorriqueñas **Ednita Nazario, Nidia Cara** e **Iris Chacón** son conocidos internacionalmente por su interpretación de canciones populares.

Tres actores mexicanos tienen fama mundial por su actuación en películas norteamericanas y dentro de su propio país: **Pedro Armendáriz, Selma Hayek** y el cómico **Cantinflas,** seudónimo de Mario Moreno.

EXERCISE A. **Subraye Ud. la palabra o expresión que correctamente complete cada frase.**

1. (José Enrique Rodó, Ricardo Güiraldes, Alonso de Ercilla) escribió una novela de la vida de los gauchos.

____

2. Una cantante del Perú que tuvo fama mundial fue (Nidia Cara, Yma Sumac, Iris Chacón).

____

3. «Los de abajo» fue escrito por (Rómulo Gallegos, David Alfaro Siquieros, Mariano Azuela).

____

4. El padre del modernismo en la poesía es (Rubén Darío, Gabriela Mistral, Agustín Lara).

____

5. Andrés Bello y Domingo Sarmiento eran dos (pintores, educadores, compositores).

____

6. Una famosa poetisa mexicana de la época colonial fue (Yma Sumac, Gabriela Mistral, Sor Juana Inés de la Cruz).

____

7. Un célebre pintor de origen cubano fue (José Clemente Orozco, David Alfaro Siqueiros, Wifredo Lam).

____

8. Un baile típico de México es (el jarabe tapatío, la rumba, la quena).

____

9. Un pianista famoso de Chile fue (Ernesto Lecuona, Cantinflas, Claudio Arrau).

____

10. «El mundo es ancho y ajeno» describe la vida y los problemas de los (indios, gauchos, actores).

____

EXERCISE B. **Combine cada persona de la columna A con las palabras que mejor se relacione en la columna B.**

	A	B
________	*1.* José Martí	*a.* poeta argentino
________	*2.* Justino Díaz	*b.* «Doña Bárbara»
________	*3.* Diego Rivera	*c.* poeta cubano
________	*4.* Cantinflas	*d.* ensayista
________	*5.* José Enrique Rodó	*e.* cantante
________	*6.* Jorge Luis Borges	*f.* compositor mexicano
________	*7.* Cesáreo Bernaldo de Quirós	*g.* «María»
________	*8.* Carlos Chávez	*h.* pintor argentino
________	*9.* Jorge Isaacs	*i.* pintor mexicano
________	*10.* Rómulo Gallegos	*j.* cómico mexicano

EXERCISE C. **Lea cada frase e indique si es cierta o falsa. Si es falsa, cámbiela para que sea cierta.**

1. Las maracas son dos palitos de madera dura.

____

2. Agustín Lara fue el compositor que escribió «Siboney».

____

3. «Tres tristes tigres» es una novela de Mario Vargas Llosa.

____

4. La novela «Cambio de piel» fue escrita por Carlos Fuentes.

____

5. Wifredo Lam fue un autor cubano.

____

6. La novela «El beso de la mujer araña» fue escrita por Manuel Puig.

____

7. José Donoso recibió el Premio Nobel de Literatura.

____

8. José José y Emmanuel son cantantes populares de Hispanoamérica.

____

9. La especialidad de Miguel Covarrubias era el mural.

____

10. Gabriela Mistral se destacó como poetisa.

____

EXERCISE D. Complete las frases siguientes.

1. En Chile el baile típico es la ______________

2. «Don Segundo Sombra», «Facundo» y «Martín Fierro» tratan de la vida de los ______________ .

3. La primera obra literaria de importancia escrita en el Nuevo Mundo fue ______________ .

4. ______________ es el autor de una famosa gramática española.

5. Uno de los mejores ejemplos de la literatura gauchesca es ______________ .

6. Para marcar el ritmo de la música se usan las ______________ .

7. ______________ fue un poeta chileno.

8. Un pintor argentino fue ______________ .

9. El tango tuvo su origen en ______________ .

10. El instrumento más popular de los países hispánicos es la ______________ .

11. ______________ fue un famoso autor peruano que escribió cuentos de la época colonial.

12. Dos bailes típicos de Cuba son ______________ y ______________ .

13. ______________ es el autor de «Cien años de soledad».

14. José Clemente Orozco fue un célebre ______________ mexicano.

15. La flauta de los indios del Perú se llama ______________ .

Part six

Comprehensive Testing:
Speaking, Listening, Reading, Writing

1. Speaking: Oral Communication Tasks [20 points]

Your teacher will administer two communication tasks. Each task prescribes a simulated conversation in which you play yourself and the teacher assumes the role indicated in the task.

Each task requires five utterances on your part. An utterance is any spoken statement that is comprehensible and appropriate and leads to accomplishing the stated task. Assume that in each situation you are speaking with a person who speaks Spanish.

2. Listening Comprehension

a. MULTIPLE CHOICE (ENGLISH) [18 points]

This part consists of nine questions. For each question, you will hear some background information in English. Then you will hear a passage in Spanish twice, followed by a question in English. Listen carefully. After you have heard the question, read the question and the four suggested answers in your book. Choose the best-suggested answer.

1. What do the teachers want to do?

1. Work with the students after school.
2. Begin a pen pal exchange for their students.
3. Arrange a trip to Costa Rica.
4. Set up a homestay for Costa Rican students.

2. What does your mother say about the dress in the window?

1. She would like to buy it.
2. It is her size.
3. She would like to wear it to a party.
4. It is too expensive.

3. What does the waiter want you to do?

1. Leave the restaurant.
2. Pay the bill.
3. Move to another table.
4. Order now.

4. Where does your friend live?

1. On the Calle Mayor.
2. Next to a restaurant.
3. On the left side of the street.
4. Past the drug store and the restaurant.

5. What does Alicia want you to do?

1. Help her clean the house.
2. Come to the party for her mother.
3. Buy a gift for her mother.
4. Go shopping with her.

6. When does your friend prefer to eat lunch?

1. At noon.
2. Before 12:00.
3. After 3:00.
4. At about 2:30.

7. How should you go to your friend's house?

1. on foot
2. by train
3. by car
4. by bus

8. Why is Gloria Acevedo being congratulated?

1. Her father just became the head technician at the radio station.
2. This is her first birthday.
3. She is going to sing with Luis Miguel and Emmanuel.
4. She is the daughter of a famous musical artist.

9. What is the topic of this announcement?

1. An outdoor celebration of Hispanic culture.
2. A street fair on 44th Street.
3. An exhibit of folkloric art.
4. A meeting of the Hispanic nations.

b. MULTIPLE CHOICE (SPANISH) [12 points]

This part consists of six questions. For each question, you will hear some background information in English. Then you will hear a passage in Spanish twice, followed by a question in Spanish. Listen carefully. After you have heard the question, read the question and the four suggested answers in your book. Choose the best-suggested answer.

1. ¿Qué anuncian?
1. Noticias sobre los desastres nacionales.
2. Información para protegerse en un desastre.
3. Folletos de promoción turística.
4. Cursos sobre los primeros auxilios.

2. ¿Qué pasa hoy en el Parque del Retiro?
1. Habrá una competencia.
2. Representarán dos obras infantiles con títeres.
3. Pasarán varios dibujos animados.
4. El alcalde va a leer unos cuentos infantiles.

3. ¿Qué le asombró a esta persona?
1. La explicación sencilla que le dieron.
2. La introducción de un nuevo medio de transporte.
3. La facilidad de manejo de este vehículo.
4. La popularidad de esta invención.

4. ¿Quiénes gozarán de esta actividad?
1. Las personas a quienes les gustan los deportes acuáticos.
2. Las personas que aprenden a pintar.
3. Las personas que trabajan cerca de la playa.
4. Las personas que no saben nadar

5. ¿De qué se trata este mensaje?
1. De una invitación a una comida.
2. De un cambio de horario.
3. De la cancelación de una cita.
4. De una inconveniencia para todo el mundo.

6. ¿Quiénes deben prestar atención a este anuncio?
1. Las personas que pasan mucho tiempo al aire libre.
2. Las personas que estudian la ciencia.
3. Las personas que se dedican a la estética.
4. Las personas que trabajan con computadoras.

3. READING COMPREHENSION

a. LONG CONNECTED PASSAGE [10 points]

This part consists of a passage followed by five questions or incomplete statements in Spanish. For each, choose the expression that best answers the question or completes the statement according to the meaning of the passage.

¿Conoce Ud. una temporada del año que sea más anhelada que la de las vacaciones? Todo el mundo suele esperar las vacaciones con entusiasmo y con grandes deseos de estar libre de la rutina diaria. Pero, al fijarnos bien en esta temporada y los preparativos que las personas hacen para disfrutarla, salimos con una perspectiva muy diferente.

El período de las vacaciones llega a ser agitado, tensionante y cansado porque esta semana significa diferentes cosas para las personas. Mucha gente deja acumularse diversas tareas para llevarlas a cabo durante esta semana disponible. Otras personas salen de la casa y viajan a otro sitio. Pero para estar completamente libre durante siete días, para muchas personas el ritmo de la oficina llega a ser frenético porque hay que dedicar diez o doce horas al día para poner en orden todos los asuntos pendientes en el trabajo. También, hay que hacer todos los preparativos para esa semana que pasarán fuera de la casa.

El acto de viajar, sea en carro, en autobús, en tren o en avión, requiere mucha preparación: lavar ropa, comprar los boletos, encontrar un mapa o plano de la ciudad a donde se va, hacer la maleta, cerrar la casa, suspender el periódico y el correo, regar las plantas, etc. Y como es la temporada de las vacaciones, las carreteras, las terminales y los aeropuertos están llenos de personas que tienen la misma intención que Ud. - ir a un lugar desconocido o volver a visitar un lugar favorito como alguna playa. El viaje ocupa todo el primer día de esa semana de libertad. Y llegan cansados por lo general.

El cambio de clima, los sonidos y ruidos distintos y desconocidos del nuevo lugar y la sensación de estar de vacaciones, hacen que las personas se despierten antes de la hora a que se acostumbran despertarse. Y ahora hay que crear una nueva rutina y acostumbrarse a ella... vestirse en seguida para salir a un restaurante para desayunarse. Además, hay muchas decisiones que tomar... ¿cómo pasar el día? ¿dónde comer? ¿ir a la playa?, etc. Por fin se deciden a ir a la playa y disfrutar del sol. Regresan al cuarto del hotel para ponerse el traje de baño, buscar una toalla y todo lo que se necesita para protegerse del sol. Llegan a la playa y se acuestan en una toalla en la arena. El cansancio que se ha acumulado de los preparativos y del viaje mismo les agobia y se quedan dormidos por largas horas en la playa. Cuando se despiertan, empiezan a sentir que tienen una quemadura de grandes proporciones. Están obligados a permanecer el resto del tiempo en la sombra y sin facilidad de movimiento por la quemadura. Entran los deseos de volver a casa.

A pesar de todo, ya de regreso a la vida normal, las personas vuelven a soñar con las próximas vacaciones.

1. ¿Por qué da la gente tanta importancia a las vacaciones?

1. Es un período de verdadero ocio.
2. Es una temporada larga y triste.
3. Es tiempo oportuno para buscar otro empleo.
4. Es una manera de liberarse de los jefes.

2. Los días anteriores al comienzo de las vacaciones se caracterizan por

1. el estrés
2. la pereza
3. la alegría
4. el miedo

3. Por lo general, las personas que salen fuera para pasar las vacaciones llegan

1. rápidamente por la eficacia de los tranportes públicos
2. a paso de tortuga porque muchas personas viajan en esta época
3. listos para divertirse el mismo día que llegan
4. desanimados por los problemas de tránsito

4. ¿Qué tienen que hacer los viajeros al llegar a su destino?

1. despertarse más tarde
2. llamar a unos amigos que viven allí
3. acostumbrarse a una nueva rutina
4. buscar a un médico

5. A pesar de todos los contratiempos que ha aguantado durante el viaje, ¿en qué piensa el viajero al regresar a casa?

1. revelar las fotos que sacó
2. entregar los regalos que compró para los parientes
3. permanecer en casa durante las próximas vacaciones
4. planear un viaje para el otro año

b. SHORT READINGS (MULTIPLE CHOICE, ENGLISH) [10 points]

This part consists of five short readings. For each selection, there is a question or incomplete statement in English. For each, choose the expression that best answers the question or completes the statement. Base your choice on the content of the reading selection.

LUNAUTO

En caso de rotura de un cristal
llame al teléfono

900 73 07 07
Llamada gratuita
524 60 18

24
horas

Primer instalador nacional de parabrisas

1. Who should pay attention to this ad?

1. Homeowners.
2. Mechanics.
3. Car owners.
4. Waiters.

El Paraíso del Jamón
San Fernando, 10 (Esquina a Gran Vía) • Tel.: 523 81 93
Todos los días 950
Menús a elegir PTAS.
4 primeros 4 segundos
2 Menús Especiales
Platos combinados desde 550 Ptas.
Especialidad en salchichas ibéricas
(Gran Variedad de Quesos • Patés)
Raciones
Pulpo gallega
Pulpo vinagreta
Callos
Almejas marinera
Ensaladilla rusa
Mejillones con tomate
Pepinillo relleno
Gambas al ajillo

2. What is the specialty of this restaurant?

1. Meals for tourists.
2. Seafood.
3. Regional dishes of Spain.
4. Fast service.

Este fin de año compre 2 y estrene 3

No pierda la oportunidad que nuestra venta de fábrica le ofrece: este fin de año lo invitamos a vestir las mejores y exclusivas marcas de ropa para dama y caballero a precios de fábrica. Además, con la compra de 2 prendas, se lleva una más completamente gratis.*

Visítenos en París No. 119, casi esquina con Centenario, de lunes a domingo de 9 a 18 horas

- trajes
- sacos
- blazers
- pantalones
- camisas
- corbatas
- chamarras
- traje sastre
- faldas
- blusas
- vestidos

*Gratis la prenda de menor precio.

Promoción valida hasta el 30 de diciembre o agotar existencia

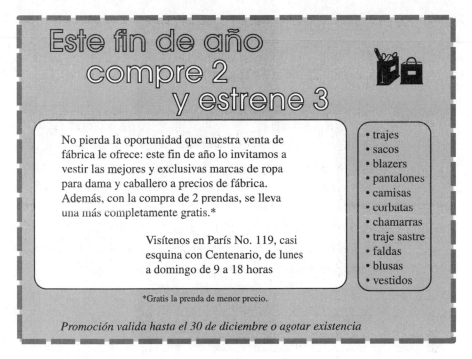

3. What is the attraction of this sale?

1. This is the store's policy for the new year.
2. The sale ends only when no stock is left.
3. It offers one article of clothing free.
4. The stock is replenished daily.

BARAJAS INFORMA

El aeropuerto de Madrid/Barajas está creciendo muy deprisa. Hace ya tiempo que se quedó pequeño. En un aeropuerto en transformación permanente, la información es vital. Vamos a ampliar los medios, para que su tránsito por el aeropuerto sea lo más cómodo posible.

Una sonrisa para ayudarle sale a su encuentro:
el equipo de Chaquetas Verdes:

Hemos reforzado el equipo de atención al público, para poder acudir allí donde surjan dada o dificultades. Usted podrá reconocerlos por sus chaquetas verdes.

4. Why has this notice been published?

1. The Barajas Madrid airport is being moved to a new location.
2. To alert the public to possible air traffic delays.
3. To publicize new services to help the traveler.
4. The uniform of the travelers' aid staff has changed.

MOVIMIENTO EN RUTA

Estamos muy cerca. Para llevarte muy lejos.

Siempre que salga a la carretera aprovéchese de la última tecnología que le ofrece Movimiento para conocer el estado de las carreteras españolas: Servicio "**Movimiento en Ruta** ". Su funcionamiento es muy sencillo. Envíe un mensaje de texto con el código de la carretera o provincia de la que desee la información al número **101**. Por ejemplo, si quiere conocer el estado de las carreteras de la provincia de Salamanca, escriba "SA" en la opción de mensajes de su Movimiento y envíelo al **101**, en pocos segundos recibirá un mensaje de texto con la información requerida en su móvil. Confíe en Movimiento y olvídese de los imprevistos.

5. This service provides information concerning

1. weather patterns
2. road conditions
3. tourist accommodations
4. air traffic

c. SLOT COMPLETION [10 points]

In the following passage there are five blank spaces numbered 1 to 5. Each blank represents a missing word or expression. For each blank space, four possible completions are provided. Only one of them makes sense in the context of the passage.

First, read the passage in its entirety to determine its general meaning. Then read it a second time. For each blank space, choose the completion that makes the best sense.

Los mayores de edad recordarán, sin duda, que el tomate era uno de los sabores ____________ (*1.*) del verano: había tomates en verano y no el resto del año. Hoy, hablar de la ____________ (*2.*) del tomate suena rarísimo, porque hay tomates todo el año. Pero es cierto que se trata de un fruto esencialmente veraniego cuando realmente apetece en ensaladas o como ____________ (*3.*) básico de un gazpacho.

El tomate procede de América, de donde se trajo ya en el siglo XVI. Hoy es fundamental en la cocina que llamamos mediterránea, compañero inseparable de las pastas. Normalmente, a un tomate tal como viene de la verdulería le sobran tres cosas: la piel, las semillas y el agua de vegetación. Al menos, pelarlos siempre nos ____________ (*4.*) otra dimensión.

Tengan en cuenta que el tomate se combina muy bien con casi todo y deben practicar usarla en nuevas recetas, especialmente durante el verano cuando los hay en gran

__________________ y a menor costo. Y siempre que puedan, háganse usted su propia salsa de
5.
tomate porque así sabrán a qué sabe de verdad.

1. 1. clásicos
2. desconocidos
3. inferiores
4. insípidos

2. 1. cultivación
2. temporada
3. venta
4. necesidad

3. 1. propósito
2. funcionario
3. toque
4. ingrediente

4. 1. ofrece
2. quita
3. distingue
4. repite

5. 1. escasez
2. producción
3. abundancia
4. conformidad

4. WRITING

a. INFORMAL NOTE [10 points]

Choose one of the topics below and write a well-organized note in Spanish as directed. Your note must consist of at least six clauses. A clause must contain a verb, a stated or implied subject, and additional words necessary to convey meaning. The six clauses may be contained in fewer than six sentences if some of the sentences have more than one clause.

EXAMPLES: One clause: Ayer fui de compras.
Two clauses: Ayer fui de compras y di con Emilio en la calle.
Three clauses: Ayer fui de compras y di con Emilio en la calle quien me invitó al cine.

Note that the salutation and closing will not count as part of the six clauses.

1. Your parents left you a note on the kitchen counter telling you the chores they wanted you to complete. Write a note in which you tell them why you didn't do the chores.

Use the following:
Salutation: Padres:
Closing: [your name]

2. You and a friend are not talking because of a misunderstanding or quarrel. Write a note to your friend in which you apologize for your actions.

Use the following:
Salutation: Estimado(a) [your friend's name]:
Closing: [your name]

b. NARRATIVE OR LETTER [10 points]

Write a well-organized composition as directed below. Choose either the narrative or the formal letter. Follow the specific instructions for the topic that you select. Each composition must consist of at least ten clauses. A clause must contain a verb, a stated or implied subject, and additional words necessary to convey meaning. The ten clauses may be contained in fewer than ten sentences if some of the sentences have more than one clause.

A. Narrative

Write a story in Spanish about the situation shown in the picture. It must be a story about the situation in the picture, not a description of the picture.

KEY WORDS:

la banda *band*	el espectador *spectator*
la bandera *flag*	el globo *balloon*
la carroza *float*	marchar *to march*
el desfile *parade*	

B. Formal Letter

Write a letter in Spanish. Follow the specific instructions. Note that the dateline, salutation, and closing will not count as part of the required ten clauses.

Your school is offering a homestay in a Spanish-speaking country. As part of the application process, you have to write a letter in which you explain why you are interested in this program. Write a letter in which you explain your reasons for applying for this homestay. Suggested subtopics are: your qualifications, reasons for wanting the homestay, what you will learn, what you will do upon returning, effect on your career goals. You may use ideas suggested by any or all of these subtopics, or may use your own ideas. Either way, you must accomplish the purpose of the letter, which is to explain your interest in this homestay experience.

Use the following:

Dateline: el _____ de _______________ de _______

Salutation: Estimado (a) Señor(a), [Muy Señores Míos]

Closing: Atentamente.

[your name]

Appendix

[1] Regular Verbs

INFINITIVE	entr**ar**	corr**er**	viv**ir**
PRESENT	entr**o**	corr**o**	viv**o**
	entr**as**	corr**es**	viv**es**
	entr**a**	corr**e**	viv**e**
	entr**amos**	corr**emos**	viv**imos**
	entr**áis**	corr**éis**	viv**ís**
	entr**an**	corr**en**	viv**en**
PRETERIT	entr**é**	corr**í**	viv**í**
	entr**aste**	corr**iste**	viv**iste**
	entr**ó**	corr**ió**	viv**ió**
	entr**amos**	corr**imos**	viv**imos**
	entr**asteis**	corr**isteis**	viv**isteis**
	entr**aron**	corr**ieron**	viv**ieron**
IMPERFECT	entr**aba**	corr**ía**	viv**ía**
	entr**abas**	corr**ías**	viv**ías**
	entr**aba**	corr**ía**	viv**ía**
	entr**ábamos**	corr**íamos**	viv**íamos**
	entr**ábais**	corr**íais**	viv**íais**
	entr**aban**	corr**ían**	viv**ían**
FUTURE	entr**aré**	corr**eré**	viv**iré**
	entr**arás**	corr**erás**	viv**irás**
	entr**ará**	corr**erá**	viv**irá**
	entr**aremos**	corr**eremos**	viv**iremos**
	entr**aréis**	corr**eréis**	viv**iréis**
	entr**arán**	corr**erán**	viv**irán**
CONDITIONAL	entr**aría**	corr**ería**	viv**iría**
	entr**arías**	corr**erías**	viv**irías**
	entr**aría**	corr**ería**	viv**iría**
	entr**aríamos**	corr**eríamos**	viv**iríamos**
	entr**aríais**	corr**eríais**	viv**iríais**
	entr**arían**	corr**erían**	viv**irían**

COMMANDS (IMPERATIVE)	entra no entres } (tú)	corre no corras } (tú)	vive no vivas } (tú)
	entrad no entréis } (vosotros)	corred no corráis } (vosotros)	vivid no viváis } (vosotros)
	entre (Ud.)	corra (Ud.)	viva (Ud.)
	entremos (nosotros)	corramos (nosotros)	vivamos (nosotros)
	entren (Uds.)	corran (Uds.)	vivan (Uds.)
PRESENT SUBJUNCTIVE	entre	corra	viva
	entres	corras	vivas
	entre	corra	viva
	entremos	corramos	vivamos
	entréis	corráis	viváis
	entren	corran	vivan
PRESENT PERFECT	he has ha hemos habéis han } entrado/corrido/vivido		
PLUPERFECT	había habías había habíamos habíais habían } entrado/corrido/vivido		

[2] STEM-CHANGING VERBS

a. -ar Verbs

INFINITIVE	pensar (e to ie)	mostrar (o to ue)	jugar (u to ue)
PRESENT	pienso	muestro	juego
	piensas	muestras	juegas
	piensa	muestra	juega
	pensamos	mostramos	jugamos
	pensáis	mostráis	jugáis
	piensan	muestran	juegan

SUBJUNCTIVE	p**ie**nse p**ie**nses p**ie**nse pensemos penséis p**ie**nsen	m**ue**stre m**ue**stres m**ue**stre mostremos mostréis m**ue**stren	j**ue**gue j**ue**gues j**ue**gue j**u**guemos j**u**guéis j**ue**guen

b. **-er** Verbs

INFINITIVE	perd**er** (**e** to **ie**)	volv**er** (**o** to **ue**)
PRESENT	p**ie**rdo p**ie**rdes p**ie**rde perdemos perdéis p**ie**rden	v**ue**lvo v**ue**lves v**ue**lve volvemos volvéis v**ue**lven
SUBJUNCTIVE	p**ie**rda p**ie**rdas p**ie**rda perdamos perdáis p**ie**rdan	v**ue**lva v**ue**lvas v**ue**lva volvamos volváis v**ue**lvan

c. **-ir** Verbs

INFINITIVE	ped**ir** (**e** to **i, i**)	sent**ir** (**e** to **ie, i**)	dorm**ir** (**o** to **ue, u**)
PRESENT	p**i**do p**i**des p**i**de pedimos pedís p**i**den	s**ie**nto s**ie**ntes s**ie**nte sentimos sentís s**ie**nten	d**ue**rmo d**ue**rmes d**ue**rme dormimos dormís d**ue**rmen
PRETERIT	pedí pediste p**i**dió pedimos pedisteis p**i**dieron	sentí sentiste s**i**ntió sentimos sentisteis s**i**ntieron	dormí dormiste d**u**rmió dormimos dormisteis d**u**rmieron

SUBJUNCTIVE	pida pidas pida pidamos pidáis pidan	**sie**nta **sie**ntas **sie**nta **si**ntamos **si**ntáis **sie**ntan	d**ue**rma d**ue**rmas d**ue**rma d**u**rmamos d**u**rmáis d**ue**rman
COMMANDS	pide / no pidas (tú) pida (Ud.) pidamos (nosotros) pedid / no pidáis (vosotros) pidan (Uds.)	**sie**nte / no **sie**ntas (tú) **sie**nta (Ud.) **si**ntamos (nosotros) sentid / no **si**ntáis (vosotros) **sie**ntan (Uds.)	d**ue**rme / no d**ue**rmas (tú) d**ue**rma (Ud.) d**u**rmamos (nosotros) dormid / no d**u**rmáis (vosotros) d**ue**rman (Uds.)

[3] Verbs with Spelling Changes

a. Verbs in **-cer** or **-cir**

INFINITIVE	ofre**cer** (**c** to **zc**)	condu**cir** (**c** to **zc**)	conven**cer** (**c** to **z**)
PRESENT	ofre**zco** ofreces ofrece ofrecemos ofrecéis ofrecen	condu**zco** conduces conduce conducimos conducís conducen	conven**zo** convences convence convencemos convencemos convencen
SUBJUNCTIVE	ofre**zc**a ofre**zc**as ofre**zc**a ofre**zc**amos ofre**zc**áis ofre**zc**an	condu**zc**a condu**zc**as condu**zc**a condu**zc**amos condu**zc**áis condu**zc**an	conven**z**a conven**z**as conven**z**a conven**z**amos conven**z**áis conven**z**an
COMMANDS	ofrece / no ofre**zc**as (tú) ofrezca (Ud.) ofre**zc**amos (nosotros) ofreced / no ofrezcáis (vosotros) ofre**zc**an (Uds.)	conduce / no condu**zc**as (tú) condu**zc**a (Ud.) condu**zc**amos (nosotros) conducid / no conduzcáis (vosotros) condu**zc**an (Uds.)	convence / no conven**z**as (tú) conven**z**a (Ud.) conven**z**amos (nosotros) convenced / no convenzáis (vosotros) conven**z**an (Uds.)

b. Verbs That Change **i** to **y**

INFINITIVE	leer	caer	oír	incluir
PRETERIT	leí leíste leyó leímos leísteis leyeron	caí caíste cayó caímos caísteis cayeron	oí oíste oyó oímos oísteis oyeron	incluí incluíste incluyó incluímos incluísteis incluyeron
PAST PARTICIPLE	leído	caído	oído	incluído

c. Verbs Ending in **-ger** or **-gir**

INFINITIVE	co**ger**	diri**gir**
PRESENT INDICATIVE	cojo coges coge cogemos cogéis cogen	dirijo diriges dirige dirigimos dirigís dirigen
PRESENT SUBJUNCTIVE	coja cojas coja cojamos cojáis cojan	dirija dirijas dirija dirijamos dirijáis dirijan

d. Verbs Ending in **-guir**

INFINITIVE	distin**guir**	
PRESENT INDICATIVE	distingo distingues distingue distinguimos distinguís distinguen	

PRESENT SUBJUNCTIVE	distin**ga** distin**ga**s distin**ga** distin**ga**mos distin**gá**is distin**ga**n

e. Verbs Ending in **-car, -gar,** and **-zar**

INFINITIVE	sac**ar** (**c** to **gu**)	pag**ar** (**g** to **gu**)	goz**ar** (**z** to **c**)
PRETERIT	sa**qué** sacaste sacó sacamos sacasteis sacaron	pa**gué** pagaste pagó pagamos pagasteis pagaron	go**cé** gozaste gozó gozamos gozasteis gozaron
SUBJUNCTIVE	sa**que** sa**que**s sa**que** sa**que**mos sa**qué**is sa**que**n	pa**gue** pa**gue**s pa**gue** pa**gue**mos pa**gué**is pa**gue**n	go**ce** go**ce**s go**ce** go**ce**mos go**cé**is go**ce**n

[4] VERBS WITH IRREGULAR FORMS

NOTE: **Only the tenses containing irregular forms are given.**

INFINITIVE	and**ar**
PRETERIT	and**uve**, and**uviste**, and**uvo**, and**uvimos**, and**uvisteis**, and**uvieron**
IMPERFECT SUBJUNCTIVE	and**uviera**, and**uvieras**, and**uviera**, and**uviéramos**, and**uviérais**, and**uvieran** and**uviese**, and**uvieses**, and**uviese**, and**uviésemos**, and**uviéseis**, and**uviesen**

INFINITIVE	cab**er**
PRESENT	**quepo**, cabes, cabe, cabemos, cabéis, caben

PRETERIT	**cupe, cup**iste, **cup**o, **cup**imos, **cup**isteis, **cup**ieron
CONDITIONAL	**cabr**ía, **cabr**ías, **cabr**ía, **cabr**íamos, **cabr**íais, **cabr**ían
PRESENT SUBJUNCTIVE	**quep**a, **quep**as, **quep**a, **quep**amos, **quep**áis, **quep**an

INFINITIVE	ca**er**
PRESENT	**caig**o, caes, cae, caemos, caéis, caen
PRETERIT	caí, caíste, ca**y**ó, caímos, caísteis, cayeron
PRESENT SUBJUNCTIVE	ca**i**ga, ca**i**gas, ca**i**ga, ca**i**gamos, ca**i**gáis, ca**i**gan
PAST PARTICIPLE	ca**í**do
GERUND	ca**y**endo

INFINITIVE	d**ar**
PRESENT	d**oy**, das, da, damos, dais, dan
PRETERIT	d**i**, d**iste**, d**io**, d**i**mos, d**i**steis, d**ie**ron
PRESENT SUBJUNCTIVE	d**é**, des, d**é**, demos déis, den

INFINITIVE	dec**ir**
PRESENT	d**ig**o, d**i**ces, d**i**ce, decimos, decís, d**i**cen
PRETERIT	**dije**, **dij**iste, **dijo**, **dij**imos, **dij**isteis, **dij**eron
FUTURE	**dir**é, **dir**ás, **dir**á, **dir**emos, **dir**éis, **dir**án
CONDITIONAL	**dir**ía, **dir**ías, **dir**ía, **dir**íamos, **dir**íais, **dir**ían
PRESENT SUBJUNCTIVE	**dig**a, **dig**as, **dig**a, **dig**amos, **dig**áis, **dig**an
COMMAND	**di** (tú), **dig**a (Ud.), **dig**amos (nosotros)

PAST PARTICIPLE	**dicho**
GERUND	diciendo

INFINITIVE	es**tar**
PRESENT	es**toy**, estás, está, estamos, estáis, están
PRETERIT	es**tuve**, estuviste, estuvo, estuvimos, estuvisteis, estuvieron
PRESENT SUBJUNCTIVE	est**é**, est**é**s, est**é**, estemos, estéis, est**é**n

INFINITIVE	hab**er**
PRESENT	**he, has, ha, h**emos, habéis, **h**an
PRETERIT	**hube, hub**iste, **hubo, hub**imos, **hub**isteis, **hub**ieron
FUTURE	**habr**é, **habr**ás, **habr**á, **habr**emos, **habr**éis, **habr**án
CONDITIONAL	**habr**ía, **habr**ías, **habr**ía, **habr**íamos, **habr**íais, **habr**ían
PRESENT SUBJUNCTIVE	**hay**a, **hay**as, **hay**a, **hay**amos, **hay**áis, **hay**an

INFINITIVE	hac**er**
PRESENT	**hag**o, haces, hace, hacemos, hacéis, hacen
PRETERIT	**hice, hic**iste, **hizo**, **hic**imos, **hic**isteis, **hic**ieron
FUTURE	**har**é, **har**ás, **har**á, **har**emos, **har**éis, **har**án
CONDITIONAL	**har**ía, **har**ías,**har**ía,**har**íamos, **har**íais, **har**ían
PRESENT SUBJUNCTIVE	**hag**a, **hag**as, **hag**a, **hag**amos, **hag**áis, **hag**an
COMMAND	**haz** (tú), **hag**a (Ud.), **hag**amos (nosotros), **hag**an (Uds.)
GERUND	**hecho**

INFINITIVE	**ir**
PRESENT	**voy, vas, va, vamos, vais, van**
IMPERFECT	**iba, ibas, iba, íbamos, ibais, iban**
PRETERIT	**fui, fuiste, fue, fuimos, fuisteis, fueron**
PRESENT SUBJUNCTIVE	**vay**a, **vay**as,**vay**a, **vay**amos, **vay**áis, **vay**an
COMMAND	ve (tú),**vay**a (Ud.), **vay**amos (nosotros), **vay**an (Uds.)
GERUND	yendo

INFINITIVE	o**í**r
PRESENT	**oig**o, **oy**es, **oy**e, oímos, oís, **oy**en
PRETERIT	oí, oíste, oyó, oímos, oísteis, oyeron
PRESENT SUBJUNCTIVE	**oig**a, **oig**as, **oig**a, **oig**amos, **oig**áis, **oig**an
COMMAND	oye (tú), oiga (Ud.), oigamos (nosotros), oigan (Uds.)
PAST PARTICIPLE	**oído**
GERUND	oyendo

INFINITIVE	pod**er**
PRESENT	p**ue**do, p**ue**des, p**ue**de, podemos, podéis, p**ue**den
PRETERIT	p**u**de, p**u**diste, p**u**do, p**u**dimos, p**u**disteis, p**u**dieron
FUTURE	**podr**é, **podr**ás, **podr**á, **podr**emos, **podr**éis, po**dr**án
CONDITIONAL	**podr**ía, **podr**ías, **podr**ía, **podr**íamos, **podr**íais, **podr**ían
GERUND	p**u**diendo

INFINITIVE	pon**er**
PRESENT	pon**g**o, pones, pone, ponemos, ponéis, ponen
PRETERIT	**pus**e, **pus**iste, **pus**o, **pus**imos, **pus**isteis, **pus**ieron
FUTURE	**pondr**é, **pondr**ás, **pondr**á, **pondr**emos, **pondr**áis, **pondr**án
CONDITIONAL	**pondr**ía, **pondr**ías, **pondr**ía, **pondr**íamos, **pondr**íais, **pondr**ían
PRESENT SUBJUNCTIVE	pon**g**a, pon**g**as, pon**g**a, pon**g**amos, pon**g**áis, pon**g**an
COMMAND	p**on** (tú), pon**g**a (Ud.), pon**g**amos (nosotros), pon**g**an (Uds.)
PAST PARTICIPLE	**puesto**

INFINITIVE	quer**er**
PRESENT	qu**ie**ro, qu**ie**res, qu**ie**re, queremos, queréis, qu**ie**ren
PRETERIT	**quise, quis**iste, **quiso, quis**imos, **quis**isteis, **quis**ieron
FUTURE	quer**ré**, quer**rás**, quer**rá**, quer**remos**, quer**réis**, quer**rán**
CONDITIONAL	quer**ría,** quer**rías,** quer**ría,** quer**ríamos,** quer**ríais,** quer**rían**
PRESENT SUBJUNCTIVE	qu**ie**ra, qu**ie**ras, qu**ie**ra, queramos, queráis, qu**ie**ran

INFINITIVE	sab**er**
PRESENT	s**é**, sabes, sabe, sabemos, sabéis, saben
PRETERIT	**supe, sup**iste, **supo, sup**imos, **sup**isteis, **sup**ieron
FUTURE	**sabr**é, **sabr**ás, **sabr**á, **sabr**emos **sabr**éis, **sabr**án
CONDITIONAL	**sabr**ía, **sabr**ías, **sabr**ía, **sabr**íamos, **sabr**íais, **sabr**ían
PRESENT SUBJUNCTIVE	**sep**a, **sep**as, **sep**a, **sep**amos, **sep**áis, **sep**an

INFINITIVE	sal**ir**
PRESENT	sal**g**o, sales, sale, salimos, salís, salen
FUTURE	**saldr**é, **saldr**ás, **saldr**á, **saldr**emos, **saldr**éis, **saldr**án
CONDITIONAL	**saldr**ía, **saldr**ías, **saldr**ía, **saldr**íamos, **saldr**íais, **saldr**ían
PRESENT SUBJUNCTIVE	sal**g**a, sal**g**as, sal**g**a, sal**g**amos, sal**g**áis, sal**g**an
COMMAND	**sal** (tú), sal**g**a (Ud.), sal**g**amos (nosotros), sal**g**an (Uds.)

INFINITIVE	s**er**
PRESENT	so**y**, **er**es, **es**, so**mos**, s**ois**, s**on**
IMPERFECT	**era, eras, era, éramos, erais, eran**
PRETERIT	**fui, fu**iste, **fue, fu**imos, **fu**isteis, **fu**eron
PRESENT SUBJUNCTIVE	**se**a, **se**as, **se**a, **se**amos, **se**áis, **se**an
COMMAND	sé (tú), s**e**an (Uds.)

INFINITIVE	ten**er**
PRESENT	ten**g**o, t**i**enes, t**i**ene, tenemos, tenéis, t**i**enen
PRETERIT	**tuv**e, **tuv**iste, **tuv**o, **tuv**imos, **tuv**isteis, **tuv**ieron
FUTURE	**tendr**é, **tendr**ás, **tendr**á, **tendr**emos, **tendr**éis, **tendr**án
CONDITIONAL	**tendr**ía, **tendr**ías, **tendr**ía, **tendr**íamos, **tendr**íais, **tendr**ían
PRESENT SUBJUNCTIVE	ten**g**a, ten**g**as, ten**g**a, ten**g**amos, ten**g**áis, ten**g**an
COMMAND	**ten** (tú), **teng**a (Ud.), **teng**amos (nosotros), **teng**an (Uds.)

INFINITIVE	tra**er**
PRESENT	tra**ig**o, traes, trae, traemos, traéis, traen
PRETERIT	**traje,** tra**j**iste, tra**jo,** tra**j**imos, tra**j**isteis, tra**j**eron
PRESENT SUBJUNCTIVE	tra**ig**a, tra**ig**as, tra**ig**a, tra**ig**amos, tra**ig**áis, tra**ig**an
PAST PARTICIPLE	tra**í**do
GERUND	tra**y**endo

INFINITIVE	val**er**
PRESENT	val**g**o, vales, vale, valemos, valéis, valen
FUTURE	**valdr**é, **valdr**ás, **valdr**á, **valdr**emos, **valdr**éis, **valdr**án
CONDITIONAL	**valdr**ía, **valdr**ías, **valdr**ía, **valdr**íamos, **valdr**íais, **valdr**ían
PRESENT SUBJUNCTIVE	val**g**a, val**g**as, val**g**a, val**g**amos, val**g**áis, val**g**an

INFINITIVE	ven**ir**
PRESENT	ven**g**o, v**i**enes, v**i**ene, venimos, venís, v**i**enen
PRETERIT	v**i**ne, v**i**niste, v**i**no, v**i**nimos, v**i**nisteis, v**i**nieron
FUTURE	**vendr**é, **vendr**ás, **vendr**á, **vendr**emos, **vendr**éis, **vendr**án
CONDITIONAL	**vendr**ía, **vendr**ías, **vendr**ía, **vendr**íamos, **vendr**íais, **vendr**ían
PRESENT SUBJUNCTIVE	ven**g**a, ven**g**as, ven**g**a, ven**g**amos, ven**g**áis, ven**g**an
COMMAND	**ven** (tú), ven**g**a (Ud.), ven**g**amos (nosotros), ven**g**an (Uds.)
GERUND	v**i**niendo

INFINITIVE	**ver**
PRESENT	veo, ves, ve, vemos, veis, ven
IMPERFECT	veía, veías, veía, veíamos, veíais, veían
PRESENT SUBJUNCTIVE	vea, veas, vea, veamos, veáis, vean
PAST PARTICIPLE	**visto**

[5] Punctuation

Although Spanish punctuation is similar to English, it has the following major differences:

(a) In Spanish, questions have an inverted question mark (¿) at the beginning and a normal one at the end.

¿Quién es? — *Who is it?*

(b) In Spanish, exclamatory sentences have an inverted exclamation point (¡) at the beginning and a normal one at the end.

¡Qué día! — *What a day!*

(c) The comma is not used before **y, e, o, u,** or **ni** in a series.

El lunes, el martes y el miércoles hay clases. — There are classes on Monday, Tuesday, and Wednesday.

(d) Spanish uses a comma with decimals where English uses a period.

3,5 (tres coma cinco) — *3.5 (three point five)*

(e) Spanish final quotation marks precede the comma or period.

Cervantes escribió «Don Quijote». — Cervantes wrote "Don Quijote."

[6] Syllabication

Spanish words are generally divided at the end of a line according to units of sound.

(a) A syllable normally begins with a consonant. The division is made before the consonant.

te-**ner**   di-**ne**-**ro**   a-**me**-**ri**-**ca**-**no**   re-**fe**-**rir**

(b) Letter combinations **ch, ll,** and **rr** are never divided.

pe-**rro**   ha-**lla**-do   di-**cho**

(c) If two or more consonants are combined, the division is made before the last consonant, except in the combinations **bl, br, cl, cr, pl, pr,** and **tr**.

tran**s-p**o**r-t**e   de**s-c**u-bie**r**-to   co**n-t**i-nuar   a**l-b**er-**c**a

BUT

ha-**bl**ar   a-**br**ir   des-**cr**i-bir   a-**pr**en-**d**er   dis-**tr**i-buir

(d) Compound words, including words with prefixes and suffixes, may be divided by components or by syllables.

sur-a-me-ri-ca-no   OR   s**u-r**a-me-ri-ca-no

mal-es-tar   OR   **ma-les**-tar

[7] STRESS

In Spanish, stress follows three general rules.

(a) If the words ends in a vowel, **n,** or **s,** the next-to-the-last syllable is stressed.

esp**a**da   des**a**stre   j**o**ven   señ**o**res

(b) If the words ends in a consonant, except **n** or **s,** the final syllable is stressed.

comprend**er**   alab**ar**   recib**ir**   señ**or**

(c) All exceptions to the above rules have a written accent mark.

s**á**bado   j**ó**venes   Ad**á**n   C**é**sar   franc**é**s

Spanish-English Vocabulary

The Spanish-English Vocabulary is intended to be complete for the context of this book.

Nouns are listed in the singular. Regular feminine forms of nouns are indicated by **(-a)** or the ending that replaces the masculine ending: **niño(-a)** or **alcalde(-esa).** Irregular noun plurals are given in full: **voz** *f.* voice; (*pl.* **voces**). Regular feminine forms of adjectives are indicated by **-a.**

ABBREVIATIONS

adj.	adjective	*irr.*	irregular
aux.	auxiliary verb	*m.*	masculine
f.	feminine	*pl.*	plural
inf.	infinitive	*sing.*	singular

a to, at; **a eso de** about (*time*); **a menudo** often
abajo below, downstairs, down
abeja *f.* bee
abierto, -a open
abogado(-a) lawyer
abrigo *m.* overcoat
abril *m.* April
abrir to open
abuela *f.* grandmother
abuelo *m.* grandfather
aburrido,-a boring
acabar to finish, end; **acabar de** to have just
acampar to camp
accidente *m.* accident
aceite *m.* oil; **aceite de oliva** olive oil
aceituna *f.* olive
aceptar to accept
acera *f.* sidewalk
acercarse to approach
acero *m.* steel
acompañar to accompany
aconsejar to advise
acontecimiento *m.* event
acordarse (de) [ue] to remember
acostarse (ue) to go to bed
actividad *f.* activity
activo, -a active
actor *m.* actor
actriz *f.* actress
actuar to act
acuarela *f.* watercolor
adelantar to advance, to move forward
adiós goodbye
admirar to admire
adolescencia *f.* adolescence
adolescente *m.* & *f.* adolescent
adorno *m.* decoration
aduana *f.* customs
aduanero(-era) customs official
aerolínea *f.* airline
aeropuerto *m.* airport
afecto *m.* affection, love
afeitarse to shave
aficionado(-a) fan
agobiar to overwhelm, to weigh down
agosto *m.* August
agradecer (zc) to thank (for)
agregar (gu) to add
agrícola agricultural
agua *f.* water; **agua mineral** mineral water
aguacate *m.* avocado
aguardar to wait (for)
agudeza *f.* sharpness
aguinaldo *m.* Christmas or New Year's gift
ahora now; **ahora mismo** right now
ahorrar to save
aire *m.* air; **al aire libre** out-of-doors
ajeno of or belonging to another, another's; foreign; different
ala *f.* wing
alabar to praise
alcalde(-esa) mayor
alcanzable attainable, reachable
alcanzar (c) to reach, to attain
aldea *f.* village, town
alegre happy
alegría *f.* joy
alejar to separate; **alejarse (de)** to move away from
alemán (*f.* alemana) German
alergia *f.* allergy
alfabeto *m.* alphabet
alfombra *f.* rug, carpet
álgebra *m.* algebra
algo something

algodón *m.* cotton
alguien someone
alguno, -a some, any
allí there
almacén *m.* department store
almohada *f.* pillow
almorzar (ue) (c) to eat lunch
almuerzo *m.* lunch
alojamiento *m.* lodging
alpargata *f.* sandal
alpinismo *m.* mountain climbing
alquilar to rent, to hire
alquiler *m.* leasing, rent
alrededor (de) around
altavoz *m.* loudspeaker
alto, -a tall; high
altura *f.* height
alumno(-a) student, pupil
alzar (c) to raise
amable friendly, nice
amanecer (zc) to dawn
amar to love
amargo, -a bitter
amarillo, -a yellow
ambicioso, -a ambitious
ambiente *m.* atmosphere, environment; **medio ambiente** environment
ambulancia *f.* ambulance
ambulante wandering
amigo(-a) friend
amistad *f.* friendship
amo(-a) master, mistress, owner, boss
amor *m.* affection, love
amoroso, -a lovable
amplio, -a large, ample
amueblar to furnish
anaranjado, -a orange
ancho, -a wide
andar (*irr.*) to walk
anhelado, -a craved, longed for
anillo *m.* ring
año *m.* year
anoche last light
anochecer to grow dark
anteayer the day before yesterday
anteojos *m. pl.* eyeglasses
antes (de) before; **cuanto antes** as soon as possible
antiguo, -a old, ancient
antipático, -a unpleasant, disagreeable
anuario *m.* yearbook
anunciar to announce
anuncio *m.* announcement
apagar (gu) to put out; **apagarse** to shut off
aparato *m.* ride
aparecer (zc) to appear
apartado *m.* box; **apartado postal** post office box
apartamento *m.* apartment
apellido *m.* last name (family name)
apenas hardly, barely
apendicitis *f.* appendicitis
apetito *m.* appetite
aplauso *m.* applause
aplicado, -a studious, smart
apoyador(-ora) supporter
apoyar to support
aprender to learn
aprisa quickly, rapidly
aprovecharse de to take advantage of
aquel that; **aquél** that one
aquí here
árabe *m. & f.* Arab
araña *f.* spider
árbol *m.* tree
arder to burn
ardilla *f.* squirrel
arena *f.* sand
arete *m.* earring
argolla *f.* wedding band
argumento *m.* theme, plot
armario *m.* wardrobe, closet
arquitecto(-a) architect
arreglar to arrange, fix
arreglo *m.* arrangement
arriba above, upstairs
arrojar to throw
arroyo *m.* stream
arroz *m.* rice
arte *f.* art; **artes industriales** shop
artesanía *f.* arts and crafts
artista *m. & f.* artist, performer
asado roasted
asamblea *f.* assembly
asar to roast
ascensor *m.* elevator
asiento *m.* seat
asistir to attend
asma *f.* asthma
aspiradora *f.* vacuum cleaner
aspirina *f.* aspirin
asustarse to be frightened
ateneo *m.* literary club
aterrizaje *m.* landing
atleta *m. & f.* athlete
atlético, -a athletic
atletismo *m.* athletics
atracciones *f. pl.* attractions; **parque de atracciones** amusement park
atravesar (ie) to cross
atreverse to dare
atún *m.* tuna fish
aula *f.* classroom
aún still, yet
aún yet
ausente absent
autobús *m.* bus
automóvil *m.* car
autopista *f.* highway
auxilio *m.* aid, help; **primeros auxilios** first aid
ave *f.* bird
avenida *f.* avenue
aventura *f.* adventure
aventurero(-era) *m.* adventurer
averiguar (gü) to investigate
avión *m.* airplane
aviso *m.* notice

ayer yesterday
ayudante *m. & f.* aide
ayudar to help
ayuntamiento *m.* town hall
azúcar *m.* sugar
azul blue
azulejo *m.* tile

babero *m.* bib
bailar to dance
baile *m.* dance
bajar to go down, descend; to lower; **bajar de peso** to lose weight; **bajar(se) de** to get off (the train, etc.)
bajo, -a short
balcón *m.* balcony
ballena *f.* whale
baloncesto *m.* basketball
bañarse to take a bath
banco *m.* bank; bench
banda *f.* band
bandera *f.* flag
baño *m.* bath; **cuarto de baño** bathroom; **traje de baño** *m.* bathing suit
banquero(-era) banker
barata *f.* sale
barato, -a inexpensive, cheap
barba *f.* beard
barbilla *f.* chin
barco *m.* boat; **barco de vela** sailboat
barrer to sweep
barrio *m.* neighborhood
barro *m.* clay
bastante enough
basura *f.* garbage
bata *f.* robe
batalla *f.* battle, fight, struggle
batear to hit (with a bat)
batido *m.* shake
baúl *m.* trunk
bebé *m.* & *f.* baby
beber to drink
bebida *f.* drink, beverage
béisbol *m.* baseball
belleza *f.* beauty
beso *m.* kiss
biblioteca *f.* library
bicicleta *f.* bicycle
biftec *m.* steak
bigote *m.* mustache
bilingüe bilingual
billete *m.* bill, ticket
biología *f.* biology
blanco, -a white
blando, -a soft
blusa *f.* blouse
boca *f.* mouth
bocado *m.* snack
bodega *f.* grocery store
boleto *m.* ticket
boliche *m.* bowling
bolígrafo *m.* ballpoint pen
bollo *m.* roll, muffin
bolos *m. pl.* bowling
bolsa *f.* purse, handbag; **Bolsa** *f.* stock market
bolsillo *m.* pocket
bombero(-era) firefighter
bondadoso, -a kind
bonito, -a pretty, beautiful
borrado, -a erased, blurred
borrar to erase
bosque *m.* woods
bota *f.* boot
botella *f.* bottle
brazo *m.* arm
brillante *m.* diamond
brincar to jump
broche *m.* brooch, pin
brócoli *m.* broccoli
brújula *f.* compass
brutalidad *f.* brutality
bucear to snorkel; to dive
buceo *m.* diving
bueno good
buey *m.* ox
bufanda *f.* scarf
buque *m.* boat, ship
burlarse (de) to make fun of
buró *m.* night stand
burro *m.* donkey
buscar (qu) to look for, seek
butaca *f.* armchair (upholstered)
buzón *m.* mailbox

caballo *m.* horse; **a caballo** on horseback
cabello *m.* hair
caber (*irr.*) to fit
cabeza *f.* head
cabina *f.* cabin, booth: **cabina telefónica** telephone booth
cabra *f.* goat
cada each, every
cadena *f.* chain
caer (*irr.*) to fall; **dejar caer** to drop
café *m.* cafe; coffee; *also adj.* brown
cafetería *f.* cafeteria
caja *f.* box; cashier, cash register, teller's window; **caja fuerte** safe
cajero(-era) cashier, teller
calcetín *m.* sock
calculadora *f.* calculator
caldo *m.* broth, soup
calendario *m.* calendar
calentar (ie) to heat
cálido, -a warm
caliente hot
callarse to be silent, keep still
calle *f.* street
callos *m. pl.* tripe (*Spain*)
calor *m.* heat; **hace calor** it is hot (*weather*); **tener calor** to be warm
calvo, -a bald
cama *f.* bed
cámara *f.* camera; chamber; **cámara de diputados** house of representatives
camarero(-era) waiter (waitress)
camarón *m.* shrimp

camarote *m.* cabin
cambiar to change
cambio *m.* change; exchange rate
caminar to walk
camino *m.* road
camión *m.* truck
camionero(-era) truck driver
camioneta *f.* station wagon, van
camisa *f.* shirt; **camiseta** T-shirt
campamento *m.* camp
campeonato *m.* championship
campesino(-a) farmer
campo *m.* country, field
caña *f.* cane; **caña de azúcar** sugar cane
canal *m.* channel (television)
canasta *f.* basket
cancha *f.* court (*sports*)
canción *f.* song
candelero *m.* candleholder
candidato(-a) candidate
canguro *m.* kangaroo
cansado, -a tired
cantante *m.* & *f.* singer
cantar to sing
canto *m.* song; singing
capacidad *f.* capacity
capítulo *m.* chapter
cara *f.* face
carabela *f.* caravel, boat
carbón *m.* coal
cariño *m.* affection, love
cariñoso, -a loving
carne *f.* meat; **carne de res** beef
carnet *m.* card; **carnet telefónico** calling card
carnicería *f.* butcher shop
carnicero(-era) butcher
caro, -a expensive
carpeta *f.* (file) folder
carpintero(-era) carpenter
carrera *f.* track; race; career, profession
carretera *f.* highway, road
carro *m.* car
carta *f.* letter
cartel *m.* poster
cartera *f.* wallet, billfold
cartero(-era) mail carrier
casa *f.* house
casado, -a married
casamiento *m.* marriage
casarse con to marry
casimir cashmere
castigar to punish
castillo *m.* castle
catedral *f.* cathedral
caucho *m.* rubber
cebolla *f.* onion
cebra *f.* zebra
ceja *f.* eyebrow
célebre famous
celoso, -a jealous
cemento *m.* cement
cena *f.* dinner, supper
cenar to eat supper
centro *m.* center, downtown; **centro comercial** mall; **centro juvenil** youth center
cepillarse to brush (one's teeth, hair, clothes)
cerca (de) near; close to
cerdo *m.* pork
cereal *m.* cereal
cereza *f.* cherry
cerrado, -a closed
cerrar (ie) to close
cesar to stop
césped *m.* lawn, grass
cesta *f.* basket
ceviche *m.* raw fish, sushi
chaleco *m.* vest
chaqueta *f.* jacket
charlar to chat
chícharo *m.* pea
chimenea *f.* fireplace
chino, -a Chinese
chisme *m.* rumor, gossip
chiste *m.* joke
chocar (qu) to crash, to collide
chocolate *m.* chocolate
chofer *m.* & *f.* driver
choza *f.* hut
chuleta *f.* chop
ciego, -a blind, visually-impaired
cielo *m.* sky
cien (ciento) one hundred; **por ciento** percent
ciencia *f.* science
científico(-a) scientist
cierto, -a sure; true; certain
cincuenta fifty
cine *m.* movies (movie theater)
cinta *f.* tape, ribbon
cinturón *m.* belt
circo *m.* circus
círculo *m.* club; **círculo de matemáticas** math club; **círculo dramático** drama club; **círculo español** Spanish club; **círculo internacional** international club
ciruela *f.* plum
cirugía *f.* surgery
cirujano(-a) surgeon
cisne *m.* swan
cita *f.* appointment, date
ciudad *f.* city
ciudadano(-a) citizen
claro, -a clear, light-colored
clase *f.* class; kind
clásico, -a classical
cliente *m.* & *f.* client, customer
clima *m.* climate
cobarde cowardly
cobrar to collect
coche *m.* car
cochero(-era) cab driver
cochino *m.* pig
cocido *m.* stew
cocina *f.* kitchen
cocinar to cook

cocinero(-era) chef, cook
cocodrilo *m.* crocodile
código *m.* code; **código postal** zip code
codo *m.* elbow
coger (j) to seize, to catch
cola *f.* line (of people); tail
colchón *m.* mattress
coleccionar to collect
colegio *m.* school, academy
colgar (ue) (gu) to hang
coliflor *m.* coliflower
colina *f.* hill
collar *m.* necklace
colocar (qu) to place, to put
colorear to color
columpio *m.* swing
comedor *m.* dining room
comentario *m.* comment
comenzar (ie, c) to begin
comer to eat
comerciante *m. & f.* merchant, businessperson
cometer to commit; **cometer un error** to make a mistake
cómico, -a funny
comida *f.* meal, food
como as; **¿cómo?** how?
cómoda *f.* dresser
cómodo, -a comfortable
compañero(-era) companion, friend
compañía *f.* company
compartimento *m.* compartment
compartir to share
compás *m.* compass; (music) beat, time
compilar to compile
comprar to buy
compras: **ir de compras** to go shopping
comprender to understand
computadora *f.* computer
comunidad *f.* community
con with
concierto *m.* concert
concluir (y) to conclude
concurso *m.* contest
conducir (zc) to lead, to drive
conejo *m.* rabbit
conferencia *f.* conference
confesar (ie) to confess
confiar (en) to rely (on), to confide (in)
congelador *m.* freezer
congreso *m.* congress; convention, meeting
conocer (zc) to know (a person)
conocido, -a known
conocimiento *m.* knowledge
conquistador(-ora) conqueror
conseguir (i) (g) to get, to obtain, to succeed in
consejero(-era) counselor
consejo *m.* advice
consentir (ie, i) to spoil
constar (de) to consist (of)
construir (y) to construct, to build
consultorio *m.* office (medical)
contaminación *f.* pollution
contar (ue) to count; to tell; **contar con** to count on
contenido *m.* content
contento, -a happy
contestar *to* answer
contigo with you
continuar (ú) to continue
contra against
contrato *m.* lease
contribuir (y) to contribute
convencer (z) to convince
conversar to converse
convidar to invite
copa *f.* (wine) glass
copiar to copy
corazón *m.* heart
corbata *f.* tie
corcho *m.* cork
cordero *m.* lamb
coreano, -a Korean
coro *m.* chorus
corregir (i) (j) to correct
correo *m.* mail, post office; **correo electrónico** e-mail
correr to run
correspondencia *f.* correspondence; **amigo por correspondencia** pen pal
corrida *f.* run, dash; **corrida de toros** bullfight
cortar to cut
corte *f.* court (house)
cortejar to court
cortés polite
cortesía *f.* courtesy
cortina *f.* curtain
cosa *f.* thing
coser to sew
costa *f.* coast
costar (ue) to cost
costumbre *f.* custom, habit
crecer (zc) to grow
creer to believe
crucero *m.* cruise
crucigrama *m.* crossword puzzle
cruzar (c) to cross
cuaderno *m.* notebook
cuadra *f.* (street) block
cuadro *m.* painting
¿cuál, -es? which?, which one(s)?
cuando when; **¿cuándo?** when?; **de cuando / de vez en cuando** from time to time
cuanto, -a as much; **¿cuánto?** how much?; **¿cuántos, -as?** how many; **¡cuánto, -a... !** how much ... !
cuarenta forty
Cuaresma *f.* Lent
cuartel *m.* barrack; **cuartel de la policía** police precinct

cuarto, -a fourth; quarter; **un cuarto** one quarter; **cuarto** *m.* room; **cuarto de baño** bathroom
cubiertos *m. pl.* cutlery, utensils
cubrir to cover
cuchara *f.* spoon
cucharada *f.* tablespoon
cucharita *f.* teaspoon
cuchichear to whisper
cuchillo *m.* knife
cuello *m.* neck
cuenta *f.* bill, (restaurant) check; account; **cuenta de ahorros** savings account; **cuenta de cheques** checking account
cuento *m.* story; **cuento infantil** childrens' story
cuero *m.* leather
cuerpo *m.* body
cuidado care; **con cuidado** carefully; **tener cuidado** to be careful
cuidar to take care of
culpa *f.* blame; **tener la culpa** to be at fault
cultivar to cultivate
cumpleaños *m.* birthday
cumplir to fulfill, to accomplish; **cumplir con la palabra** to keep one's word
cuñada *f.* sister-in-law
cuñado *m.* brother-in-law
cuota *f.* fare
cura *f.* cure; *also m.* priest
curiosidad *f.* curiosity
curioso, -a curious
curso *m.* course, class
cuyo, -a whose

dama *f.* lady; **primera dama** first lady; **juego de damas** checkers
daño *m.* harm, damage
dar to give; **darse cuenta de** to realize; **dar limosna** to give alms (make a donation)
de of, from; **de repente** suddenly
debajo de beneath, under
deber to have to (should, ought); to owe
debido a due to
débil weak
decano(-a) dean
decidir to decide
décimo, -a tenth
decir (*irr.*) to say, to tell; **decir la verdad** to tell the truth
decisión *f.* decision; **tomar una decisión** to make a decision
dedo *m.* finger; **dedo del pie** toe
defender (ie) to defend
dejar to let, allow, leave (behind)
delante de in front of, ahead of
deletrear to spell
delgado, -a thin
demasiado too much, too many
democracia *f.* democracy
demora *f.* delay
dentista *m. & f.* dentist
dentro de inside of
dependiente *m. & f.* clerk, salesperson
deporte *m.* sport
deportivo, -a sporty
depositar to deposit
depósito *m.* deposit
derecho, -a right; **derecho** straight ahead; **derecho** *m.* right
desacuerdo *m.* disagreement
desaparecer (zc) to disappear
desarrollo *m.* development
desastre *m.* disaster
desayunarse to have breakfast
desayuno *m.* breakfast
descansar to rest
descolgar (ue) (gu) to pick up (the phone)
desconocido, -a unknown
descontento, -a unhappy
descortés impolite
describir to describe
descripción *f.* description
descubridor(-ora) discoverer
descubrimiento *m.* discovery
descuento *m.* discount
desde from; since
desear to want, wish
desembocar to flow out, empty
desempleo *m.* unemployment
desgracia *f.* misfortune; **por desgracia** unfortunately
deshuesado, -a deboned
desierto *m.* desert
desilusionado, -a disillusioned
despacio slowly
despedirse (de) (i) to take leave (of), to say goodbye (to)
despegar (gu) to take off (plane)
despegue *m.* takeoff
despertarse (ie) to wake up, awaken
después later; **después de** after
destacarse to stand out
destruir (y) to destroy
desván *m.* attic
detrás (de) behind
devolver (ue) to return (something); to give back
día *m.* day; **día feriado** legal holiday; **día libre** day off; **de día** by day; **hoy día** nowadays
diamante *m.* diamond
diario, -a daily; **a diario** every day; *also m.* diary
diccionario *m.* dictionary
dicho *m.* saying
diciembre *m.* December
dictado *m.* dictation
dictador(-ora) dictator
dictadura *f.* dictatorship
diente *m.* tooth
dieta *f.* diet

difícil difficult
difunto(-a) deceased
diligente diligent, hard-working
dinero *m.* money
diputado(-a) representative
director(-ora) manager, principal
dirigir (j) to direct; **dirigirse (j) a** to make one's way toward; to address
disco *m.* record
discoteca *f.* discotheque
disculpa *f.* excuse, apology
diseñador(-ora) designer
diseñar to design
diseño *m.* drawing
disfraz *m.* disguise
disfrutar to enjoy
disminuir (y) to diminish, to decrease
disponible available
distinguir (g) to distinguish
distinto, -a different
distribuir (y) to distribute
diversión *f.* diversion; **parque de diversiones** amusement park
divertido, -a fun
divertirse (ie) to enjoy oneself
dividir to divide
doblar to fold
docena *f.* dozen
dólar *m.* dollar
doler (ue) to ache
dolor *m.* pain, ache; **dolor de cabeza** headache; **tener dolor de cabeza** to have a headache
doloroso, -a painful
domingo *m.* Sunday
dona *f.* doughnut
donde where; **¿dónde?** where?; **¿de dónde?** (from) where?; **¿a dónde?** (to) where?
dormir (ue) to sleep; **dormirse (ue)** to fall asleep
dormitorio *m.* bedroom
dote *m.* & *f.* dowry
dramaturgo(-a) playwright
ducha *f.* shower
ducharse to take a shower
duda *f.* doubt; **sin duda** undoubtedly
dudoso doubtful
dueño(-a) owner
dulce sweet; **dulces** *m.* candy, sweets
durante during
duro, -a hard

echar to throw; **echar de menos** to miss; **echar una carta** to mail; **echarse a...** to begin; **echar a perder** to spoil
economía *f.* economy
edificio *m.* building; **edificio de apartamentos** apartment house
educación *f.* education; **educación física** gym
educado, -a educated; polite
efectivo *m.* cash
eficacia *f.* efficiency
egoísta selfish
ejecutivo (-a) executive
ejercer (z) to exert; to exercise; to practice (a profession)
ejercicio *m.* exercise
ejercitar to exercise
ejército *m.* army
elector(-ora) elector, voter
elefante *m.* elephant
elegir (j) to elect, choose
elevar to raise, lift
elote *m.* green bean
embajada *f.* embassy
embajador(-ora) ambassador
embarazoso, -a embarrassing
emisión *f.* broadcast
empate *m.* tie (sports)
empezar (ie) (c) to begin
empresa *f.* business
en in, on; **en seguida** immediately
enamorarse de to fall in love with
encaje *m.* lace
encantador, -a enchanting, charming
encarcelado, -a imprisoned
encargarse (de) to take charge (of)
encender to light, to burn
encima de on top of
encontrar (ue) to find, to meet
energía *f.* energy
enero *m.* January
enfadarse to get angry
enfermedad *f.* disease, illness
enfermería *f.* infirmary; nursing
enfermero(-era) nurse
enfermo(-a) sick person, patient; *also adj.* sick, ill
enfrente in front of, opposite
enfriar to chill
ensalada *f.* salad
ensayista *m.* & *f.* essayist
enseñar to teach, show
entender (ie) to understand
enterrar (ie) to bury
entonces then
entrada *f.* entrance; admission
entrar to enter
entre between, among
entregar to deliver
entrenador(-ora) trainer, coach
entrenamiento *m.* training
entrevista *f.* interview
enviar (í) to send
envidia *f.* envy
envolver (ue) to wrap up
enojarse to get angry
época *f.* epoch, era
equipaje *m.* luggage
equipo *m.* team; equipment; **equipo de béisbol** baseball team; **equipo de fútbol** soccer team
equitación *f.* horseback riding
equivocado, -a mistaken, incorrect

equivocarse to be mistaken
error *m.* error
esbelto, -a svelt, slim
escala *f.* stop (air travel)
escalera *f.* stairs
escaparse to elope
escoger (j) to choose, to select
escolar school
esconder to hide (something)
escribir to write
escrito, -a written; **por escrito** in writing
escritor(-ora) writer
escritura *f.* writing
escuchar to listen (to)
escudero *m.* squire
escuela *f.* school; **escuela primaria** elementary school; **escuela secundaria** high school
escurrir to strain
ese that; **ése** that one
esmeralda *f.* emerald
espada *f.* sword
espalda *f.* back
español(-ola) Spanish
espantar to frighten, to scare
espejo *m.* mirror
esperar to wait for, await, hope, expect
espinaca *f.* spinach
esposa *f.* wife
esposo *m.* husband
esquí *m.* skiing; **esquí acuático** waterskiing
establecer (zc) to establish
establecimiento *m.* establishment
estación *f.* train station; season
estadio *m.* stadium
estado *m.* state
estallar to explode, to burst
estampilla *f.* stamp
estar *(irr.)* to be
estatua *f.* statue
este, -a this; **éste, -a** this one
este *m.* east
estéreo *m.* stereo
estética *f.* esthetics
estilo *m.* style
estimar to esteem
estómago *m.* stomach
estornudar to sneeze
estrecho, -a narrow
estrella *f.* star
estrenar to open (a play, a movie)
estreno *m.* opening (movie)
estricto, -a strict
estuche *m.* case
estudiante *m.* & *f.* student, pupil
estudiar to study
estudio *m.* study; den
estufa *f.* stove
examen *m.* examination, test
excursión *f.* field trip
excursionista *m.* & *f.* hiker
exigente demanding
exigir to demand
existencia *f.* stock
éxito *m.* success; **tener éxito** to be successful
explicación *f.* explanation
explicar to explain
explorador(-ora) explorer; **el niño explorador** Boy Scout
exposición *f.* exhibit, show
expulsar to expel, to eject
extinguir (g) to extinguish
extrañar to miss
extranjero(-era) foreigner; **al extranjero** abroad
extraño, -a strange, rare

fábrica *f.* factory
fabricar to manufacture
facultad *f.* faculty; **facultad de medicina** medical school
falda *f.* skirt
falta *f.* error, mistake
faltar to lack
fama *f.* fame
familia *f.* family
farmaceútico(-a) pharmacist
farmacia *f.* pharmacy, drugstore
farol *m.* street lamp
fascinar to enjoy, to like
febrero *m.* February
fecha *f.* date
felicidad *f.* happiness
felicitar to congratulate
feliz happy
feo, -a ugly
feria *f.* fair
ferretería *f.* hardware store
ferrocarril *m.* railroad
fiebre *f.* fever
fiel faithful
fieltro *m.* felt
fiesta *f.* holiday, celebration, party
fijarse en to look at
fila *f.* line (of people)
filósofo(-a) philosopher
fin *m.* end; **fin de semana** weekend; **por fin** at last; **al fin** finally
firmar to sign
física *f.* physics
flaco, -a skinny
flan *m.* custard
flor *f.* flower
florería *f.* florist shop
florero *m.* vase
fogata *f.* bonfire
folleto *m.* pamphlet
fomentar to foster, to promote
formación *f.* formation
formulario *m.* form; formula
fotografía *f.* photograph; **sacar fotografías** to take pictures
fotógrafo *m.* photographer
fracaso *m.* failure
fractura *f.* fracture
franco, -a frank
franela *f.* flannel
franqueza *f.* frankness
frase *f.* sentence
frecuencia *f.* frequency
frecuentemente frequently
fregadero *m.* kitchen sink

frenar to brake (stop)
frente *f.* forehead
frente a facing, in front of
fresa *f.* strawberry
fresco, -a fresh; also *m.* cool
frijol *m.* bean
frío *m.* cold; **hacer frío** to be cold (*weather*); **tener frío** to be cold
frito, -a fried
frontera *f.* border
fruta *f.* fruit
frutería *f.* fruit store
fuego *m.* fire
fuente *f.* fountain
fuera outside
fuerte strong
fuerza *f.* strength
función *f.* function, showing
funcionar to function, to work
fundador(-ora) founder
furia *f.* fury
furioso, -a furious
fútbol *m.* soccer; **el fútbol americano** football

gabinete *m.* cabinet
gallego, -a Galician
galleta *f.* cookie, cracker
gallina *f.* hen
gallo *m.* rooster
galón *m.* gallon
gambas *f. pl.* shrimp
gamusa *f.* suede
gana *f.* desire; **tener ganas de** to feel like
ganado *m.* cattle
ganador(-ora) winner
ganancias *f.* pl. earnings
ganar to win
garaje *m.* garage
garganta *f.* throat
gasolinera *f.* gas station
gastar to spend (money)
gasto *m.* expense
gato(-a) cat
gemelo(-a) twin
género *m.* genre
generosidad *f.* generosity
generoso, -a generous
geografía *f.* geography
gerente *m.* & *f.* manager
gimnasio *m.* gymnasium
giro *m.* money order
gitano(-a) Gypsy
globo *m.* balloon
gobernador(-ora) governor
gobernar (ie) to govern
gobierno *m.* government
gol *m.* goal (*sports*)
golf *m.* golf
goma *f.* eraser
gordo, -a fat
gorra *f.* cap
gozar de to enjoy
grabado, -a etched, recorded
grabado *m.* etching
grabar to record
gracias thank you
gracioso, -a cute, adorable
grado *m.* degree
graduarse de to be graduated from
gramática *f.* grammar
gran great
grande large, big
grandeza *f.* greatness
granja *f.* farm
gratis free (of charge)
griego, -a Greek
gripe *m.* flu
gris gray
gritar to shout
grito *m.* shout
groseramente vulgarly, impolitely
grosería *f.* vulgarity
grupo *m.* group
guante *m.* glove
guapo, -a handsome, pretty
guardar to keep; **guardar cama** to stay in bed
guardarropa *m.* checkroom
guardia *m.* & *f.* guard
guerra *f.* war
guerrillero(-era) guerrilla fighter
guía *m.* guide; *also f.* guide book; **guía telefónica** telephone book
guiar to guide, to drive (a vehicle)
guisado *m.* stew
gustar to please
gusto *m.* pleasure

haber to have (*aux. verb*)
habichuela *f.* bean
habilidad *f.* skill
habitación *f.* room
hablador, -a talkative
hablar to speak, talk
hacer *(irr.)* to make, to do; **hacer de** to act as; **hacer la(s) maleta(s)** to pack; **hacer una pregunta** to ask a question; **hacer un viaje** to take a trip; **hacerse** to become
hacha *f.* ax
hacia toward
hallar to find
hamaca *f.* hammock
hambre *f.* hunger; **tener hambre** to be hungry
hamburguesa *f.* hamburger
hasta until
hazaña *f.* deed
heladería *f.* ice-cream shop
helado *m.* ice cream; **helado, -a** iced
herencia *f.* heredity; inheritance
herida *f.* wound, injury
hermana *f.* sister
hermano *m.* brother
hermoso, -a handsome, beautiful
héroe *m.* hero
heroína *f.* heroine
hielo *m.* ice
hierba *f.* grass

hierro *m.* iron
hija *f.* daughter
hijo *m.* son; *pl.* sons, children
historia *f.* history
hockey *m.* hockey
hoja *f.* leave; sheet (of paper, etc.)
hombre *m* man
hombro *m.* shoulder
honesto, -a honest
honrado, a honorable, honest
hora *f.* hour
horario *m.* schedule; **horario de clases** class schedule
horno *m.* oven; **horno de microondas** microwave oven
hospital *m.* hospital
hotel *m.* hotel
hoy today
hoyo *m.* hole
huarache *m.* sandal
huelga *f.* strike
huérfano(-a) orphan
hueso *m.* bone
huésped *m.* & *f.* guest
huevo *m.* egg
huir (y) to flee
humanidad *f.* humanity

idioma *m.* language
iglesia *f.* church
igualmente the same to you, likewise
imaginario, -a imaginary
imaginativo, -a imaginative
imán *m.* magnet
impedir (i) to prevent
impermeable *m.* raincoat
imprenta *f.* press
impuesto *m.* tax
impulsivo, -a impulsive
inalcanzable unattainable, unreachable
incendio *m.* fire
infancia *f.* infancy
infección *f.* infection
inflación *f.* inflation
inflar to inflate
influir (y) to influence
informática *f.* computer science
ingeniero(-era) engineer
ingenuo, -a naive
inglés (*f.* **inglesa**) English
iniciar to start, begin
injusto,-a unjust
inquilino(-a) tenant
insecto *m.* insect
insistir (en) to insist on
insurrección *f.* rebellion
inteligente intelligent
intención *f.* intention
interesante interesting
intermedio *m.* intermission
interrumpir to interrupt
inundación *f.* flood
investigador(-ora) researcher
invierno *m.* winter
invitación *f.* invitation
invitar to invite
inyección *f.* injection
ir *(irr.)* to go; **irse** to leave
isla *f.* island
italiano, -a Italian
itinerario *m.* itinerary
izquierdo, -a left
jabón *m.* soap
jamás never, not . . . ever, ever
jamón *m.* ham
japonés (*f.* **japonesa**) Japanese
jardín *m.* garden
jefe *m.* chief, head; **jefe de estado** head of state
jirafa *f.* giraffe
joven young; *also m.* & *f.* young person
joya *f.* jewel
joyería *f.* jewelry store
joyero(-era) jeweler
jubilado, -a retired
judías verdes *f. pl.* green beans
juego *m.* game
jueves *m.* Thursday
juez(-a) judge
jugada *f.* play
jugador(-ora) player
jugar (ue) (gu) to play (a sport)
jugo *m.* juice
juguete *m.* toy
julio m. July
junio m. June
junto together; **junto a** beside
juventud *f.* youth

ketchup *m.* ketchup

labio *m.* lip
lado *m.* side; **al lado de** next to, alongside
ladrido *m.* bark
ladrillo *m.* brick
ladrón *m.* (*f.* **ladrona**) thief
lago *m.* lake
laguna *f.* lagoon
lamentar to be sorry about, to regret
lámpara *f.* lamp
lana *f.* wool
lancha *f.* boat
lápiz *m.* pencil
largo, -a long
lástima *f.* pity, compassion
lastimar to hurt; **lastimarse** to hurt oneself
latín *m.* Latin (language)
lavadora *f.* washing machine
lavandería *f.* laundry
lavaplatos *m.* dishwasher
lavar to wash; **lavarse** to wash oneself
lealtad *f.* loyalty
lección *f.* lesson
leche *f.* milk
lechería milk store
lechero(-era) milk deliverer
lechuga *f.* lettuce
lectura *f.* reading
leer (y) to read
legumbre *f.* vegetable
lengua *f.* tongue, language
león *m.* lion

leopardo *m.* leopard
letrero *m.* sign
levantar to raise, lift; **levantarse** to get up
ley *f.* law
leyenda *f.* legend
libertad *f.* liberty
libra *f.* pound
libre free
librería *f.* bookstore
librero *m.* bookcase
libro *m.* book
lidiar to fight
ligereza *f.* lightness
ligero, -a light (weight)
limón *m.* lemon
limonada *f.* lemonade
limosna *f.* alms
limpiar to clean
limpieza *f.* cleanliness
limpio, -a clean
lino *m.* linen
listo, -a ready; **estar listo, -a** to be ready; **ser listo, -a** to be clever
llamada *f.* call
llamar to call; **llamarse** to be named, be called
llanura *f.* plain, prairie
llave *f.* key
llavero *m.* key chain
llegada *f.* arrival
llegar to arrive
llenar to fill
lleno, -a full
llevar to carry, wear; **llevar a cabo** to carry out
llorar to cry, weep
llover (ue) to rain
lluvia *f.* rain
lobo(-a) wolf
locutor(-ora) announcer
lodo *m.* mud
lograr to achieve, to attain; to succeed in
lotería *f.* lottery
lucha *f.* battle, fight, struggle; **lucha libre** wrestling
luchar to fight
luego then
lugar *m.* place; **tener lugar** to take place
luna *f.* moon
lunes *m.* Monday
luz *f.* light

madera *f.* wood
madrastra *f.* stepmother
madrina *f.* godmother
maestro *m.* teacher
maíz *m.* corn
maleta *f.* suitcase
malo, -a evil
mañana *f.* morning; **de la mañana** A.M.; tomorrow
mancha *f.* stain, spot
mandar to send; to order
manejo *m.* handling; operation
manera *f.* way, means; **de manera...** in a . . . way
mano *f.* hand
manta *f.* blanket
mantel *m.* tablecloth
mantequilla *f.* butter
mantilla *f.* shawl
manzana *f.* apple
mapa *m.* map
maquillaje *m.* makeup
maquillarse to put on makeup
máquina *f.* machine; **máquina de contestar** answering machine
mar *m.* & *f.* sea
maratón *m.* marathon
marca *f.* brand
marcador *m.* marker
marcar (qu) to designate, to show; to dial
marcharse to go away
marido *m.* husband
mariscos *m. pl.* shellfish; seafood
marrón brown
martes *m.* Tuesday
marzo *m.* March
más more, plus
máscara *f.* mask
matemáticas *f. pl.* math
matemático(-a) mathematician
materia *f.* subject
máximo, -a maximum
mayo *m.* May
mayonesa *f.* mayonnaise
mayor older, greater
mayoría *f.* majority
mecánico(-a) mechanic
medalla *f.* medal
mediano, -a medium
medianoche *f.* midnight
medicamento *m.* medicine
medicina *f.* medicine
médico(-a) doctor
medio *m.* means, middle, half; **medio de transporte** means of transportation; *also adj.* half
mediodía *m.* noon
medir (i) to measure
mejilla *f.* cheek
mejillón *m.* mussel
mejor better, best
mejorar to improve
melocotón *m.* peach
memoria *f.* memory; **aprender de memoria** to memorize, to learn by heart
menester *m.* need; **es menester** it is necessary
menor lesser, younger
menos less, minus
mensaje *m.* message
mensajero(-era) messenger
mentir (ie, i) to lie
mentira *f.* lie
menú *m.* menu
mercado *m.* market
merecer (zc) to deserve
mermelada *f.* jam, marmalade
mes *m.* month
mesa *f.* table
mesera *f.* waitress
mesero *m.* waiter

meseta *f.* plateau
meta *f.* goal
meter to put (in); **meterse** to interfere, to meddle
metro *m.* subway
mexicano, -a Mexican
mezcla *f.* mix, mixture, blend
mezclar to mix
miedo *m.* fear; **tener miedo (de)** to fear, to be afraid
mientras while; **mientras tanto** meanwhile
miércoles *m.* Wednesday
mil one thousand
milla *f.* mile
millón *m.* million
mínimo, -a minimum
ministro(-a) minister; **primer(-a) ministro(-a)** Prime Minister
minoría *f.* minority
minusválido, -a handicapped
mirada *f.* look
mirar to look (at)
mismo, -a same; **hoy mismo** this very day
mitad *f.* half
mochila *f.* knapsack, backpack, bookbag
moda *f.* style
modo *m.* way; **de modo...** in a... way
molestar to bother, to annoy
moneda *f.* coin
mono *m.* monkey
monopatín *m.* skateboard
montaña *f.* mountain
montañoso, -a mountainous
montar to ride; **montar a caballo** to go horseback riding; **montar en bicicleta** to ride a bicycle
monumento *m.* monument
morado, -a purple
morder (ue) to bite
moreno, -a brunette
morir (ue) to die
mostaza *f.* mustard
mostrar (ue) to show
motocicleta (moto) *f.* motorcycle
mover (ue) to move
mozo *m.* waiter, server
muchedumbre *f.* crowd
mucho, -a a lot, many
mueble *m.* piece of furniture
muela *f.* molar
muelle *m.* pier
muerte *f.* death
mujer *f.* woman
muleta *f.* red flag used by bullfighters
mundial worldwide
mundo *m.* world; **todo el mundo** everyone
muñeca *f.* doll
murciélago *m.* bat
museo *m.* museum
músico *m.* musician
nacer (zc) to be born
nación *f.* nation
nacionalidad *f.* nationality
nada nothing, (not) anything; **de nada** you're welcome
nadador(-ora) swimmer
nadar to swim
nadie no one, nobody, (not) anyone
naipes *m. pl.* cards
naranja *f.* orange
nariz *f.* nose
natación *f.* swimming
naturaleza *f.* nature
neblina *f.* fog
necesitar to need
necio, -a foolish, stupid
negar (ie) (gu) to deny; **negarse a** to refuse to
negro, -a black
neumonía *f.* pneumonia
nevada *f.* snowfall
nevar (ie) to snow
ni... ni neither . . . nor . . . ; not . . . either . . . or . . . ; **ni siquiera** not even
niebla *f.* fog
nieta *f.* granddaughter
nieto *m.* grandson; *pl.* grandsons, grandchildren
nieve *f.* snow
nilón *m.* nylon
niña *f.* girl
niñez *f.* childhood
ninguno, -a no, none, (not) any
niño *m.* boy
nobleza *f.* nobility
noche *f.* night; **anoche** last night; **esta noche** tonight; **de la noche** P.M.; **de noche** by night
nombrado, -a named
nombre *m.* name; **nombre de pila** first name
norte *m.* north
nota *f.* grade; note
noticias *f. pl.* news
noticiero *m.* news show
novela *f.* novel
noveno, -a ninth
noventa ninety
novia *f.* girlfriend
noviembre *m.* November
novio *m.* boy friend
nube *f.* cloud
nudo *m.* knot
nuera *f.* daughter-in-law
nuevo, -a new
número *m.* number; **número equivocado** wrong number
numeroso, -a numerous
nunca never, (not) ever

obedecer (zc) to obey
obra *f.* work; **obra de teatro** play
obrero(-era) laborer, worker
océano *m.* ocean

ochenta eighty
ocio *m.* idleness, leisure
octavo, -a eighth
octubre *m.* October
ocupado, -a busy
odio *m.* hate
oeste *m.* west
ofrecer (zc) to offer
oído *m.* (inner) ear; hearing
oír *(irr.)* to hear
ojo *m.* eye
ola *f.* wave
oler (hue) to smell
olla *f.* jug, bowl
olvidadizo, -a forgetful
olvidar to forget
onda *f.* wave
ópera *f.* opera
operación *f.* operation
operador(-ora) operator
opuesto, -a opposite
oración *f.* sentence
ordenador *m.* computer
ordenar to order
oreja *f.* (outer) ear
orgullo *m.* pride
orgulloso, -a proud
orilla *f.* shore
oro *m.* gold
orquesta *f.* orchestra
oscuridad *f.* darkness
oscuro, -a dark
oso *m.* bear
otro, -a other, another
oveja *f.* sheep

paciente *m. & f.* patient
padecer (zc) to suffer
padrastro *m.* stepfather
padre *m.* father
padrino *m.* godfather
paella *f.* paella
pagar (gu) to pay (for)
página *f.* page
país *m.* country
paisaje *m.* landscape
pájaro *m.* bird
palabra *f.* word
palmera *f.* palm tree
palomita (de maíz) *f.* popcorn
pan *m.* bread; **pan tostado** toast; **panecillo** roll
panadería *f.* bakery
panadero(-era) (bread) baker
panecillo *m.* roll
panorámico, -a panoramic
pantalla *f.* screen
pantalón *m.* pants, trousers; **pantalón corto** shorts
pantera *f.* panther
pantimedias *f. pl.* pantyhose
pantorrilla *f.* calf
pañuelo *m.* handkerchief
papa *f.* potato; **papas fritas** french-fried potatoes
Papa *m.* Pope
papel *m.* paper; part
paperas *f. pl.* mumps
paquete *m.* package
par *m.* pair
para for
parabrisas *m.* windshield
parada *f.* stop, bus stop
paraguas *m. sing. & pl.* umbrella
parecer (zc) to seem
parecido, -a similar
pared *f.* wall
pareja *f.* couple
pariente *m. & f.* relative
parlamento *m.* parliament
párpado *m.* eyelid
parque *m.* park; **parque nacional** national park; **parque zoológico** zoo; **parque de bomberos** fire station
parte *f.* part; **en ninguna parte** not anywhere, nowhere; **en otra parte** elsewhere; **en todas partes** everywhere
partidario(-aria) fan
partido *m.* game, match; party (political)
partir to leave, depart
pasado, -a past; **el año pasado** last year
pasadomañana day after tomorrow
pasajero(-era) passenger
pasar to pass, spend (time)
pasatiempo *m.* hobby, pastime
pasearse to take a walk
paseo *m.* walk, path
pasillo *m.* hall
pasión *f.* passion
paso *m.* step
pasta *f.* macaroni
pastel *m.* cake
pastelería *f.* pastry shop
patear to kick
patín *m.* skate
patinar to skate
patio *m.* patio, schoolyard
patria *f.* native country; fatherland, mother country
pavo *m.* turkey
paz *f.* peace
peaje *m.* toll
pecho *m.* chest
pechuga *f.* chicken breast
pedir (i) to ask for, request; to order (food); **pedir prestado** to borrow
peinarse to comb one's hair
peine *m.* comb
pelar to peel
pelear to fight
peligro *m.* danger
peligroso, -a dangerous
pelo *m.* hair
pelota *f.* ball
peluche: animal de peluche stuffed animal
peluquería *f.* hair salon, barber shop
peluquero(-era) barber, hair stylist
pendiente pending

pensar (ie) to think; to intend
peor worse
pepino *m.* cucumber
pequeño, -a small
pera *f.* pear
perder (ie) to lose
perdido, -a lost
perdón *m.* apology
pereza *f.* laziness
perezoso, -a lazy
perfumería *f.* perfume shop
periódico *m.* newspaper
periodismo *m.* journalism
periodista *m.* & *f.* reporter, journalist
perla *f.* pearl
permanecer (zc) to remain
permiso *m.* permission
permitir to let, to allow, to permit
perro *m.* dog
perseguir (i) (g) to pursue
persa Persian
persona *f.* person
pertenecer (zc) to belong
pesado, -a heavy
pesas *f. pl.* weights
pesca *f.* fishing
pescado *m.* fish (out of the water)
pescador(-ora) fisherman
peso *m.* weight
pestaña *f.* eyelash
pez *m.* fish (in the water)
piano *m.* piano
picante spicy
pico *m.* peak
pie *m.* foot
piedad *f.* pity
piedra *f.* stone
piel *f.* skin; leather, fur
pierna *f.* leg
pieza *f.* piece
pijama *f.* pajama
pila *f.* battery
píldora *f.* pill
piloto *m.* & *f.* pilot
pimienta *f.* pepper
pintor(-ora) painter
pintoresco, -a picturesque
pintura *f.* paint; painting
pirámide *f.* pyramid
piscina *f.* swimming pool
piso *m.* floor, story
pizarra *f.* chalkboard
pizza *f.* pizza
planchar to iron
planeta *m.* planet
plano *m.* map (of a city)
planta *f.* plant; **planta baja** ground floor
plata *f.* silver
plátano *m.* plantain
platino *m.* platinum
plato *m.* plate, dish
playa *f.* beach
plaza *f.* square
plazo *m.* term
pluma *f.* pen; feather
población *f.* population
pobreza *f.* poverty
poco few; **dentro de poco** shortly
poder (ue) to be able, can; *also m.* power; **poder ejecutivo** executive power
poderoso, -a powerful
podrir to rot
poesía *f.* poetry
poeta *m.* poet
poetisa *f.* poet
policía *m.* police officer; *f.* the police
poliéster *m.* polyester
política *f.* politics
político(-a) politician
pollo *m.* chicken
polvo *m.* dust
pomada *f.* salve
poner *(irr.)* to put, to place; **poner la mesa** to set the table; **ponerse** to put on; to become; **ponerse rojo (-a)** to blush
por for, by, through; times (*math*)
porque because; **¿por qué?** why?
portátil portable
porteño, -a from Buenos Aires, Argentina
portero *m.* doorman
portugués, -esa Portuguese
posada *f.* inn
posponer (*irr.*) to postpone
postre *m.* dessert
practicar to practice
precio *m.* price
preciso necessary; precise
predilecto, -a favorite
preferir (ie, i) to prefer
pregunta *f.* question
preguntar to ask
premio *m.* prize; **el premio gordo** first prize, jackpot
prenda *f.* article (of clothing)
prendedor *m.* pin
prensa *f.* press, newspapers
preocupado, -a worried
preparar to prepare
presidente(-a) president
prestado, -a borrowed
prestar to lend; **prestar atención** to pay attention
prima *f.* cousin
primavera *f.* spring
primero, -a first
primo(-a) cousin
princesa *f.* princess
principiar to begin
prisa *f.* haste, promptness; **tener prisa** to be in a hurry
probar (ue) to prove, to try, to test
problema *m.* problem
producir (zc) to produce
profesión *f.* profession
profesor(-ora) teacher

profundamente deeply; soundly
profundo, -a deep
programa *m.* program, platform
programador(-ora) programmer
prohibir to forbid
prometer to promise
promoción *f.* promotion
pronosticador(-ora) forecaster
pronosticar to forecast
pronóstico *m.* forecast
pronto soon; **de pronto** suddenly; **tan pronto como** as soon as
pronunciar to pronounce
propietario(-a) owner
propina *f.* tip
propio, -a own
propósito *m.* purpose
prosperidad *f.* prosperity
protagonista *m. & f.* main character
proteger (j) to protect
provecho *m.* benefit; **buen provecho** hearty appetite
próximo, -a next
pueblo *m.* town
puente *m.* bridge
pureza *f.* purity
puerta *f.* door; gate
puerto *m.* port
puesto *m.* position, post; **puesto que** since
pulgada *f.* inch
pulmonía *f.* pneumonia
pulpo *m.* octopus
pulsera *f.* bracelet
punto *m.* sharp; **en punto** sharp
pupitre *m.* (student's) desk

que that; **¿qué?** what?, which?; **¡qué... !** what . . . !, what a . . . !, how . . . !
quebrar (ie) to break
quedar to remain; **quedarse (en)** to stay, to remain; **quedarle a uno** to have left
quehacer *m.* chore, task, errand
queja *f.* complaint
quejarse to complain
quemadura *f.* burn
quemar to burn
querer (ie) to want; to wish; to love
querido, -a dear
queso *m.* cheese
quien who; **¿quién?** who?; **¿a quién (-es)?** whom?, to whom?; **¿con quién (-es)?** with whom?; **¿de quién (-es)?** whose?, of whom?
química *f.* chemistry
quinceañero *m.* birthday party for girls turning fifteen
quinto, -a fifth
quiosco *m.* kiosk
quitar to take away; **quitarse** to take off (clothing)

ración *f.* ration
radiografía *f.* x-ray
raíz *f.* root
rapidez *f.* rapidity, quickness
rápido, -a rapid, fast; **rápidamente** rapidly, quickly
raqueta *f.* racket
rascacielos *m. sing. & pl.* skyscraper
raso *m.* satin
rato *m.* time; **pasar un buen rato** to have a good time
ratoncito *m.* mouse
razón *f.* reason; **tener razón** to be right
realizar to realize, to fulfill
rebeldía *f.* rebellion, revolt
recado *m.* message
receptor(-ora) receiver
recesión *f.* recession
receta *f.* recipe, prescription
recetar to prescribe
rechazar (c) to reject
recibir to receive
reciclaje *m.* recycling
reciclar to recycle
recoger (j) to pick up, to gather
recompensa *f.* reward
reconocer (zc) to recognize
recordar (ue) to remember
recuerdo *m.* remembrance, souvenir
recurso *m.* resource
red *f.* net
redactar to edit
reducir (zc) to reduce
referir (ie i) to tell; to narrate
refrán *m.* saying, proverb
refresco *m.* refreshment; soft drink, soda
refrigerador *m.* refrigerator
regalo *m.* gift, present
regar to water, to irrigate
régimen *m.* diet; regime
regla *f.* rule; ruler
regresar to return
reina *f.* queen
reinado *m.* reign
reinar to reign
reír(se) (i) to laugh
reja *f.* gate, wrought-iron grill
relámpago *m.* lightening
religioso, -a religious
relleno, -a stuffed
reloj *m.* watch, clock; **reloj despertador** alarm clock
relojería *f.* watch shop
relojero(-era) watchmaker
remar to row
Renacimiento *m.* Renaissance
reñir (i) to quarrel; to scold
reparar to repair
repetir (i) to repeat
reposo *m.* rest

repostería *f.* pastry shop
repostero(-era) (pastry) baker
república *f.* republic
res *f.* beef
reseña *f.* review; description
resfriado *m.* cold (illness)
resfriarse to catch a cold
resolver (ue) to solve
responder to answer
responsable responsible
respuesta *f.* answer
restaurante *m.* restaurant
resultado *m.* result
resultar to result
resumen *m.* summary
retirar to withdraw
retiro *m.* withdrawal
retrato *m.* portrait
reunión *f.* meeting
reunirse to meet
revelar to develop (film)
revisar to revise, to check
revista *f.* magazine
revolución *f.* revolution
revolver (ue) to mix
rey *m.* king
ribera *f.* shore, bank (of a river)
rico, -a rich
río *m.* river
riqueza *f.* wealth
robar to rob
rodilla *f.* knee
rogar (ue, gu) to request, to beg
rojo, -a red
romería *f.* pilgrimage, religious excursion
rompecabezas *m. sing. & pl.* puzzle
romper to break
ropa *f.* clothing
rosado, -a pink
rostro *m.* face
rotura *f.* break, crack; fracture
rubí *m.* ruby
rubio, -a blonde
ruido *m.* noise
ruidoso, -a noisy
rumano, -a Romanian
ruso, -a Russian
ruta *f.* route

sábado *m.* Saturday
saber *(irr.)* to know
sabio, -a wise
sabor *m.* flavor, taste
sabroso, -a flavorful
sacar to take out; to take (photo)
sacerdote *m.* priest
sacerdotisa *f.* priestess
saco *m.* jacket
sal *f.* salt
sala *f.* living room; **sala de clases** classroom
salchicha *f.* sausage
salida *f.* departure; exit; **salida del sol** sunrise
salir (*irr.*) to go out, to leave; **salirse con la suya** to get one's way
salsa *f.* sauce
salubridad *f.* public health
salud *m.* health
saludable healthy
saludar to greet
saludo *m.* greeting
salvaje wild, savage
salvavidas *m. & f., sing. & pl.* lifeguard
sandía *f.* watermelon
sándwich *m.* sandwich
sangre *f.* blood
santo(-a) saint
sarampión *m.* measles
sarape *m.* blanket
secador *m.* dryer; **secador de pelo** *m.* hair dryer
secadora *f.* clothes dryer
secar to dry; **secarse** to dry oneself
seco, -a dry
secretario(-a) secretary
sed *f.* thirst; **tener sed** to be thirsty
seda *f.* silk
sede *f.* seat (of government or organization)
seguir (i) (g) to follow, to continue
segundo, -a second
seguridad *f.* safety
seguro sure, safe; **seguro social** *m.* social security
selva *f.* forest, jungle
semáforo *m.* traffic light
semana *f.* week
semejante similar
senado *m.* senate
senador(-a) senator
señal *f.* signal
sentarse (ie) to sit down
sentir (ie) (i) to regret, be sorry; to feel
septiembre *m.* September
séptimo, -a seventh
ser (*irr.*) to be
serio, -a serious
serpiente *f.* snake
servilleta *f.* napkin
servir (i) to serve
sesenta sixty
setenta seventy
severo, -a severe, stern
sexto, -a sixth
siempre always
siesta *f.* nap
siguiente following
silbar to whistle
silencioso, -a quiet, silent
silla *f.* chair
sillón *m.* armchair
simpático, -a nice, pleasant
simple silly, simpleminded; simple, mere
sin without; **sin embargo** nevertheless
sinagoga *f.* synagogue

situar to place, to locate
sobre on top of; *also m.* envelope
sobresaliente outstanding
sobrina *f.* niece
sobrino *m.* nephew
sociedad *f.* society
sofá *m.* sofa
sofreír to sauté
sol *m.* sun
sólamente (sólo) only
soldado(-a) *m.* soldier
soler (ue) to be accustomed to
solo, -a alone
sombrero *m.* hat
sonar (ue) to sound
soñar (ue) to dream
sonido *m.* sound
sonreír(se) (i) to smile
sonrisa *f.* smile
sopa *f.* soup
soplar to blow
sordo, -a deaf, hearing-impaired
sorprenderse (de) to be surprised
sorteo *m.* drawing (for a raffle)
sortija *f.* ring
sótano *m.* basement
subibaja *m.* seesaw
subir to go up, climb; to raise
suburbio *m.* suburb
suceso *m.* event, occurrence
sucio, -a dirty
sudar to perspire, to sweat
sudor *m.* sweat
suegra *f.* mother-in-law
suegro *m.* father-in-law
suelo *m.* ground
sueño *m.* dream; sleep; **tener sueño** to be sleepy
suerte *f.* luck; **tener suerte** to be lucky
suéter *m.* sweater
sufrir to suffer
sugerencia *f.* suggestion
supermercado *m.* supermarket
supersticioso, -a superstitious
suplicar (qu) to implore, to beg
sur *m.* south
surtido *m.* variety, assortment
sustituir (y) to substitute
suyo, -a his, her, your, their

tacaño, -a stingy
tal such
talentoso, -a talented
talla *f.* size
tamaño *m.* size
también also, too
tampoco neither, not either; **ni yo tampoco** me neither
tanto, -a so much, so many; also *m.* score
tapiz *m.* tapestry
tardar (en) to delay (in)
tarde *f.* afternoon; late; P.M. **de la tarde**
tarea *f.* homework, assignment
tarifa *f.* rate, price
tarjeta *f.* card; **tarjeta postal** postcard
tauromaquia *f.* bull fighting
taxi *m.* taxi
taza *f.* cup
té *m.* tea
teatro *m.* theater
tecnología *f.* technology
techo *m.* ceiling, roof
tela *f.* fabric, cloth
teléfono *m.* telephone; **teléfono celular** *m.* cellular telephone
telegrama *m.* telegram
telenovela *f.* soap opera
televisión *f.* television
televisor *m.* television set
tema *m.* theme, topic
temblar (ie) to tremble
temer to fear
temor *m.* fear
temperatura *f.* temperature
templo *m.* temple
temporada *f.* time, period of time; season
temprano early
tenedor *m.* fork
tener (*irr.*) to have; **tener que** to have to
tenis *m.* tennis; *m. pl.* sneakers
tercero, -a third
tercio *m.* third; **un tercio** one-third
terciopelo *m.* velvet
terminal *f.* terminal; **terminal de autobuses** bus station
ternera *f.* veal
terraza *f.* terrace
tertulia *f.* social gathering
tía *f.* aunt
tiburón *m.* shark
tiempo *m.* time; weather; **a tiempo** on time
tienda *f.* store; **tienda de ropa** clothing store; **tienda de campaña** tent
tierra *f.* earth, ground
tigre *m.* tiger
tijeras *f.* pl. scissors
timbre *m.* bell
tímido, -a timid, shy
tintorería *f.* drycleaner
tío *m.* uncle
tirantes *m. pl.* suspenders
tirar to throw
tiras cómicas *f. pl.* comicstrips
títere *m.* puppet
titulares *m. pl.* headlines
tiza *f.* chalk
toalla *f.* towel
tobillo *m.* ankle
tocacintas *m. sing. & pl.* tape player
tocadiscos *m. sing. & pl.* phonograph
tocador *m.* dresser
tocar to play (instrument)

tocino *m.* bacon
todavía still, yet
todo, -a all, every
tomar to take, to drink; **tomar una decisión** to make a decision
tomate *m.* tomato
topacio *m.* topaz
tormenta *f.* storm
torpe clumsy
torre *f.* tower
tortuga *f.* turtle
tos *f.* cough
trabajador, -a hardworking
trabajar to work
trabajo *m.* work
traducir (zc) to translate
traer (*irr.*) to bring
traje *m.* suit; **traje de baño** bathing suit
tranquilamente tranquilly
tránsito *m.* traffic
transporte *m.* transportation
tranvía *m.* streetcar
tratado *m.* treaty
tratamiento *m.* treatment
tratar de to try to
travesura *f.* prank
travieso, -a naughty, mischievious
treinta thirty
tren *m.* train
trigo *m.* wheat
tripulación *f.* crew
triste sad
tristeza *f.* sadness
trofeo *m.* trophy
trompeta *f.* trumpet
trono *m.* throne
turista *m.* & *f.* tourist

último, -a last
ultramarino, -a overseas
uña *f.* fingernail
unidad *f.* unity
universidad *f.* university
urgencia *f.* emergency
usar to use
útil useful; **útiles** *m. pl.* school supplies
uva *f.* grape

vaca *f.* cow
vacaciones *f. pl.* vacation
vacío, -a empty
vacuna *f.* vaccine
valentía *f.* bravery, valor
valer (*irr.*) to be worth
valiente brave
valor *m.* value
vapor *m.* ship, boat
variar to vary
varicela *f.* chicken pox
variedad *f.* variety
varios, -as several
vaso *m.* drinking glass
vecindario *m.* neighborhood
vecino, -a neighbor
veinte twenty
vela *f.* candle
velocidad *f.* speed
vencedor(-ora) winner
vencer (z) to conquer, defeat; end
vendedor(-ora) salesperson
vender to sell
venir (*irr.*) to come
ventana *f.* window
ventanilla *f.* window (for service); small window
ver to see, to watch
veraniego, -a summer
verano *m.* summer
verdad *f.* truth
verdadero, -a true
verde green
verdulería *f.* vegetable shop
verduras *f. pl.* greens, vegetables
vergüenza *f.* shame
vestido *m.* dress
vestirse (i) to dress oneself; to get dressed
vez *f.* time; **a veces** sometimes; **rara vez** seldom; **tal vez** perhaps
viajar to travel
viaje *m.* trip
viajero(-era) *m.* traveler
vicepresidente, -a vice president
vicio *m.* vice
vida *f.* life
videocasetera *f.* VCR
videojuego *m.* video game
vidrio *m.* glass
viejo, -a old
viento *m.* wind; **hacer viento** to be windy
viernes *m.* Friday
violeta purple
virtud *f.* virtue
visitar to visit
vista *f.* view, vision
vivir to live
vivo, -a alive
vocabulario *m.* vocabulary
volar (ue) to fly
volcán *m.* volcano
voleibol *m.* volleyball
volver (ue) to return
voz *f.* voice
vuelo *m.* flight

ya already; **ya no** no longer

zafiro *m.* sapphire
zanahoria *f.* carrot
zapatería *f.* shoe store
zapatero(-era) shoemaker
zapato *m.* shoe
zorra *f.* fox
zumbido *m.* buzz

English-Spanish Vocabulary

The English-Spanish Vocabulary includes only those words that occur in the English-to-Spanish exercise.

a lot mucho
about unos
absent ausente
accompany: to accompany acompañar
act: to act like hacer de
address dirección *f.*; **to address** dirigirse a
afraid: to be afraid tener miedo de
after después de
afternoon tarde *f.*
again otra vez, de nuevo; volver a + *inf.*
ago hace... días (meses, años, *etc.*)
air aire *m.*
almost casi
alone solo, -a
aloud en voz alta
among entre
ancient antiguo
angry: to become angry enojarse, enfadarse
another otro
answer: to answer contestar
applaud: to applaud aplaudir
appreciate: to appreciate agradecer, apreciar
arrive: to arrive llegar
as tan... como; **as many . . . as** tantos, -as... como
ask: to ask preguntar; **to ask for** pedir
assignment tarea *f.*
attend: to attend asistir
attendance asistencia *f.*
author autor(-ora)
autumn otoño *m.*

backpack mochila *f.*
bad malo, -a
banner bandera *f.*
bark: to bark ladrar
basement sótano *m.*
become: to become llegar a ser, ponerse, hacerse
before antes de
begin comenzar (ie) (c), empezar (ie) (c), principiar
beginning principio *m.*
bellboy botones *m. sing.*
best mejor
better mejor
bill cuenta *f.*
bird pájaro *m.*
blanket cobija *f.*
blond rubio, -a
bored aburrido, -a
born: to be born nacer (zc)
break: to break romper, quebrar
breakfast desayuno *m.*
bring: to bring traer, llevar
broom escoba *f.*
brunette moreno, -a
build: to build construir (y)
building edificio *m.*
bus autobús *m.*
but pero
camera cámara *f.*
cancel: to cancel cancelar, anular
candidate candidato(-a)
candle vela *f.*
century siglo *m.*
certain cierto, -a
chambermaid camarera *f.*
change cambio *m.*; **to change** cambiar; **to change one's mind** cambiar de opinión
character personaje *m.*
charge: to charge cobrar
chef cocinero(-a)
chess ajedrez *m.*
choose: to choose escoger (j)
Christmas Navidad *f.*
city ciudad *f.*
civilization civilización *f.*
class clase *f.*
clean limpio; **to clean** limpiar
close: to close cerrar
coach entrenador(-a)
coat abrigo *m.*
colleague colega *m.* & *f.*
colorful colorido, -a
comb peine *m.*; **to comb one's hair** peinarse
comfortable cómodo, -a
commentary comentario *m.*
commit: to commit cometer
competition competencia *f.*
complete: to complete completar, terminar

construct: to construct construir (y)
contaminate: to contaminate contaminar
convince: to convince convencer (z)
cool fresco; **to be cool** hacer fresco (*weather*)
corner *(street corner)* esquina *f.*; rincón *m.*
cosmopolitan cosmopolita
cost: to cost costar (ue)
country campo *m.*; **(nation)** país *m.*
courteous cortés; de manera cortés
critic crítico *m.* & *f.*
cut: to cut cortar

daily diario
darkness oscuridad *f.*
day día *m.*
daybreak: at daybreak al amanecer
December diciembre
decoration adorno *m.*
defect falta *f.*
demanding exigente
deserve: to deserve merecer
desk escritorio *m.*
develop: to develop desarrollar
different diferente, distinto, -a
difficult difícil
dinner cena *f.*
discuss: to discuss discutir
dish plato *m.*
divide: to divide dividir
dog perro *m.*
doll muñeca *f.*
door puerta *f.*
doorman portero *m.*
doubt duda *f.*; **to doubt** dudar
doubtful dudoso
dream sueño *m.*; **to dream** soñar (ue) con
dress vestido *m.*; **to dress oneself** vestirse
drink: to drink beber, tomar
during durante

each cada
early temprano
earn: to earn ganar
elect: to elect elegir (j)
electricity electricidad *f.*; luz *f.*
empire imperio *m.*
employ: to employ emplear, usar
employee empleado(-a)
end fin *m.*; **to end** terminar, acabar, concluir (y)
English inglés (*f.* inglesa)
enjoy: to enjoy gozar de; **to have a good time** divertirse (ie, i)
entire entero, todo
European europeo, -a
every cada
everything todo
example ejemplo *m.*
exercise ejercicio *m.*
exhibit exposición *f.*, exhibición *f.*
experience experiencia *f.*
explain: to explain explicar

factory fábrica *f.*
fair justo,-a; recto, -a
fall otoño *m.*; **to fall** caer; **to fall asleep** dormirse (ue) (u)
famous famoso, -a
fan aficionado(-a), fanático(-a)
father padre *m.*
festival fiesta *f.*
few poco
finally por fin
finish: to finish terminar, acabar
first primero, -a
flashlight linterna *f.*
follow: to follow seguir (i)
food comida *f.*
fool tonto, inocente; **April Fools Day** Día de los Inocentes
forecast pronóstico *m.*; **to forecast** pronosticar (qu)
French francés (*f.* francesa)
frequently a menudo
friend amigo(-a)
friendly amigable, amable
fun: to make fun of burlarse de
funny cómico, -a

game juego *m.*, partido *m.*
garbage basura *f.*
garden jardín *m.*
gardener jardinero(-era)
generally generalmente, por lo general
get: to get into subir a; **to get up** levantarse
gift regalo *m.*
go: to go ir; **to go out** salir
goodbye adiós; **to say goodbye** despedirse
government gobierno *m.*
grass césped *m.*
green verde
greet: to greet saludar
guest huésped *m.* & *f.*
guide guía *m.* & *f.*

hair pelo *m.*
hall pasillo *m.*
Halloween Día de las Brujas *m.*
hang: to hang colgar (ue) (gu)
happy alegre, contento, feliz
hard duro; mucho
help: to help ayudar
hide: to hide esconder
homeowner dueño de casa *m.*
hope esperanza *f.*; **to hope** esperar
hostel hostería *f.*, albergue *m.*
house casa *f.*

immediately en seguida, inmediatamente
include: to include incluir (y)
independence independencia *f.*
information información *f.*
insist: to insist on insistir en
intend: to intend pensar (ie)
introduce: to introduce presentar
itinerary itinerario *m.*

July julio *m.*

key llave *f.*
kind bondadoso, -a
knock: to knock tocar, llamar
know: to know (something) saber; **to know (someone)** conocer

lamp lámpara *f.*
language idioma *m.*, lengua *f.*
large grande
late tarde
lawyer abogado(-a)
lead: to lead conducir (zc)
learn: to learn aprender
leave irse, marcharse, salir; **to leave something (behind)** dejar
letter carta *f.*; **letter opener** abrecartas *m.*
lightning relámpago *m.*
like: to like gustar
live: to live vivir
lobby vestíbulo *m.*
long largo
look: to look at mirar; **to look for** buscar
lose: to lose perder
loud fuerte
love: to love amar
luggage maleta *f.*; equipaje *m.*

machine máquina *f.*
mail correo *m.*; **to mail** echar al correo
main principal
mall centro comercial *m.*
manager gerente *m.* & *f.*
many muchos, -as
means modo *m.*
meanwhile mientras tanto
meet: to meet encontrar (ue)
member miembro *m.* & *f.*, socio *m.* & *f.*
message recado *m.*, mensaje *m.*
mile milla *f.*
mischievious travieso, -a
mistake error *m.*, falta *f.*; **to be mistaken** equivocarse
money dinero *m.*
month mes *m.*
most más
mother madre *f.*
mountain montaña *f.*
move: to move mover (ue)
museum museo *m.*

name nombre *m.*
nature naturaleza *f.*
near cerca de
need necesidad *f.*; **to need** necesitar
neighborhood barrio *m.*
neither tampoco
never nunca, jamás
nevertheless sin embargo
new nuevo, -a; **New Year's** Año Nuevo
news noticia *f.*
newspaper periódico *m.*
next próximo; **the next day** al día siguiente; **next to** al lado de, junto a
nice simpático, -a
night noche *f.*; **last night** anoche
nightfall: at nightfall al anochecer
no one nadie
noise ruido *m.*
noon mediodía *m.*
nothing nada
novel novela *f.*
now ahora
number número *m.*

obtain: to obtain conseguir
offer: to offer ofrecer (zc)
office oficina *f.*
often a menudo
old viejo, -a
older mayor
open: to open abrir
operator operador(-ora); **telephone operator** telefonista *m.* & *f.*
opportunity oportunidad *f.*
ourselves nosotros; nosotros mismos
outdoors al aire libre
outside afuera

pack: to pack empacar, hacer la(s) maleta(s)
parent padre *m.*, madre *f.*; **parents** padres *m. pl.*
participate: to participate participar
pay: to pay pagar (gu); **to pay attention** prestar atención
people gente *f.*
perhaps quizá, tal vez
photograph fotografía *f.*
place lugar *m.*, sitio *m.*; **to take place** tener lugar; **to place** colocar (qu), poner
plan proyecto *m.*; **to plan** pensar (ie)
plant: to plant plantar, cultivar
play: to play (music) tocar (qu); **(to play a game or sport)** jugar (ue) (gu)
player jugador(-a)
please por favor
polite cortés

pool piscina *f.*
porch balcón *m.*, terraza *f.*
practice práctica *f.*; **to practice** practicar (qu)
praise: to praise alabar
prefer: to prefer preferir (ie, i)
prepare: to prepare preparar
pretty bonito, -a
prize premio *m.*
promise: to promise prometer
proud orgulloso, -a
public público, -a
punish: to punish castigar

quickly rápidamente

racket raqueta *f.*
rain lluvia *f.*; **to rain** llover (ue)
read: to read leer
realistic realista, verdadero, -a
recognize: to recognize reconocer (zc)
recommend: to recommend recomendar (ie)
record disco *m.*
regret: to regret sentir (ie, i)
remain: to remain permanecer (zc), quedarse
respect: to respect respetar
respond: to respond responder, contestar
result resultado *m.*
review: to review repasar
road carretera *f.*
room cuarto *m.*
rule regla *f.*
run: to run correr

saint santo, -a
same mismo, -a
schedule horario *m.*
school escuela *f.*; **elementary school** escuela primaria *f.*; **high school** escuela secundaria *f.*
scream grito *m.*; **to scream** gritar
seat asiento *m.*
seem: to seem parecer
seize: to seize coger (j)
seldom rara vez
serious serio, -a
serve: to serve servir (i)
set juego *m.*
several varios, unos
share: to share compartir
shop: to shop ir de compras
short bajo, -a
show: to show mostrar (ue), enseñar
shower: to shower ducharse
shut : to shut cerrar (ie); **to shut off** apagar (gu)
silent: to be silent callarse
sit: to sit down sentarse (ie)
sleep: to sleep dormir (ue, u)
slowly despacio, lentamente
small pequeño, -a
sneakers zapatos de tenis *m. pl.*
snow nieve *f.*; **to snow** nevar (ie)
someone alguien
something algo
sometimes a veces
soon pronto
soup sopa *f.*
spacious amplio, -a
Spain España
Spanish español
speak: to speak hablar
special especial
specialize: to specialize especializarse
spend: to spend time pasar; **to spend money** gastar
sport deporte *m.*
spring primavera *f.*
stairs escalera *f.*
start out: to start out ponerse en camino
stay: to stay (in) quedarse (en), permanecer (zc)
sternly severamente
stop: to stop dejar de, cesar de
story cuento *m.*
street calle *f.*
student estudiante, alumno(-a); *also adj.* estudiantil
study: to study estudiar
suddenly de pronto, de repente, repentinamente
suggest: to suggest sugerir (ie, i)
summer verano *m.*
sun sol *m.*; **to be sunny** hacer sol
support apoyo *m.*; **to support** apoyar
surprise sorpresa *f.*; **to surprise** sorpenderse (de)
sweep: to sweep barrer
swim: to swim nadar

take: to take tomar; **to take off** quitarse; **to take pictures** sacar fotografías
talkative hablador(-ora)
tall alto, -a
task tarea *f.*
team equipo *m.*
technique técnica *f.*
telephone teléfono *m.*
there allí, allá
thing cosa *f.*
think: to think creer, pensar (ie)
thunder trueno *m.*
thunderstorm tormenta *f.*
ticket boleto *m.*, billete *m.*
time tiempo *m.*; hora *f.*; vez *f.*; **on time** a tiempo; **What time is it?** ¿Qué hora es?; **to have a good time** divertirse (ie, i), pasar un buen rato
timid tímido, -a
tired cansado, -a; **to be tired** estar cansado, -a

title título *m.*
today hoy
together junto
tomorrow mañana
too también
tour excursión *f.*
toy juguete *m.*
traffic tráfico *m.*, tránsito *m.*
train tren *m.*
trait característica *f.*
transportation transporte *m.*
tree árbol *m.*
trip viaje *m.*
try: to try (to) tratar de
type clase *f.*, tipo *m.*

umpire árbitro *m.*
under debajo de
understand: to understand comprender, entender (ie)
unoccupied desocupado, -a
usually generalmente

vacation vacaciones *f. pl.*
videogame videojuego
visit visita *f.*; **to visit** visitar
vote voto *m.*; **to vote** votar

wait: to wait (for) esperar
waiter mesero *m.*
walk andar (*irr.*), caminar, pasearse; **to take a walk** dar un paseo
want: to want desear, querer (ie)
water agua *f.*; **to water** regar (ie) (gu)
wear: to wear llevar, usar
weather tiempo *m.*
Wednesday miércoles *m.*
week semana *f.*
well bien
white blanco, -a
willingly de buena gana
win: to win ganar
winter invierno *m.*
word palabra *f.*; **to keep one's word** cumplir con la palabra
work: to work trabajar
worker trabajador(-ora)
worried preocupado, -a
worse peor
worthwhile: to be worthwhile valer la pena

year año *m.*
younger menor; **younger than** menor que
youngest menor; **the youngest** el / la menor, los / las menores

FRANCIA
PORTUGAL
ESPAÑA
Madrid
Barcelona
Islas Baleares
ITALIA
Sevilla

Index